CONSUMER LAW AND PRACTICE

AUSTRALIA
The Law Book Company
Sydney

CANADA
The Carswell Company
Ontario

INDIA
N.M. Tripathi (Private) Ltd
Bombay
Eastern Law House (Private) Ltd
Calcutta
M.P.P. House
Bangalore
Universal Book Traders
Delhi

ISRAEL
Steimatzky's Agency Ltd
Tel Aviv

PAKISTAN
Pakistan Law House
Karachi

CONSUMER LAW AND PRACTICE

Third edition

By

ROBERT LOWE, LL.B.
Solicitor

and

GEOFFREY WOODROFFE, M.A. (Cantab.)
*Solicitor, Professor Associate and Director of the Centre
for Consumer Law, Brunel University*

LONDON
SWEET AND MAXWELL
1991

First edition 1980
Second edition 1985
Third edition 1991

Published by
Sweet & Maxwell Ltd., of
South Quay Plaza, 183 Marsh Wall, London E14 9FT
Computerset by
MFK Typesetting Ltd., Hitchin, Herts.
Printed by
Richard Clay Limited
Bungay, Suffolk.

A CIP Catalogue Record
for this book is available
from the British Library

ISBN 0 421 43950-5

PREFACE

The nemesis inflicted on authors of legal text books for their hubris in putting pen to paper is that the book is likely to be out of date before it is published. In the preface to the second edition in March 1985 we wrote that the introduction of strict liability for producers and the 1979 draft directive were "bogged down in the battlefield of development risks". The week before the book's publication in August the directive was adopted!

The EC Directive on Liability for Defective Products led inevitably to the Consumer Protection Act 1987. It is the 1987 Act which has resulted in the most significant legislative changes discussed in this third edition. Part I of the Act is concerned with product liability, while Part II contains the important provisions on product safety (including the new "general safety requirement"). The law on misleading prices has also undergone major surgery with the repeal of section 11 of the Trade Descriptions Act 1968 and its replacement by the more sweeping provisions contained in Part III.

The other main statutory reforms also emanated from the European Community. The 1984 Directive on Misleading Advertisements resulted in the Control of Misleading Advertisement Regulations 1988, while the 1985 Doorstep Selling Directive was implemented by the Consumer Protection (Cancellation of Contracts Concluded away from Business Premises) Regulations 1987.

There was also considerable judicial activity in the field of consumer protection. The Court of Appeal for the first time demonstrated that "merchantable quality" extends to cosmetic defects (*Rogers* v. *Parish*) and gave a very wide meaning to "dealing as consumer" in the Unfair Contracts Terms Act 1977 (*R & B Customs Brokers* v. *UDT*). The House of Lords also turned its attention to the 1977 Act in *Smith* v. *Bush* when considering the reasonableness test in the context of the provision of services and liability for negligence, and in the same case decided that the boundaries of tort included the relationship between ordinary house purchasers and their mortgagees' surveyors. In *Interfoto* v. *Stiletto* the Court of Appeal sharpened the weapon of incorporation for use in attacking exemption clauses and other unusual or onerous terms. Finally, attention hardly needs to be drawn to *Bernstein* v. *Pamson Motors*, a decision much criticised by the consumer movement on the loss of the right to reject by the "acceptance" of goods.

v

The European Community will continue to influence consumer law in this country, as can be seen from the draft directives on General Product Safety, Unfair Terms and Suppliers of Services (discussed in Chapter 24) and from the Directive on Package Holidays to be implemented shortly. However, "home grown" legislation is imminent too. The domestic scene has shown a dramatic change in the political attitude to consumers, highlighted by the Conservative Government's "Citizen's Charter" launched by the Prime Minister on July 22, 1991.

Finally, a short curtain call. Our thanks to Malcolm Leder (Middlesex Polytechnic) and Richard Bragg (University of Manchester) for their helpful suggestions at proof stage; to many individuals at the Office of Fair Trading and the Department of Trade and Industry for information on recent developments; to Jeremy Lowe, whose eagle eye spotted a number of errors on the proofs; and to the editorial and production staff at Sweet and Maxwell for preparing the tables and index and generally trying to keep us on target.

The law is intended to be accurate as at July 1, 1991.

July 29, 1991   *Robert Lowe*
                                              Geoffrey Woodroffe

PREFACE TO THE FIRST EDITION

There are many ways of writing a book on consumer protection. One can trace the historical development; one can analyse the economic and social effects; one can deal with the subject from a comparative point of view. In this book we have decided to concentrate on practical problems and remedies. The book is written primarily for law students and for those who are called upon to advise on consumer problems, whether legal or para-legal practitioners. We hope that it will also be useful to persons in industry and their legal advisers as an indication of the growing battery of controls—civil, criminal and administrative—which the law now imposes on business activity. With this aim in mind we have tried to adopt a very practical approach.

A further problem for writers on this subject is that of selection. The term "consumer protection" has no precise definition and it could quite properly be given an immensely wide meaning. Thus every citizen of this country is a consumer, or potential consumer, of welfare benefits, public utilities, health services, educational services and so on. Then again it can be argued that the term "consumer protection" should include the law relating to the supply of housing. Another relevant area is the law of competition which has an underlying consumer protection philosophy. Finally, we have had Government regulation of business activity and in particular we have had price control. In view of our basic approach outlined above we have decided not to deal in any detail with these wide areas. Indeed, we shall concentrate on the types of problem most likely to arise where an individual consumer orders goods or services from a supplier who then proceeds to render defective performance or no performance at all.

Our remedies-based approach has influenced the structure of this book. Part I is entitled "The Consumer and the Civil Law" and deals with such matters as defective performance of contracts to supply goods or services, product liability, the remedies available to the consumer, attempts to exclude them and finally the all-important question of how the remedies can be enforced. Special attention is given to the methods of extra-legal enforcement provided by the growing number of voluntary Codes of Practice. Part II of the book is entitled "The Consumer and the Criminal Law"; special consideration is given to the Trade Descriptions Act 1968 and there is also a chapter dealing with compensation orders. Part III of the book describes the most significant development of consumer protection—administrative control under the Fair Trading Act 1973. Part IV contains nine chapters dealing with "Consumer Protection in Credit Transactions." The book ends with a chapter entitled "The EEC Dimension."

This is a new venture and we would welcome suggestions for improvement. In the meantime we would like to thank the many people who took the trouble to read parts of the typescript and to answer our questions. Special thanks are due to a number of individuals at the Office of Fair Trading, Department of Trade, National Consumer Council, Society of Motor Manufacturers and Traders, Motor Agents Association and the Manchester Arbitration Scheme. The views which they expressed are necessarily personal ones but nevertheless we have found them of great value. We would also like to thank Bill Thomas (solicitor), Valerie Chiswell (consumer adviser), Malcolm Leder (Senior Lecturer at Middlesex Polytechnic), and Peter Chiswell, Peter Hawkins, Tony King, and Chris Whitehouse (all at the College of Law). All of them made very helpful suggestions and assisted in the tiresome task of proof reading.

At the time of going to press there is a Bill before Parliament entitled the Sale of Goods Bill. This is a pure consolidation measure which does not make any changes in the law. The future of the London Small Claims Court, which is discussed in Chapter 9, is still in the balance; we understand that a grant of £5,000 will enable it to survive.

We have tried to state the law as at October 1, 1979.

Robert Lowe
Geoffrey Woodroffe

CONTENTS

Preface		v
Preface to the First Edition		vii
Table of Cases		xiii
Table of Statutes		xxiii
Table of Statutory Instruments		xxx

1	INTRODUCTION	1

PART I: THE CONSUMER AND THE CIVIL LAW

2	"THEY SAY IT ISN'T MINE"	9
	1. Does the buyer get title?	9
	2. Buyer's rights against seller	22
	3. Improvements and repairs	24
3	"IT'S A GOOD LITTLE BUS"	27
	1. Mere puff	28
	2. Misrepresentation	29
	3. Liability in tort for negligence	31
	4. Contractual terms	35
	5. Description	36
	6. Other supply contracts	40
4	"IT DOESN'T WORK"	41
	1. The problem	41
	2. Sale of goods	42
	3. Hire-purchase	55
	4. Work and Materials	55
	5. Hire	57
5	"IT WILL COST £1,000 TO MAKE THEM SAFE"	59
	A. Defective Goods	59
	1. Introduction	59
	2. Manufacturers' Guarantees	60
	B. Dangerous Goods	63
	1. Introduction	63
	2. Part I of the Consumer Protection Act 1987	63
	3. Negligence	73

6   "DO I HAVE TO PAY?"   79
      1. I never ordered these goods   79
      2. I have changed my mind   81
      3. When I opened the box the plates were broken   84
      4. The plumber was a cowboy   90
      5. They turned up late   91
      6. The price seems rather high   92
7   "WHAT ARE MY REMEDIES?"   95
      1. Remedies for misrepresentation   95
      2. Remedies for breach of contract   99
      3. Remedies in tort   115
8   "THEY SAY THAT I HAVE SIGNED AWAY MY RIGHTS"   117
      1. Judicial control of exemption clauses   118
      2. Unfair Contract Terms Act 1977   126
      3. Other controls   145
      4. The EEC Dimension   146
9   "HOW DO I ENFORCE MY RIGHTS?"   147
      1. How to start   147
      2. Codes of practice   148
      3. Arbitration   184
      4. Proceedings in the county court   186

    PART II: THE CONSUMER AND THE CRIMINAL
    LAW

10 INTRODUCTION   193
11 "THE DESCRIPTION MISLED ME"   195
      1. Introduction   195
      2. Goods   200
      3. Services   214
      4. Defences   220
      5. Enforcement   226
      6. Penalties   227
      7. Civil remedies   228
      8. Prices: Consumer Protection Act 1987, Part III   229
12 "THE GOODS AREN'T SAFE"   243
      1. Introduction   243
      2. Consumer Protection Act 1987, Part II   245
13 CRIME AND COMPENSATION   257
      1. Introduction   257
      2. Powers of Criminal Courts Act 1973   258
      3. Breach of statutory duty   262

PART III: ADMINISTRATIVE CONTROL

14 FAIR TRADING 267
    1. Introduction 267
    2. Part II—Adverse consumer trade practices 269
    3. Part III—Persistently unfair traders 282
    4. Misleading Advertisements 286

PART IV: SPECIAL PROTECTION IN CREDIT TRANSACTIONS

15 THE BACKGROUND TO CONSUMER CREDIT 295
    1. Introduction 295
    2. Consumer Credit Act 1974—Ten Preliminary Points 296
16 "WHAT AGREEMENTS ARE CAUGHT BY THE ACT?" 301
    1. Regulated agreements 301
    2. Partially regulated agreements 305
    3. Exempt agreements 306
    4. Linked transactions 310
17 CONTROL OF BUSINESS ACTIVITIES 313
    1. Licensing 313
    2. Advertisements and quotations 317
    3. Canvassing 320
18 "I CAN'T REMEMBER WHAT I SIGNED" 323
19 "CAN I GET OUT OF THE AGREEMENT?" 331
    1. Withdrawal 331
    2. Rescission and repudiation 332
    3. Cancellation 332
    4. Termination 338
20 "THE GOODS ARE DEFECTIVE" 341
    1. Cash sale—unconnected lender 341
    2. Cash sale—connected lender 341
    3. Credit sale and conditional sale 345
    4. Hire-purchase 345
    5. Hire 346
21 "I HAVE LOST MY CREDIT CARD" 347
22 "I CAN'T AFFORD TO PAY" 351
23 "I WANT TO SEE MY CREDIT FILE" 365
24 THE EEC DIMENSION 369
    1. The Treaty of Rome 369
    2. Three draft directives 372

xii CONTENTS

APPENDIX 1: THREE SELECTED CODES OF PRACTICE 383
    1. Code of practice for the motor industry 383
    2. A.B.T.A. tour operators' code of conduct 393
    3. R.E.T.R.A. code of practice for the selling and
       servicing of electrical and electronic appliances 405

APPENDIX 2: ADDRESSES OF TRADE ASSOCIATIONS SPONSORING CODES OF PRACTICE AGREED WITH THE OFFICE OF FAIR TRADING 415

APPENDIX 3: THE INSURANCE OMBUDSMAN'S BUREAU 421

Index 425

TABLE OF CASES

PAGE

ADAMS v. Richardson & Starling [1969] 1 W.L.R. 1645; 113 S.J. 282; [1969] 2 All
E.R. 1221 (C.A.) 137

Ailsa Craig Fishing Co. Ltd. v. Malvern Fishing Co. and Securicor (Scotland)
[1983] 1 W.L.R. 964; (1983) 127 S.J. 508; [1983] 1 All E.R. 101; (1983) 80
L.S.Gaz. 2516 .... 125, 142

Aluminium Industrie Vaassen B.V. v. Romalpa Aluminium Ltd. [1976]
1 W.L.R. 676; 120 S.J. 95; [1976] 2 All E.R. 552; [1976] 1 Lloyd's Rep.
443 85

Amos v. Melcon (Frozen Foods) (1985) 149 J.P. 712; (1985) 149 J.P.N. 667;
(1985) 4 Tr.L. 247, D.C. 224

Andrews v. Hopkinson [1957] 1 Q.B. 229; [1956] 3 W.L.R. 732; 100 S.J. 768;
[1956] 3 All E.R. 422 .... 28, 60, 74, 346

Andrews Bros. (Bournemouth) Ltd. v. Singer & Co. Ltd. [1934] 1 K.B. 17;
[1933] All E.R. Rep. 479; 103 L.J.K.B. 90; 150 L.T. 172 124

Anglo-Continental Holidays Ltd. v. Typaldos Lines (London) Ltd. [1967] 2
Lloyd's Rep. 61; 111 S.J. 599 134

Apollo Leasing Ltd. v. Scott [1986] Consumer Credit Law Reports 1 305

Arcos Ltd. v. Ronaasen [1933] A.C. 470; [1933] All E.R. Rep. 646; 102 L.J.K.B.
346; 149 L.T. 98; 77 S.J. 99 38

Ardath Tobacco Ltd. v. Ocker (1931) 47 T.L.R. 177 15

Armour v. Thyssen A.G. [1990] 3 W.L.R. 810; [1990] 3 All E.R. 481 85

Ashby v. Tolhurst [1937] 2 K.B. 242; [1937] 2 All E.R. 837; 106 L.J.K.B. 783; 156
L.T. 518; 53 T.L.R. 770 126

Ashington Piggeries v. Christopher Hill [1972] A.C. 441; [1971] 2 W.L.R. 1051;
115 S.J. 223; [1971] 1 All E.R. 847 .... 40, 44, 54

Astral, The (1981), unreported 201

BADHAM v. Lambs Ltd. [1946] K.B. 45; [1945] 2 All E.R. 295; 115 L.J.K.B. 180;
173 L.T. 139 263

Badische Anilin und Soda Fabrik v. Basle Chemical Works [1898] A.C. 200; 67
L.J. Ch 141; 77 L.T. 573; 46 W.R. 255; 14 T.L.R. 82 88

Bambury v. Hounslow L.B.C. [1971] R.T.R. 1 (D.C.) 220

Barge v. British Gas Corp. (1983) 81 L.G.R. 53 (D.C.) 227

Barker v. Bell [1971] 1 W.L.R. 983; 115 S.J. 364; [1971] 2 All E.R. 867 (C.A.) 21

Bartlett v. Marcus (Sidney) [1965] 1 W.L.R. 1013; 109 S.J. 451; [1965] 2 All E.R.
753 (C.A.) 49

Batty v. Metropolitan Realisations [1978] Q.B. 554; [1978] 2 W.L.R. 500; (1977)
122 S.J. 63; [1978] 2 All E.R. 445 115

Beale v. Taylor [1967] 1 W.L.R. 1193; 111 S.J. 668; [1967] 3 All E.R. 253 (C.A.) 37

Beckett v. Cohen [1972] 1 W.L.R. 1593; 116 S.J. 882; [1973] 1 All E.R. 120;
(1972) 71 L.G.R. 46 (D.C.) 218

—— v. Kingston Bros. (Butchers) Ltd. [1970] 1 Q.B. 606; [1970] 2 W.L.R. 558;
[1970] 1 All E.R. 715; 68 L.G.R. 244 .... 212, 221

Beer v. Walker (1877) 46 L.J.Q.B. 677; 37 L.T. 278; 41 J.P. 728; 25 W.R.
880 .... 50, 88

Belvoir Finance Co. Ltd. v. Cole (Harold G.) & Co. [1969] 1 W.L.R. 1877; [1969]
2 All E.R. 904 13

PAGE

Bentinck Ltd. *v.* Cromwell Engineering Co. Ltd. [1971] 1 Q.B. 324; [1970] 3 W.L.R. 1113; 114 S.J. 823; [1971] 1 All E.R. 33; [1971] R.T.R. 7 (C.A.) 359

Bentley (Dick) Productions *v.* Smith (Harold) (Motors) [1965] 1 W.L.R. 623; 109 S.J. 329; [1965] 2 All E.R. 65 (C.A.) 30, 34, 35

Bernstein *v.* Pamson Motors (Golders Green) Ltd. [1987] 2 All E.R. 220; [1987] R.T.R. 384; (1987) 6 T.L.R. 33 .... 47, 48, 106, 108, 113, 114

Birkenhead & District Co-operative Society Ltd. *v.* Roberts [1970] 1 W.L.R. 1497; 114 S.J. 703; [1970] 3 All E.R. 391; 68 L.G.R. 744 (D.C.) 221, 222

Bishopsgate Motor Finance Corp. Ltd. *v.* Transport Brakes Ltd. [1949] 1 K.B. 322; [1949] L.J.R. 741; 65 T.L.R. 66; 93 S.J. 71; [1949] 1 All E.R. 37 .... 9, 15, 16

Blakemore *v.* Bellamy [1983] R.T.R. 303 (D.C.); (1983) 147 J.P. 89 199

Bliss *v.* South East Thames Regional Health Authority [1987] I.C.R. 700; [1985] I.R.L.R. 308 (C.A.) 114

Bolton *v.* Mahadeva [1972] 1 W.L.R. 1009; 116 S.J. 564; [1972] 2 All E.R. 1322 (C.A.) 115

Bourhill *v.* Young [1943] A.C. 92; [1942] 2 All E.R. 396; 111 L.J.P.C. 97; 167 L.T. 261; 86 S.J. 349 79

Breed *v.* Cluett [1970] 2 Q.B. 459; [1970] 3 W.L.R. 76; 114 S.J. 453; [1970] 2 All E.R. 662; 68 L.G.R. 604 214

Bristol Tramways etc Carriage Co. Ltd *v.* Fiat Motors Ltd. [1910] 2 K.B. 831; [1908–10] All E.R. Rep. 113; 79 L.J.K.B. 1107; 103 L.T. 443; 26 T.L.R. 629 (C.A.) 52

British Airways Board *v.* Taylor [1976] 1 W.L.R. 13; (1975) 120 S.J. 7; [1976] 1 All E.R. 65; [1976] Lloyd's Rep. 167; (1975) 62 Cr.App.R. 174 219

British Gas Corporation *v.* Lubbock [1974] 1 W.L.R. 37; 117 S.J. 833; [1974] 1 All E.R. 188; (1973) 72 L.G.R. 231; [1973] Crim.L.R. 775 (D.C.) 213

Brown & Son Ltd *v.* Craiks [1970] 1 W.L.R. 752 (H.L.) 47

Buckley *v.* La Réserve [1959] Crim.L.R. 451 263

Bunge Corporation *v.* Tradax Export S.A. [1981] 1 W.L.R. 711; (1981) 125 S.J. 373; [1981] 2 All E.R. 540; [1981] Lloyd's Rep. 1 (H.L.) 92

Business Application Specialists *v.* Nationwide Credit Corporation [1988] R.T.R. 332; *The Times,* April 27, 1988 50

Butterworth *v.* Kingsway Motors [1954] 1 W.L.R. 1286; 98 S.J. 717; [1954] 2 All E.R. 694 109

CANDLER *v.* Crane Christmas & Co. [1951] K.B. 164; [1951] 1 T.L.R. 371; 95 S.J. 171; [1951] 1 All E.R. 426 31

Caparo Industries plc *v.* Dickman [1990] 2 W.L.R. 358 (H.L.) 32, 34

Capital Finance Co. Ltd. *v.* Bray [1964] 1 W.L.R. 323; 108 S.J. 95; [1964] 1 All E.R. 603 (C.A.) 359

Car & Universal Finance Co. *v.* Caldwell [1965] 1 Q.B. 525; [1964] 2 W.L.R. 600; 108 S.J. 15; [1964] 1 All E.R. 290 .... 17, 20

Carlos Federspiel & Co. S.A. *v.* Twigg (Charles) Ltd. [1957] 1 Lloyd's Rep. 240 ... 87

Carr *v.* Broderick & Co. Ltd. [1942] 2 K.B. 275; [1942] 2 All E.R. 441; 111 L.J.K.B. 667; 167 L.T. 335 359

Castle Phillips Finance Co. Ltd. *v.* Williams [1986] Consumer Credit Law Reports 43 362

Cehave N.V. *v.* Bremer Handelsgesellschaft GmbH; Hansa Nord, The [1976] Q.B. 44; [1975] 3 W.L.R. 447; 119 S.J. 678; [1975] 3 All E.R. 739 ... 36, 103

Central Newbury Car Auctions Ltd. *v.* Unity Finance Ltd. [1957] 1 Q.B. 371; [1956] 3 W.L.R. 1068; 100 S.J. 927; [1956] 3 All E.R. 905 11

Chapelton *v.* Barry U.D.C. [1940] 1 K.B. 532; [1940] 1 All E.R. 356; 109 L.J.K.B. 213; 162 L.T. 169; 104 J.P. 165; 56 T.L.R. 331; 84 S.J. 185 .. 120

Charge Card Services, *Re* [1988] 3 W.L.R. 764; (1988) 138 New L.J. 201; (1988) B.C.C. 524; [1988] 3 All E.R. 702 344

Charnock *v.* Liverpool Corporation and Another [1968] 1 W.L.R. 1498; 112 S.J. 781; [1968] 3 All E.R. 473 91

PAGE

Chartered Trust p.l.c. v. Pitcher [1988] R.T.R. 72; [1988] T.L.R. 97; (1987) 131
  S.J. 503; (1987) 84 L.S.Gaz. 1147 (C.A.) 359
Clough Mill Ltd. v. Martin [1985] 1 W.L.R. 111; (1984) 128 S.J. 850; [1984] 3 All
  E.R. 982; (1985) 82 L.S.Gaz. 116 85
Coldunell v. Gallon [1986] Q.B. 1184; [1986] 2 W.L.R. 466; (1986) 130 S.J. 88;
  [1986] 1 All E.R. 429 363
Coppen v. Moore (No 1) [1898] 2 Q.B. 300 201
Corfield v. Sevenways Garage Ltd. [1985] R.T.R. 109 (D.C.); (1984) 148 J.P.
  684; (1985) 4 Tr.L. 172 208
—— v. Starr [1981] R.T.R. 380 211
Cottee v. Seaton (Douglas) (Used Cars) [1972] 1 W.L.R. 1408; 116 S.J. 821;
  [1972] 3 All E.R. 750; [1972] R.T.R. 509 .... 203, 225
Coupe v. Guyett [1973] 1 W.L.R. 669; 117 S.J. 415; [1973] 2 All E.R. 1058; 71
  L.G.R. 355; [1973] R.T.R. 518 226
Cremdean Properties Ltd. v. Nash (1977) 244 E.G. 547 (C.A.) 30, 139
Crook v. Howells Garages [1980] R.T.R. 434 (D.C.) 223
Croshaw v. Pritchard & Renwick (1899) 16 T.L.R. 45 93
Crowther v. Shannon Motor Co. [1975] 1 W.L.R. 30; [1975] 1 All E.R. 139;
  [1975] R.T.R. 201; [1975] 1 Lloyd's Rep. 382 49
Curtis v. Chemical Cleaning and Dyeing Co. [1951] 1 K.B. 805; [1951] 1 T.L.R.
  452; 95 S.J. 253; [1951] 1 All E.R. 631 124

D. & F. ESTATES LTD. v. Church Commissioners [1989] A.C. 177; [1988] 2
  E.G.L.R. 213 73
Daniels & Daniels v. White Ltd. and Tarbard [1938] 4 All E.R. 258; 160 L.T. 128;
  82 S.J. 912 77
Davie v. New Merton Board Mills [1959] A.C. 604; [1959] 2 W.L.R. 331; 103 S.J.
  177; [1959] 1 All E.R. 346 76
Davies v. Sumner [1984] 1 W.L.R. 1301; (1984) 128 S.J. 814; [1984] 3 All E.R.
  831; (1985) 149 J.P. 110 .... 45, 132, 133, 198, 200, 202
Dennant v. Skinner and Collom [1948] 2 K.B. 164; [1948] 2 K.B. 164; [1948]
  L.J.R. 1576; [1948] 2 All E.R. 29 85
Department of the Environment v. Thomas Bates & Son Ltd. [1991] 1 W.L.R.
  73; [1990] 2 All E.R. 943 (H.L.) 77
Derry v. Peek (1889) 14 App. Cas. 337; 58 L.J. Ch. 864; 61 L.T. 265; 54 J.P. 148;
  38 W.R. 33; 5 T.L.R. 625 96
Director General of Fair Trading v. Smiths Bakeries (Westfield) Ltd., The
  Times, May 11, 1978 286
—— v. Tobyward Ltd. [1989] 1 W.L.R. 517; (1989) S.J. 184; [1989] 2 All E.R.
  266 290
Doble v. Greig (David) Ltd. [1972] 1 W.L.R. 703; 116 S.J. 217; [1972] 2 All E.R.
  195; [1972] Crim.L.R. 265 (D.C.) 235
Donnelly v. Rowlands [1970] 1 W.L.R. 1600; 114 S.J. 863; [1971] 1 All E.R. 9; 69
  L.G.R. 42 (D.C.) 206
Donoghue v. Stevenson [1932] A.C. 562; 101 L.J.P.C. 119; 48 T.L.R. 494; 37
  Com. Cas. 350; 28, 31, 73
Doyle v. Olby (Ironmongers) Ltd. [1969] 2 Q.B. 158; [1969] 2 W.L.R. 673; 113
  S.J. 128; [1969] 2 All E.R. 119 96
Du Jardin v. Beadman Bros. [1952] 2 Q.B. 712; [1952] 1 T.L.R. 1601; 96 S.J. 414;
  [1952] 2 All E.R. 160 19

EAST v. Maurer [1991] 1 W.L.R. 461 96
Eastern Distributors v. Goldring [1957] 2 Q.B. 600; [1957] 3 W.L.R. 237; 101 S.J.
  553; [1957] 2 All E.R. 525 .... 12, 326, 354, 359
Edgington v. Fitzmaurice (1885) 29 Ch.D. 459; [1881–85] All E.R. Rep. 856; 55
  L.J.Ch. 650; 53 L.T. 369; 50 J.P. 52 216
Elphick v. Barnes (1880) 5 C.P.D. 321; 40 L.J.Q.B. 698; 44 J.P. 651; 29 W.R.
  139 86

PAGE

Evans v. Triplex Safety Glass Co. [1936] 1 All E.R. 283 .... 74, 75
Evans (J.) & Son (Portsmouth) v. Merzario (Andrea) [1976] 1 W.L.R. 1078; 120
    S.J. 734; [1976] 2 All E.R. 930; [1976] 2 Lloyd's Rep. 165 124

FARNWORTH FINANCE FACILITIES v. Attryde [1970] 1 W.L.R. 1053; 114 S.J.
    354; [1970] 2 All E.R. 774 (C.A.) 108, 109
Fibrosa Spolka Akcyjna v. Fairbairn, Lawson Combe Barbour Ltd. [1943] A.C.
    32; [1942] 2 All E.R. 122; 111 L.J.K.B. 433; 167 L.T. 101; 58 T.L.R. 308   89
Financings Ltd. v. Stimson [1962] 1 W.L.R. 1184; [1962] 3 All E.R. 386   89
Fisher v. Bell [1961] 1 Q.B. 394; [1960] 3 W.L.R. 919; 125 J.P. 101; 104 S.J. 981;
    [1960] 3 All E.R. 731 203
—— v. Harrods Ltd. [1966] 1 Lloyd's L.R. 500; 110 S.J. 133; 116 New L.J. 919   76
Fletcher v. Budgen [1974] 1 W.L.R. 1056; 118 S.J. 498; [1974] 2 All E.R. 1243;
    [1974] R.T.R. 471 213
Folkes v. King [1923] 1 K.B. 282 13
Forward Trust Ltd. v. Whymark [1989] 3 W.L.R. 1229 (C.A.); (1989) 133 S.J.
    1577; [1989] L.S.Gaz. December 20 354
Frost v. Aylesbury Dairy Co. [1905] 1 K.B. 608; [1904–07] All E.R. Rep. 132; 74
    L.J.K.B. 366; 92 L.T. 527, 53 W.R. 354 .... 43, 44

GARDINER v. Gray (1815) 4 Camp. 144; 171 E.R. 46 46
Geddling v. Marsh [1920] 1 K.B. 668; [1920] All E.R. Rep 631; 89 L.J.K.B. 526;
    122 L.T. 775; 36 T.L.R. 337 45
Godley v. Perry [1960] 1 W.L.R. 9; 104 S.J. 16; [1960] 1 All E.R. 36 113
Grant v. Australian Knitting Mills Ltd. [1936] A.C. 85; [1935] All E.R. Rep. 209;
    105 L.J.P.C. 6; 154 L.T. 18; 52 T.L.R. 38; 79 S.J. 815 .... 46, 50, 77
Greenwood v. Bennett [1973] 1 Q.B. 195; [1972] 3 W.L.R. 691; 116 S.J. 762;
    [1972] 3 All E.R. 586; [1972] R.T.R. 535 .... 24, 25
Grenfell v. E.B. Meyrowitz Ltd. [1936] 2 All E.R. 1313 39
Griffiths v. Peter Conway Ltd. [1939] 1 All E.R. 685 54

HADLEY v. Baxendale (1854) 9 Exch. 341; [1843–60] All E.R. Rep 461; 23
    L.J.Ex. 179; 23 L.T.O.S. 69; 18 Jur. 358; 2 W.R. 302 .... 111, 112
Hall v. Wickens Motors (Gloucester) [1972] 1 W.L.R. 1418; 116 S.J. 744; [1972]
    R.T.R. 519; [1972] Crim.L.R. 652 .... 203, 214, 215
Hammertons Cars v. Redbridge London Borough Council [1974] 1 W.L.R. 484;
    118 S.J. 240; [1974] 2 All E.R. 216; [1974] Crim.L.R. 241 261
Harlingdon and Leinster Enterprises Ltd. v. Christopher Hull Fine Art Ltd.
    [1990] 3 W.L.R. 13; [1990] 1 All E.R. 737 .... 37, 47, 98
Harris v. Wyre Forest D.C. [1990] 1 A.C. 831 .... 32, 33, 34, 129, 143
Havering London Borough Council v. Stevenson [1970] 1 W.L.R. 1375; [1971]
    R.T.R. 58 .... 133, 198, 199
Hayes v. James & Charles Dodd (A Firm) [1990] 2 All E.R. 815 (C.A.) 114
Head (Philip) & Sons v. Showfronts Ltd. (1969) 113 S.J. 978; [1970] 1 Lloyd's
    Rep. 140 87
Healy v. Howlett [1917] 1 K.B. 337; 86 L.J.K.B. 252; 116 L.T. 591 87
Hedley Byrne & Co. Ltd. v. Heller & Partners Ltd. [1964] A.C. 465; [1963] 3
    W.L.R. 101; 107 S.J. 454; [1963] 2 All E.R. 575; [1963] 1 Lloyd's Rep.
    485 .... 27, 29, 32, 34, 35, 346
Heil v. Hedges [1951] 1 T.L.R. 512; 95 S.J. 140 50
Heilbut, Symons & Co. v. Buckleton, Symons & Co. v. Buckleton [1913] A.C.
    30 35
Helby v. Matthews [1895] A.C. 471; 64 L.J.O.B. 465; 72 L.T. 841; 60 J.P. 20 . 19
Henderson & Co. v. Williams [1895] 1 Q.B. 521; 64 L.J.Q.B. 308; 72 L.T. 98; 43
    W.R. 274 12
Heywood v. Wellers [1976] Q.B. 446; [1976] 2 W.L.R. 101; (1975) 120 S.J. 9;
    [1976] 1 All E.R. 300; [1976] 2 Lloyd's Rep. 88 113

PAGE

Hill v. Crowe (James) (Cases) [1978] I.C.R. 298; [1978] 1 All E.R. 812; [1977] 2
Lloyd's Rep. 450 77
Hollier v. Rambler Motors (AMC) Ltd. [1972] 2 Q.B. 71; [1972] 2 W.L.R. 401;
(1971) 116 S.J. 158; [1972] 1 All E.R. 399 124
Holloway v. Cross [1981] 1 All E.R. 1012; 125 S.J. 46; [1981] R.T.R. 146 206
Hongkong Fir Shipping Co. v. Kawasaki Kisen Kaisha [1962] 2 Q.B. 26; [1962] 2
W.L.R. 474; 106 S.J. 35; [1962] 1 All E.R. 474; [1961] 2 Lloyd's Rep.
478 .... 102, 103
Houghland v. Low (Luxury Coaches) Ltd. [1962] 1 Q.B. 694; [1962] 2 W.L.R.
1015; 106 S.J. 243; [1962] 2 All E.R. 159 86
Howard v. Harris (1884) C. & E. 253 79
Howard Marine and Dredging Co. Ltd. v. Ogden & Sons (Excavation) Ltd.
[1978] Q.B. 574; [1978] 2 W.L.R. 515; (1977) 122 S.J. 48; [1978] 2 All E.R.
1134; [1978] 1 Lloyd's Rep. 334 .... 29, 97
Hughes v. Hall [1981] R.T.R. 430; (1981) 125 S.J. 255 275

INGRAM v. Little [1961] 1 Q.B. 31; [1960] 3 W.L.R. 504; 104 S.J. 704; [1960] 3 All
E.R. 332 16,17
Interfoto Picture Library Ltd. v. Stileto Visual Programmes Ltd. [1988] 2 W.L.R.
615; (1988) 132 S.J. 460; [1988] 1 All E.R. 348; [1988] L.S.Gaz. March 2,
45 121

JACKSON v. Chrysler Acceptances [1978] R.T.R. 474 114
—— v. Horizon Holidays [1975] 1 W.L.R. 1468; 119 S.J. 759; [1975] 3 All E.R. 92
(C.A.) 43, 114, 259
—— v. Rotax Motor Co. Ltd. (1910) 2. K.B. 937; 80 L.J.K.B. 38; 103 L.T. 411
(C.A.) 46
Jarvis v. Swan Tours [1973] 1 Q.B. 233; [1972] 3 W.L.R. 954; 116 S.J. 822; [1973]
1 All E.R. 71 (C.A.) 113, 259

KARFLEX LTD. v. Poole [1933] 2 K.B. 251; [1933] All E.R. Rep. 46; 102
L.J.K.B. 475; 149 L.T. 140 24
Karsales (Harrow) Ltd. v. Wallis [1956] 1 W.L.R. 936; 100 S.J. 548; [1956] 2 All
E.R. 866 (C.A.) 40, 125, 128
Kat v. Diment [1951] 1 K.B. 34; 66 T.L.R. (Pt. 2) 474; 114 J.P. 472; 94 S.J. 596;
[1950] 2 All E.R. 657 205
Kay v. Ayrshire and Arran Health Board [1987] 2 All E.R. 417 (H.L.) 64
Ketley (A.) v. Scott [1981] I.C.R. 241 363
Kinchin v. Ashton Park Scooters (1984) 148 J.P. 540; (1984) 134 J.P.N. 459
(D.C.) 220
Koufos v. Czarnikow Ltd. (The Heron II) [1969] 1 A.C. 350; [1967] 3 W.L.R.
1491; S.J. 848 111

LAMBERT v. Lewis [1982] A.C. 225; [1981] 2 W.L.R. 713; [1981] 1 All E.R. 1185;
[1981] Lloyd's Rep. 17 reversing [1980] 2 W.L.R. 229 (C.A.) 35, 51, 75
Langridge v. Levy (1838) 4 M. & W. 337 96
Leaf v. International Galleries [1950] 2 K.B. 86; 66 T.L.R. (Pt. 1) 1031; [1950] 1
All E.R. 693 98
Leather Funwear, The Times, June 14, 1973 214
Leaves v. Wadham Stringer (Clifton) Ltd. [1980] R.T.R. 308 47
Lee v. York Coach and Marine [1977] R.T.R. 35 .... 49, 108, 113
Lemy v. Watson [1915] 3 K.B. 731 205
L'Estrange v. Graucob [1934] 2 K.B. 394; [1934] All E.R. Rep. 16 ; 103 L.J.K.B.
730; 152 L.T. 164 .... 119, 123
Lewis v. Averay [1973] 1 W.L.R. 510; 117 S.J. 188; [1973] 2 All E.R. 229 17
Lill (K.) Holdings (t/a Stratford Motor Corp.) v. White [1979] R.T.R. 120
(D.C.) 212

PAGE

Lockett v. A. M. Charles Ltd. [1938] 4 All E.R. 170; 159 L.T. 547; 55 T.L.R. 22;
82 S.J. 951 43
London Wine Company (Shippers), Re (1986) 126 N.L.J. 977; 1986 P.C.C. 121 87
Long v. Jones, *The Times*, March 6, 1990 14
—— v. Lloyd [1958] 1 W.L.R. 753; 102 S.J. 488; [1958] 2 All E.R. 402 ..... 97, 106
Lowe v. Lombank [1960] 1 W.L.R. 196; 104 S.J. 210; [1960] 1 All E.R. 611 .. 54

M.F.I. WAREHOUSES v. Nattrass [1973] 1 W.L.R. 307; (1972) 117 S.J. 143;
[1973] 1 All E.R. 762; [1973] Crim.L.R.196 (D.C.) 215
M/S Aswan Engineering Establishment Co. v. Lupdine Ltd. [1987] 1 W.L.R. 1;
[1987] 1 All E.R. 135; (1987) 6 T.L.R. 1; (1986) 130 S.J. 712; [1986] 2
Lloyd's Rep. 347 .... 47, 54
McCutcheon v. MacBrayne (David) [1964] 1 W.L.R. 125; 108 S.J. 93; [1964] 1
All E.R. 430; [1964] 1 Lloyd's Rep. 16 120
McGuire v. Sittingbourne Co-Operative Society Ltd. [1976] 120 S.J. 197; [1976]
Crim.L.R. 268 (D.C.) 222
McWilliams v. Arrol (Sir William) & Co. [1962] 1 W.L.R. 295; 106 S.J. 218; 1962
S.C. 70; 1962 S.L.T. 121 77
Mash & Murrell v. Emanuel (Joseph) (I.) [1962] 1 W.L.R. 16; 105 S.J. 1007;
[1962] 1 All E.R. 77n; [1961] 2 Lloyd's Rep. 46 50
Mason v. Burningham [1949] 2 K.B. 545; [1949] L.J.R. 1430; 65 T.L.R. 466; 93
S.J. 496; [1949] 2 All E.R. 134 .... 23, 25, 113
May and Butcher v. R. [1934] 2 K.B. 17; n: 103 L.J.K.B. 556; n: 151 L.T. 246
(H.L.) 92
Mendelssohn v. Normand [1970] 1 Q.B. 177; [1969] 3 W.L.R. 139; (1969) 113
S.J. 263; [1969] 2 All E.R. 1215 (C.A.) 124
Metsoja v. Norman (H.) Pitt & Co. (1989) 8 Tr.L.R. 155; (1989) 153 J.P.N. 630
(D.C.) 318
Millars of Falkirk Ltd. v. Turpie (1976) S.L.T. 66 47
Mitchell (George) (Chesterhall) v. Finney Lock Seeds [1983] 2 A.C. 803; [1983] 3
W.L.R. 163; [1983] 2 All E.R. 737; [1983] 2 Lloyd's Rep. 272 ...... 125, 140
Moorcock, The (1889) 14 P.D. 64; [1886–90] All E.R. Rep. 530; 58 L.J.P. 73; 60
L.T. 654; 37 W.R. 439; 5 T.L.R. 316; 6 Asp. M.L.C. 373 (C.A.) 151
Moore v. Fox (R.) & Sons [1956] 1 Q.B. 596; [1956] 2 W.L.R. 342; [1956] 1 All
E.R. 182; [1956] 1 Lloyd's Rep. 129 76
Moore & Co. and Landauer & Co., Re [1921] 2 K.B. 519; [1921] All E.R. Rep.
466; 90 L.J.K.B. 731; 125 L.T. 372; 37 T.L.R. 452 39
Moorgate Mercantile Co. v. Twitchings [1977] A.C. 890 (H.L.) 11
Morgan Crucible Co. v. Hill Samuel Bank Ltd. and Others [1991] 1 All E.R. 148
(C.A.) 34
Munro v. Willmott [1949] 1 K.B. 295; [1949] L.J.R. 471; 64 T.L.R. 627; 92 S.J.
662; [1948] 2 All E.R. 983 24
Murphy v. Brentwood D.C. [1990] 3 W.L.R. 415; [1990] 2 All E.R. 908 (H.L.) 77
Myers (G.H.) & Co. v. Brent Cross Service Co. [1934] 1 K.B. 46; [1933] All E.R.
Rep. 9; 103 L.J.K.B. 123; 150 L.T. 96 56

NAISH v. Gore [1971] 3 All E.R. 737; [1972] R.T.R. 102; [1972] J.C.L. 80
(D.C.) 223, 224
National Employers' Mutual General Insurance Association v. Jones [1990] 1
A.C. 24; [1988] 2 W.L.R. 952; [1988] 132 S.J. 658; [1988] 2 All E.R. 425;
[1988] R.T.R. 289 19
Naughton v. O'Callaghan [1990] 3 All E.R. 191 .... 97, 99
Newell and Taylor v. Hicks (1984) 128 S.J. 63; (1984) 148 J.P. 308; (1984) 81
L.S.Gaz. 354; [1984] R.T.R. 135 (D.C.) 219
Newham London Borough Council v. Singh (1988) 152 J.P. 239; (1988) 52 J.P.N.
206; [1988] R.T.R. 359 (D.C.) 202
Newman v. Hackney London Borough Council (1982) 80 L.G.R. 611; [1982]
R.T.R. 296 (D.C.) 208

PAGE

New Zealand Shipping Co. Ltd. *v.* Satterthwaite & Co. Ltd. [1975] A.C. 154;
[1974] 2 W.L.R. 865; 118 S.J. 387; [1974] 1 All E.R. 1015 . . . .　123

Newtons of Wembley *v.* Williams [1965] 1 Q.B. 560; [1964] 3 W.L.R. 888; 108
S.J. 619; [1964] 3 All E.R. 532 . . . . 17, 19, 20

Nichol *v.* Godts (1854) 10 Exch. 191; 2 C.L.R. 1468; 23 L.J. Ex. 314; 23 L.T.O.S.
162 . . . .　124

Norman *v.* Bennett [1974] 1 W.L.R. 1229; 118 S.J. 697; [1974] 3 All E.R. 351;
[1974] R.T.R. 441; 72 L.G.R. 676 . . . . 209, 211

Norman (Alec) Garages Ltd. *v.* Phillips (1984) 148 J.P. 741; [1985] R.T.R. 164;
(1985) 4 Tr.L. 21 (D.C.) . . . .　200

OLGEIRSSON *v.* Kitching [1986] 1 W.L.R. 304; (1986) 130 S.J. 110; (1985) 150
J.P. 117; [1986] 1 All E.R. 746 . . . .　225

Olley *v.* Marlborough Court Hotel [1949] 1 K.B. 532; [1949] L.J.R. 360; 65
T.L.R. 95; 93 S.J. 40; [1949] 1 All E.R. 127 . . . . 120, 121

Oscar Chess Ltd. *v.* Williams [1957] 1 W.L.R. 370; 101 S.J. 186; [1957] 1 All E.R.
325 . . . .　29

Overbrooke Estates Ltd. *v.* Glencombe Properties Ltd. [1974] 1 W.L.R. 1335;
118 S.J. 775; [1974] 3 All E.R. 511 . . . . 125, 139

PARSONS (LIVESTOCK) LTD. *v.* Uttley Ingham & Co. [1978] 1 Q.B. 791; [1977] 3
W.L.R. 990; (1977) 121 S.J. 811; [1978] 1 All E.R. 525; [1977] 2 Lloyd's
Rep. 522 (C.A.) 111, 115

Parker *v.* South Eastern Rly. Co. (1877) 2 C.P.D. 416; [1874–80] All E.R. Rep.
166; 46 L.J.Q.B. 768; 36 L.T. 540; 41 J.P. 644 . . . .　122

Payne *v.* Cave (1789) 3 Term Rep. 148; [1775–1802] All E.R. Rep. 492; 100 E.R.
502 . . . .　203

Pearson *v.* Rose & Young [1951] 1 K.B. 275; 66 T.L.R. (Pt. 2) 886; 94 S.J. 778;
[1950] 2 All E.R. 1027 . . . .　13

Pepper *v.* Healey [1982] R.T.R. 411 (C.A.) . . . .　188

Pharmaceutical Society of G.B. *v.* Boots Cash Chemists (Southern) [1952] 2
Q.B. 799; [1953] 2 W.L.R. 427; 117 J.P. 132; 97 S.J. 149; [1953] 1 All E.R.
482 . . . .　203

Phillips *v.* Britannia Hygienic Laundry Co. [1923] 2 K.B. 832; [1923] All E.R.
Rep. 1227; 93 L.J.K.B. 5; 129 L.T. 777; 39 T.L.R. 530; 68 S.J. 102 . . . .　263

Phillips Products Ltd. *v.* Hyland [1987] 1 W.L.R. 659; (1985) 129 S.J. 47; [1987] 2
All E.R. 620; (1988) 4 Const. L.J. 53 . . . . 129, 139, 141

Photo Production *v.* Securicor Transport [1980] A.C. 827; [1980] 2 W.L.R. 283;
(1980) 124 S.J. 147; [1980] 1 All E.R. 556; [1980] 1 Lloyd's Rep. 545
(H.L.) 125, 141

Preist *v.* Last [1903] 2 K.B. 148; 72 L.J.K.B. 657; 89 L.T. 33; 51 W.R. 678; 19
T.L.R. 527; 47 S.J. 566 (C.A.) . . . .　54

QUALCAST (WOLVERHAMPTON) LTD. *v.* Haynes [1959] A.C. 743; [1959] 2
W.L.R. 510; 103 S.J. 310; [1959] 2 All E.R. 38 . . . .　77

Queensway Discount Warehouses Ltd. *v.* Burke (1986) 150 J.P. 17; (1985) 149
J.P.N. 783 (D.C.) . . . .　204

R. *v.* Breeze [1973] 1 W.L.R. 994; [1973] 2 All E.R. 1141; [1973] Crim.L.R.
458 . . . . 198, 214

—— *v.* Clarksons Holidays (1972) 116 S.J. 728; (1972) 57 Cr.App.R. 38; 71
L.G.R. 1; [1972] Crim.L.R. 653 (C.A.) . . . .　218

—— *v.* Coventry City Justices, *ex p.* Farrand [1988] R.T.R. 273; (1988) 152 J.P.
26; (1987) 151 J.P.N. 702 (D.C.) . . . .　208

—— v. Daly [1974] 1 W.L.R. 133; (1973) 118 S.J. 66; [1974] 1 All E.R. 290 . .　260

—— *v.* Ford Motor Co. [1974] 1 W.L.R. 1220; 118 S.J. 596; [1974] 3 All E.R.
489; [1974] R.T.R. 509 . . . . 202, 213

PAGE

R. v. Haesler [1973] Crim.L.R. 586; [1973] R.T.R. 486. (C.A.) 203, 228
—— v. Hammertons Cars Ltd. [1976] 1 W.L.R. 1243; 120 S.J. 553; [1976] 3 All
    E.R. 758; [1976] R.T.R. 516; (1976) Cr.App.R. 234 ...... 208, 209, 210, 228
—— v. Hewitt, *The Times*, June 21, 1991 (C.A.) 228
—— v. Inner London Justices, *ex p.* Wandsworth L.B.C. [1983] R.T.R. 425
    (D.C.) 205
—— v. Johnstone (1982) 4 Cr.App.R. (S) 141; [1982] Crim.L.R. 537 (C.A.) . 261
—— v. Kneeshaw [1975] Q.B. 57; [1974] 2 W.L.R. 432; 118 S.J. 218; [1974] 1 All
    E.R. 896 260
—— v. McCullough (1982) 4 Cr.App.R. (S) 98 (C.A.); [1982] Crim.L.R.
    461 (D.C.) 261
—— v. McIntosh [1973] Crim.L.R. 378 261
—— v. Modupe, *The Times,* February 27, 1991 (C.A.) 323
—— v. Morgan (1982) 4 Cr.App.R. (S) 358 (C.A.) 261
—— v. Southwood [1987] 1 W.L.R. 1361; (1987) 131 S.J. 1038; [1987] 3 All E.R.
    556; (1987) 85 Cr.App.R. 272; [1987] R.T.R. 273 .... 208, 220
—— v. Thomson Holidays Ltd. [1974] Q.B. 592; [1974] 2 W.L.R. 371; [1974] 1
    All E.R. 823; (1973) 58 Cr.App.R. 429 .... 218, 227, 228, 260
—— v. Vivian [1979] 1 W.L.R. 291; (1978) 122 S.J. 680; [1979] 1 All E.R. 48;
    [1979] R.T.R. 106; (1978) 68 Cr.App.R. 53 260
R. & B. Customs Brokers Co. v. United Dominions Trust (Saunders Abbott
    (1980) Ltd., third party) [1988] 1 W.L.R. 321; (1988) 132 S.J. 300; [1988] 1
    All E.R. 847; [1988] R.T.R. 134; (1988) L.S.Gaz. March 16, 42 .... 132, 138,
    200
Reardon Smith v. Hansen-Tangen [1976] 1 W.L.R. 989; 120 S.J. 719 39
Reid v. Metropolitan Police Commissioner [1973] 1 Q.B. 551; [1973] 2 W.L.R.
    576; [1973] 2 All E.R. 97 .... 15, 16
Richmond upon Thames L.B.C. v. Motor Sales (Hounslow) Ltd. [1971] R.T.R.
    116; 69 L.G.R. 266; 115 S.J. 156 .... 223, 224
Rickards (Charles) v. Oppenheim [1950] 1 K.B. 616; 66 T.L.R. (Pt. 1) 435; 94
    S.J. 161; [1950] 1 All E.R. 420 92
Riley v. Webb [1987] Crim.L.R. 477; (1987) 151 J.P. 327; (1987) 6 T.L.R. 92 . 254
Rogers v. Parish (Scarborough) [1987] Q.B. 933; [1987] 2 W.L.R. 353; (1987) 131
    S.J. 223; [1987] 2 All E.R. 232; [1987] R.T.R. 312 ... 46, 47, 48, 50, 110
Rondel v. Worsley [1969] 1 AC. 191; [1967] 3 W.L.R. 1666; 111 S.J. 927; [1967] 3
    All E.R. 993 91
Rotherham Metropolitan B.C. v. Raysun (U.K.) Ltd. *The Times*, April 27, 1988
    (D.C.) 224
Rowland v. Divall [1923] 2 K.B. 500; [1923] All E.R. Rep. 270; 92 L.J.K.B. 1041;
    129 L.T. 757; 67 S.J. 703 (C.A.) 23, 109
Royscott Trust Ltd. v. Rogerson [1991] 3 W.L.R. 57 97
Ruben v. Faire Bros. [1949] 1 K.B. 254; [1949] L.J.R. 800; 93 S.J. 103; [1949] 1
    All E.R. 215 105
Ryan v. Mutual Tontine Westminster Chambers Ass. [1893] 1 Ch. 116; 62
    L.J.Ch. 252; 67 L.T. 820; 41 W.R. 146; 9 T.L.R. 72; 37 S.J. 45 (C.A.) . 100

SAMUELS v. Davis [1943] 1 K.B. 526; [1943] 2 All E.R. 3; 112 L.J.K.B. 561; 168
    L.T. 296 (C.A.) 56
Saunders v. Anglia Building Society (No. 2) [1971] A.C. 1039; [1971] 2 W.L.R.
    349; 22 P.C.R. 300 119
Scott v. Avery (1856) 5 H.L.C. 811; [1843–60] All E.R. Rep. 1; 25 L.J.Ex. 308; 28
    L.T.O.S. 207 185
Scruttons v. Midland Silicones Ltd. [1962] A.C. 446; [1962] 2 W.L.R. 186; 106
    S.J. 34; [1962] 1 All E.R. 1 123
Shaw v. Commissioner of Police of the Metropolis [1987] 1 W.L.R. 1332; [1987] 3
    All E.R. 405; (1987) 131 S.J. 1357; 10
Sherratt v. Geralds The American Jewellers Ltd. (1970) 114 S.J. 147; 68 L.G.R.
    256 (D.C.) 213
Simmons v. Potter [1975] Crim.L.R. 354; [1975] R.T.R. 347 (D.C.) 212

PAGE

Simmons v. Ravenhill (1984) 148 J.P. 109; [1984] R.T.R. 412; (1984) 3 Tr.L.R.
   29; [1983] Crim.L.R. 749 (D.C.) 224
Smeaton Hanscombe & Co. Ltd v. Setty (Sassoon) Sons & Co. (No. 1) [1953] 1
   W.L.R. 1468; 97 S.J. 562; [1953] 2 All E.R. 1471; [1953] 2 Lloyd's Rep.
   580 125
Smith v. Eric S. Bush; Harris v. Wyre Forest District Council [1990] 1 A.C. 831;
   [1989] 2 W.L.R. 790; (1989) 133 S.J. 597; (1989) 87 L.G.R. 685; [1989] 2
   All E.R. 514 .... 32, 33, 34, 129, 143
Snow (John) & Son Ltd. v. Woodcroft Ltd. [1958] B.C.L.C. 48 119
South Western General Property Co. v. Marton (1982) 263 E.G. 1090; (1983) 2
   T.L.R. 14 144
Southern Water Authority v. Carey [1985] 2 All E.R. 1077 123
Southwark London Borough Council v. Charlesworth [1983] C.L.Y. 3311;
   (1983) 2 T.L.R. 93 (D.C.) 248
Spencer v. Claude Rye (Vehicles) Ltd., The Guardian, December 19, 1972 ... 47
—— v. Cosmos Air Holidays, The Times, December 6, 1989 (C.A.) 114, 144
Spurlinj v. Bradshaw [1956] 1 W.L.R. 461; 100 S.J. 317; [1956] 2 All E.R. 121;
   [1956] 1 Lloyd's Rep. 392 .... 120, 122
Square v. Model Farm Dairies (Bournemouth) Ltd. [1939] 2 K.B. 365; [1939] 1
   All E.R. 259; 108 L.J.K.B. 198; 160 L.T. 165; 83 S.J. 152 .... 263, 264
Stadium Finance Ltd. v. Robbins [1962] 2 Q.B. 664; [1962] 3 W.L.R. 453; 106
   S.J. 369; [1962] 2 All E.R. 633 14
Stag Line v. Tyne Ship Repair Group; Zinnia, The [1984] 2 LL.L.R. 211; (1985) 4
   Tr.L. 33 .... 124, 142
Stennett v. Hancock and Peters [1939] 2 All E.R. 578; 83 S.J. 379 74
Stevenson v. Beverley Bentinck Ltd. [1976] 1 W.L.R. 483; 120 S.J. 197; [1976] 2
   All E.R. 606; [1976] R.T.R. 543 21
Stewart v. Reavell's Garage [1952] 2 Q.B. 545; [1952] 1 T.L.R. 1266; 96 S.J. 314;
   [1952] 1 All E.R. 1191 57
Stone v. Burn [1911] 1 K.B. 927; [1908–10] All E.R. Rep. 477; 80 L.J.K.B. 560;
   74 J.P. 456 206
Suisse Atlantique Société D'Armement Maritime S.A. v. N.V. Rotterdamsche
   Kolen Centrale [1967] 1 A.C. 361; [1966] 2 W.L.R. 944; 110 S.J. 367;
   [1966] 2 All E.R. 61 125
Sunair Holidays Limited v. Dodd [1970] 1 W.L.R. 1037; 114 S.J. 372; [1970] 2 All
   E.R. 410; 68 L.G.R. 550 .... 215, 216

TARLETON ENGINEERING CO. LTD. v. Nattrass [1973] 1 W.L.R. 1261; 117 S.J.
   745; [1973] 3 All E.R. 699; [1973] R.T.R. 435; 72 L.G.R. 56 .... 202, 209
Tesco Supermarkets v. Nattrass [1972] A.C. 153; [1971] 2 W.L.R. 1166; 115 S.J.
   285; [1971] 2 All E.R. 127; 69 L.G.R. 403 .... 222, 223, 231
Texas Homecare v. Stockport M.B.C. [1987] Crim.L.R. 709; [1988] T.L.R. 59;
   (1988) 152 J.P. 83; (1988) 152 J.P.N. 110 224
Thompson v. London, Midland & Scottish Railway Co. [1930] 1 K.B. 41; 98
   L.J.K.B. 615; 141 L.T. 382 119
Thornett & Fehr v. Beers & Son. [1919] 1 K.B. 486; 88 L.J.K.B. 684; 120 L.T.
   570; 24 Com.Cas. 133 52
Thornton v. Shoe Lane Parking Co. Ltd. [1971] 2 Q.B. 163; [1971] 2 W.L.R. 585;
   (1970) 115 S.J. 75; [1971] 1 All E.R. 686; [1971] R.T.R. 79 .... 120, 121, 122

U.C.B. LEASING v. Holtom [1987] R.T.R. 362; [1988] T.L.R. 97; (1987) New
   L.J. 614 (C.A.) 114
U.D.T. v. Taylor (1980) S.L.T. 18 344
Ultramares Corporation v. Touche (1931) 255 N.Y. Rep. 170, cited in Candler v.
   Crane Christmas [1951] 2 K.B. 164; [1951] 1 T.L.R. 371; 95 S.J. 171;
   [1951] 1 All E.R. 426 31
United Scientific Holdings Ltd. v. Burnley Borough Council; Cheapside Land
   Development Co. v. Messels Service Co. [1978] A.C. 904; [1977] 2
   W.L.R. 806; (1977) 121 S.J. 223; (1977) 33 P. & C.R. 220 92

PAGE

Vacwell Engineering Co. Ltd. v. B.D.H. Chemicals Ltd. [1971] 1 Q.B. 88;
  [1969] 3 W.L.R. 927; 7 K.I.R. 286 .... 75, 111
Vigers v. Cook [1919] 2 K.B. 475; 88 L.J.K.B. 1132; 121 L.T. 357; 35 T.L.R. 605;
  63 S.J. 702 172

Wait, Re [1927] 1 Ch. 606; [1926] All E.R. Rep. 433; 71 S.J. 56: 100
Waldron-Kelly v. British Railway Board [1981] 3 Cur. Law 33 145
Wallis Son and Wells v. Pratt and Haynes [1911] A.C. 394; [1911–13] All E.R.
  Rep. 989; 80 L.J.K.B. 1058; 105 L.T. 146 123
Walker v. Boyle [1982] 1 W.L.R. 495; (1981) 125 S.J. 724; [1982] 1 All E.R. 634;
  (1982) 44 P. & C.R. 20 144
Waltham Forest London Borough Council v. Wheatley (T.G.) (Central Garage)
  Ltd. (No. 2) [1978] R.T.R. 333; [1977] Crim.L.R. 761 (D.C.) 210, 211
Walton v. British Leyland (unreported) 76
Wandsworth L.B.C. v. Bentley [1980] R.T.R. 429 (D.C.) 223
Ward (R.V.) v. Bignall [1967] 1 Q.B. 534; [1967] 2 W.L.R. 1050; 111 S.J. 190;
  [1967] 2 All E.R. 449 (C.A.) 85
Warman v. Southern Counties Car Finance Corp. [1949] 2 K.B. 576; [1949]
  L.J.R. 1182; 93 S.J. 319; [1949] 1 All E.R. 711 24
Watson v. Buckley Osborne & Co. [1940] 1 All E.R. 174 56
Watts v. Spence [1976] Ch. 165; [1975] 2 W.L.R. 1039; 119 S.J. 168; [1975] 2 All
  E.R. 528 97
Westminster City Council v. Alan (Ray) Manshops [1982] 1 W.L.R. 383; (1982)
  126 S.J. 115; [1982] 1 All E.R. 771; [1982] Crim.L.R. 309 (D.C.) 219
White v. Warwick (John) [1953] 1 W.L.R. 1285; 97 S.J. 740; [1953] 2 All E.R.
  1021 124
Wilson v. Rickett Cockerell & Co. Ltd. [1954] 1 Q.B. 598; [1954] 2 W.L.R. 629;
  98 S.J. 233; [1954] 1 All E.R. 868 45
Wings Ltd. v. Ellis [1985] A.C. 272; [1984] 3 W.L.R. 965; (1984) 128 S.J. 766;
  (1985) 149 J.P. 33; [1984] 3 All E.R. 577 .... 182, 216, 218, 221, 228
Woodar Investment Development v. Wimpey Construction U.K. [1980] 1
  W.L.R. 277; (1980) 124 S.J. 184; [1980] 1 All E.R. 571 (H.L.) 43
Woodman v. Photo Trade Processing Ltd., Times Business News, June 20,
  1981 .... 145, 176
Worcester Works Finance Ltd. v. Cooden Engineering Ltd. [1972] 1 Q.B. 210;
  [1971] 3 W.L.R. 661; 115 S.J. 605; [1971] 3 All E.R. 708 18
Wormell v. R.H.M. Agriculture (East) [1987] 1 W.L.R. 1091; (1987) 131 S.J.
  1085; [1987] 3 All E.R. 75; [1988] T.L.R. 114; (1987) 84 L.S.Gaz 2197 . 55
Wren v. Holt [1903] 1 K.B. 610; 72 L.J.K.B. 340; 88 L.T. 282; 67 J.P. 191; 51
  W.R. 435 74
Wright v. Dunlop Rubber Co. Ltd. and I.C.I. (1972) Vol. XIII, Knights Indus-
  trial Reports 255. (C.A.) 76

Yeoman Credit Ltd. v. Apps [1962] 2 Q.B. 508; [1961] 3 W.L.R. 94; 105 S.J.
  567; [1961] 2 All E.R. 281 114
Yugotours v. Wadsley [1988] Crim.L.R. 623 (D.C.) 217

Zawadski v. Sleigh (1975) 119 S.J. 318; [1975] R.T.R. 113; [1975] Crim.L.R.
  180 (D.C.) 211
Zinnia, The. See Stag Line v. Tyne Ship Repair Group 124, 142

TABLE OF STATUTES

PAGE

1542 Laws in Wales Act (34 & 35
Hen. 8 c. 26) 15
1862 Merchandise Marks Act (25
& 26 Vict. c. 88) 196
1887 Merchandise Marks Act (50
& 51 Vict. c. 28) 196
s. 17 .... 229, 264
1889 Factors Act (52 & 53 Vict. c.
45)—
s. 1 12
s. 2 .... 12, 22
(1) 13
(2) 13
1893 Sale of Goods Act (56 & 57
Vict. c. 71) .. 37, 45, 52, 407
s. 13 282
s. 14 282
(2) 200
s. 55 135
(3)–(11) 274
1933 Local Government Act (23
& 24 Geo. 5 c. 51) ... 197
1943 Law Reform (Frustrated
Contracts) Act (6 & 7
Geo. 6 c. 40) 89
1953 Merchandise Marks Act (1
& 2 Eliz. 2 c. 48) 196
1954 Hire-Purchase Act (2 & 3
Eliz. 2 c. 51) 1
1955 Food and Drugs Act (4 & 5
Eliz. 2 c. 16) 263, 286
1957 Occupiers' Liability Act (5
& 6 Eliz. 2 c. 31) . 126, 130,
146
s. 2(2) 128
1961 Carriage by Air Act (9 & 10
Eliz. 2 c. 27) 146
Consumer Protection Act
(9 & 10 Eliz. 2 c. 40) .. 244,
247
s. 50(5) 247
1963 Weights and Measures Act
(c. 31) 193, 196
1964 Hire-Purchase Act (c. 53) . 1
s. 28 21
Pt. III 10, 20, 21, 22
1965 Hire-Purchase Act (c. 66) .. 296,
302, 326, 333, 339, 358
1967 Misrepresentation Act (c.
7) 1, 35, 395, 400

PAGE

1967 Misrepresentation Act—
cont.
s. 1 99
ss. 2, 3, 4, 6, 7 and 8 ... 139
s. 2 29
(1) 27, 30, 34, 96, 97
(2) 96, 98, 99
s. 3 .... 138, 139, 145, 342
s. 11 139
(1) 139
1968 Trade Descriptions Act (c.
29) .. 1, 5, 28, 132, 133, 161,
182, 194, 195, 196, 197,
200, 243, 257, 258, 259,
265, 271, 280, 284, 288,
315, 317, 389, 395, 400
s. 1 .... 197, 200, 203, 212,
214, 215, 217, 226, 233,
282
(1) 198, 199, 200, 205
(a) and (b) 207
(a) 201, 208, 213,
220, 225
(b) 202, 203, 206,
208, 209, 210,
211, 213, 220,
224, 225
s. 2 205
(1) 203, 204, 205, 207
(c) 213
(e) 213
(j) 207, 208
(2) 203, 204
(3) 203, 204
(4) 204
(5) 204
s. 3(1) 206
(2) and (3) 206
(3) 207
(4) 204
s. 4 .... 201, 202, 207
(1)(b) 208
(c) 207
(2) 196, 201
(3) 202
s. 5 207
(2) 207
s. 7 205

PAGE

1968 Trade Descriptions Act—
      cont.
      s. 11 ..... 197, 219, 222, 230,
                  231, 232, 235, 237
          (2) 235, 282
      s. 14 ..... 151, 197, 198, 214,
                  215, 218, 219, 220,
                  226, 229, 232, 233,
                  237, 259, 260
          (1) 214, 218, 219
              (a) 216, 217
              (b) 217, 219
          (2)(b) 215
      s. 18 228
      ss. 19(1), (2) and (4) ... 227
      s. 20 .... 222, 233
      s. 23 ..... 197, 203, 212, 213,
                  222, 224, 225, 226, 242
      s. 24 ..... 212, 217, 221, 225,
                  226, 229
          (1) ... 212, 220, 221, 224,
                  241, 224, 225
              (a) 222, 241
              (b) 222, 223
          (2) 222
          (3) 220, 224
      s. 25 .... 220, 226
      s. 26 227
          (1) 227
      s. 27 227
      s. 28 227
      s. 35 .... 229, 264
      s. 39 208
      Civil Evidence Act (c. 64)—
      s. 11 261
1969 Employers'   Liability
      (Defective   Equip-
      ment) Act (c. 37) 76
1971 Consumer Protection Act
      (c. 15) 244
      Unsolicited Goods and
      Services Act (c. 30) .. 1, 79
      s. 1 ....
          (1) 80
      s. 2 80
      s. 6 80
      Civil Aviation Act (c. 75) . 395,
                                    400
1972 Road Traffic Act (c. 20) .. 146
      Defective Premises Act (c.
      35) 146
      European Communities
      Act (c. 68)—
      s. 2(2) 287
      Local Government Act (c.
      70) 5
      Criminal Justice Act (c. 71) 258

PAGE

1973 Supply of Goods (Implied
      Terms) Act (c. 13) ... 1, 24,
      103, 109, 135, 273, 324, 407
      ss. 8–11 345
      s. 9 .... 40n
      s. 10 .... 41, 55n
      Fair Trading Act (c. 41) .. 1, 3,
      148, 230, 265, 267, 296
      s. 1 268
      s. 2 269
          (1) 154, 231, 268
              (b) 283
          (3) 231, 268, 272, 278
      s. 3 269
      s. 12 269
      s. 13 270
          (a) 274
      s. 14 .... 269, 270
      s. 15 270
      s. 16 270
      s. 17 .... 269, 270, 271
          (2) 270, 274
      s. 20 271
      s. 21 271
      s. 22 271
      s. 23 272
      s. 25 272
      s. 26 272
      s. 27 272
      s. 28 272
      s. 29 272
      s. 34 .... 151, 285
          (1) 282, 283, 285
          (2) 284
          (3) 284
          (4) 284
      s. 35 285
      s. 37 285
      s. 38 286
          (2), (7) 286
      s. 39 286
      s. 40 286
      s. 41 285
      s. 124(1) 153, 267
          (3) 148, 267
      s. 130 5
      s. 132 272
      s. 137 198
          (2) 283
          (5) 286
      Pt. II 5, 43, 148, 194,
      231, 269, 270, 271, 272, 278
      Pt. III 3, 150, 152, 269,
                     280, 283, 285
      Sched. 4 270
      Sched. 5 270
      Sched. 6 271
      Powers of Criminal Courts
      Act (c. 62) 28, 194, 228,
                       258, 262, 317
      s. 35 298
          (1) 258

PAGE

1973 Powers of Criminal Courts
Act—cont.
(3) 259
(4) 261
s. 38(2) 261
1974 Prices Act (c. 24) 231
Health and Safety at Work
etc. Act (c. 37)—
s. 6 .... 243, 246
Consumer Credit Act
(c. 39) 1, 3, 4, 5, 10, 20,
45, 55, 83, 84, 109, 127,
146, 150, 194, 254, 265,
267, 282, 289, 295, 296,
325, 345, 346
s. 4 154
s. 8 301
(2) 302
(3) 301
s. 9(3) 302, 308
(4) 302
s. 10(1)(a) 302
(3) 303
s. 11 299
ss. 12–13 .... 303, 304
s. 14(1) 347
(2) 347
s. 15 .... 301, 304
(2) 301
s. 16 .... 301, 306, 324
s. 17 305
(3) 306
s.19 .... 310, 337
(3) 310
s. 20 308
s. 21 314
ss. 22–24 313
s. 22(2) 315
s. 23(2) 315
s. 25 315
(1)(a) 315
(2) 315
s. 27 20
s. 29 298
ss. 31–33 315
s. 32 298
s. 40 316
s. 41 315
s. 43(3)(b) 317
s. 46 .... 28, 318
s. 48 298
(1)(b) 320
s. 49 320
(2) 320
s. 50(1) 321
(2) 321
s. 51 347
s. 52 319
s. 55 324

PAGE

1974 Consumer Credit Act—
cont.
s. 56 .... 342, 343, 345
(1)(c) 342
(2) 342
(3) 342
s. 57 .... 331, 351
(2) 331
(3) 331
ss. 58–65 323
s. 58(1) 324
s. 59(1) 331
s. 60 325
(1) 326
s. 61 .... 325, 326
(1)(a) 353
(2) 324
(4) 324
ss. 62–63 326
ss. 62–65 328
s. 62 .... 334, 353
(1) 327
(2) 327
s. 63 .... 334, 335, 353
(1) 327
(2) 327
(a) 327
(b) 327
(3) 334
(4) 348
s. 64 334
(1) 353
(a) 334
(b) 334
(2) 348
(4) 335
s. 65 .... 323, 351, 360
s. 66 ...... 348, 349
ss. 67–73 333
s. 67 .... 81, 324
s. 68 335
s. 69 335
(1) 310
(2)(b) 338
(4) 336
s. 70(1)(b) 336
(c) 336
(2) 336
(5) 349
s. 71 .... 336, 337
s. 72 .... 337, 338
s. 73 338
(2) 338
s. 74(2) 334
s. 75 ...... 164, 181, 304, 342,
343, 344
(1) 343
(2) 344
(3) 343

PAGE

1974 Consumer Credit Act—
cont.
s. 75(5) 344
ss. 77–79 .... 305, 328, 329
ss. 77–80 323
s. 77(1)(a) 305
s. 78(4) 328
s. 80 329
s. 81 361
(2) 361
s. 84 .... 348, 349
(1) 349
(2) 349
(3) 349
(4) 349
(5) 349
s. 85 348
s. 87 .... 356, 360
s. 88 356
s. 89 357
s. 90 .... 358, 359
(2) 359
(3) 359
s. 91 .... 357, 358
s. 92 360
(1) 358
(2) 358
(3) 263, 354, 358
s. 94 354
s. 95 354
s. 97 356
ss. 99–100 .... 338, 339
ss. 99–101 338
s. 99 359
(2) 339
s. 100(1) 339, 340
(2) 339, 359
(4) 339
(5) 339
s. 101 .... 338, 340
(3) 340
(7) 340
(8) 340
s. 102 332
ss. 105–110 329
s. 127 356
(1) 352
(2) 352
(3) and (4) 353
s. 129 ..... 352, 356, 357, 360
s. 132 360
s. 133 360
(3) 360
s. 135 .... 352, 360
(1) 352
(2) 352
(3) 352
s. 136 .... 352, 353
ss. 137–140 361

PAGE

1974 Consumer Credit Act—
cont.
s. 138 .... 361, 362
s. 139(1) 362
(2) 362
(5) 362
s. 145 314
(1)(e) 365
(8) 366
ss. 147–150 313
s. 148 316
s. 149 316
s. 152 319
s. 157(1) 366
(2) 366
(3) 366
s. 158 .... 366, 368
(3) 366
s. 159 366
(2) 367
(3) 367
(5) 367
s. 160 366
s. 166 315
s. 167(2) 28, 320
s. 170 .... 298, 321
(3) 298, 354
s. 171(7) 362
s. 173(1) 358
(1) and (2) 298
(3) .. 298, 316, 323, 351,
358, 359
s. 175 332
s. 182(2) 328
s. 188(3) 297
s. 189 ..... 198, 297, 305, 318,
335, 347
(1) 297
(2) 314
Pts. V–IX 323
Pt. VIII 365
Sched. 1 .... 298, 316
Sched. 2 .... 297, 303, 305
Sched. 3 297
para. 17(2) 329
Sched. 4 .... 19, 55
Solicitors Act (c. 47) 146
1977 Torts (Interference with
Goods) Act (c. 32)—
s. 6(1) 25
(2) 25
(3) 25
Unfair Contract Terms Act
(c.50) ... 1, 5, 45, 61, 117,
118, 122, 123, 125,
126, 133, 139, 140,
145, 159, 194, 257,
273, 277, 296, 373,
374, 375, 395
s. 1(1) 129
(3) 127
ss. 2–3 161

PAGE

1977 Unfair Contract Terms
         Act—*cont.*
      ss. 2–4 127
      ss. 2–7 127
      s. 2 ... 126, 128, 130, 138, 243
         (1) 121, 128
         (2) 137, 374, 380
      ss. 3, 4, 5, 6 and 7 130
      s. 3 ..... 6, 130, 134, 179, 183
         (2) 374
      s. 4 137
         (1) 137
      s. 5 .... 128, 137, 138
         (1) 138
         (2)(*a*) 138
         (3) 138
      s. 6 .... 135, 136, 137, 138,
                       140, 273, 274
         (2) 132, 275
            (*a*) 276
         (3) 141
      s. 7 .... 128, 136, 138, 140
         (3) 141
            (A) 136
         (4) 136, 141
      s. 8 .... 99, 138, 342
      s. 11(1) 138
         (3) 140
         (4) 142
         (5) 140
      s. 12 .. 131, 133, 134, 135, 136,
              185, 200, 249, 273, 274
         (1)(*a*) 132
            (*b*) 132
         (2) 131
         (3) 132
      ss. 13, 14 and 15 135
      s. 13 .... 136, 137
         (1) 128, 129
         (2) 129
      s. 14 .... 127, 283
         (2) 136
      s. 15 136
      s. 20 141
      s. 21 141
      Sched. 2 140
1978 Consumer Safety Act (c.
         38) 2, 244, 245
      s. 1 244
      s. 3(1) 244
      s. 5(1) 245
1979 Weights and Measures Act
         (c. 45) 193
      Sale of Goods Act (c. 54) .36, 59,
              160, 170, 243, 257, 263,
              315, 343, 345, 383, 384,
                            385, 386
      s. 3 321
      s. 7 89

PAGE

1979 Sale of Goods Act—*cont.*
      s. 8 92
      s. 10(3) 55
      ss. 11, 13 28
      s. 11(3) 102
         (4) 104, 110, 345
      ss. 12–14 .... 135, 341
      s. 12 .... 11, 24, 25
         (1) 22
         (2) 22
         (3) 23
      ss. 13–15 273
      s. 13 ...... 36, 39, 40, 98, 275,
                            276, 284
         (1) 38
         (3) 37, 276
      s. 14 .... 40, 41, 42, 53
         (1) 42
         (2), (3) 284
         (2) 44, 54, 74, 88, 276
            (*a*) 51
            (*b*) 51, 276
         (3) ... 53, 54, 55, 132, 276
         (5) 42, 43
         (6) 46, 47, 54
      s. 15 103
      ss. 16–18 84
      s. 16 87
      s. 17 .... 85, 88
      s. 18 .... 85, 87, 88
         r. 1 .... 18, 299
      s. 20 86
         (1) 84
      s. 21(1) 10, 11
      s. 22(1) 14
      s. 23 .... 16, 17, 97
      s. 24 .... 18, 22
      s. 25(1) 18, 22
      s. 30 110
      s. 31(2) 104
      s. 32(2) 88
      s. 34 .... 104, 105
      s. 35 .... 106, 107, 108
         (1) 104, 105
      s. 36 111
      s. 51(2) 112
         (3) 112
      s. 52 100
      s. 53(2) 113
         (3) 113
      s. 54 .... 103, 112
      s. 59 108
      s. 61 ...... 35, 84, 86, 100
         (1) 102
      Pt. I 63
1980 Magistrates' Courts Act (c.
         43)—
      s. 40 258
      s. 76 261
      Limitation Act (c. 58)—
      s. 11 72

PAGE

1981 Broadcasting Act (c. 68) ..   288
1982 Civil Jurisdiction and
        Judgments Act 1982
        (c. 27)—
     Sched. 1 .... 67, 69
     Supply of Goods and
        Services Act (c. 29) ... 2, 4,
            103, 109, 136, 151, 278
        s. 2   24
        s. 3   40
        s. 4 .... 41, 56
        s. 7   24
        s. 8   40
        s. 9 .... 41, 57
        s. 12(4)   90
        ss. 13–15 .... 90, 103
        s. 13 .... 56, 90, 91, 130
        s. 14   91
        s. 15   93
     Criminal Justice Act (c.
        48)—
        s. 67   258
     Insurance Companies Act
        (c. 50)   424
1984 Food Act (c. 30)   193
     Data Protection Act (c. 35)   368
        s. 21   368
        s. 22   368
        s. 23   368
     Cable and Broadcasting Act
        (c. 46)   288
1985 Companies Act (c. 6)—
        s.224   423
1986 Consumer Safety (Amend-
        ment) Act (c. 29)   245
     Building Societies Act (c.
        53)   306
     Financial Services Act (c.
        60) 83, 291
1987 Minors Contracts Act
        (c. 13)   321
     Banking Act (c. 22)   83
     Consumer Protection Act
        (c. 43) . 2, 44, 115, 194, 245,
            246, 247, 249, 252,
            262, 376, 377, 378,
                    395, 400
        s. 1(1)   63
           (2)   66
        s. 2(1)   64
           (2) 69, 70, 71
           (3) 69, 70
           (4)   66
           (5)   70
        s. 3   67
           (2)(a)   249
        s. 4(1)   70
              (e)   72
           (2)   71
        s. 5 .... 64, 73,

PAGE

1987 Consumer Protection Act—
        cont.
        s. 5(2)   65
           (3)(a)   249
           (4)   65
        s. 6(7) 67, 69
        s. 10 .... 232, 250
           (1)   249
           (2)(b)   250
           (3) 250, 252
           (4) 251, 254
           (5)   251
           (7) 248, 249
        s. 11 .... 69, 252
           (1)(b)   252
           (2)   252
           (5) 252, 253
           (7)   248
        s. 12   252
           (5)   254
        s. 13(1)(a)   253
        s. 14(1)   253
           (7)   253
        s. 16   253
        s. 19   246
           (1)   246
           (2)   247
        s. 20 ...... 219, 232, 236, 239,
                    240, 242
           (1) 232, 233, 234,
                    239, 240
           (2) 233, 236, 239
           (6)   234
        s. 21   236
           (1) 235, 237
           (3)   237
        s. 22   237
        s. 23 .... 237, 238
           (1)   238
           (2)   239
           (3)   238
        s. 24   240
        s. 25   232
           (1)   239
           (2)   239
        s. 26 ...... 232, 237, 240, 241
        s. 27(1)   254
           (2)   254
        s. 28   254
        s. 29   254
        s. 30   254
        s. 39 .... 240, 241
           (1) 241, 254
           (2) and (3)   241
           (2)   254
           (4)   241
        s. 40   242
           (1)   242
           (2)   233

PAGE

1987 Consumer Protection Act—
cont.
    s. 41(1) 255, 263
        (3) 255
        (4) 255
    s. 45 .... 66, 246
        (1) 248
        (2) 248
    s. 46 .... 66, 71, 246
        (1) 248
        (5) 248
    s. 50(7) 73
    Pt. I 6, 59, 63, 73, 243,
        246, 249, 254, 372
    Pt. II 3, 194, 240, 241,
        243, 245, 246
    Pt. III 194, 195, 220, 229,
        232, 240, 241, 254,
        282, 289
    Pt. IV 242

PAGE

1988 Consumer Arbitration
    Agreements Act (c.
    21) 2, 185
    s. 1 185
    s. 3 185
    s. 4 185
    Legal Aid Act (c. 34) 186
    s. 8 186
        (5) 186
    s. 9(6) 186
    s. 10 186
    s. 14 186
    s. 15(2) 187
    s. 16 187
        (6) 187
    Road Traffic Act (c. 52)—
    s. 75 263
1990 Food Safety Act (c. 16) .. 3, 193
    s. 14 193
    Courts & Legal Services
    Act (c. 41) 310
    s. 62 91

TABLE OF STATUTORY INSTRUMENTS

PAGE

1976 Consumer Credit Licensing (Appeals) Regulations 1976 (S.I. 1976 No. 837) 315

Mail Order Transactions (Information) Order 1976 (S.I. 1976 No. 1812) 279

Consumer Transactions (Restrictions on Statements) Order 1976 (S.I. 1976 No. 1813) . 134, 160, 274, 278

Art. 2(1) 274

Art. 3 .... 274, 277

(a) 274

(b), (c) & (d) 275

Art. 4 276

Art. 5 277

1977 Consumer Credit (Credit Reference Agency) Regulations 1977 (S.I. 1977 No. 329) 366

reg. 2 366

reg. 3 366

reg. 4 367

Sched. 2 366

Consumer Credit (Conduct of Business) (Credit Reference Agencies) Regulations 1977 (S.I. 1977 No. 330)—

reg. 2 366

reg. 3 366

reg. 5 367

Business Advertisements (Disclosure) Order 1977 (S.I. 1977 No. 1918) 43, 280

Art. 2(1) 280

1978 Consumer Transactions (Restrictions on Statements) (Amendment) Order 1978 (S.I. 1978 No. 127) 274

1979 Price Marking (Bargain Offers) Order 1979 (S.I. 1979 No. 364) 231, 232, 268

1979 Price Marking (Bargain Offers) (Amendment) Order 1979 (S.I. 1979 No. 633) 231, 232

1980 Consumer Credit (Total Charge for Credit) Regulations 1980 (S.I. 1980 No. 51)—

reg. 2(1)(d) 309

reg. 4 308

reg. 5 308

reg. 7 309

reg. 8 309

reg. 9 309

reg. 15 310

Consumer Credit (Exempt Advertisements) Order 1980 (S.I. 1980 No. 53) 317

Consumer Credit (Advertisements) Regulations 1980 (S.I. 1980 No. 54) 318

1982 Supply of Services (Exclusion of Implied Terms) Order 1982 (S.I. 1982 No. 1771) 90

1983 Consumer Credit (Agreements to enter Prospective Agreements) (Exemptions) Regulations 1983 (S.I. 1983 No. 1552) 331

Consumer Credit (Agreements) Regulations 1983 (S.I. 1983 No. 1553) 326

regs. 2–5 326

reg. 6 326

reg. 6(2) 326

reg. 11(e) 328

Consumer Credit (Credit-Token Agreements) Regulations 1983 (S.I. 1983 No. 1555)—

reg. 2 349

Consumer Credit (Guarantees and Indemnities) Regulations 1983 (S.I. 1983 No. 1556) 329

PAGE

1983 Consumer Credit (Cancel-
        lation Notices and
        Copies of Documents)
        Regulations 1983 (S.I.
        1983 No. 1557) ... 328, 334,
                                               335
        reg. 5   335
        reg. 6   335
      Consumer Credit (Notice of
        Cancellation Rights)
        (Exemptions) Regula-
        tions 1983 (S.I. 1983
        No. 1158)   335
      Consumer Credit (Repay-
        ment of Credit on Can-
        cellation) Regulations
        1983 (S.I. 1983 No.
        1559)   337
      Consumer Credit (Linked
        Transactions) (Exemp-
        tions)   Regulations
        1983 (S.I. 1983 No.
        1560) 310, 336
      Consumer Credit (Enforce-
        ment Default and Ter-
        mination   Notices)
        Regulations 1983 (S.I.
        1983 No. 1561)   356
      Consumer Credit (Rebate
        on Early Settlement)
        Regulations 1983 (S.I.
        1983 No. 1562)   355
        reg. 5   355
        reg. 6   355
      Consumer Credit (Settle-
        ment   Information)
        Regulations 1983 (S.I.
        1983 No. 1564)   356
      Consumer Credit (Pre-
        scribed Periods for
        Giving Information)
        Regulations 1983 (S.I.
        1983 No. 1569)—
        reg. 2   328
      Consumer Credit (Run-
        ning-Account Credit
        Information) Regula-
        tions 1983 (S.I. 1983
        No. 1570)   328
      Consumer Credit (Increase
        of Monetary Amounts)
        Order 1983 (S.I. 1983
        No. 1571) 340, 349

PAGE

1983 Consumer Credit (Increase
        of Monetary Limits)
        Order 1983 (S.I. 1983
        No. 1878)   343
1984 Criminal Penalties etc.
        (Increase) Order 1984
        (S.I. 1984 No. 447) ..   228,
                                               258
1985 Supply of Services (Exclu-
        sion of Implied Terms)
        Order 1985 (S.I. 1985
        No. 1)   91
1987 Approval of Safety Stan-
        dards Regulations 1987
        (S.I. 1987 No. 1911) .   251
      Consumer Protection (Can-
        cellation of Contracts
        Concluded away from
        Business   Premises)
        Regulations 1987 (S.I.
        1987 No. 2117) . 81, 332, 372
        reg. 4   333
        reg. 9   305
1988 Control of Misleading
        Advertisement Regu-
        lations 1988 (S.I. 1988
        No. 915) 4,
                                  287, 317, 372,
                                         395, 400
        Art. 2   289
          (2)   289
        Art. 6   290
1989 Consumer Credit (Exempt
        Agreements) Order
        1989 (S.I. 1989 No.
        869)   306
        Art. 3(1)(a)(i)   307
              (ii)   307
          (b)   307
      Consumer Credit (Quota-
        tions) Regulations
        1989 (S.I. 1989 No.
        1126)   319
        reg. 2(2)   319
        reg. 4(1)(b)   319
1991 Credit Cards (Price Dis-
        crimination) Order
        1991 (S.I. 1991 No.
        2159)   240

CHAPTER ONE

INTRODUCTION

"The bottle started to leak as I was putting it into my bag"
"The central heating isn't working"
"The holiday was ruined"
"The car has been off the road for a month"
"The underpants had too much sulphite"
"There were worms in the pork chops"

This book is concerned with complaints which consumers may have against a supplier of goods or services and with the remedies available to them. It is a vast subject and, as indicated in the preface,[1] it is necessary to curtail it.

In the words of the Molony Committee on Consumer Protection (1961) "the consumer, unlike some classes with claims on public bounty, is everybody all the time." In the present book, however, the word "consumer" will be used to describe a customer who buys for personal use and not for business purposes.[2]

A number of learned writers, *e.g.* Borrie and Diamond in their excellent book *The Consumer, Society and the Law*, have traced the history of the subject and have shown that, although the subject is comparatively new, its roots are old. Thus the law has imposed duties on persons exercising certain callings for many centuries (*e.g.* innkeepers and carriers). Nevertheless, the explosion of interest in consumer matters is very much a creature of the second half of the twentieth century. We can see this simply by looking at the dates of some of the principal reforming statutes:

Hire-Purchase Acts 1954 and 1964
Misrepresentation Act 1967
Trade Descriptions Act 1968
Unsolicited Goods and Services Act 1971
Fair Trading Act 1973
Supply of Goods (Implied Terms) Act 1973
Consumer Credit Act 1974
Unfair Contract Terms Act 1977

---

[1] *Ante*, p. v.
[2] Note, however, the extended meaning of "consumer" in the Consumer Credit Act 1974, *post*, pp. 296–297.

1

Consumer Safety Act 1978
Supply of Goods and Services Act 1982
Consumer Protection Act 1987
Consumer Arbitration Agreements Act 1988

What is the reason for this tremendous upsurge of activity? The answer is two-fold—a combination of new business methods and changing social attitudes. The key factors on business methods are to be found in the complexity of the goods themselves and in the changing forms of advertising and distribution. To quote again from the Molony Report (p. 31):

> "[The last half century] has seen a growing tendency for manufacturers ... to appeal directly to the public by forceful national advertising and other promotional methods ... a further influence during the same period has been the development of a mass market for extremely complex mechanical and electrical goods. ... Their performance cannot in some cases be accurately established by a short trial; shortcomings of design are not apparent to the inexpert eye; inherent faults may only come to light when the article breaks down after a period of use."

In other words, the need for what is called consumer protection has become far greater because the consumer is no longer in a position to rely on his own judgment when buying a complex article.

The second motivating force is the general move from individualism to collectivism. The twentieth century has seen not only consumer protection but also the Rent Acts, Financial Services Act, the large volume of legislation protecting employees and, of course, the welfare state. The extent to which some of these measures hamper business activity is, of course, a matter of keen political debate.

The international dimension

A modern textbook[3] has demonstrated that the judiciary of the United States has been a long way ahead of this country in recognising and dealing with consumer problems. In particular, the American courts have increased the manufacturer's liability in two respects (1) by moving from negligence liability to strict liability and (2) by breaking the shackles of the privity of contract rule.

The subject of consumer protection is also very much alive in the European Community and other Western countries. In the second edition of this book we referred to EC initiatives in four areas— product liability, cancellation of "doorstep" sales, misleading adver- tisements and consumer credit. Since then the first three of them have

---

[3] A. M. Clark, *Product Liability*, pp. 13–21. The policy aspects are particularly instructive.

found their way into English law as a result of one Act and two statutory instruments and they will be considered in Chapters 5, 6 and 14. It is clear that further developments are in the pipeline and that English lawyers and advisers must be constantly aware of actual (and proposed) developments in Brussels. The matter is dealt with in the final chapter of this book.

Consumer protection agencies

There are a very large number of bodies concerned with consumer protection matters and they can be divided into Government Departments, Government-sponsored bodies, local authorities and voluntary bodies.

(a) *Government Departments*

As a result of the 1979 general election, the Department of Prices and Consumer Affairs was absorbed into the Department of Trade and Industry; that Department now has an Under Secretary of State for Industry and Consumer Affairs. Among its principal duties are the making of regulations under the Consumer Credit Act 1974 and the Consumer Protection Act 1987, Part II.[4] In addition the Home Office has responsibilities in certain areas, including firearms and explosives, and the Ministry of Agriculture, Fisheries and Food has a number of duties under the Food Safety Act 1990.

Closely linked with the Department of Trade and Industry is the Office of Fair Trading which was set up as a result of the Fair Trading Act 1973. The extensive powers and duties of the Director General will be discussed later in this book. The bulk of the provisions in the Act are concerned with restrictive practices, monopolies and mergers but the Director General of Fair Trading is also given very extensive powers in relation to consumer protection matters. His duties include:

  (i) keeping under review the commercial supply of goods and services to consumers in the United Kingdom;
 (ii) making recommendations to the Department of Trade and Industry—either if asked to do so or on his own initiative;
(iii) taking action against individual traders who have persisted in a course of conduct which is unfair to consumers[5];
 (iv) providing information to the public;
  (v) encouraging trade associations to prepare codes of practice for their members.[6]

In other words he is a statutory watchdog who can take action if

---

[4] *Post*, pp. 245 and 297.
[5] Fair Trading Act 1973, Pt. III, *post*, p. 282.
[6] '*Post*, p. 148.

undesirable trade practices come to his notice. He has also been given very extensive powers to supervise and control the consumer credit industry under the Consumer Credit Act 1974. His principal weapon of control lies in the operation of the licensing system; every trader who carries on a consumer credit or consumer hire business needs a licence[7] and the Director General is responsible for the grant, renewal, suspension and revocation of licences. He is also responsible, along with trading standards inspectors, for the enforcement of the Act by criminal proceedings. The Consumer Credit Act is examined in Part IV of this book. The most recent addition to his powers is to be found in the Control of Misleading Advertisement Regulations 1988 which will be discussed in Chapter 14.

(b) *Government-sponsored bodies*

The Consumer Council, set up as a result of the Molony Committee recommendations, was abolished by the Conservative Government in 1971, but a new body—named the National Consumer Council—was set up by the Labour Government in 1974 and is financed by a Government grant. It has no executive power and does not deal with individual complaints. Its principal functions are to act as a pressure group to represent the consumer interest in negotiations with Government and other bodies. It gives an immensely wide meaning to the term "consumer"; thus it has published papers dealing with security of tenure for tenants and with the powers of the police. The relatively generous help given to the National Consumer Council can be contrasted with the very inadequate funds made available for legal aid.[8] A report of the Council "Service Please" by Lantin and Woodroffe led directly to the passing of the Supply of Goods and Services Act 1982.

The Department of Trade and Industry also makes a grant to the British Standards Institute. This voluntary body has been in existence for more than 75 years, and one of its functions is to lay down uniform specifications for certain products. If a product bears a B.S.I. "kite mark" this means that it has been tested by B.S.I. Regular spot checks will follow and the mark will be withdrawn if these prove unsatisfactory.

(c) *Local authorities*

The county councils and the London boroughs make two major contributions to consumer protection. First they employ trading standards inspectors (their former name was weights and measures inspectors) who have extensive responsibilities in the enforcement of the

---

[7] *Post*, p. 313.
[8] See an article in [1978] L.S.Gaz. 822.

Trade Descriptions Act 1968, the Consumer Credit Act 1974 and Part
II of the Fair Trading Act 1973. In all these cases they must give the
Director General of Fair Trading notice of an intended prosecution[9]
and they will also keep him informed of undesirable trade practices
which come to their notice.

The second major field of local authority involvement lies in the
field of consumer advice. Consumer Advice Centres have been set up
in many parts of the country under the Local Government Act 1972.
They give pre-shopping advice and they also give advice on complaints. Sometimes they take up individual complaints with the object
of achieving a satisfactory settlement but they do not normally assist in
litigation if a settlement proves impossible.

(d) *Voluntary bodies*

The Consumers' Association is widely known for its comparative
testing of goods and services. The results are published in *Which?* and
are clearly of great value to prospective consumers. The Association is
very active in promoting legislation dealing with consumer affairs.
Thus it played a large part in seeing the Unfair Contract Terms Act
1977 on to the statute book and is pressing for legislation to improve
the buyer's right to reject (see *post*, p. 108).

There are also a number of consumer groups at local level; their
main function is to carry out research into the quality of local services
and to publish the results of these surveys to their members. There is a
central co-ordinating body known as the National Federation of Consumer Groups and it is believed that total membership of the groups is
in the region of 2,000.

Finally we should mention trade and professional associations (*e.g.*
the Retail Motor Industry Federation or the Association of British
Travel Agents). These are in no sense consumer protection agencies
but many of them operate voluntary conciliation and arbitration procedures. A consumer with a complaint may well find that an approach
to the relevant association may produce a more satisfactory outcome
than embarking on the hazards of litigation. The codes of practice and
arbitration procedures operated by a number of associations are
examined in Chapter 9 of this book.[10]

One important aspect of the voluntary procedures referred to above
has been the creation of an "Ombudsman" for particular industries.
The Insurance Ombudsman's Bureau was set up, on a voluntary basis,
in 1981. Similar bodies now exist in relation to banking, building
societies, pensions and unit trusts. The Insurance Ombudsman's
powers (and those of the others) stem from the terms of his appointment which are set out in Appendix 3.

[9] See, *e.g.* Fair Trading Act 1973, s.130.
[10] *Post*, p. 148.

Part I

THE CONSUMER AND THE CIVIL LAW

The civil law assists the consumer by imposing certain obligations on manufacturers and suppliers of goods and services and by restricting attempts to exclude or cut down these obligations or the remedies available on breach.

It must be said at once that the law relating to many of these obligations is in a very uncertain state. Two particularly thorny questions are (1) when are goods unmerchantable and (2) when does the buyer lose his right of rejection by "accepting" the goods? There is also the question of "reasonableness" under section 3 of the Unfair Contract Terms Act where, for example, a builder seeks to avoid liability for delay or non-performance.[1] When one thinks of the many millions of consumer contracts concluded each day this absence of authority may seem surprising. A charitable view would be that traders, for reasons of commercial goodwill, settle all genuine complaints without litigation. A more realistic view is that consumers are deterred from bringing proceedings by a variety of factors including ignorance, lethargy and cost.

In Chapters 2–4 we shall consider the consumer's rights against his *immediate supplier* of goods for failure to pass title, to deliver the goods contracted for or to deliver goods of the right quality and fitness. Then in Chapter 5 we shall consider his rights against the *manufacturer (and other suppliers in the distribution chain)* both under the general law and under Part I of the Consumer Protection Act 1987. Chapter 6 deals with a number of common consumer problems including defective performance, late delivery and disputes about the price. In Chapter 7 we shall analyse and explain the remedies available to the consumer and to members of his family. This will be followed in Chapter 8 by an examination of exemption clauses. In Chapter 9 we shall discuss the various ways in which the consumer can seek redress

---

[1] The Unfair Contract Terms Act 1977 and the emerging case law is examined in Chap. 8.

for his complaint. This will include voluntary arbitration and adjudication procedures and arbitration in the county court. The special rules relating to credit transactions (involving an amalgam of civil, criminal and administrative matters) will be dealt with in Part IV of this book.

CHAPTER TWO

"THEY SAY IT ISN'T MINE"

(1) A owns a diamond ring. B steals it and sells it to C who sells it to D. The police have now traced the ring and have seized it from D's home. (2) E takes his car to F, a car dealer, and says "Find me a buyer but don't sell for less than £1,000." F sells to G for £600 and disappears. (3) H, a finance house, supply a car to I on hire-purchase. Before completing her payments I sells the car to J, a motor dealer, who lets the car out to K on a fresh hire-purchase agreement. H now claim from K the unpaid balance due on the original agreement.

In unravelling this type of problem three closely connected principles must be distinguished:
1. Does any buyer acquire title to the goods?
2. What are the rights as between each buyer and seller? This question will usually only be relevant in advising a buyer who has not acquired title.
3. What are the rights of a buyer who has spent money on improving the goods?

In this chapter it is proposed to deal separately with these three questions.

1. DOES THE BUYER GET TITLE?

Where goods are sold by a non-owner the law is faced with a clear policy choice. Lord Denning M.R. has described it[1]:

> "In the development of our law two principles have striven for mastery. The first is for the protection of property; no one can give a better title than he himself possesses.[2] The second is for the protection of commercial transactions; the person who takes in good faith and for value without notice should get a good title."

Faced with this choice the law has developed in a piecemeal and haphazard way with a basic rule protecting property and a number of exceptions protecting commercial transactions. The Crowther Committee on Consumer Credit described the rules as "arbitrary and

---

[1] *Bishopsgate Motor Finance Corp. Ltd.* v. *Transport Brakes Ltd.* [1949] 1 K.B. 322, 336–337.
[2] This is commonly referred to as the *"nemo dat"* rule, *i.e. nemo dat quod non habet.*

capricious" and pointed out that their application depended "not on principles of equity or justice but on fine technicalities which have little rhyme and less reason."[3]

The nemo dat rule

With this warning we can examine the relevant provisions. The cornerstone is to be found in section 21(1) of the Sale of Goods Act 1979. It reads:

> Subject to this Act, where the goods are sold[4] by a person who is not their owner, and who does not sell them under the authority or with the consent of the owner, the buyer acquires no better title to the goods than the seller had, unless the owner of the goods is by his conduct precluded from denying the seller's authority to sell.

If we revert to our three examples, the effect of section 21(1) is that the goods will still belong to A, E and H unless someone along the line acquired title under one of the exceptions to the basic rule. We must now consider the scope and extent of these exceptions.

Does an exception apply?

Let us first list the principal exceptions:

- (i) Sale under order of court.
- (ii) Sale under a common law or statutory power.
- (iii) Sale with the owner's consent.
- (iv) Sale where the owner is precluded from denying the seller's right to sell ("estoppel").
- (v) Disposition by a mercantile agent.
- (vi) Sale in market overt.
- (vii) Sale under a voidable title.
- (viii) Disposition by a seller in possession.
- (ix) Disposition by a buyer in possession.
- (x) Disposition of a motor vehicle under Part III of the Hire-Purchase Act 1964 (as re-worded by the Consumer Credit Act 1974).

It is now proposed to examine some of the more important of these exceptions. Nearly all of the examples chosen relate to motor cars; this is clearly the area where the consumer is most likely to buy goods which turn out to have been stolen. There is substantial overlap between these provisions and it is often advisable to plead more than one.

---

[3] Report, p. 178.
[4] "Sold" does not cover an agreement to sell by the intermediate seller: *Shaw* v. *Commissioner of Police of the Metropolis* [1987] 1 W.L.R. 1332 (C.A.).

(i) *Is the owner estopped?*

Section 21 itself displaces the basic *nemo dat* rule where the owner, by his conduct, is precluded from denying the seller's right to sell. The courts have construed this provision in a fairly narrow way. In the words of Lord Wilberforce:

> "English law has generally taken the robust line that the man who owns property is not under a general duty to safeguard it and that he may sue for its recovery any person into whose hands it has come."[5]

In *Central Newbury Car Auctions Ltd.* v. *Unity Finance Ltd.*[6]:

> A distinguished looking swindler wished to acquire a car from Central Newbury Car Auctions on hire-purchase terms and intimated that he was prepared to leave his own car in part exchange. He filled up an application form for a hire-purchase agreement. If the deal went through the dealer would sell to a finance company who would let the car to him on hire-purchase. Central Newbury allowed him to take the new car and its registration book away. Within a very short time it was discovered that (i) he had given a false name, address and employer (ii) the car which he had left in part exchange did not belong to him and (iii) he had sold the new car to Unity Finance. Central Newbury sued Unity Finance for the return of the car.

It was the classic situation; which of two innocent parties should suffer for the fraud of a third? Many people would agree with Lord Denning that the loss should fall on Central Newbury in view of their carelessness in parting with the car. Nevertheless this was a minority view; the majority in the Court of Appeal applied what Lord Wilberforce has described as the "robust" view.[7] All that Central Newbury had done was to hand over physical possession; that was not conduct which precluded them from setting up their ownership; the car was still theirs. The only right of Unity Finance would be an action against the swindler under section 12 of the Sale of Goods Act[8] and this would almost certainly be worthless.

In the more recent case of *Moorgate Mercantile Co.* v. *Twitchings*[9]:

> Finance companies set up a company called HPI and ninety-eight per cent. of all finance companies belonged to it. The object was to register subsisting hire-purchase agreements—some four and a half million—and to pass on information to motor dealers who were associated members. Any dealer who was considering buying a car could contact HPI to find

---

[5] *Moorgate Mercantile Co.* v. *Twitchings* [1977] A.C. 890, 902.
[6] [1957] 1 Q.B. 371.
[7] See above.
[8] *Post*, pp. 22–24.
[9] [1977] A.C. 890.

out whether a hire-purchase agreement relating to that car was registered. Several thousand enquiries were made each day. The M. Finance Co. entered into a hire-purchase agreement, but for some unexplained reason they failed to register it with HPI. The hirer offered to sell the car to T, a dealer. T contacted HPI and was told that nothing had been registered. He then bought the car from the hirer. M. Finance Co. claimed that the car was still theirs. The House of Lords, by a majority, upheld this claim.

The case was fought on two grounds—estoppel and negligence. As to estoppel the question was twofold: (i) were HPI the agents of the finance companies? (ii) did their answers amount to a representation that no finance company had an interest in the car? By a majority of four to one (Lord Salmon dissenting) the House of Lords gave a negative answer to both of these questions. The other argument was negligence—the M. Finance Company owed a legal duty of care to dealers and were in breach of that duty. This argument was accepted by the Court of Appeal and by Lords Salmon and Wilberforce but the majority of the House of Lords rejected it. One of the main reasons which influenced the majority was the fact that (i) membership of HPI was voluntary and (ii) there was no duty to register agreements. Neither of these arguments appears totally convincing but they indicate that the owner of goods will seldom lose his ownership by reason of carelessness, even though this causes serious loss to an innocent buyer. We shall see later that HPI can also be used by a prospective private buyer.[10]

The only type of case where the owner may be estopped is where he makes a positive representation that the seller owns the goods[11] or where he signs a document which clearly conveys that impression.[12]

(ii) *Was there a disposition by a mercantile agent?*

We have seen that the mere delivery of possession does not preclude the owner from setting up his ownership. There is, however, one statutory exception. The basic effect of section 2 of the Factors Act 1889 is that if the owner transfers possession to a "mercantile agent," this may amount to a representation that the agent has authority to sell. If the agent then sells in the ordinary course of business, the owner may lose his ownership even though the agent went beyond his instructions.

The Act of 1889 starts by defining a mercantile agent. By section 1:

> "Mercantile agent" shall mean a mercantile agent having in the customary course of his business as such agent authority to sell goods, or to consign

---

[10] *Post*, pp. 21–22.
[11] See *Henderson* v. *Williams* [1895] 1 Q.B. 521.
[12] See *Eastern Distributors* v. *Goldring* [1957] 2 Q.B. 600.

goods for the purpose of sale, or to buy goods, or to raise money on the security of goods.

Then comes the key provision. By section 2(1):

> Where a mercantile agent is, with the consent of the owner, in the possession of goods . . . any sale, pledge or other disposition of the goods, made by him when acting in the ordinary course of business of a mercantile agent, shall . . . be as valid as if he were expressly authorised by the owner of the goods to make the same; provided that the person taking under the disposition acts in good faith, and has not at the time of the disposition notice that the person making the disposition has not authority to make the same.

This section could apply to the second example at the beginning of this chapter.[13] If the agent receives instructions not to sell for less than £1,000 or if he is merely instructed to take offers, the buyer will usually not be aware of these restrictions and will get a good title under section 2 even though the agent exceeded his authority.

The sale by the agent must be in the ordinary course of business and the buyer must have no notice of the restrictions on the agent's authority. In practice these points are unlikely to give rise to difficulty. There are, however, two other points which could defeat the buyer's claim. Thus:

(a) The section will only apply if the agent was in possession *in his capacity of mercantile agent*. It would not apply if, for example, a garage which happened to be a mercantile agent received a car for servicing or repair and then sold it.[14]

(b) The agent must have received possession of the goods with the owner's consent. The mere fact that consent was obtained by fraud[15] or that consent has ended[16] does not affect the buyer unless he knows of this—an obviously sensible rule. On the other hand, the owner may decide to keep the registration document and/or the ignition key. What happens if he accidentally leaves them with the dealer or in the car? In *Pearson* v. *Rose and Young*[17]:

> The owner of a car instructed a dealer to obtain offers. He never intended to hand over the registration book but by mistake he left it in the dealer's

---

[13] *Ante*, p. 9.

[14] See, *e.g. Belvoir Finance Co. Ltd.* v. *Harold G. Cole & Co. Ltd.* [1969] 1 W.L.R. 1877.

[15] *Folkes* v. *King* [1923] 1 K.B. 282; but perhaps the position would be different if the owner was under a fundamental mistake as to the agent's identity. See *Benjamin on Sale of Goods*, (3rd ed.), para. 526.

[16] Act of 1889, s.2(2).

[17] [1951] 1 K.B. 275.

showroom. The dealer sold the car with its registration book to a buyer. The Court of Appeal held that (i) in the case of a second hand car the words "goods" included the registration book and the consent of the owner must extend to the registration book as well as to the car itself (ii) there had been no consent to the handing over of the book (iii) the dealer must therefore be treated as if he had sold the car without the book (iv) such a sale would not be in the ordinary course of business (v) consequently the buyer obtained no title under section 2.[18]

(iii) *Was the sale in market overt?*

This is probably the most ancient of all the *nemo dat* exceptions, dating back to the sixteenth century. It is riddled with technical rules and anomalies and has little to do with the realities of modern commercial life. The rule is set out in section 22(1) of the Sale of Goods Act 1979 as follows:

> Where the goods are sold in market overt, according to the usage of the market, the buyer acquires a good title to the goods, provided he buys them in good faith and without notice of any defect or want of title on the part of the seller.

This section could be relevant to the first of the examples at the beginning of this chapter.[19] In one sense it is wider than any other of the *nemo dat* exceptions. In the two which we have already considered and in the four which we still have to consider[20] there has been a direct relationship between the owner and the seller. Market overt is the only exception where such a relationship may be entirely absent. A sale by a thief may pass title.

To find out whether the consumer (or one of his predecessors in title) got a market overt title a number of questions have to be asked. Title will only pass if the answer to all the questions is "yes."

(a) Did the sale take place in market overt? A market overt is a market or fair established by charter or custom[21]; there is a very ancient custom that every shop in the City of London is market overt.

(b) Were the goods of a kind normally dealt with in the market?

(c) Did the sale take place "according to the usage of the market"? Thus the section would not apply to a private sale at a market where goods were normally sold only by auction.

---

[18] See also *Stadium Finance Ltd.* v. *Robbins* [1962] 2 Q.B. 664 (C.A.) (book accidentally left in car; key not handed over at all; buyer from agent not protected).

[19] *Ante*, p. 9.

[20] *Post*, pp. 16–22.

[21] For the latest re-statement of the relevant rules, see *Long* v. *Jones, The Times*, March 6, 1990 (sale from private stall adjoining a market; not market overt; so buyer not protected). See also *R.* v. *Wheeler, The Times*, December 5, 1990.

(d) Was the sale public and open in the public part of the market or shop? It is necessary that the goods themselves should be displayed there and not only a sample. It must also be shown that the sale is *by* the shopkeeper and not *to* him.[22]

(e) Was the sale between sunrise and sunset? In one of the few modern cases on market overt this point was crucial and the buyer lost because the sale to him took place before sunrise.[23]

(f) Did the buyer take in good faith and without notice of any defect in the seller's title?

(g) Did the sale take place in England? There is no market overt in Wales (Laws in Wales Act 1542), nor does it apply in Scotland.

These points can now be illustrated by considering two of the very few modern market overt cases to reach the courts.

In *Bishopsgate Finance Co. Ltd.* v. *Transport Brakes Ltd.*[24]

> X had a car on hire-purchase with no right to sell. He took it to Maidstone market, unsuccessfully tried to sell it by auction and eventually sold it privately there. The finance company who had let it to X claimed it from the buyer. The claim failed.

The Court of Appeal found that Maidstone market had been running since 1747 and they had little difficulty in finding that it was market overt. It was also proved that cars were regularly sold there both by auction and privately. Hence the sale in this case was "according to the usage of the market" and the buyer acquired title.

In a more recent case involving candelabra a claim of market overt title failed. In *Reid* v. *Metropolitan Police Commissioner*[25] the facts were vividly described by the Master of the Rolls:

> "The centre-piece of this story is a pair of candelabra, made of well-cut glass, each supporting two candles with sparkling pear-drops all about. . . . In December 1969 this lovely pair of candelabra stood on the table of Mr. Reid. . . . He and his wife went away for the week-end. During their absence thieves broke in and ransacked the house. They took many things. In their haul they stole the pair of Adam candelabra. The next we hear of them is two months later. This time it is at the New Caledonian Market in Southwark. That market is open every Friday from seven in the morning onwards, but dealers go there before that time so as to get the best bargains. It is the early bird that catches the worm. On Friday, February 13, 1970 Norman Cocks, an art dealer, the defendant went early to the market. It was still only half-light. The sun had not risen. He saw a man putting up a stall. . . . On the stall there was a cardboard box. . . . Wrapped up in a newspaper there were the main parts of a pair of

[22] *Ardath Tobacco Ltd.* v. *Ocker* (1931) 47 T.L.R. 177.
[23] See below.
[24] [1949] 1 K.B. 322.
[25] [1973] Q.B. 551.

> candelabra. . . . He did not ask the man where he got them from. No one ever asks questions of that kind in the market. . . . Mr. Cocks said 'I'll give you £200.' The man agreed."

Some time later, when Mr. Cocks was negotiating a re-sale, Mr. Reid appeared and claimed that the candelabra were the ones which had been stolen from his house. The police took them away and the ownership was fought out between Reid and Cocks. The Court of Appeal held that as Cocks had bought before sunrise, he acquired no market overt title. Consequently the candelabra still belonged to Reid.

In both of these cases the buyers were commercial buyers. It will be appreciated that if either of them had resold the goods to a consumer then (i) in the *Bishopsgate* case the first buyer's market overt title would have passed to the consumer and (ii) in the *Reid* case the consumer would acquire no title unless the sale *to him* was in market overt or unless one of the other *nemo dat* exceptions applied. The market overt rules apply equally to private and business buyers.

(iv) *Did the seller have a voidable title?*

Where a contract is voidable (*e.g.* for misrepresentation) it is a valid contract until the innocent party takes steps to set it aside, *i.e.* rescinds the contract. The remedy of rescission is an equitable one and in certain cases it will not be possible to rescind. One such case is concerned with third party rights—once a third party has acquired rights under the voidable contract it will be too late to rescind it. This principle now appears in section 23 of the 1979 Act as follows:

> When the seller of goods has a voidable title to them, but his title has not been avoided at the time of the sale, the buyer acquires a good title to the goods, provided that he buys them in good faith and without notice of the seller's defect of title.

In virtually all the reported cases under this section the goods were obtained as a result of a fraudulent misrepresentation. The position of the ultimate buyer depends on a highly technical rule—was the title to the fraudulent buyer *voidable* for misrepresentation or *void* for mistake? In the well-known case of *Ingram* v. *Little*[26]:

> Three ladies agreed to sell a car to a man who called himself "Hutchinson." They were reluctant to take a cheque from him but he gave them the initials and address of a real Hutchinson. After checking in the telephone directory they let him take the car away in return for a cheque. He sold the car to a buyer; the cheque was dishonoured. The Court of Appeal held that (i) the offer to sell was made to Hutchinson and could not be accepted by anyone else; (ii) consequently the contract with the rogue was void; (iii) consequently section 23 did not apply and the buyer acquired no title.

[26] [1961] 1 Q.B. 31.

Some years ago, the Law Reform Committee recommended that the fraudulent person should always be treated as having a *voidable* title, so that the ultimate buyer would be protected. No such legislation has been enacted but the courts have, in effect, achieved this result. In the more recent case of *Lewis* v. *Averay*[27] the facts were somewhat similar to those in *Ingram* v. *Little* but the decision went the other way. In that case:

> A rogue calling himself Green—a well known television actor—induced the owner of a car to sell it to him in return for a cheque. He resold the car to a buyer. The cheque was dishonoured.

The Court of Appeal held that the rogue had a voidable title, with the result that section 23 protected the buyer. They treated *Ingram* v. *Little* as a case turning on very special facts and they laid down the broad principle that where the parties were face to face, the seller would normally be treated as intending to deal with the actual person in front of him. If this intention was brought about by fraud or by a trick this would make the transaction voidable but not void.

Section 23 does not apply if the owner has avoided the contract *before* the resale takes place. In general the innocent party must give notice of rescission and this can raise a practical problem, since not all fraudulent buyers supply their sellers with an address. In *Car and Universal Finance Co.* v. *Caldwell*[28] the Court of Appeal held that avoidance was possible in this type of case without notifying the fraudulent buyer. In that case the seller reported the matter to the police and the AA as soon as the cheque was dishonoured and asked them to trace the car. It was held that his conduct did amount to an avoidance of contract. The practical effect of this case has however been largely undermined by the later case of *Newtons of Wembley Ltd.* v. *Williams* which is considered later in this chapter.[29]

(v) *Did the seller remain in possession after a previous sale?*

We have seen that the owner of goods may lose his ownership if he transfers possession to a mercantile agent who disposes of them in the ordinary course of business.[30] We now meet two further cases where ownership and possession are split. The first concerns a sale where the buyer becomes the owner but the seller retains possession. Let us assume that X, an antique dealer, agrees to sell to Y an antique vase. Y agrees to collect it on the following day. By mistake the dealer sells the same vase to Z who pays for it and takes it away. On these facts the first

---

[27] [1973] 1 Q.B. 198.
[28] [1965] 1 Q.B. 525.
[29] *Post*, p. 19.
[30] *Ante*, p. 12.

sale may have initially passed the ownership to Y[31] but nevertheless the second sale, coupled with delivery, may have then passed the ownership to Z. The authority for this is section 24 of the Sale of Goods Act 1979 which reads as follows:

> Where a person having sold goods continues or is in possession of the goods . . . the delivery or transfer by that person or by a mercantile agent acting for him of the goods . . . under any sale, pledge or other disposition thereof to any person receiving the same in good faith and without notice of the previous sale, has the same effect as if the person making the delivery or transfer were expressly authorised by the owner of the goods to make the same.

Thus in advising Z one would start by claiming that X was still the owner at the time of the sale to him. If this is not so (see above) Z may acquire title under section 24, provided that the sale to him was coupled with delivery. After earlier doubts it now seems clear that the nature of X's possession is immaterial—he may be in possession as seller, as repairer, as warehouseman or in any other capacity.

As already stated[32] these rules are highly technical. Consider the following problem:

> X sells a car to Y as a result of a fraudulent misrepresentation made by Y. Y pays by cheque. Y sells to Z and retains possession. When Y's cheque is dishonoured X comes to Y's premises. Y allows X to take the car back in return for a promise by X not to enforce the cheque.

The sale from Y to Z gave Z a title under section 23.[33] After that sale Y became a "seller in possession." The return of the car to X amounts to a delivery under a "sale, pledge *or other disposition*" within section 24. Consequently title is re-transferred to X.[34]

(vi) *Was the sale by a buyer in possession?*

Section 25(1) is the exact converse of section 24. It is again concerned with a split between ownership and possession but this time it is the seller who retains ownership and the buyer who obtains possession. There is, in fact, a very substantial overlap with section 23. Let us assume that A buys a car from B and pays by cheque. The contract provides that no property shall pass to A until the cheque is cleared. A obtains possession of the car with B's consent, and sells and delivers the car to C. A's cheque is dishonoured. Although C bought from a non-owner he may acquire title under section 25(1). The section reads as follows:

---

[31] s.18, r. 1, *post*, p. 85.
[32] *Ante*, p. 9.
[33] *Ante*, p. 16.
[34] See *Worcester Works Finance Ltd.* v. *Cooden Engineering Co. Ltd.* [1972] 1 Q.B. 210 (C.A.).

> Where a person having bought or agreed to buy goods obtains, with the consent of the seller, possession of the goods ... the delivery or transfer by that person, or by a mercantile agent acting for him, of the goods ... under any sale, pledge or other disposition thereof, to any person receiving the same in good faith and without notice of any lien or other right of the original seller in respect of the goods, shall have the same effect as if the person making the delivery or transfer were a mercantile agent in possession of the goods ... with the consent of the owner.

This provision has been before the courts on a number of occasions and the following points emerge.

(a) The section only applies where a person has bought or agreed to buy goods. It does not apply where, for example, the goods have been let out on hire-purchase[35] or stolen.[36] Similarly, a buyer under a conditional sale agreement within the Consumer Credit Act 1974 is *not* (for this purpose) a person who has "agreed to buy" so that a transfer by him will not enjoy the protection of the section.[37]

(b) The first buyer must obtain possession with the *consent* of the seller; this includes consent obtained by fraud.[38]

(c) The section can apply even where the first buyer has obtained a voidable title and even if the disposition by him takes place *after* his title has been avoided (see below).

(d) What is the meaning of the obscure words "shall have the same effect as if the person making the delivery or transfer were a mercantile agent in possession ... with the consent of the owner"? In *Newtons of Wembley Ltd.* v. *Williams*[39] the Court of Appeal reached the astonishing conclusion that the disposition by the first buyer must be in the ordinary course of business of a mercantile agent—even though that buyer is not such an agent! In that case:

A agreed to buy a Sunbeam Rapier car from Newtons of Wembley. The contract provided that no property should pass to the buyer until his cheque was cleared. When the cheque was dishonoured Newtons took steps to trace the car and recover it. A then sold it to B in an open-air market in Warren Street. B resold it to Williams. A pleaded guilty to obtaining the car by false pretences and Newtons of Wembley sued Williams for the return of the car. The claim was unsuccessful.

The Court of Appeal held that A was a buyer in possession; even

---

[35] *Helby* v. *Matthews* [1895] A.C. 471.
[36] *National Employers' Mutual General Insurance Association* v. *Jones* [1990] 1 A.C. 24 (H.L.). Lord Goff's judgment contains a clear, historical analysis of this and related statutory exceptions.
[37] See Consumer Credit Act 1974, Sched. 4.
[38] *Du Jardin* v. *Beadman Bros.* [1952] 2 Q.B. 712.
[39] [1965] 1 Q.B. 560.

though he was not a mercantile agent the sale to B was in the ordinary course of business of a mercantile agent; B took in good faith; accordingly B acquired a good title which he could pass on to Williams.

It will be appreciated that the first transferee from the original buyer must take "in good faith." This condition was satisfied in this case but not in the earlier case of *Car and Universal Finance Co. Ltd.* v. *Caldwell.*[40] The effect of the *Newton* decision is to severely restrict the practical consequences of the original seller avoiding a voidable title acquired by the fraudulent buyer.

(vii) *Was there a disposition of a motor vehicle held on hire-purchase or conditional sale?*

The final rule which may protect the consumer was introduced by Part III of the Hire-Purchase Act 1964 and verbal amendments were made to it by the Consumer Credit Act 1974. The provision was introduced after an earlier proposal had been rejected, for administrative reasons, by the finance companies. This would have provided for the retention of the registration books by the companies and the issue of cards to the hirers. One of the real problems in this area of law is that many people ignore the warning in the registration document that "The Registered Keeper is not necessarily the legal owner."

Part III applies if the following conditions are satisfied:

(a) a motor vehicle is let out on hire-purchase or agreed to be sold under a conditional sale agreement; and
(b) the hirer or buyer ("the debtor") disposes of it before the property has passed to him.

The Act then makes a distinction between:

(a) a disposition to a *private purchaser*; and
(b) a disposition to a *trade or finance purchaser*.

In the former case the purchaser may get a good title. In the words of section 27 of the 1964 Act (in its amended form):

> Where the disposition . . . is to a private purchaser, and he is a purchaser of the motor vehicle in good faith without notice of the hire-purchase or conditional sale agreement (the "relevant agreement") that disposition shall have effect as if the creditor's title to the vehicle had been vested in the debtor immediately before that disposition.

Two points can be made here. First, the private purchaser must have no actual notice of a subsisting hire-purchase or conditional sale agree-

---

[40] *Ante*, p. 17.

ment.[41] Secondly, the "creditor's title" means the title of the person who was described as the creditor in the hire-purchase or conditional sale agreement (*i.e.* the person who made the relevant agreement as owner or seller).

> Suppose that X, a thief, sells a car to Y not in market overt. Y lets it on hire-purchase to Z and Z sells it to A. Even if A takes in good faith he will only get the title which was vested in Y. Since Y had no title, the section does not protect A.

If we now assume that the hirer or buyer disposes of the vehicle to a trade or finance purchaser, that purchaser has no Part III protection (presumably because he will be able to use the HPI facilities[42]) but if further dispositions take place the Act protects the *first private purchaser* if he takes in good faith and without notice. It, therefore, becomes crucial to find out whether the original transferee was a trade or finance purchaser. A trade purchaser is defined as a person who at the time of the disposition carries on a business of buying motor vehicles for sale,[43] while a finance purchaser is one who provides finance by buying motor vehicles and letting them out under hire-purchase or conditional sale agreements. Any other purchaser is a private purchaser. The following points can be important:

(i) "Private purchaser" is much wider than "private person"; thus many large public companies will enjoy the "private purchaser" protection of the Act.

(ii) If the purchaser is a trade or finance purchaser, he will not have Part III protection even if he buys for his private use.

(iii) The term "disposition" can include a fresh hire-purchase agreement. Thus in the third example at the beginning of this chapter[44] the ultimate hirer will be entitled to remain in possession under Part III even though he finds out about the original agreement before completing his payments.

Two final points can be made. First, there are bound to be serious practical problems in proving that the vehicle was transferred by the hirer or buyer to a private purchaser. The purchaser's job is made somewhat easier by a series of rebuttable presumptions which are to be found in section 28 of the 1964 Act. Secondly, one must always bear in mind that prevention is better than cure. A member of the public who is considering buying a car can always check with HPI.[45] HPI make

---

[41] *Barker* v. *Bell* [1971] 1 W.L.R. 983 (C.A.).
[42] *Ante*, p. 11.
[43] This may be a part-time business: *Stevenson* v. *Beverley Bentinck Ltd.* [1976] 1 W.L.R. 483 (C.A.).
[44] *Ante*, p. 9.
[45] *Ante*, pp. 11–12.

their information available to the AA, RAC and Citizens Advice Bureaux.

Hire-purchase generally

X lets out goods to Y on hire-purchase and it then transpires that X is not the owner of the goods. A number of the provisions discussed in this chapter refer to a "disposition" and this is clearly wide enough to cover a hire-purchase agreement. Thus Y could, in appropriate cases, claim the protection of section 2 of the Factors Act,[46] section 24 or 25(1) of the Sale of Goods Act[47] or Part III of the Hire-Purchase Act. He would also be protected if X had a voidable title, since it will be too late for the original owner to rescind the agreement once third party rights have been acquired.[48]

2. Buyer's Rights Against Seller

We have dealt at some length with the *nemo dat* rules because it is likely that the real battle in practice is likely to be fought between the original owner and the buyer. We must now consider the position as between buyer and seller. The general principle is clear enough; under a contract of sale the transfer of ownership from seller to buyer is a fundamental term around which the whole contract revolves. Section 12(1) spells out the seller's basic obligation:

> In a contract of sale, other than one to which subsection (3) below applies, there is an implied condition on the part of the seller that in the case of a sale, he has a right to sell the goods, and in the case of an agreement to sell, he will have a right to sell the goods at the time when the property is to pass.

In addition, section 12(2) implies warranties that

> (a) the goods are free, and will remain free until the time when the property is to pass, from any charge or encumbrance not disclosed or known to the buyer before the contract is made, and
> (b) the buyer will enjoy quiet possession of the goods except so far as it may be disturbed by the owner or other person entitled to the benefit of any charge or encumbrance so disclosed or known.

These provisions have been before the courts on a number of occasions and the following points emerge from the cases:

(1) If the goods are delivered in such a form that any sale can be stopped by an injunction there is no "right to sell."

---

[46] *Ante*, p. 13.
[47] *Ante*, pp. 17–20.
[48] *Ante*, p. 16.

(2) If the seller is in breach of this essential condition, the buyer can recover the price even though he has used the goods for a considerable time.[49] The basis of his claim is a "total failure of consideration." If he asks for the return of the price his right will crystallise and will not be affected by anything done *after* this to cure the defect. If the principle of "total failure" were applied literally it would enable a buyer of stolen wine to have the best of both worlds—consume the wine and get his money back on discovering the theft![50]

(3) If the buyer has incurred other expenses, *e.g.* the cost of necessary repairs, these can also be claimed from the seller.[51]

An unsettled question is the precise relationship between section 12 and the *nemo dat* exceptions considered earlier in this chapter. If the seller had no title he would technically have no *right* to sell, even though the effect of the sale would be to pass title to the buyer. Nevertheless, it is inconceivable that a court would allow a claim based on "total failure of consideration" if the buyer got exactly what he paid for, *i.e.* the property in the goods. If, however, he was put to trouble and expense in proving his title he might well have a claim.

Can sections 12(1) and 12(2) be excluded?

There may be cases where the seller of goods is uncertain as to whether or not he has a right to sell and he may wish the buyer to bear this risk. Section 12(3) allows the seller to give a more limited undertaking in a case where there appears from the contract or is to be inferred from its circumstances an intention that the seller should transfer only such title as he or a third person may have. In this type of case the basic title obligations referred to above are replaced by two implied warranties, *i.e.*:

(4) ... that all charges and encumbrances known to the seller and not known to the buyer have been disclosed to the buyer before the contract is made.

(5) ... that none of the following will disturb the buyer's quiet possession of the goods, namely—

    (a) the seller;

    (b) in a case where the parties to the contract intend that the seller should transfer only such title as a third person may have, that person;

    (c) anyone claiming through or under the seller or that third person otherwise than under a charge or encumbrance disclosed or known to the buyer before the contract is made.

---

[49] *Rowland* v. *Divall* [1923] 2 K.B. 500 (C.A.).

[50] If the true owner re-appeared he could, of course, sue the buyer for conversion.

[51] *Mason* v. *Burningham* [1949] 2 K.B. 545.

Subject to this, section 12 cannot be excluded.

Hire-purchase

The Supply of Goods (Implied Terms) Act 1973 implies title provisions into hire-purchase agreements.[52] These are similar to those implied in a sale of goods and only one point calls for brief mention. Under the 1973 Act the condition of "right to sell" is a condition that the owner will have a right to sell when the property is to pass (this usually occurs when the hirer has completed his payments). It seems, however, that the hirer may be in an even stronger position under a term implied at common law, *i.e.* that the owner has the right to sell at the time of delivery to the hirer.[53] A breach of the condition gives the hirer the right to recover all his payments with no set-off for user.[54]

Other contracts

There may be other cases where a contract is made involving the transfer of ownership of goods to the buyer. Examples include contracts for work and materials (installation of central heating, double glazing, etc.) and contracts of exchange. The obligations as to the right to sell, quiet possession and freedom from encumbrances are similar to those implied in a sale of goods (see section 2 of the Supply of Goods and Services Act 1982). In contrast, the contract of hire does not involve the transfer of ownership at all and consequently the only "title" terms are (a) a condition that the owner has the right to transfer possession and (b) a warranty for quiet possession (section 7 of the 1982 Act).

3. IMPROVEMENTS AND REPAIRS

S sells goods to B who spends £200 on repairs and improvements. It then transpires that the goods belong to C who claims them, or their value, from B. It has been well established for many years that, in assessing damages for conversion, credit must be given for improvements made by the defendant.[55] In *Greenwood* v. *Bennett*[56] this principle was applied in interpleader proceedings between the owner and the improver. This seems fair enough but one point is unclear; if the owner seizes the goods from the improver, does the improver have a cause of action to recover the cost of the improvements from the owner? No English authority supports such a claim, although Lord

[52] s.8.
[53] *Karflex Ltd.* v. *Poole* [1933] 2 K.B. 251.
[54] *Warman* v. *Southern Counties Finance Corporation* [1949] 2 K.B. 576 (C.A.).
[55] *Munro* v. *Willmott* [1949] 1 K.B. 295.
[56] [1973] 1 Q.B. 195.

Denning M.R. suggested (*obiter*) that such a claim would be allowed on the basis of unjust enrichment.[57]

The principle of *Greenwood* v. *Bennett* now appears in statutory form in section 6(1) of the Torts (Interference with Goods) Act 1977. It reads:

> If in proceedings for wrongful interference against a person (the "improver") who has improved the goods, it is shown that the improver acted in the mistaken but honest belief that he had a good title to them, an allowance shall be made for the extent to which, at the time as at which the goods fall to be valued in assessing damages, the value of the goods is attributable to the improvement.

The section goes on to give a similar right to a subsequent buyer who acted in good faith.[58] If the buyer then sues his seller under section 12 of the Sale of Goods Act[59] the seller can claim a similar reduction provided that he acted in good faith.[60]

> O owns a car which is stolen by T who sells it to A. It is worth £200 but A increases its value to £900. He then sells it to B for £900. O claims the car from B.

If we assume that O has been the owner at all material times, the court may well order O to pay B the sum of £700 (the improvement figure reflected in the price paid by B to A) as a condition of getting the car back. In the result, B is out of pocket to the tune of £200. If he then sues A for the return of the £900 it seems only right that his claim should be limited to £200 and (assuming that A acted in good faith) section 6(3) allows such a reduction.

Two final points may be made. It will be seen that the section uses the words "if in proceedings . . . against a person." In other words it does not create a new cause of action. If the owner seizes the goods from the improver, there is nothing in the Act to give the improver a claim against the owner.[61] Secondly the right to claim compensation for improvements will only be relevant where the improver or his successor in title is liable to the owner and it will not be relevant where the improver or his successor in title has himself become the owner under one of the *nemo dat* exceptions discussed at the beginning of this chapter.

[57] For further discussion, see (1973) 36 M.L.R. 89.
[58] s.6(2).
[59] *Ante*, pp. 22–23.
[60] s.6(3).
[61] He may of course have a claim against the seller—see *Mason* v. *Burningham* n. 51, *supra*.

CHAPTER THREE

"IT'S A GOOD LITTLE BUS"

(1) During negotiations for the sale of a car the dealer says to the consumer "it's a good little bus—I'd stake my life on it." The consumer then takes the car on hire-purchase from a finance company. The steering is defective and the consumer is injured.

(2) The vendor of a site of a petrol filling station tells the prospective purchaser that it should have a throughput of 200,000 gallons per year. This is far too high and the purchaser suffers severe financial loss.

(3) A prospective hirer of barges asks the owner how much they could carry and the owner replies "1,600 tonnes." The hirer makes the contract but the statement is wrong and the hirer refuses to pay the hire charges.

The supplier of goods is likely to make extravagant claims about them before or during negotiations. What are the remedies of the consumer if, as in the three cases cited, the statement turns out to be wrong? The position depends on how the statement is classified. There are at least five possibilities:

(a) the statement may be nothing more than "trader's puff." In this case the consumer has no remedy.

(b) the statement may be an actionable misrepresentation; in this case the consumer may have (i) a right to rescind the contract unless it is too late to do so; (ii) a right to damages at common law if the supplier was fraudulent; (iii) a right to damages under section 2(1) of the Misrepresentation Act 1967 unless the supplier can prove that he had reasonable grounds for believing, and did believe, the statement to be true.

(c) it may be a negligent misstatement giving rise to an action for damages in tort. This branch of the law of negligence is based on the House of Lords decision in *Hedley Byrne & Co. Ltd.* v. *Heller & Partners Ltd.*,[1] but the law has been developing slowly and the precise scope of liability has still to be determined.

(d) it may be a contractual term. In this case the consumer can claim damages; whether he can also treat the contract as discharged depends upon the importance of the term and upon the seriousness and the consequences of the breach.

---

[1] [1964] A.C. 465.

27

(e) it may form part of the description of the goods (this overlaps with (d) above). If this is so, a breach will be a breach of condition and the consumer can choose between (i) treating the contract as repudiated and claiming damages and (ii) affirming the contract and claiming damages.[2] Until recently the term "description" has been given a very wide meaning but it seems that the pendulum is now swinging the other way.[3]

It remains to add that the supplier may be in breach of the Trade Descriptions Act 1968[4] and a criminal conviction could lead to an award of compensation under the Powers of Criminal Courts Act 1973.[5] Further, if the statement is a credit advertisement within the Consumer Credit Act 1974 the provisions of sections 46 and 167(2) of that Act must be borne in mind. These matters are considered in later parts of this book.

1. MERE PUFF

The praising of goods by a prospective supplier is a universal fact of commercial life and the lifeblood of the advertising industry. The following phrases are typical:

"the most popular bike in Britain"
"clean, healthy and alive"
"super value for money"
"the bathroom bargain of the year."

This is typical sales patter; it is not intended to give rise to legal liability and it does not do so. The difficulty is to know where to draw the line between (a) mere puff and (b) a representation or a term. In the above examples the statements were vague and not specific; as soon as the supplier makes an inaccurate specific statement, for example, as to measurements or ingredients, the consumer should have little difficulty in proving an actionable misrepresentation or breach of a contractual term. In an early case a seller of port who described it as "superior old port" was held liable as the maker of a contractual promise. More recently in *Andrews* v. *Hopkinson*,[6] the facts of which appear in example 1,[7] the dealer who described the car as a "good little bus" was liable for breach of a collateral contract (and also in tort under the rule in *Donoghue* v. *Stevenson*).[8]

---

[2] Sale of Goods Act 1979, ss.11, 13.
[3] See *post*, p. 39.
[4] *Post*, p. 197.
[5] *Post*, p. 258.
[6] [1957] 1 Q.B. 229.
[7] *Ante*, p. 27.
[8] [1932] A.C. 562, *post*, pp. 31 and 73.

2. MISREPRESENTATION

A misrepresentation can broadly be described as a half-way house between mere puff and a contractual term. The essence of a misrepresentation is that it is a statement made *before* the making of the contract which *induces* the other party to enter into the contract. There can, of course, be an overlap between a misrepresentation and a contractual term; a dealer may represent a car as being a 1977 model and this may later be incorporated into the contract. Subject to this, a mere pre-contractual inducement is less potent than a term of the contract itself.

Until the 1960s it was often vital for the injured party to prove that the statement was something more than a misrepresentation; the reason was that the only remedy for misrepresentation was the equitable remedy of rescission, with no right to damages unless there was fraud. If it was too late to rescind the innocent party might find himself with no remedy at all. This is what happened in *Oscar Chess Ltd.* v. *Williams*[9] where the following facts arose:

> A consumer who was buying a car was asked by the dealer to state the age of the car which he was giving in part-exchange. He said that it was a 1948 model, as appeared from the registration book. In fact it was a 1939 model and the dealer suffered loss in that the part-exchange allowance was too high. He sued the buyer for damages.

The Court of Appeal held that the statement made by Mr. Williams was a mere representation and not a contractual warranty. Accordingly, as the law then stood, no damages could be awarded. In the words of Lord Denning M.R.:

> "If, however, the seller, when he states a fact, makes it clear that he has no knowledge of his own but has got his information elsewhere and is merely passing it on it is not so easy to infer a warranty."

On these particular facts the result of this case might be the same today even after the changes made by section 2 of the Misrepresentation Act 1967 (as the consumer could prove reasonable grounds for his belief) and even after *Hedley Byrne* v. *Heller*.[10]

If the parties are on an equal bargaining footing the courts may again be reluctant to find a contractual promise. Thus in *Howard Marine and Dredging Co. Ltd.* v. *Ogden & Sons (Excavation) Ltd.*,[11] the facts of which appear in example 3 at the beginning of this chapter,[12] the

---

[9] [1957] 1 W.L.R. 370.
[10] *Post*, pp. 32–35.
[11] [1978] Q.B. 574.
[12] *Ante*, p. 27.

statement about the barge capacity was held to be non-contractual; in this case, however, the hirers recovered damages under section 2(1) of the Misrepresentation Act.[13]

If, however, we turn to the normal dealer-consumer situation a statement made by the dealer will frequently be classified as a contractual promise because of the dealer's special knowledge. In *Dick Bentley* v. *Harold Smith Ltd.*[14]:

> A dealer told a prospective buyer that the engine of a second-hand car had done 20,000 miles. It was later discovered that the engine had done 100,000 miles. The buyer claimed damages.

The Court of Appeal gave judgment for the buyer. Here was a statement about a matter within the special knowledge of the seller. It was a contractual warranty and the seller was liable for breach of it.

In this type of case, therefore, the plaintiff should allege in the alternative (i) a contractual term (ii) a misrepresentation and (iii) a negligent statement.[15] The advantage of (i) is that the consumer will be entitled to damages for *any* breach of the term, even though the maker had reasonable grounds for believing the statement to be true.

The various remedies available for misrepresentation will be further considered[16] but before leaving misrepresentation three further points can be made:

(a) It may be necessary to distinguish a representation of *fact* from a mere statement of *opinion*—a problem which can cause particular difficulty on a sale of a painting which is attributed to an old master.

(b) Whether a person relies on the statement is a question of fact. The maker of a statement cannot avoid liability simply by saying "the accuracy of this statement is not guaranteed and the buyer should make his own enquiries." If, in such a case, the buyer *does* rely on the statement he will have the usual remedies for misrepresentation if the statement is incorrect.[17]

(c) The action for damages for misrepresentation is only available where the statement was made by the other party to the contract. Thus it would not be available if, for example, a consumer bought from a retailer in reliance on a statement made by the manufacturer. There may, however, be a claim against the manufacturer if a collateral contract can be established or if he is liable in negligence under the rules discussed below.

---

[13] *Post*, p. 97.
[14] [1965] 1 W.L.R. 623.
[15] *Post*, p. 32.
[16] *Post*, p. 95.
[17] *Cremdean Properties Ltd.* v. *Nash* (1977) 244 E.G. 547 (C.A.).

3. LIABILITY IN TORT FOR NEGLIGENCE

The history of the law of tort is one of gradual and cautious development. Although the industrial revolution started in the eighteenth century, it was not until 1932 that the modern law of negligence was born. Until then it was widely accepted that where A negligently performed a contract with B and thereby caused loss to C, A was not liable to C. It was not until *Donoghue* v. *Stevenson*[18] that the House of Lords, by a bare majority, came down in favour of a more realistic approach. In that case the House decided that in certain circumstances the manufacturer of a product owed a duty of care to the ultimate consumer. The case is also a landmark because Lord Atkin laid down his famous "neighbour" test as the basis of liability in negligence. He said:

"The liability for negligence . . . is no doubt placed upon a general public sentiment of moral wrongdoing for which the offender must pay. But acts or omissions which any moral code would censure cannot in a practical world be treated so as to give a right to every person injured by them to demand relief. In this way rules of law arise which limit the range of complainants and the extent of their remedy. The rule that you are to love your neighbour becomes in law—you must not injure your neighbour; and the lawyer's question, Who is my neighbour? receives a restricted reply. You must take reasonable care to avoid acts or omissions which you can reasonably foresee would be likely to injure your neighbour. Who, then, in law, is my neighbour? The answer seems to be—persons who are so closely and directly affected by my act that I ought reasonably to have them in contemplation as being so affected when I am directing my mind to the acts or omissions which are called in question."

Despite *Donoghue* v. *Stevenson* there were, and still are, important areas of non-liability. In particular the courts were very reluctant to hold that a careless statement causing economic loss gave rise to legal liability; the plaintiff could not succeed merely by proving that he was a "neighbour" of the defendant within Lord Atkin's test. The reason for this refusal to apply *Donoghue* v. *Stevenson* to statements was their potentially lethal effect. A distinguished American judge referred to the "three indeterminates"—a careless statement might make the maker liable "in an indeterminate amount for an indeterminate time to an indeterminate class."[19] The refusal of the law to provide a remedy was not without its critics. In *Candler* v. *Crane Christmas*[20] Lord Denning adopted a statement from an earlier case that:

"A country whose administration of justice did not afford redress in a case of the present description would not be in a state of civilization."

[18] [1932] A.C. 562.
[19] Cardozo C.J. in *Ultramares Corporation* v. *Touche* (1931) 255 N.Y. Rep. 170, cited in *Candler* v. *Crane Christmas, infra.*
[20] [1951] K.B. 164, 176 (a powerful dissenting judgment).

It was not until 1964 that the House of Lords altered the law. The case of *Hedley Byrne & Co. Ltd.* v. *Heller and Partners Ltd.*[21] shows a cautious approach and it is difficult to extract one really clear-cut principle from the five speeches. In one sense all the pronouncements in the *Hedley Byrne* case were *obiter* because the actual decision was that the defendants were absolved from liability because of a disclaimer. The facts were as follows:

> The plaintiffs were advertising agents. They placed orders on behalf of E. Ltd. with various newspapers and television. They were personally liable to the sellers of the advertising space and they were anxious to make sure that E. Ltd. were financially sound. The plaintiffs' bankers got in touch with the defendants who were the bankers of E. Ltd. The defendants gave favourable references "without responsibility." The plaintiffs thereupon made the contracts. The references turned out to be unjustified and the plaintiffs lost £17,000 on the contracts. They sued the defendants on the references. The House of Lords gave judgment for the defendants.

Lord Reid pointed out that a duty of care existed if there was a "special relationship"; he considered that this could be proved

> "where it is plain that the party seeking information or advice was trusting the other to exercise such a degree of care as the circumstances required, where it was reasonable for him to do that, and where the other gave the information or advice when he knew or ought to know that the enquirer was relying on him."

It is clear from a careful reading of the speeches that the key factor was an assumption of responsibility. In the words of Lord Morris:

> "My Lords, it seems to me that if A assumes a responsibility to B to tender him deliberate advice, there could be a liability if the advice is negligently given."

The case was decided in favour of the bank because (a) the disclaimer made it clear that no responsibility was being assumed and (b) even without such disclaimer it could well be argued that the only duty expected in this type of case was a duty to be honest.

In all the decided cases since 1964 the defendants supplied information in answer to an enquiry or in the course of professional duties and the most recent cases[22] indicate that a private consumer (especially at the lower end of the market) is more likely to succeed than a businessman or professional investor; the "reliance" factor mentioned above will often be crucial. The cases of *Smith* v. *Bush* and *Harris* v. *Wyre Forest D.C.*[23] were heard together because similar issues arose. The facts were as follows:

---

[21] [1964] A.C. 465.

[22] Five of them related to auditors. The leading case on non-liability of auditors is undoubtedly *Caparo Industries plc* v. *Dickman* [1990] 2 A.C. 605 (H.L.).

[23] [1990] 1 A.C. 831. The "disclaimer" aspect of the case is considered in Chapter 8, *post*, p. 143.

Mrs. Smith and Mr. and Mrs. Harris applied for mortgages for house purchase. In both case they paid to the lenders a non-returnable fee for a valuation. In one case the valuer was an independent surveyor and in the other he was an in-house surveyor employed by the lender. In both cases they negligently overvalued the property by failing to discover defects and the buyers suffered loss. Mrs. Smith was shown a copy of the valuer's report; the Harrises were not.

In both cases the lenders were under a statutory duty to cause a valuation to be made but the House of Lords held that this was irrelevant. They unanimously held that the negligent surveyor was liable to Mrs. Smith and that the council who made the advance to the Harrises were liable for the negligence of their surveyor. What emerges from the case is that the "assumption of responsibility" test is not the true one—or rather the question should be "in what circumstances will a negligent party be *deemed* to have assumed responsibility?" The language of the three substantive speeches is cautious. Lord Templeman said (at p. 800):

"In general, I am of the opinion that in the absence of a disclaimer of liability the valuer who values a house for the purposes of a mortgage, knowing that the mortgagee will rely and the mortgagor will probably rely on the valuation, knowing that the purchaser mortgagor has in effect paid for the valuation, is under a duty to exercise reasonable skill and care and that duty is owed to both parties to the mortgage for which the valuation was made."

The speech of Lord Griffiths shows a typical judicial reluctance to extend the scope of liability. He said (at pp. 815–816):

"I therefore return to the question in what circumstances should the law deem those who give advice to have assumed responsibility to the person who acts upon the advice? I would answer—only if it is foreseeable that if the advice is negligent the recipient is likely to suffer damage, that there is a sufficiently proximate relationship between the parties *and that it is just and reasonable to impose the liability*" (italics supplied).

Finally, Lord Jauncey of Tullichettle stressed the reliance factor in the following passage (at p. 822):

"The four critical facts [in the Smith case] are that the appellants knew from the outset:
  (1) that the report would be shown to Mrs. Smith;
  (2) that Mrs. Smith would probably rely on the valuation contained therein in deciding whether to buy the house without obtaining an independent valuation;
  (3) that if in these circumstances the valuation was, having regard to the actual condition of the house, excessive, Mrs. Smith would be likely to suffer loss; and
  (4) that she had paid to the building society a sum to defray the appellants' fee."

After stating that these facts gave rise to a duty of care both to the building society and to Mrs. Smith he added:

> "It is critical to this conclusion that the appellants knew that Mrs. Smith would be likely to rely on the valuation without obtaining independent advice."

In a more recent case[24] (involving a company take-over by a person who had relied on statements made by the company's financial advisers) Hoffman J. was asked to apply the principles set out above so as to impose negligence liability on the advisers. He declined to do so and in an illuminating passage he stressed the "consumer" aspect of the *Smith* and *Harris* cases. He distinguished *Smith* from the case before him as follows (at p. 335):

> "First, Mr. Smith [*sic*] had paid for the survey; although he had no contract with the surveyor, the relationship was, as Lord Templeman said, "akin to contract." [The take-over bidder], on the other hand, had not paid for the audit.
> Second, the typical plaintiff in a *Smith* v. *Bush* type case is a person of modest means and making the most expensive purchase of his or her life. He was very unlikely to be insured against the manifestation of inherent defects. The surveyor can protect himself relatively easily by insurance. The take-over bidder, on the other hand, is an entrepreneur taking high risks for high rewards and while some accountants may be able to take out sufficient insurance, others may not.
> Third, the imposition of liability on surveyors would probably not greatly increase their insurance costs and push up the cost of surveys because the typical buyer who relies on a building survey is buying a relatively modest house. Take-overs on the Stock Exchange involve huge amounts and the effects on accountants' insurance and fees are unpredictable."

This "economic" distinction is not an absolute one. Thus an auditor who prepares and certifies the accounts of a company does not thereby owe a legal duty of care to individual shareholders[25] and there is no distinction for this purpose between a private and a commercial investor.

What is the relevance of all this to supplies of goods? If the statement is made by the supplier it may be useful to plead *Hedley Byrne* as an alternative to other forms of liability. It is unlikely, however, to add a great deal to consumers' chances of success, as the facts will usually disclose a *Bentley* v. *Smith* contractual term[26] or an actionable misrepresentation under section 2(1) of the Misrepresentation Act 1967[27]

---

[24] *Morgan Crucible Co.* v. *Hill Samuel Bank Ltd. and Others* [1990] 3 All E.R. 330. The Court of Appeal subsequently held that, on the case as pleaded, a duty of care *might* arise—see [1991] 1 All E.R. 148.

[25] *Caparo Industries plc* v. *Dickman* [1990] 2 A.C. 605 (H.L.).

[26] *Ante*, p. 30.

[27] *Ante*, p. 27 and *post*, p. 95.

as well as a *Hedley Byrne* duty situation. Apart from the inherent uncertainty of establishing such a duty, the plaintiff is on stronger ground under the Misrepresentation Act because under that Act the burden is on the defendant to prove that he had reasonable grounds for believing the statement to be true. There is, however, a possibility that a *Hedley Byrne* claim could be pursued where the consumer has relied on a statement made by the manufacturer (for example, in sales literature or in a leaflet giving instructions for use). There is no doubt, however, that this would represent a major extension of the *Hedley Byrne* rule and in the only modern case in which the matter was raised the claim was rejected.[28]

4. Contractual Terms

We have already seen that a statement made during negotiations may sometimes be classified as a contractual term.[29] When will this occur? The leading case is *Heilbut, Symons & Co.* v. *Buckleton*[30] where Lord Moulton said:

> "An affirmation at the time of the sale is a warranty, provided it appears on evidence to be so intended."

The key word here is the word "intended" and the courts apply an objective test; they do not look into the minds of the parties but at their conduct. In the words of Lord Denning M.R.:

> "If an intelligent bystander would reasonably infer that a warranty was intended, that will suffice."[31]

To avoid confusion it must be stressed that the word "warranty" has at least two meanings. In the above examples it is used in its normal sense to mean "a term" or "a contractual promise." There is, however, a second meaning which is used in the Sale of Goods Act 1979. By section 61:

> warranty . . . means an agreement with reference to goods which are the subject of a contract of sale, but collateral to the main purpose of such contract, the breach of which gives rise to a claim to damages, but not to a right to reject the goods and treat the contract as repudiated.

In other words it means a minor term.

---

[28] *Lambert* v. *Lewis* [1980] 2 W.L.R. 299, 328 (C.A.) (the claim was actually brought by an intermediate dealer). In the House of Lords the case was decided on a different point. See also *post*, p. 51.
[29] *Ante*, p. 27.
[30] [1913] A.C. 30.
[31] *Dick Bentley* v. *Harold Smith* [1965] 1 W.L.R. 623, 627.

If an express statement is classified as a contractual term we have seen that the innocent party can claim damages. Can he also treat the contract as repudiated and reject the goods? The answer is that he may be able to do so, provided that he has been substantially deprived of what he bargained for. Under the Sale of Goods Act 1979 terms are classified as conditions or warranties but it has recently been held by the Court of Appeal that this rigid classification is not exhaustive.[32] The court held that there were intermediate stipulations (sometimes called "innominate terms") where the right to reject depended on the consequences of the breach. This decision helps to bring the law of sale of goods more into line with the rest of the law of contract and with the reasonable expectations of the parties.

5. DESCRIPTION

The final possibility is that the statement formed part of the description of the goods. By section 13 of the Sale of Goods Act 1979:

(1) Where there is a contract for the sale of goods by description, there is an implied condition that the goods will correspond with the description.
(2) If the sale is by sample, as well as by description, it is not sufficient that the bulk of the goods corresponds with the sample if the goods do not also correspond with the description.
(3) A sale of goods is not prevented from being a sale by description by reason only that, being exposed for sale or hire, they are selected by the buyer.

The section is largely self-explanatory. Thus if a handbag is described as "leather" there will be a breach of section 13 if it is plastic; if a car is described as a 1989 model there is a breach of section 13 if it is a 1986 model; if the seller agrees to sell "woollen underpants" he will be in breach if the material is cotton, rayon or linen. In this type of case the section adds nothing to the general law. It is a central obligation of the seller to supply the goods contracted for and he is guilty of non-performance if he fails to do so.

We now have to consider two problems, namely:

(1) What is a sale by description?
(2) What stipulations form part of the contract description?

What is a sale by description?

The courts have given a wide meaning to this term—in the words of the Law Commission "It [is] to all intents and purposes comprehensive." The following examples show how wide it is.

---

[32] *Cehave N.V.* v. *Bremer Handelsgesellschaft GmbH* [1976] Q.B. 44.

(a) Sales of purely generic goods, *e.g.* "50 rolls of hand-blocked wallpaper."
(b) Sales of specific goods which the buyer has not seen where he is relying on the description ("my 1988 wooden skis, ideal for Alpine downhill skiing").
(c) Sales of specific goods which the buyer has seen if they are sold as goods answering a description ("Canadian salmon").[33]
(d) Goods selected by the buyer at a self-service store or supermarket. This is the effect of section 13(3).[34] Thus if a tin on a supermarket shelf is labelled "Scotch salmon" and it contains Canadian salmon there will be a breach of section 13—so also if a label wrongly states the ingredients or quantity.

The principle that goods can describe themselves was affirmed by the courts in the remarkable case of *Beale* v. *Taylor*[35] where the following facts occurred:

> The plaintiff saw an advertisement "Herald convertible white 1961." He went to see it and saw a "1200" disc on the rear of the car. He agreed to buy it for £190 in the belief that he was buying a 1961 Triumph Herald model. Unfortunately, he was only half right; the front part consisted of an earlier model which had been welded on to the rear end of a 1961 Herald 1200. He claimed damages from the seller, but the county court judge dismissed the claim. The Court of Appeal allowed his appeal.

The court held that the combined effect of the advertisement and the disc was that the seller was offering to sell a 1961 Herald. This was, therefore, a sale by description and the seller was in breach of section 13. Damages were agreed at £125 (the price less the scrap value to the buyer).

It is not clear from the judgments whether the buyer would have succeeded on the strength of the disc alone. It is clear, however, that if a seller says to the buyer "I am offering to sell this to you—I am making no representations and you must exercise your own judgment," there would not be a sale by description. It was presumably on this ground that the county court judge had given judgment for the seller. This principle was recently applied and extended to a case[36] where the seller started by telling the buyer that he had come to sell two paintings by

---

[33] The relationship between s.13 and "bought as seen" has recently been considered by the Divisional Court, *post*, p. 275.
[34] This "supermarket" rule was first introduced in 1973 as an amendment to the original Sale of Goods Act 1893 to reflect the changing pattern of retail trading.
[35] [1967] 1 W.L.R. 1193.
[36] *Harlingdon and Leinster Enterprises Ltd.* v. *Christopher Hull Fine Art Ltd.* [1990] 3 W.L.R. 13. The legal effect of attribution may depend on whether the buyer was (as here) a dealer or a private buyer (*ibid.*). Note the strong and convincing dissenting judgment by Stuart-Smith L.J.

one Gabrielle Munter and then went on to say that he was not an
expert in these matters and knew nothing about that particular artist.
In holding that this was *not* a sale by description, Nourse L.J. in the
Court of Appeal said (at p. 18):

> "Authority apart, those words [*i.e.* section 13(1)] would suggest that the
> description must be influential in the sale, not necessarily alone, but so as
> to become an essential term, *i.e.* a condition, of the contract. Without
> such influence a description cannot be said to be one *by* which the contract
> for the sale of goods is made."

Accordingly, the buyer will fail if, viewed objectively, the court is
satisfied that he did not rely on the description.

What statements form part of the description?

Until recently the courts have given an extremely wide meaning to
the term "description." The term has been held to include such matters
as the quantity, the measurements, the manner of packing and even
the date of shipment. The practical result of this can be very serious
from the seller's point of view and unduly favourable to the buyer. We
have seen that if the goods do not comply with their description there is
a breach of "condition"; this means that the buyer can reject the goods,
even though he has suffered no loss. In the leading case of *Arcos Ltd.*
v. *Ronaasen*[37]:

> Sellers sold a quantity of wooden staves to the buyers. The thickness was
> given as half an inch. When the goods were delivered the arbitrator found
> that (i) only 5 per cent. were half an inch thick; (ii) a large proportion were
> between half an inch and nine-sixteenths of an inch; (iii) some were
> between nine-sixteenths and five-eighths of an inch; (iv) a very small
> proportion were more than five-eighths of an inch; (v) the staves were fit
> for the buyer's purpose and commercially within, and merchantable
> under, the contract specification. Despite the finding in (v) the buyer
> claimed that he was entitled to reject them. The High Court, the Court of
> Appeal and the House of Lords upheld the buyer's claim.

The judgments in the House of Lords are brief but they emphasize
the need for strict compliance. In the words of Lord Buckmaster[38]:

> "If the article they have purchased is not in fact the article that has been
> delivered, they are entitled to reject it, even though it is the commercial
> equivalent of that which they have bought."

Lord Atkin, in a well-known passage, commented that:

> "If the written contract specifies conditions of weight, measurement and

---

[37] [1933] A.C. 470.
[38] *Ibid.* at p. 474.

the like, these conditions must be complied with. A ton does not mean about a ton, or a yard about a yard. Still less, when you descend to minute measurements does half an inch mean about half an inch. If the seller wants a margin he must and in my experience does stipulate for it."

He did, however, go on to add that:

"No doubt there may be microscopic deviations which businessmen, and therefore lawyers will ignore."

Another well-known illustration of the doctrine of strict compliance is *Re Moore & Co. and Landauer & Co.*[39] which, like the previous case, reached the courts via an arbitrator.

Sellers agreed to sell tinned fruit in boxes containing 30 tins. When delivered some contained only 24 tins. The arbitrator found that there was no difference in the market value of the goods whether they were packed 24 tins or 30 tins in a case. The Court of Appeal upheld a claim by the buyer that he was entitled to reject the entire consignment.

It may be, however, that the position is changing. In a passage which can be equally relevant to consumer cases Lord Wilberforce said this:

"Some of these cases . . . I find to be excessively technical and due for fresh examination in this House. Even if a strict and technical view must be taken as regards the description of unascertained future goods (*e.g.* commodities) as to which each detail of the description may be assumed to be vital, it may be, and in my opinion is, right to treat other contracts of sale of goods in a similar manner to other contracts generally so as to ask *whether a particular item in a description constituted a substantial ingredient of the "identity" of the thing sold, and only if it does to treat it as a condition.*[40] (*italics supplied*)

Special meaning

If words have acquired a special trade meaning there will be no breach of section 13 if they answer that meaning. Thus in the case of *Grenfell* v. *E.B. Meyrowitz Ltd.*[41] it was proved that the words "safety glass" had acquired a special meaning and that this was known to the buyer. It was held that the sellers were not in breach of section 13 when they supplied "safety glass" goggles which corresponded to the special trade meaning.

Relationship between description and fitness

A final question which can be important for the consumer relates to

[39] [1921] 2 K.B. 519.
[40] *Reardon Smith* v. *Hansen-Tangen* [1976] 1 W.L.R. 989, 998 (H.L.).
[41] [1936] 2 All E.R. 1313.

the distinction between description and fitness for purpose. If goods
are unfit for the buyer's particular purpose can he allege that there is a
breach of section 13 or must he rely on the condition of fitness for
purpose under section 14 (which is considered in Chapter 4)? This is
yet another problem where the law is uncertain; the practical importance lies in the sphere of private sales.

> Suppose that the seller of a house agrees to sell to the buyer his furniture,
> lawnmower and television set. Both the lawnmower and the television set
> break down almost immediately and a cocktail cabinet collapses shortly
> afterwards.

As the law stands at the moment it is very unlikely that the buyer
would have any remedy against the seller. Section 14 only applies to a
sale "in the course of a business." There is nothing to suggest that any
of the goods have been misdescribed. One point which is clear is that
unfitness for one particular use does not amount to a breach of section
13. Thus "herring-meal" is still "herring-meal" even if it has defects
making it lethal when fed to mink.[42] If, however, the goods have only
one use (*e.g.* "touring skis") it might be arguable that fitness for
purpose forms an intrinsic part of the description. Perhaps the courts
might adopt the words spoken by Birkett L.J. in another context that
"a car which will not go is not a car at all."[43]

6. OTHER SUPPLY CONTRACTS

Where goods are let out on hire-purchase the condition as to description is identical to that for sale of goods.[44] An identical condition also
applies in other cases where the property in goods is transferred to the
customer (notably contracts of exchange and contracts for work and
materials)[45] and in cases of hire.[46]

[42] *Ashington Piggeries* v. *Christopher Hill* [1972] A.C. 441.
[43] *Karsales (Harrow) Ltd.* v. *Wallis* [1956] 1 W.L.R. 936, 942.
[44] Supply of Goods (Implied Terms) Act 1973, s.9.
[45] Supply of Goods and Services Act 1982, s.3.
[46] *Ibid.* s.8.

CHAPTER FOUR

"IT DOESN'T WORK"

1. THE PROBLEM

(1) A buys a dishwasher. It fails to work. The seller calls on numerous occasions to try to put it right. It invariably breaks down again after a few days.

(2) B orders central heating which is installed by X. The radiators leak and damage the carpet.

(3) C takes his suit to the cleaners. It comes back in a ruined condition.

(4) D buys a pair of new patent leather shoes for a party. The soles come away from the uppers almost immediately and D is unable to wear them.

(5) E takes his car to a garage for repair. The garage puts in faulty brake linings and E is injured when the brakes fail.

By far the most common consumer complaint is that the goods or services were not up to the expected standard. How does the law protect the consumer? There are three sets of provisions which may give him rights against the supplier:

(a) Section 14 of the Sale of Goods Act 1979 (as amended) is vitally important if the contract was a contract of sale.

(b) Section 10 of the Supply of Goods (Implied Terms) Act 1973 contains virtually identical provisions relating to hire-purchase agreements.

(c) Sections 4 and 9 of the Supply of Goods and Services Act 1982 contain virtually identical provisions in relation to other contracts for the transfer of goods (exchange, work and materials, etc.) and contracts of hire.

Until the passing of the 1982 Act it used to be important to distinguish clearly between a contract of sale of goods on the one hand and a contract for work and materials (central heating, double glazing, loft conversion, etc.) on the other. The need for a clear distinction has been reduced considerably in relation to quality and fitness but it can still be important for other purposes—including the "nemo dat" rules discussed in Chapter 2.

2. SALE OF GOODS

The general position

If the contract is for the sale of goods the obligations of the seller are governed by section 14 of the Sale of Goods Act 1979 which is one of the most important provisions of the Act.[1] Unfortunately, the Act was drafted before the consumer explosion of the present century and the language of the Act (*e.g.* "merchantable quality") is more appropriate to a contract between two businessmen than to a contract between a businessman and a consumer. This point will come out even more strongly when we examine the question of remedies.[2] We shall see that the two remedies which the consumer most wants—a right to have the defective goods repaired or replaced by the seller—are not provided for by the Act. Both of these matters (merchantability and remedies) have been thoroughly examined by the Law Commission and their Report *Sale and Supply of Goods*[3] will be referred to at appropriate places in this chapter.

Let the buyer beware

In the light of what has been said above, the early law developed on the basis that it was for the parties to make their own bargain—it was up to the buyer to decide whether the goods were merchantable and fit before he agreed to buy them. The principle ("*caveat emptor*" or "let the buyer beware") has been severely eroded but is not entirely extinct. By section 14(1):

> Except as provided by this section . . . there is no implied condition or warranty about the quality or fitness for any particular purpose of goods supplied under a contract of sale.

We shall see that the Act protects the consumer if the seller sells in the course of a business. If, however, the seller is a private seller the principle of *caveat emptor* may still apply.

> Suppose that A, a private individual, sells a hedgecutter to B. It is in poor condition and breaks down after a few days. In the absence of any express promise or representation B has no claim against A.

The distinction then is between a sale "in the course of a business" and a sale which is not in the course of a business. There is one hybrid situation; what about a dealer who sells in the course of a business as agent for a private seller? Section 14(5) makes it clear that the seller must endeavour to bring this fact to the buyer's notice. It provides that:

---

[1] See Law Commission Report No. 24, p. 9.
[2] *Post*, p. 101.
[3] Law Com. No. 160, Scot. Law Com. No. 104 (1987).

[The conditions of quality and fitness] apply to a sale by a person who in the course of business is acting as agent for another as they apply to a sale by a principal in the course of a business except where that other is not selling in the course of a business and either the buyer knows that fact or reasonable steps are taken to bring it to the notice of the buyer before the contract is made.

Presumably the seller should instruct the dealer to inform prospective buyers of his private status; the dealer might then have to indemnify the seller against liability arising through failure to perform this duty.

Section 14(5) is concerned with the case where a private seller appears to be selling in the course of a business. What about the converse case—trade sellers masquerading as private sellers? An enquiry under Part II of the Fair Trading Act 1973 disclosed that some motor traders were guilty of this practice—they advertised their cars for sale in newspapers and gave only their private addresses. Such practices are now a criminal offence.[4]

Privity of contract

The conditions of merchantable quality and fitness are implied *as between seller and buyer*. If, for example, a lady buys an unmerchantable washing machine and gives it to her daughter as a present, the daughter has no claim against the supplier if it breaks down. The mother would have a claim but she might find it difficult to prove damage flowing from the breach (although she might have a claim if she paid for the cost of repairs).[5] The question of "who made the contract?" may also be relevant if, for example, a group of people go to a restaurant for a meal. It seems that the restaurant makes a contract with each of them, so that each of them would be entitled to claim damages if the food supplied were unmerchantable.[6]

Questions of agency must also be borne in mind in this connection. A woman who does the shopping may do so as agent for her husband or cohabitee, so that *he* would have a claim in contract if the goods turn out to be defective. There is no agency case (so far) the other way round. Thus if the man buys typhoid-infected milk which injures his wife it was held in *Frost* v. *Aylesbury Dairy Co.*[7] that the husband has a claim in contract. In modern social conditions it might well be possible for the courts to hold that the husband was buying for himself and as agent for his wife. An argument on these lines should certainly be tried

---

[4] Business Advertisements (Disclosure) Order 1977, *post*, p. 280.
[5] See *Jackson* v. *Horizon Holidays* [1975] 1 W.L.R. 1468 where the Court of Appeal allowed a contracting party to recover damages for a third party's loss. But see the comments of Lord Wilberforce in *Woodar Investment Development* v. *Wimpey Construction U.K.* [1980] 1 W.L.R. 277 (H.L.).
[6] *Lockett* v. *A.M. Charles Ltd.* [1938] 4 All E.R. 170.
[7] [1905] 1 K.B. 608.

in appropriate cases; if it were accepted it could loosen the shackles of the privity rule.

Strict liability

The practical importance of the point just mentioned lies in the concept of strict liability. Section 14(2) says "are of merchantable quality." It is clear from the case of *Frost* v. *Aylesbury Dairy Co.* (*supra*) that the absence of negligence is no defence; the seller will not be able to avoid liability by proving that he neither knew, nor ought to have known, of the defect.

If, however, the privity rules bar a claim in contract an injured plaintiff will have to bring proceedings in *tort*. This used to mean having to prove negligence—by no means an easy task. However, since the arrival of the Consumer Protection Act 1987 and the imposition of strict (or at least semi-strict) liability on producers and some distributors the plaintiff's position has improved significantly.[8]

Merchantable quality

The implied condition of merchantable quality should be of great importance to the consumer. Unfortunately, it is beset with difficulties. Section 14(2) reads as follows:

> Where the seller sells goods in the course of a business, there is an implied condition that the goods supplied under the contract are of merchantable quality, except that there is no such condition—
> (a) as regards defects specifically drawn to the buyer's attention before the contract is made; or
> (b) if the buyer examines the goods before the contract is made, as regards defects which that examination ought to reveal.

In advising a consumer a number of points must be considered. In particular:

(a) Was the sale in the course of a business?
(b) What is the meaning of "goods supplied"?
(c) Are the goods unmerchantable?
(d) Do either of the exceptions apply?

(a) *Are the goods supplied "in the course of a business"?*

In the vast majority of cases this should present no problems. A consumer buying from a shop, warehouse or mail order firm will have no difficulty in clearing this hurdle. The mere fact that the seller is handling a particular product for the first time is immaterial.[9] What is

---

[8] *Post*, pp. 63 *et seq.*
[9] See Lord Wilberforce in *Ashington Piggeries* v. *Christopher Hill* [1972] A.C. 441, 494.

less clear is whether a supplier must be a dealer in that particular class of goods. In a Report published in 1969 the Law Commission gave the example of a coal merchant selling off one of his lorries; presumably a sale of a cash register by a shop-keeper or surplus office furniture by a solicitor would fall within the same category. There is, however, no judicial authority to confirm the view that such sales are "in the course of" a business merely because the seller is a business and cases on exemption clauses[10] and trade descriptions[11] point in the opposite direction.

Other borderline cases can be imagined. What about goods sold at a charity, tennis club bazaar or jumble sale? It could be argued that such a "one-off" activity is not a business sale. Again, if a dentist or an accountant sells his private car, the mere fact that he sometimes used it for business would not, it is believed, make it a sale "in the course of a business." The Act itself merely provides that the term "trade" includes a profession and the activities of a local authority, government department or statutory undertaker. The concept of "business" is also central to the Unfair Contract Terms Act 1977[12] and to the Consumer Credit Act 1974[13] and both of these Acts merely give a limited definition similar to the one referred to above.

(b) *What is the meaning of "goods supplied"?*

The courts have given a sensible answer to this question by giving the words their normal meaning. Thus the condition of merchantable quality can apply not only to the *contents* of a bottle or tin but also to the *container, i.e.* the bottle or tin itself, even if it has to be returned—it is still "supplied" under the contract.[14] Similarly, if the goods actually supplied contain a foreign body (for example, a worm, a snail, a piece of glass or a detonator) the totality of the goods supplied may be unmerchantable.[15]

(c) *When are goods unmerchantable?*

This is the crucial question and in practice it is often extremely hard to answer. The Sale of Goods Act 1893 contained no definition and dicta in a number of cases were not always easy to reconcile. Eventually in 1973 a statutory definition was inserted and this now appears

---

[10] See *R & B Customs Brokers Ltd.* v. *UDT* [1988] 1 W.L.R. 321 (C.A.) (shipping brokers bought car for use by a director; held that they had bought "as consumer" and not "in the course of a business"; accordingly a purported exemption clause was void: see Chap. 8).

[11] See *Davies* v. *Sumner* [1984] 3 All E.R. 831 (H.L.), *post*, pp. 198–199.

[12] *Post*, p. 132.

[13] *Post*, p. 314.

[14] *Geddling* v. *Marsh* [1920] 1 K.B. 668.

[15] See the interesting case of *Wilson* v. *Rickett Cockerell & Co. Ltd.* [1954] 1 Q.B. 598 where a detonator was mistakenly included in a bag of coalite.

in section 14(6). Unfortunately this has not resolved all the problems, although in *Rogers* v. *Parish (Scarborough) Ltd.*[16] Mustill L.J., stressing that the 1973 Act was an amending Act, said hopefully:

> "The language of s.14(6) is clear and free from technicality, and it should be sufficient in the great majority of cases to enable the fact-finding judge to arrive at a decision without exploring the intricacies of the prior law."

In advising the consumer three particular problems stand out, namely:

(i) If a new article is delivered with minor defects, does that make it unmerchantable?

(ii) What standard is required for second-hand goods?

(iii) For how long must the goods remain merchantable?

In practice the seller may be willing to deal with the matter for reasons of commercial goodwill but if he refuses to do so the buyer may face an uphill task—and a potentially expensive one. No doubt this helps to explain the popularity of manufacturers' guarantees.

Section 14(6) provides that:

> Goods of any kind are of merchantable quality . . . if they are as fit for the purpose or purposes for which goods of that kind are commonly bought as it is reasonable to expect having regard to any description applied to them, the price (if relevant) and all the other relevant circumstances.

It is clear from this definition that if the goods are unfit for their only proper use, they will not be merchantable. If a thermos flask breaks when it is filled, if a piece of a jigsaw puzzle is missing, if wallpaper cannot be stuck to the wall, the seller is liable. In the words of Lord Ellenborough in an early case[17]

> "The purchaser cannot be expected to buy the goods to lay them on the dunghill."

Again in the well-known "sulphite in the pants" case of *Grant* v. *Australian Knitting Mills Ltd.*[18] Lord Wright commented that

> "it [merchantable quality] does mean that the article sold, if only meant for one particular use, is fit for that use."[19]

Before considering the three problems mentioned above various other points can be made. First, the definition uses the word "are." This confirms the ruling in *Jackson* v. *Rotax Motor Co. Ltd.*[20] that if

[16] [1987] 2 W.L.R. 353, 357.
[17] *Gardiner* v. *Gray* (1815) 4 Camp. 144.
[18] [1936] A.C. 85.
[19] *Ibid.* at p. 100.
[20] [1910] 2 K.B. 937.

goods are unmerchantable, the mere fact that they can be made merchantable by a simple process is immaterial and it is very doubtful whether the seller can legally rectify the defect after the buyer's rejection of the goods. Secondly, the reference to price supports what Lord Reid said in *Brown & Son Ltd.* v. *Craiks*,[21] namely that if a particular description covers different qualities of goods, a buyer who pays a price appropriate to a *superior* quality can reasonably expect to receive that quality, and can regard the goods as unmerchantable if he receives an inferior quality. Thirdly, what about goods bought at a "sale" at reduced prices? There is no reported case on this point but a buyer should have no difficulty in satisfying a court that the "sale" aspect is irrelevant; it results from a commercial decision to dispose of surplus stock and it cannot in any way be relied on by the seller to justify the supply of inferior goods.

Finally, what is the meaning of "fit for the purpose or purposes" in section 14(6)? Does it mean that multi-purpose goods will be unmerchantable if they have defects rendering them unfit for some (but not all) of their normal purposes? Such an interpretation would involve a major change in the law and the Court of Appeal has recently confirmed that the statutory wording introduced in 1973 has not had this effect; in other words multi-purpose goods will only be unmerchantable if they are unfit for *all* their normal purposes.[22]

Minor and cosmetic defects. In a report[23] published by the Consumers' Association in 1979 it was pointed out that the statutory definition was unsatisfactory in two respects. In the first place, it concentrates excessively on the fitness of the goods for their purpose and ignores aesthetic considerations and appearance (dents, scratches, etc.). Secondly, the reference to the standard which a buyer might reasonably expect could open the door to an argument that a buyer could not complain if his new car had "teething troubles" since it was widely known that all new cars had them. The Law Commission Report[24] refers to a number of cases which lend some support to these fears[25] but in two recent cases these fears have been largely laid to rest. The leading modern case on the point is *Rogers* v. *Parish (Scarborough) Ltd.*[26]

---

[21] [1970] 1 W.L.R. 752 (H.L.). If, however, the buyer relies entirely on his own judgment, the mere fact that he makes a bad bargain will not give rise to a claim: *Harlingdon Enterprises Ltd.* v. *Christopher Hull Fine Art Ltd.*, *ante*, p. 37.

[22] *M/S Aswan Engineering Establishment Co.* v. *Lupdine Ltd.* [1987] 1 W.L.R. 1 (C.A.).

[23] "Merchantable Quality—What does it mean?"

[24] Law Com. No. 160, p. 9.

[25] *Millars of Falkirk Ltd.* v. *Turpie* (1976) S.L.T. (Notes) 66; *Spencer* v. *Claude Rye (Vehicles) Ltd. The Guardian* December 19, 1972; *Leaves* v. *Wadham Stringer (Cliftons) Ltd.* [1980] R.T.R. 308.

[26] [1987] 2 W.L.R. 353. The other case is *Bernstein* v. *Pamson Motors (Golders Green) Ltd.* [1987] 2 All E.R. 220 which is also of great interest on the question of remedies— see *post*, p. 106.

Mr. Rogers bought a Range Rover for £16,000 under a conditional sale agreement. It was sold as new but it had defects in the engine, gearbox and bodywork and the oilseals were unsound at vital junctions. In the six months following delivery Mr. Rogers drove the car some 5,500 miles while unsuccessful efforts were made to rectify the defects. At the end of that period he rejected the car and claimed the return of his payments and damages on the basis that the car was unmerchantable.

Counsel for the sellers argued that since the car was roadworthy, the defects did not make it unmerchantable. The judge at first instance accepted this view but the Court of Appeal rejected it and found in favour of Mr. Rogers. In a passage which is certain to be quoted by advisers in this type of case Mustill L.J. said (at p. 359):

> "Starting with the purpose for which 'goods of that kind' are commonly bought, one would include in respect of any passenger vehicle not merely the buyer's purpose of driving the car from one place to another *but of doing so with the appropriate degree of comfort, ease of handling and reliability and, one might add, of pride in the vehicle's outward and interior appearance* (italics supplied). What is the appropriate degree and what relative weight is to be attached to one characteristic of the car rather than another will depend on the market at which the car is aimed.
>
> "To identify the relevant expectation one must look at the factors listed in the subsection. First, the description applied to the goods. In the present case the vehicle was sold as new. Deficiencies which might be acceptable in a secondhand vehicle were not to be expected in one purchased as new. Next, the description 'Range Rover' would conjure up a particular set of expectations, not the same as those relating to an ordinary saloon car, as to the balance between performance, handling, comfort and resilience. The factor of price was also significant. At more than £16,000 this vehicle was, if not at the top end of the scale, well above the level of the ordinary family saloon. The buyer was entitled to value for his money."

Even if the car is in the middle or lower end of the market it will still be unmerchantable if (1) the defects have a knock-on effect so that the car can never be restored to its previous condition, or (2) the defects (*e.g.* oil leak) render it dangerous to drive the car.[27]

Effect of guarantee. In the *Rogers* case (*supra*) counsel for the sellers raised a further point—namely that a car was not rendered unmerchantable by defects which the buyer was entitled to have rectified free of charge under the manufacturer's guarantee (or warranty). Mustill L.J. was unimpressed. He said (at p. 360):

> "Can it really be right to say that the reasonable buyer would expect less of his new Range Rover with a warranty than without one? Surely the warranty is an addition to the buyer's rights, not a subtraction from them,

---

[27] See the judgment of Rougier J. in the *Bernstein* case cited in n. 26.

and, it may be noted, only a circumscribed addition since it lasts for a limited period and does not compensate the buyer for consequential loss and inconvenience.

"If the defendants are right a buyer would be well advised to leave his guarantee behind in the showroom. This cannot be what the manufacturers and dealers intend or what their customers reasonably understand."

Second-hand goods. There have been four fairly recent cases dealing with "merchantability" of second-hand cars. The first was *Bartlett* v. *Sidney Marcus*[28] where the following facts arose:

> The plaintiff bought a second-hand Jaguar car for £950. It was pointed out that the clutch was in need of repair, but the defect was believed to be a small one and the price was reduced accordingly. After driving for 300 miles the plaintiff took the car to a garage who found that the defect was more serious than the plaintiff expected. The cost of repairs came to £84 and the plaintiff claimed this amount from the seller.

The county court judge gave judgment for the buyer but the Court of Appeal allowed the seller's appeal. On the question of merchantability Lord Denning M.R. pointed out that:

> "on the sale of a second-hand car, it is merchantable if it is in usable condition, even if not perfect. . . . A buyer should realise that when he buys a second-hand car defects may appear sooner or later and, in the absence of an express warranty, he has no redress."

In *Crowther* v. *Shannon Motor Co.*,[29] which was also concerned with a second-hand Jaguar, the buyer was more successful.

> The car was eight years old; the engine had done 82,165 miles; the buyer paid a price of £390. He drove the car for another 2,300 miles in three weeks. Then the engine expired. The evidence showed that (a) the engine was in a "clapped out" state when the car was sold to the buyer; (b) the buyer of a Jaguar car could reasonably expect the engine to do 100,000 miles. On these facts the Court of Appeal held that the seller was liable.

In the third case the buyer scored a somewhat Pyrrhic victory. The case was *Lee* v. *York Coach and Marine*[30] and the facts were as follows:

> Mrs. Lee bought a second-hand Morris 1100 for £355. Almost immediately it developed defects and it was off the road for a considerable time when the sellers sought unsuccessfully to mend the defects. After seven weeks her solicitors wrote to the sellers saying "we must ask you please to remedy all these defects without delay or to refund £355 to Mrs. Lee." The sellers then offered to do some further work on the car; a Department of Environment examiner found very serious defects, and two weeks later

[28] [1965] 1 W.L.R. 1013.
[29] [1975] 1 W.L.R. 30.
[30] [1977] R.T.R. 35.

a further letter was written by the solicitors. "Mrs. Lee would have been justified in rescinding the contract on that basis—that is on the basis that the car was unroadworthy—in our opinion she may still be entitled to do so." Four months later the buyer brought an action claiming the return of the price. The evidence showed (*inter alia*) that the brakes were so poor that they could not have survived an attempt to test them.

The Court of Appeal held that the car, being unsafe to be driven, was clearly unmerchantable. They also held, however, that neither of the solicitor's letters amounted to a rejection of the car. By the time that the buyer finally sought to reject (the start of the proceedings) it was too late to reject.[31] Accordingly, she was only entitled to damages and the figure of £100 was not disputed. Presumably Mrs. Lee would have seen very little of the £100 since the court made no order for costs in the Court of Appeal.

Finally, in the most recent case[32] the Court of Appeal have applied the *Rogers* ruling (*ante*) that roadworthiness was not the correct test. Each case would turn on the application of the statutory definition to the particular facts and on the extent to which the actual condition of the vehicle matched the buyer's reasonable expectations.

Merchantability—acts to be done before use. If both parties contemplate that some act will be done to the goods before use they must be merchantable *after* this has been done but not necessarily before. Thus in *Heil* v. *Hedges*[33] the buyer of pork chops failed to cook them properly and became ill as the result of the chops becoming infected by worms. Had she cooked them properly the infection would not have occurred. Her claim for damages failed. On the other hand in the underpants case[34] the pants were sold for immediate use. Therefore the fact that the sulphite might have been removed by washing was held to be irrelevant.

Merchantability—for how long? It is clear from commercial cases involving the sale of rabbits and potatoes that if defects appear soon after purchase this may show that the goods were unmerchantable at the time of the contract.[35] What does that mean in the consumer context? A vacuum cleaner breaks down after one month, a freezer after two months, a carpet starts to wear away after three months and a dishwasher breaks down after 18 months. The consumer *may* be able to show that the goods were not merchantable right at the beginning

[31] See *post*, p. 106.
[32] *Business Application Specialists* v. *Nationwide Credit Corporation* [1988] R.T.R. 332.
[33] [1951] 1 T.L.R. 512.
[34] *Grant* v. *Australian Knitting Mills* [1936] A.C. 85.
[35] See *Beer* v. *Walker* (1877) 46 L.J.Q.B. 677; *Mash & Murrell* v. *Joseph I. Emanuel Ltd.* [1961] 1 All E.R. 485.

but it will not be easy. If the seller wishes to resist a claim, he will point out that all sorts of things could have caused the breakdown and that it is up to the buyer to produce evidence linking the breakdown to the condition of the goods when he bought them. The buyer will argue, "I used the goods in the normal way—a freezer should not break down after only two months." The Act does not spell out any obligation of durability but a recent case lends support to the consumer's argument of unmerchantability. In *Lambert* v. *Lewis*[36]—a case concerning a commercial vehicle—Lord Diplock said:

> "The implied warranty [*sic*] of fitness for a particular purpose ... is a continuing warranty that the goods will continue to be fit for that purpose for a reasonable time after delivery. ... What is a reasonable time will depend on the nature of the goods but I would accept that in the case of the coupling the warranty was still continuing up to the date, some three to six months before the accident, when it first became known to the farmer that the handle of the locking mechanism was missing."[37]

Nevertheless there is considerable uncertainty in this area (especially at the level of consumer complaints) and the Law Commission recommend[38] an express reference to durability in the Act.

Spare parts. A consumer may find that his goods become useless because, for example, the retailer does not have a supply of spare parts and the manufacturer has discontinued that particular product or has gone out of business altogether. There is no legal obligation on the seller to carry spare parts[39]—although some trade associations have adopted Codes of Practice which require their members to do so.[40]

(d) *Do either of the exceptions apply?*

The first exception in section 14(2)(*a*) applies where defects are *specifically* drawn to the buyer's attention before the contract is made. This could apply if, for example, a defective clutch or a dent or scratch or other defect was pointed out to the buyer—perhaps with an abatement in price. This is quite common where stores sell shop-soiled showroom models at a discount with labels drawing attention to the particular damage. There could, of course, be room for argument— the buyer might say "the seller told me that the clutch was rather worn but I had no idea I would have to spend £250 on it a week after buying the car."

The second exception in section 14(2)(*b*) relates to examination

---

[36] [1981] 2 W.L.R. 713.
[37] At p. 720.
[38] *Op. cit.* at pp. 10, 31–33.
[39] See Law Com. No. 160, p. 34.
[40] See *post*, p. 101.

where the buyer has examined the goods *before* the making of the contract. The condition does not apply as regards defects which that examination ought to reveal. Two points can be made with regard to this exception. First, it only applies to a buyer who has *actually* examined the goods—not to a buyer who has declined an opportunity to do so. Secondly, what is the meaning of "defects which that examination ought to reveal?" This wording was first introduced in 1973 and differs slightly from the wording of the original 1893 Act, *i.e.* "defects which such examination ought to have revealed." In either case the words appear to refer solely to the examination actually made. If, for example, the buyer of a handbag only examines the outside, he will still be able to complain if on arriving home he finds that the inside has numerous defects including a broken zip (but he could not claim for an external defect which he should have seen, *e.g.* a broken handle). There is a Court of Appeal case which appears to confirm this view.[41] However, in *Thornett & Fehr* v. *Beers & Son*[42] Bray J. at first instance appeared to treat the words "such examination" as if they read "a reasonable examination." He held that (a) the buyers had examined the goods; (b) an examination would "in the ordinary way" have revealed the defect; (c) accordingly, the condition was not implied.

It is possible that this decision is wrong on the wording of the Act and it appears to be inconsistent with the *Bristol Tramways* case (which was not cited). It can also be argued that if the case was wrong on the original wording of the Act, it may well be even more incorrect on the amended wording. Thus, the courts may well refuse to follow it.

(e) *The Law Commission*

The Law Commission have acknowledged that there is no magic formula to cover all cases. They recommend that the words "merchantable quality" be replaced by a more modern phrase such as "acceptable quality." This basic principle should be amplified with a list of aspects of quality[43]:

    (a) their fitness for all their common purposes;
    (b) their appearance and finish;
    (c) their freedom from minor defects;
    (d) their safety;
    (e) their durability.

An attempt in 1990 to introduce these reforms as part of the Consumer Guarantees Bill—a Private Members' Bill—failed at the last ditch

---

[41] *Bristol Tramways* v. *Fiat Motors* [1910] 2 K.B. 831.
[42] [1919] 1 K.B. 486.
[43] *Op. cit.* at p. 66.

because of Government objections to other provisions in the Bill. We consider it likely that the Law Commissions' recommendations will be given legislative effect before the new decade is much older.

Fitness for particular purpose

Section 14 of the Sale of Goods Act implies a condition of reasonable fitness as well as the condition of merchantable quality which has just been considered. Section 14(3) reads as follows:

> Where the seller sells goods in the course of a business and the buyer, expressly or by implication, makes known
>   (a) to the seller or
>   (b) where the purchase price or part of it is payable by instalments and the goods were previously sold by a credit-broker to the seller, to that credit-broker
> any particular purpose for which the goods are being bought, there is an implied condition that the goods supplied under the contract are reasonably fit for that purpose, whether or not that is a purpose for which such goods are commonly supplied, except where the circumstances show that the buyer does not rely, or that it is unreasonable for him to rely, on the skill or judgment of the seller or credit-broker.

What is the relationship between the two conditions? It can be argued that in the case of "single purpose" goods section 14(3) is completely unnecessary because the concept of "fitness" is built into the definition of merchantable quality.[44] Thus, if a catapult or a drill breaks when it is first used, or if a hot water bottle bursts, it is neither "merchantable" nor "fit." In the previous discussion on new and second-hand cars no distinction has been drawn between the two conditions because the test to be applied is basically the same.

It should also be mentioned that a number of rules are common to both subsections. Thus (a) in both cases liability is strict[45]; (b) in both cases the seller is only liable if he supplied the goods "in the course of a business"; (c) both conditions apply to all goods "supplied" under the contract; (d) in both cases the condition only applies as between seller and buyer; and (e) in both cases the seller may be relieved from liability if the buyer fails to do something to the goods before use.[46]

What then is the need for section 14(3)? The key is to be found in the words "any *particular* purpose . . . whether or not that is a purpose for which such goods are commonly supplied."

> Suppose that a law student goes to a bookseller and says "I want to buy some books which are suitable for the Solicitors examinations." The seller supplies books which are only suitable for the Bar or University examinations.

---

[44] *Ante*, p. 46.
[45] *Ante*, p. 44.
[46] See *ante*, p. 50.

On these facts the seller would clearly be liable under section 14(3); but there might well be no breach of section 14(2).

The subsection applies where the purpose is made known expressly or by implication. In the case of single purpose goods such as weed-killer, a bun or a hot water bottle, the buyer does not have to go through the ritual of spelling out his purpose—this will be implied because it is self-evident.[47] In this type of case the courts would not give much weight to a clause in a standard form contract (even if signed by the buyer) stating that "the buyer has not made known the purpose for which the goods are required." This type of clause was used in the hire-purchase case of *Lowe* v. *Lombank*,[48] a case involving a car with numerous defects. The Court of Appeal found no difficulty in holding that the supplier (the finance company) was liable under the implied condition of fitness. The purpose was obvious and the clause was inconsistent with the facts. If, however, the purpose is a special one (for example, a textbook suitable for a particular course) then the seller will be liable only if that purpose was *expressly* made known. In *Griffiths* v. *Peter Conway Ltd.*[49]:

> A lady bought a Harris tweed coat. She had an abnormally sensitive skin and contracted dermatitis from wearing the coat. The evidence showed that the coat would not have caused problems apart from this one special fact. It was held that as this fact had not been disclosed to the seller he was not liable.

Reliance

The condition of fitness is not implied if the seller can prove that the buyer did not rely on the seller's skill or judgment. Thus, suppose that John, an amateur jeweller, goes to a general hardware store and asks for glue suitable for jewellery-making. The seller might say "I have no idea whether this brand is suitable—you must decide for yourself and not rely on me." In such a case he might escape liability under section 14(3) (and perhaps also under section 14(2) since the circumstances surrounding the purchase would be one of the "circumstances" in section 14(6)). The buyer's reliance on the seller's skill or judgment may well be partial. If the goods turn out to be unfit for the buyer's particular purpose, the seller will be liable unless he can prove that the defect fell outside the area of reliance.[50]

Warnings and instructions

If the instructions supplied with the goods are wrong or misleading

---

[47] See *Preist* v. *Last* [1903] 2 K.B. 148—the well-known case of a bursting hot water bottle.

[48] [1960] 1 W.L.R. 196.

[49] [1939] 1 All E.R. 685. See also *M/S Aswan Engineering Establishment Co.* v. *Lupdine Ltd.* [1987] 1 W.L.R. 1.

[50] *Ashington Piggeries Ltd.* v. *Christopher Hill Ltd.* [1972] A.C. 441.

this can make the goods unfit for their purpose. If, however, there is a clear warning (*e.g.* "Do not use after July 1") a buyer who ignores this cannot complain merely because the damage which he suffers is different from that mentioned in the warning.[51]

Credit-broker

The term "credit-broker" is taken from the Consumer Credit Act 1974 which is considered in Part IV of this book (*post*, p. 295). The type of case contemplated by section 14(3) is that of a consumer who goes to a dealer and tells the dealer the purpose for which he wants the goods. The dealer then sells the goods on to a finance house which in turn sells the goods to the consumer on instalment terms. Although the consumer has bought the goods from the finance company (which he has probably never heard of until they write to him demanding payment) he will enjoy the protection of section 14(3) if he makes his purpose known to the dealer (credit-broker) unless he did not rely, or if it was not reasonable for him to rely, on the credit-broker's skill or judgment.

The Law Commission

In their Report No. 160, which has been discussed earlier in this chapter in relation to merchantable quality, the Law Commission do not make any proposals for the amendment of the fitness condition in section 14(3). There are, however, a number of proposals in relation to remedies and these will be dealt with in Chapter 7.

3. HIRE-PURCHASE

The implied terms as to fitness and quality are virtually the same as in sale of goods.[52] The hire-purchaser will usually conduct the negotiations with a "credit-broker" (see above) and once again it is sufficient if he notifies his purpose to that credit-broker.[53]

4. WORK AND MATERIALS

We have seen earlier in this chapter that certain contracts may be classified as contracts for "work and materials" rather than "sale of goods." Contracts to repair a house or car, or to insulate a loft, are

---

[51] *Wormell* v. *RHM Agriculture (East)* [1987] 1 W.L.R. 1091 (herbicide failed to kill farmer's wild oats because it was used too late in the season).

[52] See Supply of Goods (Implied Terms) Act 1973, s.10, as redrafted in Schedule 4 to the Consumer Credit Act 1974.

[53] s.10(3).

obvious examples. In the words of Stable J. in a case where a hair-dresser applied a hair dye to the head of a customer:

> "[It] is really half the rendering of services and, in a sense, half the supply of goods."[54]

The law applies different standards to the two halves of the contractual obligation. On the first half (*i.e.* the provision of work) there is an implied duty to take reasonable care[55]; on the second half (*i.e.* the provision of materials) there is strict liability under section 4 of the Supply of Goods and Services Act 1982 in respect of merchantable quality and fitness for purpose.

The Act confirms the common law position; thus in *Samuels* v. *Davis*[56] the defendant was liable when the denture which he had made made did not fit the mouth of the plaintiff's wife. The Court of Appeal found it unnecessary to decide whether it was a sale of goods or work and materials contract. The important point is that the dentist was liable even though the county court judge had found that he was not negligent. The court approved the reasoning in the earlier Divisional Court case of *GH Myers & Co.* v. *Brent Cross Service Co.*[57] In that case:

> The plaintiff asked the defendant to "knock-in" the engine of his car and to renew any parts which required replacement. In the course of the work the defendant bought six connecting rods and fitted them. Owing to a latent defect one of the rods broke and damage of nearly £70 was caused. When the plaintiff claimed damages, the defendant argued that he was not liable because the defect could not have been discovered by the exercise of reasonable care and skill. The defence was rejected.

The Divisional Court made it clear that if the consumer relied on the repairers' skill and judgment then liability was strict. In the words of du Parcq J.:

> "I think that the true view is that a person contracting to do work and supply materials warrants that the materials which he uses will be of good quality and reasonably fit for the purpose for which he is using them, unless the circumstances of the contract are such as to exclude any such warranty. There may be circumstances which would clearly exclude it. A man goes to a repairer and says "repair my car; get the parts from the makers and fit them." In such a case it is made plain that the person ordering the repairs is not relying upon any warranty, except that the parts

---

[54] *Watson* v. *Buckley Osborne & Co.* [1940] 1 All E.R. 174, 180.
[55] Supply of Goods and Services Act 1982, s.13. *Post*, p. 90.
[56] [1943] K.B. 526.
[57] [1934] 1 K.B. 46. The principles set out in this judgment are now statutory—see Supply of Goods and Services Act 1982, s.4. A detailed discussion can be found in Woodroffe, *Goods and Services—the New Law*, Chap. 3.

used will be parts ordered and obtained from the makers. On the other hand if he says "do the work—fit any necessary parts" he is in no way limiting the person doing the repair work, and the person doing the repair work is in my view liable if there is any defect in the materials supplied, even if it was one which reasonable care would not have discovered."

Thus, for example, the repairer will be liable where the defect was due to the faulty work of a sub-contractor—unless this was a person selected by the customer.[58]

5. Hire

Until recently the rules relating to the merchantability or fitness of goods let out on hire were somewhat uncertain but the matter is now governed by section 9 of the Supply of Goods and Services Act 1982. Once again the rules are virtually identical to those which apply to sale, hire-purchase and the "materials" element of work and materials contracts.[59]

[58] *Stewart* v. *Reavell's Garage* [1952] 2 Q.B. 545.
[59] See Woodroffe, *ante*, n. 55.

Chapter Five

"IT WILL COST £1,000 TO MAKE THEM SAFE"

Scheme of this chapter

In the previous chapter we examined the consumer's rights against his immediate supplier where the goods were faulty. In this chapter we move further afield to consider the consumer's rights against other persons in the distribution chain—including in particular the manufacturer. Such rights can be important for at least three reasons:

1. A buyer may find that his rights under a manufacturer's guarantee are easier to enforce than his Sale of Goods Act rights against his supplier where he may have considerable difficulty in proving that the goods were unmerchantable.
2. A supplier may be unable to meet the claim—perhaps because he has gone out of business.
3. The injured party may not have a contract at all; thus a badly constructed car may cause death or injury to passengers and pedestrians while a child may suffer pre-natal injuries caused by a drug supplied to the mother.

This chapter will deal first with *defective* goods and then with *dangerous* goods. The distinction is crucial.

Example 1

A buys goods from B. They are of very poor quality and useless to A unless he spends money on repairing them. The goods are *defective*.

Example 2

The goods in the previous example cause death or personal injury or damage to other property. The goods are *dangerous*.

A. DEFECTIVE GOODS

1. Introduction

It is clear from the decided cases that the law of negligence will not help the consumer in this situation and it is equally clear that Part I of the Consumer Protection Act 1987 (*post*, p. 63) will not help either. That leaves just two rights which exist side by side—a claim under the contract of supply[1] (which we have considered in Chapter 4) and a claim under a manufacturer's guarantee.

2. MANUFACTURERS' GUARANTEES[2]

The nature of a guarantee

A guarantee is familiar to millions of consumers and it has become an integral part of the purchase of durable goods. The manufacturer usually agrees to replace defective parts within a specified time (for example, 12 months). The attraction of this for the consumer may be cut down by further clauses requiring the consumer to pay the cost of carriage and sometimes even the cost of labour. Subject to this, a guarantee can have very real commercial advantages for both parties. For the manufacturer it helps to promote his product and the card which the customer signs and returns may be valuable for the purposes of market research. For the customer, the guarantee may be a valuable way of sidestepping the hazards of litigation, especially as the remedy which he *really* wants—repair or replacement—is not available against the retailer.[3]

There have been very few cases on guarantees and their precise legal status is uncertain.[4] As a matter of strict legal analysis the problem is one of offer, acceptance and consideration. Is there a contract if the consumer is unaware that the guarantee exists when he buys the goods? What is the consideration to support the manufacturer's promise? In practical terms, it is highly unlikely that these matters will ever be litigated; it is difficult to imagine a manufacturer giving a guarantee and then refusing to honour it. The legal points might one day be taken by a liquidator of the guarantee-giving manufacturer. If the points ever did come to court it is likely that the courts would uphold the guarantee as a collateral contract, the consideration being the customer's purchase of the goods from the retailer. The onus will be on the buyer to prove that he knew of the guarantee when he bought the goods; in practice it should not be difficult for him to prove this, especially as the guarantee often forms part of the advertising and promotional material.

---

[1] Or possibly under a collateral contract: consider Example 1 on p. 27 and *Andrews* v. *Hopkinson* [1957] 1 Q.B. 229.

[2] In practice guarantees are sometimes also given by retailers and by suppliers of services (see, *e.g.* the Codes of Practice relating to motor vehicles and electrical appliances, *post*, pp. 160, 170).

[3] *Post*, p. 101. For the interrelationship between guarantees and the condition of merchantable quality see, *ante*, p. 48.

[4] See the O.F.T. Discussion Paper "Consumer Guarantees" published in August 1984, at pp. 21–25.

The legal liability of the manufacturer can also be established in another way. The consumer is sometimes asked to complete and return a card containing market research questions, *e.g.* "how did you learn of this product?" or "what persuaded you to buy it?" or "did you compare this unit with other models?" The act of the consumer in completing and returning the card may itself be consideration to support the manufacturer's promise.

The value of the guarantee to the consumer depends on its terms. The most generous ones prove that:

> If owing to a defect in workmanship or material your appliance breaks down within 6 [or 12] months of purchase we will repair or replace it free of charge.

We have seen, however, that the consumer may sometimes be required to pay the cost of transporting the goods; occasionally he even has to pay the cost of labour which can render the guarantee virtually useless. There is also the possibility that the manufacturer may say "there is nothing wrong with this appliance—you have mishandled it." (A similar argument is sometimes advanced by a seller when a buyer complains that the goods are unmerchantable.) In such a case the consumer might have to negotiate an independent examination of the goods, with the manufacturer paying the whole or part of the cost. The provisions of the various Codes of Practice (*e.g.* for electrical goods) should also be borne in mind.

Statutory provisions relating to guarantees

It was noted at the beginning of this chapter that there is still widespread misunderstanding about who is legally responsible for defective products. Perhaps this ignorance may be lessened as the result of an Order made in 1976 whereby a supplier commits a criminal offence if a document setting out his obligations (*e.g.* the guarantee) fails to draw the consumer's attention to his rights against the retailer.[5]

Another feature of guarantees aroused fierce criticism in the past; many guarantees were used not to extend the customer's rights (as he not unreasonably expected) but to cut them down. The Unfair Contract Terms Act 1977 now makes void such exemption clauses in consumer guarantees.[6]

Further reforms?

A discussion paper published by the Office of Fair Trading in August 1984 highlights some of the main problem areas. Attention is drawn in particular to the following matters:

[5] *Post*, p. 277.
[6] *Post*, p. 137.

1. The consumer may buy an "extended guarantee" or "extended warranty" which may become worthless if the "guarantor" goes out of business during the extended period.
2. Guarantors delay in dealing with complaints and in carrying out or authorising repairs.
3. Consumers take guarantees at their face value (with bland assurances as to "peace of mind")—only to find later, when they seek to enforce them, that the small print makes them far narrower than expected; the guarantee may, for example, exclude liability for consequential loss and a warranty for a second-hand car will almost certainly not extend to the clutch.
4. A consumer wishing to sell a house or car with the benefit of a long-term guarantee may find, to his horror, that it is not transferable.

The paper contains proposals to strengthen the consumer's position in all these areas and to make him more aware of what his rights are and against whom. In the case of extended warranties and long term guarantees it is proposed that the consumer should have a direct contractual relationship with a duly authorised insurer. These proposals have been incorporated in the Code of Practice for Mechanical Breakdown Insurance Schemes, but this covers motor vehicles only.[7]

Consumer Guarantees Bill

In 1990 the National Consumer Council initiated an attempt to encourage the provision of guarantees by obtaining sponsors for a Private Member's Bill. The Consumer Guarantees Bill would have compelled manufacturers of specified consumer products (*e.g.* cars, cookers and televisions) to inform the public whether or not their products were covered by a "consumer guarantee" lasting for at least a year. The Bill also contained the Law Commission's proposed reforms set out in their Report *Sale and Supply of Goods*.[8] The Bill was entirely killed off by the Government's opposition to the guarantee clauses, but will doubtless be revitalised in the not too distant future in an amended and circumscribed form.

Conclusion

It cannot be stressed too strongly that any rights which the consumer may have under a manufacturer's guarantee do *not* cut down his rights against the supplier. In virtually all cases retailers seek to create the false impression in the minds of their customers that the legal responsibility is that of the manufacturer. The consumer must be on his guard against this and must be prepared to say (in a loud voice if necessary) "it's *your* responsibility under the Sale of Goods Act." The question of remedy enforcement is considered in greater detail in Chapter 9.

[7] *Post*, p. 163.
[8] *Ante*, p. 52.

B. DANGEROUS GOODS

1. INTRODUCTION

In the previous edition of this book it was pointed out that proposals to alter manufacturer's liability from negligence to strict liability had been made by no less than four different bodies—the Law Commission, the Pearson Commission, the Council of Europe and the EC. At the time of publication (March 1, 1985) some seven years had gone by without any progress; negotiations on the EC draft directive were stalled over the so-called "development risks" defence. It was, however, only a matter of months before a workable compromise emerged and on July 25, 1985 the EC Council of Ministers adopted the Product Liability Directive whereby Member States were required to pass the appropriate legislation by July 30, 1988 (but with the option of excluding the development risks defence). The United Kingdom responded before the deadline by passing the Consumer Protection Act 1987. Part I is designed to implement the Directive and came into force on March 1, 1988.

It is important to appreciate that Part I exists side by side with the general law of contract and negligence. In a contract case the consumer will have his (largely non-excludable) rights under the Sale of Goods Act, etc., and in this situation the 1987 Act is virtually irrelevant. As regards non-contractual claims the basic rule is that the consumer will be in a stronger position under the Act because the need to prove negligence has disappeared. The provisions of Part I will be examined in detail in the next section of this chapter. It will be seen that there are some situations where the Act does not apply and in these cases the non-contractual consumer will have to fall back on the general law of negligence, which will be briefly considered in the final part of this chapter.

2. PART I OF THE CONSUMER PROTECTION ACT 1987 ("THE ACT")

We have seen that Part I is designed to give effect to the EC Product Liability Directive and section 1(1) expressly so provides. These Directives generally start off with a large number of recitals and the second recital of this one states that:

> Whereas liability without fault on the part of the producer is the sole means of adequately solving the problem, peculiar to our age of increasing technicality, of a fair apportionment of the risks inherent in modern technological production.

In the light of the provision of section 1(1) above the adviser must refer to the Directive if the drafting of the Act is in any way ambiguous.

The basic rule

By section 2(1):

> Subject to the following provisions of this Part, where any damage is caused wholly or partly by a defect in a product, every person to whom subsection (2) applies shall be liable for the damage.

Thus in advising the consumer a number of questions must be asked:

1. Has a *product* been *supplied*?
2. If yes, did it contain a *defect*?
3. If yes, did the defect cause *damage*?
4. If yes, is it the *type* of damage to which the Act applies?
5. If yes, *who* is liable to the consumer?
6. Are there any *defences* which may cut down the consumer's rights?
7. Are there any special *time limits* for bringing a claim?
8. Was the product first supplied after March 1, 1988?

Burden of proof

The Act is silent on this but on general principle the burden will fall on the plaintiff. This is reinforced by Article 4 of the Directive which states that:

> The injured person shall be required to prove the damage, the defect and the causal relationship between defect and damage.

In practical terms the abolition of the need to prove negligence may be of limited value because the task of proving causation (which still exists) can be equally difficult—especially in medical and pharmaceutical cases.[9]

It will be appreciated from the wording of section 2(1) that partial causation is sufficient.

Example 3

Goods manufactured by M injure C; this is due partly to the goods being defective and partly to C not following M's instructions. C can recover damages from M under the Act—but subject to a reduction for contributory negligence under section 6(4).

What damage is covered by the Act?

Section 5, which is based on Article 9, makes it clear that only three

---

[9] See, *e.g. Kay* v. *Ayrshire and Arran Health Board* [1987] 2 All E.R. 417 (H.L.) (penicillin given to child; child became deaf; causal link not proved).

types of damage are covered, namely death, personal injury and damage to "private" (as opposed to business) property, *i.e.* property is excluded if at the time of the loss or damage it is not—

(a) of a description of property ordinarily intended for private use, occupation or consumption; and
(b) intended by the person suffering the loss or damage mainly for his own private use, occupation or consumption.

Example 4

A defective heater explodes and damages X's office premises. He cannot recover under the Act.

Two other restrictions must be noted. First (and this is an echo of the distinction between defective and dangerous goods)[10] the Act does not cover loss of or damage "to the product itself" or to "the whole or any part of any product which has been supplied with the [defective product] comprised in it."[11]

Example 5

C buys a defective car. It crashes and injures C. The car is a write-off. C can recover for his injuries but not for the cost of replacing the car.

Example 6

Suppose in the above example the accident is caused by a defective tyre. If the tyre formed part of the car as originally supplied the answer is the same as in Example 5. If, on the other hand, the tyre was fitted at a later date the car replacement cost will be "damage to any property" and recoverable under the Act.

The second restriction (designed to exclude small claims) is set out in section 5(4); the Act will not apply where the total damages awarded, exclusive of interest, in respect of *property* do not exceed £275. What if the damages are, say, £1,000? The wording of the Act is unambiguous—no deduction is made and £1,000 would be awarded. However, Article 9(*b*) talks of "a lower threshold of 500 ECU." It could be argued—and the French version of the EC Directive and the EC Commission support this view—that a deduction should be made from *every* award in respect of property. It will be interesting to see how the courts interpret this provision.

It is clear from the wording that any reduction for contributory negligence must be made first.

Example 7

C's damages in respect of private property are assessed at £500 but this

---

[10] *Ante*, p. 59.
[11] S.5(2).

figure falls to be reduced by 50 per cent. for contributory negligence so that the final figure is £250. The Act does not apply.

Was the damage caused by a defective product?

In order to answer this question we must start by asking two questions, namely:

(a) What is a product?
(b) When is a product defective?

What is a product?

Section 1(2) provides that the term "product" means any goods or electricity and it is clear that components are included.

> *Example 8*
>
> CM supplies a defective component to M who incorporates it into a product which he then supplies to D. Both CM and M have supplied a "product" and, if the component makes M's product defective, both CM and M are liable under the Act.

The term "goods" is defined in section 45 to include "substances,[12] growing crops and things comprised in land by virtue of being attached to it and any ship, aircraft or vehicle." What about houses and land? The effect of section 46 is that the seller of a house built with defective bricks does not supply "goods," but if the house collapses and causes "damage,"[13] the brick manufacturer can be liable to the injured party under the Act.

Agricultural products

Although the definition of "goods" includes crops (see above), section 2(4) creates an important (and politically sensitive) exception from liability. It excludes liability under the Act "in respect of any defect in any game or agricultural produce if the only supply . . . by that person to another was at a time when it had not undergone an industrial process."[14]

> *Example 9*
>
> Farmer F grows and supplies defective peas to P who processes them and sells them to a restaurant. C, a customer, eats them and becomes ill. P is liable to C under the Act (even though the defect is unconnected with the processing). F is not liable.

The Act does not define "industrial process" directly but its meaning can be gleaned from the definition of "producer" which includes

---

[12] This is not itself defined in the Act.
[13] *Ante*, p. 64.
[14] This is one of the cases where the injured party must fall back on his rights under the general law of negligence—*post*, p. 73.

(c) in the case of a product which has not been manufactured, won or abstracted but essential characteristics of which are attributable to an industrial or other process having been carried out (for example, in relation to agricultural produce) the person who carried out that process.

Thus a court may decide that the key factor is whether the alleged "processing" is something which alters the essential characteristics of the product so that washing and packing might not qualify (with the result that the statutory immunity would be preserved). It may also be significant that the word "industrial" does not appear in the Directive which uses the wider term "initial processing" in Article 2. Finally, the Government has expressed the view that the "process" must be something applied to the product *after* it has become a product so that, for example, spraying growing crops or injecting hormones into live animals would not qualify. It is by no means certain that a court would uphold this view.

Is the product defective?

Section 3 rephrases Article 6 of the Directive in the following words:

(1) Subject to the following provisions of this section, there is a defect in a product for the purposes of this Part if the safety of the product is not such as persons generally are entitled to expect; and for these purposes "safety," in relation to a product, shall include safety in respect to [components] and safety in the context of risks of damage to property, as well as in the context of risks of death or personal injury.

(2) In determining . . . what persons generally are entitled to expect . . . all the circumstances shall be taken into account, including—

   (a) the manner in which, and purposes for which, the product has been marketed, its get-up, the use of any mark in relation to the product, any instructions for, or warnings with respect to, doing or refraining from doing anything with or in relation to the product;

   (b) what might reasonably be expected to be done with or in relation to the product; and

   (c) the time when the product was supplied by its producer to another;

and nothing in this section shall require a defect to be inferred from the fact alone that the safety of a product which is supplied after that time is greater than the safety of the product in question.

The above definition of "defective goods" is broadly similar to the definition of "unmerchantable goods"[15] with the key word "safe"

---

[15] *Ante*, p. 46.

substituted for "fit." However, one major distinction must be reiterated. Whereas merchantable quality covers both unsafe and shoddy, poor quality products, "defective" goods in the 1987 Act mean only unsafe or dangerous products; so "defective" is used in an unusually narrow sense. The following points can be made:

(1) "Persons generally" can be contrasted with "a person" in Article 6 of the Directive; the expectation standard will be an objective one in the light of the matters mentioned in the section—notably any safety representations in advertising material.

(2) A warning can make a product safe—provided that it is sufficiently clear; conversely the absence of a warning can make it unsafe. The massive (and so far inconclusive) cigarette litigation in the United States has largely turned on the warning factor—although (quite apart from this) the difficulty of proving a causal link between smoking the particular brand of cigarettes and lung cancer might well be insuperable.

(3) The question of what safety persons are entitled to expect brings in what is known as the "cost-benefit" analysis. In relation to medicines a D.T.I. explanatory note contains the following passage:

> "Establishing the existence of a defect in a medicine administered to a patient is complicated by the fact that not only is the human body a highly complex organism, but at the time of treatment it is already subject to an adverse pathological condition. . . .
> The more active the medicine, and the greater its beneficial potential, the more extensive its effects are likely to be, and therefore the greater the chances of an adverse effect. A medicine used to treat a life-threatening condition is likely to be much more powerful than a medicine used in the treatment of a less serious condition, and the safety that one is reasonably entitled to expect of such a medicine may therefore become correspondingly lower."

(4) The relevant time for assessing the safety factor (and this is important for two reasons) is the time when the product was supplied by its *producer*—not by the retailer. This is often called "the state of the art" factor.

Example 10

In April 1988 M sells to D a car manufactured by him. In August 1988 D sells it to R who sells it to C in 1992. While C is driving the car it veers out of control and P is injured. In considering the safety aspects two questions arise, namely (1) what degree of safety could reasonably be expected of a four-year-old car? and (2) what were the relevant safety standards in

April 1988? The fact that safer models have been introduced since that time is irrelevant.

Whom can the consumer sue under the Act?

Section 2(2) imposes liability on:

(1) the "producer" (see below).
(2) any person who, by putting his name on the product or using a trade mark or other distinguishing mark in relation to the product, has held himself out as the producer of the product.

Example 11

S, a supermarket, puts its own brand mark on a bottle of wine which it sells to B. Unknown to the seller the wine has been mixed with antifreeze. C becomes violently ill when drinking the "wine" at B's house. C can sue S under the Act. But if S makes it clear that a third party is the producer, *e.g.* with a label stating "produced for S by M," S is not caught—there is no "holding out."

(3) any person who imported the goods into a Member State of the EC from a place outside the Member States in order, in the course of a business, to supply it to another.

Example 12

F, a French company, imports lethal toys from Taiwan which it then exports to England where one is sold by R to C. C's child is injured.
The English importer is *not* liable under the Act because he imported the toys from another Member State (*i.e.* France). F, however, *is* liable under the Act and he can be sued in England.[16]

(4) A person to whom section 2(3) applies—see below.

Returning to paragraph (1) above, section 1(2) defines a "producer" in relation to a product as—

(a) the person who manufactured it;
(b) in the case of a substance which has not been manufac- tured but has been won or abstracted, the person who won or abstracted it (this covers mining and quarrying);
(c) in any other case, a person who has applied an industrial or other process affecting the essential characteristics of the product.[17]

---

[16] Under the EC Jurisdiction and Judgments Convention (see Schedule 1 to the Civil Jurisdiction and Judgments Act 1982) a defendant domiciled in a Contracting State can be sued in tort in another Contracting State where the damage is suffered (see Article 5). A claim under Part I of the Act is a claim in tort—see s.6(7). The Act gives the injured consumer a wide choice of where to sue (this is known as "forum shopping"); this can be important because the development risks defence (*post*, p. 71) applies in some EC countries but not all.

[17] *Ante*, p. 67.

The section 2(3) defendant

There may well be cases where the injured party will have great difficulty in identifying the "producer" or the person importing the product into a Member State. To deal with this situation section 2(3) allows him to seek information from another supplier in the chain and makes that other supplier liable if the information is not supplied. Such liability will arise if the following conditions are satisfied:

(1) the injured party asks the supplier to identify one or more of the persons listed in section 2(2) (*ante*, p. 69)—whether still in existence or not; and

(2) the request is made within a reasonable time after the damage and at a time when it is not reasonably practicable for the person making the request to identify all those persons; and

(3) the supplier fails within a reasonable time after receiving the request either to comply with the request or to identify the person who supplied the product to him.

Example 13

The facts are as in Example 12 except that the only person known to the injured party is the retail supplier R. The injured party can ask R to identify the manufacturer and/or the EC-importer. R can supply this information or alternatively he can say "I bought from X Ltd." (whereupon the injured party can approach X Ltd. with a similar request). If R does neither of these things within a reasonable time he will be liable under the Act.

Conclusion

It will be apparent that the injured consumer has a large number of persons to sue—especially bearing in mind the co-extensive liability of a component supplier and an end-product supplier. He can sue them alone or together and their liability is joint and several; each of them is liable to him for the full amount of his "damage" (see s.2(5)).

What defences are available?

Section 4(1) lists six possible defences, *viz.*

(a) That the defect is attributable to compliance with any statutory or EC *requirement*;

(b) That the person proceeded against did not at any time supply the product to another.

Example 14

M manufactures a crane. While it is being tested, it crashes and P is killed. P's estate has no claim under the Act.

The term "supply" is widely defined in section 46. In a hire-purchase case involving dealer—hire-purchaser—finance company the section provides that the *dealer* (and not the finance company) is to be treated as supplying the product to the hire-purchaser—which is what happens in practice (although not in law).

(c) That the only supply was not in the course of the supplier's business *and* that either section 2(2) does not apply to that person or does so only as the result of things done otherwise than with view to profit.

Example 15

Mrs. Jones makes jam for a private function. The jam is defective and a guest is taken ill. There is no liability under the Act.

(d) That the defect did not exist in the product at the relevant time.[18]

Example 16

M supplies perishable goods to C, a carrier. The goods deteriorate solely because the ventilation in C's lorry breaks down. They were not defective when they left M. M is not liable under the Act.

Example 17

M manufactures a car and sells it to D. D sells it to C. C has it serviced by S. C crashes because S left the wheel nuts loose. M is not liable.

(e) That the state of scientific and technical knowledge at the relevant time was not such that a producer of products of the same description as the product in question might be expected to have discovered the defect if it had existed in his products while they were under his control.

It will be recalled that the dispute over this *"development risks"* defence was the prime reason why the EC draft directive took nearly 10 years to become a Directive. There was strong lobbying from United Kingdom industries (especially pharmaceuticals) on the basis that without such a defence research and development would be severely hampered. The argument on the other side is equally compelling—such a defence would leave victims of a future Thalidomide-type tragedy without a remedy. In the event the Council adopted a compromise—the defence was introduced by Article 7(e) but individual Member States were left free to exclude it (Article 15(1)(b)) and a few of them have exercised their right to do so.

---

[18] "Relevant time" means the time when the "producer" supplied it to another: s.4(2).

The drafting of this provision was hotly debated in Parliament and the Government forced through the present wording in the dying days of the 1986–87 session just before the 1987 General Election. It is widely felt that the wording is less strict than Article 7(e) of the Directive[19] which reads:

> that the state of scientific and technical knowledge at the time when he put the product into circulation was not such as to enable the existence of the defect to be discovered.

There is an immense gap between what a producer might be *"expected"* to discover in a particular sector of industry and what he *could* ("enable") discover with all the technical resources available. Presumably the point is academic since an English court would construe s.4(1)(*e*) so as to give effect to the Directive.[20]

(f) That the defect:
  (i) constituted a defect in a subsequent product in which the product in question (*i.e.* a component) was comprised; and
  (ii) was wholly attributable to the design of the subsequent product or to compliance with instructions given by the producer of the subsequent product.

Example 18

CM supplies a component to M. The component makes the end product faulty but only because M's design is faulty. CM is not liable.

When must the claim be brought?

There are two rules—a consumer rule and an overriding supplier rule. For the *injured party* the basic limitation period is three years from (1) the date on which the cause of action accrued or (2) (if later) the date on which he first discovered (or should have discovered) the relevant facts.[21] There is no distinction between injury and property damage—the period is the same in both cases.

As regards the *supplier* there is a 10 year cut off period for each supplier.[22] This "period of repose," as it is called in the United States, relates to the particular product, not to the product line; so producers must keep precise records (showing the exact date when each item was sold) to enable them to rely on this provision.

---

[19] The European Commission is taking proceedings against the U.K. Government for failing to implement the Directive correctly.
[20] See s.1(1), *ante*, p. 63.
[21] Sched. 1, para. 1, amending Limitation Act 1980, s.11.
[22] *Ibid.*

Example 19

CM supplies a component to M in April 1988. M sells the end product to R in April 1989.

The 10 year period expires in April 1998 as regards CM and in April 1999 as regards M. The fact that no injury has occurred by the cut-off date is immaterial.

Commencement of Part I

As previously mentioned Part I came into force on March 1, 1988 and by section 50(7) it does not apply to any product which was supplied by its producer before that date.

Example 20

Yen, a Japanese manufacturer, sells a product to its United States distributor in February 1988. In April 1988 it is exported to the United Kingdom. The Act does not apply.

3. NEGLIGENCE

It will be appreciated that there will be a limited number of cases where the regime introduced by the Act will not apply and in these cases the injured party must fall back on the general law of negligence. This will be so where, for example:

(1) the product was first supplied before March 1, 1988;
(2) the "primary agricultural produce" exemption applies;
(3) the damage sustained by the plaintiff (*e.g.* to business property) is not covered by the Act;
(4) the damage to property is £275 or less;
(5) the claim is out of time.

In considering negligence we must stress once again what we said at the beginning of this chapter—namely the crucial distinction between defective or shoddy goods and dangerous goods. The courts have always been very cautious to extend the boundaries of liability and one weapon which they have used has been the weapon of "economic loss." They have held that where the only damage is to the product itself, this loss is "economic" and not recoverable in the tort of negligence.[23]

In relation to dangerous goods the starting point must be the so-called "narrow rule" in *Donoghue* v. *Stevenson*.[24] The principle of law was stated by Lord Atkin in the following well-known passage:

---

[23] The first of three recent House of Lords cases on this point (all concerned with defective construction of buildings) is *D. & F. Estates Ltd.* v. *Church Commissioners* [1989] A.C. 177. Note the similar exclusion under the Act: s.5 *ante*, p. 65.
[24] [1932] A.C. 562.

> "A manufacturer of products, which he sells in such a form as to show that he intends them to reach the ultimate consumer in the form in which they left him with no reasonable possibility of intermediate examination, and with the knowledge that the absence of reasonable care in the preparation or putting up of the products will result in an injury to the consumer's life or property, owes a duty to the consumer to take that reasonable care."

Lord Atkin added that this was a self-evident proposition which no one who was not a lawyer would for one moment doubt.

The duty outlined above is merely one particular type of "duty situation" in the context of the general law of negligence. The cases decided since 1932 show a gradual extension of liability. Thus:

(1) There is no limit to the type of goods covered by the rule. Examples include hair dye, underpants, cars, lifts and even a tombstone.

(2) Liability has been extended beyond manufacturers to cover, for example, repairers and assemblers. In one case even a car dealer was held liable.[25]

(3) The word "consumer" is not confined to the ultimate buyer; it means anyone likely to be injured by the lack of reasonable care. Perhaps the best illustration is provided by *Stennett* v. *Hancock and Peters*[26] where part of the wheel of a lorry came off and struck a pedestrian on the pavement. She recovered damages from the second defendant who had negligently repaired the wheel shortly before the accident.

(4) The "possibility of an intermediate examination" will only defeat the claim if there was a real likelihood of a type of examination which would (or should) reveal the defect. Thus in *Evans* v. *Triplex Safety Glass Co.*[27] the buyer of a Vauxhall car was injured when the windscreen shattered. His action against the manufacturers of the windscreen failed for various reasons; one reason was the likelihood of an intermediate examination by Vauxhall before it was fitted into the car; another reason was a failure to prove that the windscreen was defective when it left the manufacturer.

This case can be contrasted with the sale of goods case of *Wren* v. *Holt*[28] where beer containing arsenic was sold by a publican to a customer. The case was fought on section 14(2) of the Sale of Goods Act[29] and the publican was liable even though the customer had examined the beer before drinking it; the

---

[25] *Andrews* v. *Hopkinson* [1957] 1 Q.B. 229.
[26] [1939] 2 All E.R. 578.
[27] [1936] 1 All E.R. 283.
[28] [1903] 1 K.B. 610.
[29] *Ante*, pp. 44, 51.

defect was not discoverable by any normal examination. Presumably the same reasoning would have applied if the buyer had sued the brewer, *i.e.* the manufacturer would have been liable if negligence could have been proved.

Proof of negligence and causation

As the law stands at present the task facing the injured consumer is not an easy one. He must prove (a) that the product was defective when it left the manufacturer; (b) that this was due to negligence and (c) that this was the cause of his injury. If the article is completely destroyed in the accident, the plaintiff's task may well be insuperable unless the court is prepared to make a dangerous use of circumstantial evidence.

Was the product defective?

In many cases this should present no problem; a bun containing a stone, a loaf of bread containing a cigarette butt or a car with faulty brakes—these are obvious examples. There may, however, be other cases which are less obvious. Thus in *Evans* v. *Triplex Safety Glass Co.*, the facts of which have already been given,[30] the plaintiff failed to prove that the windscreen was dangerous when it left the manufacturer.

In the examples previously given (for example, arsenic in the beer)[31] the product was out of line with the general run of goods produced by the manufacturers. Alternatively, it may be possible to argue that there is a fault in manufacture or design affecting all goods of a particular type. The cost of such a finding could be potentially astronomic for the manufacturer and for intermediate suppliers; they could be faced with a very large number of claims when the decision became known, or they might have to call in all the defective goods for repair. In view of this the courts (both here and in the United States) have been cautious to base a negligence finding on this ground. There have however been cases in which the injured party has been successful. Thus in *Lambert* v. *Lewis*[32] the manufacturer of a defective towing hitch which broke and caused a serious accident was held liable to the victims because its design was negligent.

Has the manufacturer been negligent?

This question and the previous one are closely linked. Thus in *Vacwell Engineering Co. Ltd.* v. *B.D.H. Chemicals Ltd.*[33] the defendants, who manufactured a chemical, were liable in negligence for

[30] *Ante*, p. 74.
[31] *Ibid.*
[32] [1982] A.C. 225. See *ante*, pp. 35 and 51.
[33] [1971] 1 Q.B. 88.

failing to appreciate, and to warn prospective users, that contact with water could lead to an explosion. Similarly, in *Wright* v. *Dunlop Rubber Co. Ltd. and ICI*[34] the Court of Appeal held that ICI were liable in negligence for continuing to market a product with knowledge that it constituted a serious health hazard. Finally in *Fisher* v. *Harrods Ltd.*[35] Mrs. Fisher recovered damages from Harrods when they sold an untested bottle of cleaning fluid to her husband. She suffered personal injury when it came into contact with her eyes.

The duty owed by the manufacturer does not involve him in strict liability—it is merely a duty to take reasonable care. This is particularly relevant where a manufacturer of (say) a car buys brake linings or wheel bearings[36] which prove to be defective and cause injury to the ultimate consumer. A case from another branch of the law of negligence (employer's liability) is highly relevant here. In *Davie* v. *New Merton Board Mills*[37] an employer supplied his employee with a tool which the employer had bought from a reputable supplier. The tool had a latent defect which the employer had no means of discovering. The employee was injured when the tool broke and he sued the employer for damages for negligence. The House of Lords dismissed the claim on the ground that the employer had not been negligent. In the employment field the principle underlying this case has been reversed by statute[38] but in the product liability field the principle still stands. If the manufacturer has an adequate inspection system and an adequate system for checking faults this may well be sufficient.

As already stated, the onus of proving negligence is on the injured party and it can be immensely difficult, especially in the case of a highly complex piece of equipment or a chemical or drug. Evidence of previous accidents caused by the same product is highly relevant and should be sought. Sometimes the facts themselves point to negligence; if a consumer loses a tooth through eating a bun containing a stone this suggests that the manufacturer had been negligent and, under the doctrine of *res ipsa loquitur*, the manufacturer will have to adduce evidence from which the inference of negligence can be rebutted.[39] He may say "the defect was in a component and I myself took all reasonable care" or even "I have no idea how the acid got into the lemonade bottle but I had a foolproof system of inspection" (this latter argument

[34] (1972) Vol. XIII, Knights Industrial Reports 255.
[35] [1966] Lloyds L.R. 500.
[36] But in *Walton* v. *British Leyland* (*unreported*) the defendants were liable in negligence for failure to recall cars when they discovered unexpected defects in wheel bearings.
[37] [1959] A.C. 604.
[38] Employers' Liability (Defective Equipment) Act 1969.
[39] *Moore* v. *R. Fox & Son* [1956] 1 Q.B. 596.

was successfully raised in *Daniels* v. *White Ltd. and Tarbard*[40] but the decision has been criticised and is unlikely to be followed).[41]

When studying all the vast number of reported cases on negligence (perhaps far too many are reported) one point must never be forgotten; whether a defendant has performed his duty of care is a pure question of fact and a decision on this point is not a binding precedent for any future case.[42]

Did the defendant's negligence cause the plaintiff's injury?

The injured plaintiff must be able to prove a causal link between the defect, the negligence and his injury. This again can be a difficult matter in practice and the result of the case may turn on the inferences which the court is willing to draw from the facts. In the leading case of *Grant* v. *Australian Knitting Mills*[43] where the plaintiff, a doctor, contracted dermatitis, the Privy Council accepted his argument that it was caused by an excess of sulphite in underpants manufactured by the defendants. The court reached this decision even though the evidence showed that more than four million of these pants had been sold without complaint. On the other hand, the plaintiff will fail if the injury would have occurred in any event. Thus, to borrow again from employment law, an employer is generally not liable for failing to provide safety equipment if he can show that the employee would not have worn it.[44] Similarly, a manufacturer of a car will not be liable for faulty brakes if the plaintiff was driving so fast that the accident would have occurred even if the brakes had been in perfect working order.

For what damage can the plaintiff recover?

Reverting once again to the defective/dangerous dichotomy, the final question relates to *potentially* dangerous goods. On which side of the line do they fall? Can the buyer of a car claim in negligence for the cost of repairing brakes in order to avert a serious accident? In the previous edition of this book we expressed the view that such a claim should be allowed but in two very recent cases the House of Lords have classified such repair costs as irrecoverable economic loss.[45]

---

[40] [1938] 4 All E.R. 258. See also *ante*, p. 43, n. 6.
[41] For a recent case where the court refused to follow the *Daniels* decision see *Hill* v. *James Crowe (Cases) Ltd.* [1978] 1 All E.R. 812.
[42] *Qualcast (Wolverhampton) Ltd.* v. *Haynes* [1959] A.C. 743.
[43] *Ante*, p. 46.
[44] *Qualcast (Wolverhampton) Ltd.* v. *Haynes* [1959] A.C. 743; *McWilliams* v. *Arrol* [1962] 1 W.L.R. 295 (H.L.).
[45] *Murphy* v. *Brentwood D.C.* [1990] 3 W.L.R. 415; *Department of the Environment* v. *Thomas Bates & Son Ltd.* [1990] 3 W.L.R. 457. These building cases would be decided differently if the provisions of the draft EC Services Directive become law: *post*, p. 378.

CHAPTER SIX

"DO I HAVE TO PAY?"

If the supplier of goods or services is guilty of a misrepresentation or a serious breach of contract the consumer may be able to rescind the contract or treat it as repudiated. In either case this will relieve him of his obligation to pay the price. Some examples of this were examined in Chapters 2–4 and the matter will be considered again in Chapter 7. This chapter is concerned with a group of six unrelated but important topics on which the consumer may seek legal advice. The topics are:

1. Delivery of unordered goods.
2. Cancellation of contracts made away from business premises.
3. Loss or damage of goods after contract but before delivery.
4. Unsatisfactory performance of services.
5. Late performance.
6. A dispute about the price.

1. I NEVER ORDERED THESE GOODS

An aggressive salesman may try to boost his sales by delivering goods which the customer has never ordered, followed by an invoice demanding payment. He clearly hopes that the consumer will be induced, by a combination of ignorance, lethargy and fear, to pay the price. Some years ago there was a considerable outcry at these and similar practices, and there was a growing demand for legislation to curtail them. Eventually a Bill was introduced into Parliament and this passed into law as the Unsolicited Goods and Services Act 1971.

Before considering this Act it may be useful to dispose of one problem which has arisen under the general law: is the consumer legally liable if the goods are lost or damaged while they are in his possession? Under the tort of negligence the plaintiff must prove that the defendant owed him a legal duty of care.[1] A person receiving unordered goods is known as an "involuntary bailee" and does not owe a duty of care. Therefore he will generally not be liable for accidental loss or damage.[2] On the other hand he may be liable for the tort of conversion if he deliberately destroys the goods or converts them to his

---

[1] *Bourhill* v. *Young* [1943] A.C. 92.
[2] See *Howard* v. *Harris* (1884) C. & E. 253.

own use. Where is the line to be drawn? Thus, if a tradesman delivers an unordered ten-volume encyclopaedia the consumer might well be liable if he puts them outside his house and allows them to disintegrate. The editors of a leading textbook[3] have suggested that the consumer might be entitled to destroy the goods in an emergency.

The Act of 1971

The sanctions provided by this Act are both civil and criminal. The *civil* sanction is that, as between himself and the sender, the recipient can:

> use, deal with or dispose of [the goods] as if they were an unconditional gift to him, and any right of the sender to the goods shall be extinguished.[4]

The recipient will have these rights if the following conditions are satisfied:

(1) the goods were sent to him without any prior request made by him or on his behalf[5];

(2) they were delivered or sent to him with a view to his acquiring them;

(3) he had no reasonable cause to believe that they were sent with a view to their being acquired for the purposes of a trade or business;

(4) the consumer has neither agreed to acquire the goods nor agreed to return them;

(5) (a) during the period of six months beginning with the date of receipt the sender did not take possession and the recipient did not unreasonably refuse to permit him to do so; or

(b) the recipient served a notice in writing on the sender, stating that the goods were unsolicited and giving the address where they could be collected, and during a period of 30 days from the giving of the notice the sender did not take possession and the recipient did not unreasonably refuse to permit him to do so.

Thus if the recipient serves a notice on April 2 saying, "I didn't order these goods—take them away" and the sender ignores the notice, the goods will become the property of the recipient on May 3.

The *criminal* sanction is provided in section 2 which is confined to persons acting in the course of a trade or business. The section deals

---

[3] *Winfield and Jolowicz on Tort* (13th ed.), p. 473.
[4] s.1(1).
[5] See 1971 Act, s.6.

with a trader who makes a demand for payment for goods where (a) the goods are unsolicited goods and (b) he has no reasonable cause to believe that there is a right to payment. An offence is also committed where a person, in such a case, (i) asserts a right to payment or (ii) threatens to bring legal proceedings or (iii) places, or threatens to place, the name of any person on a defaulters' list or (iv) invokes, or threatens to invoke, any other collection procedure.

2. I Have Changed My Mind

In the previous edition of this book we referred to an EC draft directive which conferred cancellation rights for contracts "which have been negotiated away from business premises." We commented then on this somewhat surprising approach and in the event a number of changes were made before it was adopted as Council Directive 85/577 on December 20, 1985. It has now been incorporated into English law by the Consumer Protection (Cancellation of Contracts Concluded away from Business Premises) Regulations 1987.[6]

Relationship with Consumer Credit Act

Since May 17, 1985 a consumer has had the right to cancel a regulated consumer credit or consumer hire agreement (subject to minor exceptions) where oral representations were made in his presence and the prospective agreement is signed by the debtor or hirer away from business premises (as defined). This right is conferred by section 67 of the Consumer Credit Act 1974.[7] It is clear from the Regulations that section 67 and the new cancellation right conferred by the Regulations are intended to be mutually exclusive (see Reg. 4).

What agreements are caught?

Subject to what has been said above, and subject also to the exceptions set out below, the Regulations (which are aimed at cold callers and high-pressure doorstep salesmen) apply to a contract for the supply by a trader of goods or services to a consumer where the *contract* is made in any of the following cases:

(a) during an "unsolicited visit" by a trader to the consumer's home or the home of another person or to the consumer's place of work.

(b) during a visit to such premises by the trader at the express request of the consumer where the contract relates to goods or

---

[6] S.I. 1987 No. 2117 (as amended).
[7] *Post*, p. 332.

services not comprised in the request and the consumer at the time of the request did not know, and could not reasonably have known, that those other goods or services formed part of the trader's business activities.

Example 1

Albert invites Bert (a central heating specialist) to his home to discuss the installation of central heating. Unknown to Albert, Bert also sells double glazing and Albert signs (at his home) a double glazing contract. The Regulations will apply unless Albert should have known this.

(c) after an *offer* by the consumer was made at such premises or under (d) below.

Example 2

Following a "cold call" by Charles to David's place of work David offers to acquire a personal computer on hire-purchase terms. The contract itself is concluded a week later at Charles' shop. The Regulations apply.

(d) during an excursion organised by the trader away from his business premises.

Example 3

A timeshare company organises a visit to one of its sites. While relaxing in a restaurant after the visit a customer is induced to sign a time share contract. The Regulations apply.

Business "consumers"

Even if the consumer carries on a business, the Regulations will still apply if in making the contract he is acting for purposes which can be regarded as outside his business.

Unsolicited

In general a contract is not caught by the Regulations if the consumer takes the initiative by inviting the trader to his home. If, however, an unsolicited telephone call from the trader ("I can come to see you") provokes the invitation, then the Regulations can apply.[8]

Excepted contracts

Reg. 3(2) contains a long list of contracts to which the Regulations do not apply. They include:

---

[8] Reg. 3(3).

(1) contracts for the sale of an interest in land, leases and land mortgages;
(2) a bridging loan linked to land purchase;
(3) building contracts (but contracts for the supply of building materials *are* caught);
(4) food, drink and other goods intending for current consumption in the household and supplied by regular roundsmen;
(5) contracts of insurance;
(6) investment agreements under the Financial Services Act 1986 and deposit agreements under the Banking Act 1987.

The cancellation notice

Any agreement to which the Regulations apply is unenforceable against the consumer unless the trader has delivered to him a notice in writing, informing him of his right to cancel and containing the information (including a cancellation form) set out in the Schedule to the Regulations. This notice must be given at the time of the contract or, in offer cases,[9] at the time of the offer.

Time for cancellation

The consumer can cancel by serving a notice in writing (not necessarily in the form set out in the Schedule) within seven days following the making of the contract.[10] It is important to note that a posted notice takes effect at the time of posting—even though it never reaches the trader (see Reg. 4(7)).

Example 4

Fred (the representative of a local store) visits George at his home and persuades George to sign an agreement for a charge card (this being outside the Consumer Credit Act). The contract is made on April 1. The last day for cancellation is April 8.

Effect of cancellation

The rules are very similar to those under the Consumer Credit Act.[11] Thus:

(a) the cancelled contract is treated as if it had never been made and any security is extinguished;
(b) sums paid by the consumer are repayable to him and he can refuse to hand over the goods (in legal terminology he has a "lien" over them) until those sums have been repaid;

[9] See (c) above.
[10] *Cf.* the 5 day period in relation to consumer credit: *post*, p. 335.
[11] *Post*, p. 336.

(c) subject to exceptions, he must have the goods available for collection by the dealer;

(d) where the consumer has already had the benefit of a loan or overdraft, then cancellation will not extinguish his repayment obligation. Reg. 6 contains special rules for computation of interest similar to those in Consumer Credit Act cancellation cases.

3. WHEN I OPENED THE BOX THE PLATES WERE BROKEN

We have already seen that where goods are supplied in the course of a business, they must be of merchantable quality. What happens if they were clearly merchantable at the time of the contract but are accidentally damaged or destroyed at a later date? The basic rules in the Sale of Goods Act 1979 are straightforward but their application in practice is far from easy.

The basic rule as to risk

Section 20(1) of the Act provides as follows:

> Unless otherwise agreed, the goods remain at the seller's risk until the property in them is transferred to the buyer, but when the property therein is transferred to the buyer, the goods are at the buyer's risk whether delivery has been made or not.

So the key question for the consumer is—had the property passed to him when the loss or damage occurred? If the answer is "yes," then (unless otherwise agreed) the risk will also have passed to him and he must bear the loss; this means that, for example, he will remain liable to pay the contract price. Most consumers would be very surprised to learn that the property (*i.e.* ownership) had passed to them before delivery, but in many cases this will in fact be so.

When does property pass?

The rules as to the passing of property are to be found in sections 16–18 of the Act. The essential distinction is between specific and unascertained goods and it will be convenient to deal with these matters first.

(a) **Specific goods.** These are defined by section 61 "as goods identified and agreed on at the time a contract of sale is made." The obvious example is goods selected by the buyer in a shop, showroom or store.

(b) **Unascertained goods.** This term is not defined in the Act but it is clear that the terms "specific" and "unascertained" are mutually exclusive. Thus, goods are "unascertained" if they are purely generic, as where a buyer gives an order for "two tons of coal" or for a car or a freezer like the one on display in the showroom. Goods are also unascertained if they form part of a larger consignment which is specified in the contract, as where a buyer agrees to buy "ten bottles of wine from the case in the seller's warehouse."

Passing of property—specific goods

The basic rule of section 17 is that property passes when the parties intend it to pass. There is nothing in the Sale of Goods Act to prevent an agreement that "no property in the goods shall pass until the buyer has paid the price." Such a clause, or an extension of it,[12] is frequently inserted into commercial contracts and this can give rise to many legal, financial and accounting problems.[13]

Then again if the price is payable by instalments, there may be a clause that ownership shall remain with the seller until the final instalment has been paid. Such an agreement is known as a "conditional sale agreement."[14] Apart from these cases, it is unusual to have an express passing of property clause in a consumer sale agreement and we must therefore examine the first four rules of section 18. These rules govern the passing of property in specific goods where no contrary intention appears. The courts have held that a "contrary intention" will only oust the statutory rules if present at the time of the contract.[15] The four rules can be summarised as follows:

Rule 1. In the usual case of an unconditional contract for the sale of specific goods in a deliverable state, the property passes to the buyer when the contract is made. This rule applies to the vast majority of retail sales. Thus if a consumer goes to a store, selects a suite of furniture and agrees to have it delivered in a week's time, the property and risk will pass to the buyer as soon as the contract has been made. If, therefore, the contents of the showroom are destroyed by fire, or damaged by vandals, at any time after the contract the buyer must bear the loss and must pay the agreed price for the lost or damaged goods. In other words, the insurable risk was on him as from the making of the contract. It has, however, been suggested that the courts will be very ready to infer an intention (ousting the statutory rule) that property is not to pass until delivery or payment.[16] A well-advised consumer of a

---

[12] *e.g.* "the property in the goods shall remain in the seller until all sums due from the buyer to the seller under this or any other contract shall have been paid." See now *Armour* v. *Thyssen AG* [1990] 3 All E.R. 481 (H.L.) where an extended clause of this type was upheld.

[13] See *Aluminium Industrie Vaassen BV* v. *Romalpa Aluminium Ltd.* [1976] 1 W.L.R. 676 and, more recently, *Clough Mill Ltd.* v. *Martin* [1984] 3 All E.R. 982 (C.A.).

[14] *Post*, p. 299.

[15] *Dennant* v. *Skinner* [1948] 2 K.B. 164.

[16] *Per* Diplock L.J. in *R.V. Ward Ltd.* v. *Bignall* [1967] 1 Q.B. 534, 545.

domestic appliance should try to insert a clause that the risk shall not pass to the buyer until the goods have been installed in his home; in the case of a car he should try to agree that the risk should remain with the seller until delivery by which time the buyer should have insured it.

Rule 2. If a contract for the sale of specific goods requires the seller to do something to put the goods into a deliverable state, the effect of rule 2 is that no property passes to the buyer until the seller has done this *and* the buyer has notice thereof. If we turn to section 61 we will find that goods are in "a deliverable state" when they are in such a state that the buyer would under the contract be bound to take delivery of them. Thus if the seller agreed to enlarge a watchstrap or ring, or to install a sunroof in a car, the risk would remain on the seller until the buyer has received notice that this work has been done.

It will be observed that the Act uses the clear and positive words "the buyer has notice thereof." Thus, if the seller sends off a letter saying that the work has been done this would not, of itself, pass the property and risk.

Rule 3. In the rather less common case where the seller has to do some act to ascertain the price (for example, weighing or measuring the goods), the effect of rule 3 is that property does not pass to the buyer until the seller has done this and the buyer has notice thereof.

Rule 4. If the buyer agrees to take goods on approval or on sale or return (for example, some bottles of wine for a party) the effect of rule 4 is that the property will pass to the buyer (a) if he intimates acceptance or otherwise adopts the transaction, or (b) if he retains the goods beyond the stipulated time or, if no time has been stipulated, beyond a reasonable time without intimating rejection.

An extreme example of the risk rules can be seen from the early case of *Elphick* v. *Barnes*[17] where a horse, which was delivered on sale or return, died during the approval period without the buyer's fault. It was held that the buyer was not bound to pay the price.

It should be added that all these rules as to risk pre-suppose that the loss or damage was purely accidental. The principle is underlined by the two further subsections of section 20 which read as follows:

(2) But where delivery has been delayed through the fault of either buyer or seller the goods are at the risk of the party at fault as regards any loss which might not have occurred but for such fault.
(3) Nothing in this section shall affect the duties and liabilities of either seller or buyer as a bailee of the goods for the other party.

A bailment would arise if, for example, the seller of goods agreed to store them for the buyer. If the goods were lost or damaged, the onus would be on the seller (as bailee) to disprove negligence.[18]

---

[17] (1880) 5 C.P.D. 321.
[18] See, *e.g. Houghland* v. *Low (Luxury Coaches) Ltd.* [1962] 1 Q.B. 694.

Passing of property—unascertained goods

If a buyer agrees to buy "ten rolls of wallpaper" or "twenty square metres of carpet," this would be a contract for the sale of unascertained goods. Bearing in mind the basic rule that risk passes with property[19] we must start with section 16 which provides that:

> Where there is a contract for the sale of unascertained goods no property in the goods is transferred to the buyer unless and until the goods are ascertained.

Thus, if in the above example, the manufacturer of carpet sends a large roll to the seller, no property can pass to the buyer until a piece measuring twenty square metres has been cut and set aside for the buyer's contract, *i.e.* until the goods are "*ascertained*".

We can now turn to section 18, **rule 5**, which applies where no contrary intention appears. It reads as follows:

> (1) Where there is a contract for the sale of unascertained or future goods by description, and goods of that description and in a deliverable state[20] are unconditionally appropriated to the contract, either by the seller with the assent of the buyer, or by the buyer with the assent of the seller, the property in the goods then passes to the buyer and the assent may be express or implied and may be given either before or after the appropriation is made.
>
> (2) Whether, in pursuance of the contract, the seller delivers the goods to the buyer or to a carrier or other bailee . . . for the purpose of transmission to the buyer, and does not reserve the right of disposal, he is to be taken to have unconditionally appropriated the goods to the contract.

Three points call for comment. First, rule 5(2) refers to delivery of "the goods" to the carrier. Thus, if the seller merely delivers a larger consignment (of which the buyer's goods form an unascertained part) section 16[21] will apply. The result is that the property and risk remain with the seller; if therefore they are lost or damaged before becoming ascertained the buyer can reject them.[22]

Secondly, there must be an unconditional "*appropriation*." The mere fact that the seller sets them aside is not enough because he may change his mind. To constitute appropriation:

> "the parties must have had, or be reasonably supposed to have had an intention *to attach the contract irrevocably to those goods* so that those goods and no others are the subject of the sale and become the property of the buyer"[23] (italics supplied).

---

[19] *Ante*, p. 84.

[20] *Philip Head* v. *Showfronts Ltd.* [1970] 1 Lloyd's Rep. 140. See also *The London Wine Company (Shippers)* (1986) 126 N.L.J. 977 for a good, modern illustration of goods remaining unascertained despite the issue of "documents of title" to buyers.

[21] *Supra.*

[22] *Healy* v. *Howlett* [1917] 1 K.B. 337.

[23] *Per* Pearson J. (as he then was) in *Carlos Federspiel & Co. S.A.* v. *Twigg (Charles) Ltd.* [1957] 1 Lloyd's Rep. 240, 255 where the authorities are fully reviewed.

Thirdly, there is the question of consent. If the buyer orders goods by post, does he automatically consent in advance to the seller's appropriation? If this is so, then the risk will be on the buyer before he ever sees the goods—a clearly unreasonable result since he will usually not be in a position to insure them. Even here, however, the buyer is not entirely without a remedy. He might, for example, be able to prove that the seller has failed to make a reasonable contract of carriage.[24] In such a case the buyer can refuse delivery or he can claim damages from the seller—even if the loss or damage was not causally connected with the seller's default. Secondly, the buyer may have rights under section 14(2)[25] if the condition of the goods at the time of delivery suggests that they were not merchantable at the time of the contract and so were not fit to travel.[26]

The question of when property and risk pass where a consumer orders goods from a mail order house has never been expressly decided. In one case a commercial buyer ordered goods from a Swiss seller and it was held by the House of Lords that property passed to the buyer as soon as the goods were posted by the seller.[27] This case, if applied to the consumer mail order purchase, would produce a result which is out of line with the reasonable expectation of most consumers[28] and, as already stated, it can be most unfair to the consumer.[29] The *Badische Anilin* case was not a risk case at all and it turned on a point of patent law. The courts could always side-step this decision by finding an implied "contrary intention" under section 17 which would oust section 18 altogether.

Effect of risk rules

The Act, the cases and the textbooks are remarkably silent on the precise operation of the risk rules in the case of damage. A distinction can be drawn between (a) total destruction, and (b) damage.

(a) *Total destruction*

If the goods are totally destroyed either physically or commercially, they can be said to "perish." In advising the consumer in a case where the goods have perished after the making of the contract we must again distinguish between specific and unascertained goods.

(i) If specific goods perish, without the fault of either party, after[30] contract but before the risk has passed to the buyer, the con-

---

[24] s.32(2).
[25] *Ante*, p. 50.
[26] See, *e.g.* the pre-Act case of *Beer* v. *Walker* (1877) 46 L.J.Q.B. 677 (rabbits go putrid on the Brighton train; condition of merchantable quality broken).
[27] See *Badische Anilin und Soda Fabrik* v. *Basle Chemical Works* [1898] A.C. 200.
[28] See *Which?* May 1978, p. 316.
[29] See above.
[30] *Cf.* s.6, which deals with goods perishing *before* contract, *i.e. res extincta* and common mistake.

tract is avoided.[31] Thus if, in the example cited above,[32] the jeweller's entire stock is destroyed by an accidental fire before he has given notice that the enlarged ring is ready, the provisions of section 7 will apply. Further, the perishing of specific goods is not a case to which the Law Reform (Frustrated Contracts) Act 1943 applies so that the effects of frustration will be governed by the common law rules. Accordingly, since the contract is avoided by section 7, the buyer will not have to pay the price; if he has paid it or some of it, he can recover it because the consideration has failed[33]; he cannot claim damages for non-delivery. The unfortunate seller cannot sue for the price, nor can he claim any payment for work done by him on the goods before the fire broke out.

(ii) When we turn to unascertained goods we must draw yet another distinction. In the case of purely generic goods (*e.g.* "twenty square metres of Wilton carpet") no question of perishing can arise. If the goods which the seller intends to supply cease to be available, the seller must find the goods from another source or pay damages for non-delivery, unless he has covered himself by an effective exemption clause.[34] If, however, the source of the goods is specified in the contract (*e.g.* "ten bottles of wine from the case in my warehouse") the destruction of the source after contract but before the risk has passed to the buyer will frustrate the contract. The position of the parties is similar to that under section 7[35] except that the Act of 1943 will regulate the rights of the parties so that adjustments for expenses incurred, and benefits received, are possible.

(b) *Damage*

What happens if goods are accidentally damaged while they are still at the seller's risk? This problem could arise if, *e.g.* the furniture ordered by the buyer is damaged when the delivery van is involved in a road accident for which the seller is not responsible. Presumably the buyer can refuse to accept the damaged goods and then bring an action for non-delivery. The precise nature and the precise legal basis of the buyer's rights do not appear to have been analysed in any reported case; perhaps it is based on an implied undertaking by the seller that the quality of the goods delivered will correspond precisely with the quality of the goods when the buyer agreed to take them.[36]

[31] s.7.
[32] *Ante*, p. 86.
[33] *Fibrosa Spolka Akcyjna* v. *Fairbairn, Lawson Combe Barbour Ltd.* [1943] A.C. 32.
[34] *Post*, p. 130.
[35] *Supra.*
[36] For a somewhat similar principle in a slightly different context see *Financings Ltd.* v. *Stimson* [1962] 1 W.L.R. 1184 (C.A.)—damage to car between hirer's initial offer and its acceptance by the finance company.

4. THE PLUMBER WAS A COWBOY

The contract of "work and materials" (installation of central heating, double-glazing, etc.) was briefly examined in Chapter 4.[37] It will be recalled that such a contract can be divided into two parts—the "goods" part and the "work" part and the legal rules for the two parts are different (although in practice the difference may well be slight). The "work" part of such a contract can be classified as a contract for services. The list of such contracts includes repair, decoration, servicing, maintenance, cleaning, building, storage, carriage of goods and passengers, insurance, the provision of accommodation, entertainment and the whole range of professional services—legal, banking, accountancy, medical, dental, surveying, valuing and so on. A report published by the National Consumer Council ("*Service Please*")[38] in 1981 highlighted three main areas of dissatisfaction—the quality of the work, the time it took to do it and the cost. This section of this chapter is only concerned with the first of these—unsatisfactory performance. The Report referred to above shows that, for example:

1. Out of 50 garages only two came anywhere near to carrying out a full service in line with the maker's specifications.[39]
2. Out of 10 repair men called in to mend defective washing machines only two did so effectively.
3. A "plumber" connected an office coffee machine to a lavatory pipe.

Until fairly recently there was no statutory obligation on the supplier of a service to carry out his work with reasonable care and skill but this has now been rectified by section 13 of the Supply of Goods and Services Act 1982.[40] It reads:

> In a contract for the supply of a service where the supplier is acting in the course of a business there is an implied term that the supplier will carry out the service with reasonable care and skill.

The section was intended to confirm and codify the existing common law. It was not intended to enlarge existing areas of liability. Accordingly, section 12(4) gives the Secretary of State power to make orders excluding particular groups of persons from the "services" provisions of the Act (*i.e.* ss.13–15). An Order has been made (S.I. 1982 No. 1771) which provides that section 13 shall not apply to the following services:

(i) the services of an advocate in court or before any tribunal,

[37] *Ante*, p. 55.
[38] *Ante*, p. 4.
[39] See *Motoring Which*, January 1981.
[40] For the background to, and commentary on, the 1982 Act see Woodroffe, *Goods and Services—The New Law* (1982 Sweet & Maxwell).

inquiry or arbitration or in carrying out any preliminary work directly affecting the conduct of the hearing[41]; or

(ii) the services rendered to a company by a director of the company in his capacity as such.

A second Order (S.I. 1985 No. 1) has been made taking arbitrators outside the scope of section 13.[42]

We revert now to the basic question—does the consumer have to pay the price if the work of the plumber, electrician, etc., is unsatisfactory? In the vast majority of cases the answer will be "no"; the plumber, etc., will be in breach of the implied duty of care and skill under section 13 and the consumer may well be able to treat himself as discharged from the contract altogether or alternatively he can set off his claim for damages against the claim for the charge or fee. The matter is examined more fully in Chapter 7 (*post*, p. 101).

5. THEY TURNED UP LATE

Late performance, whether by sellers, electricians, builders, plumbers, carriers or holiday operators, is a frequent source of complaint by consumers. The legal principles governing this topic can be summarised as follows:

(1) If the contract specifies a date for performance, a supplier of goods or services who fails to perform by that date will be liable for damages for breach of contract (unless this liability has been effectively excluded or unless the contract is frustrated). This claim for damages can be pleaded by way of set-off or counter-claim in an action by the supplier for the price.[43]

(2) If the contract does not specify a date for performance the supplier must perform within a "reasonable" time.[44] The question of reasonableness is a question of fact[45]; even a long delay will not necessarily amount to a breach of contract if it was due to circumstances beyond the supplier's control. In one case a car owner took his car to a garage for repair following an accident. A normally competent repairer would have taken five weeks; the garage gave priority to other work and took eight weeks. It was held by the Court of Appeal that they had failed to carry out the work within a reasonable time and were therefore liable in damages.[46]

---

[41] See *Rondel* v. *Worsley* [1969] 1 A.C. 191 for the advocate's immunity in such cases. The immunity is not limited to barristers: Courts and Legal Services Act 1990, s.62.
[42] Whether an arbitrator has immunity from negligence claims is still unsettled. See (1991) 141 N.L.J. 633 and cases there cited.
[43] For the assessment of damages, see *post*, p. 111.
[44] See now section 14 of the Supply of Goods and Services Act 1982 which applies this rule where services are supplied in the course of a business.
[45] *Ibid.*
[46] *Charnock* v. *Liverpool Corporation and Another* [1968] 1 W.L.R. 1498; s.14 (*supra*) would now apply to such a case.

(3) Can the consumer go further and claim to be discharged from the contract altogether? This depends on whether time is "of the essence," *i.e.* a vital term or, in sale of goods language, a condition. The following statement in *Halsbury's Laws of England* has recently received judicial approval:

> Time will not be considered to be of the essence unless (1) the parties expressly stipulate that conditions as to time must be strictly complied with, or (2) the nature of the subject-matter of the contract or the surrounding circumstances show that time should be considered to be of the essence.[47]

It is probably true to say that under a contract to supply goods or services to a consumer a failure to observe the agreed performance date is not of itself a repudiation of the contract. There can, of course, be difficult cases; what about an operator who agrees to provide his client with a 15-day holiday in Majorca starting on August 1, but is prevented from carrying out that obligation by reason of industrial action for which he is not responsible? It could be argued that if he is unable to transport his clients on August 1, he will have broken an essential term of the contract which enables the clients to treat the contract as discharged; alternatively, it might be argued that the contract has been frustrated.[48]

(4) If a reasonable time has elapsed, or if the breach of an essential time clause has been waived, the consumer can serve a notice fixing a time for performance. The time limit in this notice must itself be a reasonable one, but subject to this the consumer can treat the contract as discharged if the supplier fails to perform by the date specified in the notice.[49]

Thus the consumer should always make it clear, in appropriate cases, that the date for performance is vital, *e.g.* by stating expressly that "time is of the essence."

6. THE PRICE SEEMS RATHER HIGH

In the case of sale of goods it is fairly rare to find an agreement without a price; indeed the absence of a price may indicate that the parties are still negotiating and that consequently there is no contract at all.[50] Section 8 of the 1979 Act, which is more appropriate to a commercial

---

[47] *Halsbury's Laws of England* (4th ed.), Vol. 9, para. 481, approved by Lord Simon in *Universal Scientific Holdings Ltd.* v. *Burnley Council* [1978] A.C. 904 (H.L.). See also *Bunge Corporation* v. *Tradax S.A.* [1981] 1 W.L.R. 711 (H.L.)

[48] In practice the contract will usually deal with the matter in accordance with the Codes of Practice discussed in Chap. 9, *post*, p. 147.

[49] *Charles Rickards Ltd.* v. *Oppenheim* [1950] 1 K.B. 616 (C.A.).

[50] *May and Butcher* v. *R.* [1934] 2 K.B. 17.

contract, provides that the price can be fixed by the contract itself, or in manner thereby agreed, or by usage. It then goes on to provide that if the price is not fixed in this way the buyer must pay a reasonable price.

In the case of services, it is rather more common to call in a repairer, or to take a suit to the cleaners or a car for a service without agreeing a price in advance. In such a case the supplier is entitled to claim a reasonable charge.[51] This, of course, is much easier said than done. If a consumer feels that the price is too high the onus will be on him to find expert evidence to substantiate his claim. He will also be put to great practical inconvenience if the supplier has the goods in his possession and refuses to release them until he has been paid. The consumer should also be very careful to limit his potential liability. Instead of saying "the car is starting badly—put it right" he should say "tell me if the work is going to cost more than £50."

Incidentally, what about an "estimate?" If an estimate amounts to an offer which is accepted, the estimate will become the contract price.[52] This, however, is rather unusual and the general rule is that the estimate is not legally binding; if however the estimate is a long way short of the final bill, the court might take the estimate into account in fixing a "reasonable price." In contrast, a quotation is more likely to be an offer to do the job for the quoted price.[53]

Can a supplier of services claim an additional amount if additional work is required? This again depends on what the parties have agreed. If, for example, a builder is employed to convert a loft the onus will be on him to ensure that the work will comply with the local bye-laws and building regulations. If it turns out that the local authority require extra work to be done (for example, fireproofing) he will generally be unable to recover any additional payment for this extra work from the owner—he should have checked on the point before fixing his price.

There may also be special rules to protect the consumer in particular professions. Thus, for example, a client who is dissatisfied with a solicitor's bill for non-contentious business can insist that the solicitor has the bill assessed by the Law Society (a "remuneration certificate") or by an official of the court (a "taxation" of the bill).

---

[51] See now the Supply of Goods and Services Act 1982, s.15. Provided that there is a "contract" for the service it does not have to be in the course of a business—although it usually is.

[52] *Croshaw* v. *Pritchard* (1899) 16 T.L.R. 45.

[53] See, *e.g.* Motor Industry Code, *post*, p. 160, and contrast the Consumer Credit (Quotation) Regulations, *post*, p. 319. See further the discussion and cases cited in Woodroffe, *Goods and Services—The New Law* (1982 Sweet & Maxwell), pp. 37–39.

CHAPTER SEVEN

"WHAT ARE MY REMEDIES?"

In the previous five chapters we have considered some of the supplier's basic obligations. We now come to the subject of remedies which, as stated in the preface, is what this book is all about; it is also the area in which the consumer is most likely to seek legal advice. In practice three questions most frequently arise, namely (a) what are the consumer's remedies (b) can they be excluded, and (c) how can they be enforced? These topics are considered in this chapter and the two following ones.

One preliminary point can be made. This chapter and the next one are concerned with questions of strict law. In Chapter 9 we shall see that in many cases consumers may be able to sidestep the worry, uncertainty and expense of litigation as a result of voluntary codes of practice drawn up by a number of trade and professional associations with the encouragement of the Office of Fair Trading. We shall also see that a complaint to a trading standards inspector can lead to a prosecution in certain cases and that this, in turn, can lead to a compensation order.[1]

This chapter is divided into three parts, namely:

1. Remedies for misrepresentation
2. Remedies for breach of contract
3. Remedies in tort.

The Law Commission Report No. 160[2] (which has already been considered when dealing with merchantable quality in Chapter 4) will be considered again in appropriate places in this chapter.

1. REMEDIES FOR MISREPRESENTATION

The remedies for misrepresentation can be summarised as follows:

(1) Fraudulent misrepresentation:
    (a) damages in tort for deceit;
    (b) rescission.
(2) Negligent misrepresentation:

---

[1] *Post*, pp. 227 and 258.
[2] *Ante*, pp. 42 *et seq.*

> > (a) damages under section 2(1) of the Misrepresentation Act 1967;
> > (b) rescission (or damages in lieu under section 2(2) of the 1967 Act).
> (3) "Innocent" misrepresentation (*i.e.* neither fraudulent nor negligent):
> > rescission (or damages in lieu under section 2(2) of the 1967 Act).

These matters will now be considered.

Fraudulent misrepresentation

A person commits the tort of deceit (or fraud) if he makes a false statement of fact knowingly, or without belief in its truth, or recklessly (*i.e.* careless whether true or false) with the intention that it should be acted upon by the plaintiff who does act on it and thereby suffers damage.[3] In practice, fraud is notoriously hard to prove. If, however, the consumer can prove that, for example, the dealer deliberately misrepresented the age or mileage of a car then, as we have seen, he may have the remedies of damages and/or rescission.[4] If he rescinds the contract he can claim to be put back into his pre-contractual position, so that, for example, he can recover any part of the price which he has paid. The action for damages can be considered (a) if the innocent party does not wish to rescind or (b) if it is too late to rescind[5] or (c) if he has suffered damage over and above the price.

What is the measure of damages for fraudulent misrepresentation? The rules are designed to prove compensation for all loss flowing directly from the fraud, whether reasonably foreseeable or not. Thus, in a sale of goods or land the starting point is the difference (if any) between the price paid by the consumer and the true value of the goods or land.[6] Money spent on repair and improvement before discovering the fraud can also be recovered[7] but not damages for loss of bargain.[8] Damages for personal injury or damage to property can also be recovered.[9]

Negligent misrepresentation

Until the passing of the Misrepresentation Act 1967 the court had no general power to award damages for a non-fraudulent misrepresentation—hence the importance of proving that there had been a breach

---

[3] See the leading case of *Derry* v. *Peek* (1889) 14 App.Cas. 337 (H.L.).
[4] *Ante*, p. 27.
[5] See *post*, p. 97.
[6] *Doyle* v. *Olby (Ironmongers) Ltd.* [1969] 2 Q.B. 158—a case of the sale of a business.
[7] *Ibid.*
[8] *East* v. *Maurer* [1991] 1 W.L.R. 461 (another business sale—damages awarded for the profits which the plaintiff would have earned if the false statement had not been made).
[9] *Langridge* v. *Levy* (1838) 4 M. & W. 337—exploding gun.

of a contractual term.[10] A Law Reform Committee recommended a change in the law and accordingly section 2(1) of the 1967 Act was passed to give a statutory right to damages in certain cases. It reads:

> Where a person has entered into a contract after a misrepresentation has been made to him by another party thereto and as a result thereof he has suffered loss then if the person making the representation would be liable in damages in respect thereof had the representation been made fraudulently, that person shall be so liable notwithstanding that the misrepresentation was not made fraudulently, unless he proves that he had reasonable grounds to believe and did believe up to the time that the contract was made that the facts represented were true.

It is clear from the case of *Howard Marine & Dredging Co. Ltd.* v. *A. Ogden & Son (Excavation) Ltd.*[11] that a section 2(1) claim is a claim in tort, and the approach in relation to a claim for damages is the same as for fraud.[12] We have seen that the object of damages in tort is to put the innocent party in the same position *as if the contract had never been made*. This can be contrasted with a different rule in contract where the damages are designed to put the innocent party in the same position *as if the contract had been performed*. Thus damages for loss of bargain are appropriate to contract but not to tort; the case of *Watts* v. *Spence*,[13] where damages for loss of bargain were awarded under section 2(1) of the 1967 Act, may well be wrongly decided.

Rescission

We can now turn to the equitable remedy of rescission. This has already been mentioned[14] and it only remains to consider the cases where it is not available. There are four well-established bars to rescission and these can be summarised as follows:

(a) where the parties can no longer be restored to their previous position. Thus the right to rescission would disappear if goods were destroyed before the buyer had elected to rescind;

(b) where third party rights have been acquired. Perhaps the clearest example is where B, by misrepresentation, persuades S to sell the goods to B and then resells the goods to C[15];

(c) where the innocent party has affirmed the contract with knowledge of the misrepresentation[16];

---

[10] *Ante*, p. 30.

[11] [1978] Q.B. 574. See also *Naughton* v. *O'Callaghan* [1990] 3 All E.R. 191 (misdescription of racehorse).

[12] *Ibid.* at p. 197. See also *Royscot Trust Ltd.* v. *Rogerson* [1991] 3 W.L.R. 57 (C.A.).

[13] [1976] Ch. 165.

[14] *Ante*, p. 96.

[15] See Sale of Goods Act 1979, s.23, *ante*, p. 16.

[16] *Long* v. *Lloyd* [1958] 2 All E.R. 402. *Cf.* Acceptance and loss of the right to reject for breach of condition, where knowledge is irrelevant: *post*, p. 106.

(d) where the innocent party has been guilty of unreasonable delay. In the well-known case of *Leaf* v. *International Galleries*,[17] the buyer of a painting which was described as by J. Constable sought to rescind for misrepresentation five years after making the contract on discovering that it was the work of another artist. The Court of Appeal held that it was far too late to rescind. In the words of Jenkins L.J.:

> "If he is allowed to wait five, ten or twenty years and then re-open the bargain, there can be no finality at all."

If the buyer had claimed damages under section 13 of the Sale of Goods Act[18] the claim would presumably have been unanswerable.

Statutory restriction on rescission

If none of these four bars apply, the general rule is that the innocent party can rescind the contract. The exercise of this remedy can have far-reaching results.

> Suppose that P buys a house from V for £20,000. V makes a non-fraudulent misrepresentation relating to the drains; the defect will cost £200 to put right. V has spent the whole of the £20,000 in buying another house.

If P were to rescind, V would have to find £20,000 (and might well be rendered homeless) because of a statement which caused damage of only £200. It was clearly with this kind of case in mind that section 2(2) of the Misrepresentation Act was enacted. It provides that:

> where a person has entered into a contract after a misrepresentation has been made to him otherwise than fraudulently, and he would be entitled, by reason of the misrepresentation, to rescind the contract, then, if it is claimed in any proceedings arising out of the contract, that the contract ought to be or has been rescinded, the court or arbitrator may declare the contract subsisting and award damages in lieu of rescission, if of opinion that it would be equitable to do so, having regard to the nature of the misrepresentation and the loss that would be caused by it if the contract was upheld, as well as to the loss that rescission would cause to the other party.

Thus, in the above example, the court might refuse rescission and award P damages of £200.

This power to award discretionary damages only applies where a

---

[17] [1950] 2 K.B. 86.
[18] *Ante*, p. 36. But see *Harlingdon and Leinster Enterprises* v. *Christopher Hull Fine Art* (*ante*, p. 37).

person "would be entitled . . . to rescind the contract." It would seem that the operative time is the time of the hearing. If by that date the right to rescind has already been lost (see *ante*, p. 97), the innocent party would not be "entitled" to rescind, and accordingly the court would no longer be able to award damages instead.

"Innocent" misrepresentation

If the misrepresentation is neither fraudulent nor negligent, the only possible remedy is rescission. This is subject to the usual equitable bars[19] and the court's discretionary powers under section 2(2) to award damages in lieu of rescission.

Exclusion clauses

A clause excluding liability for misrepresentation or cutting down the consumer's remedies for misrepresentation is only valid if it satisfies the test of "reasonableness."[20]

Misrepresentation and breach of contract

It is clear from section 1 of the Misrepresentation Act 1967 that the innocent party will have remedies for misrepresentation even though the representation has become a term of contract. The precise relationship between the two sets of remedies has yet to be worked out but presumably they are complementary.[21] It has recently been held that a clause stating "this agreement contains the whole contract between the parties" does not oust a claim for misrepresentation.[22] The court expressly decided that such a clause was not an exemption clause within section 8 of the Unfair Contract Terms Act 1977 (*post*, p. 138), but presumably the reasoning in this case would apply to an exemption clause.

2. REMEDIES FOR BREACH OF CONTRACT

This topic will be considered under four main headings, namely:

(1) Can I make him perform the contract?
(2) Can I have the goods repaired or replaced?
(3) Can I get my money back?
(4) Can I get compensation?

(1) Can I make him perform the contract?

Let us suppose that a consumer has ordered goods from a supplier,

---

[19] *Ante*, p. 97.
[20] *Post*, p. 138.
[21] See *Naughton* v. *O'Callaghan*, *ante*, p. 97, n. 10.
[22] *McGrath* v. *Shah* (1988) 57 P. & C.R. 452.

or work from a builder, and the supplier or builder has failed to turn up to do it. We have already seen that the consumer may be able to serve a notice making time of the essence; if the supplier or builder then fails to perform by the stipulated date the consumer may be able to treat the contract as discharged.

Let us suppose, however, that the consumer does not want to do this—what he wants is to compel the supplier or builder to perform the contract. In practical terms this may be more trouble than it is worth—the consumer may be better advised to obtain the goods or work elsewhere and claim compensation from the defaulting party.[23] If, however, the consumer insists on performance can the law help him? Historically the courts of common law granted only the remedy of damages, but the courts of equity supplemented this by granting decrees of specific performance in cases where damages would not be an adequate remedy. In the case of sale of goods the power to award specific performance is now enacted in section 52 of the Sale of Goods Act 1979 as follows:

> In any action for breach of contract to deliver specific or ascertained goods the court may, if it thinks fit, on the plaintiff's application . . . direct that the contract shall be performed specifically, without giving the defendant the option of retaining the goods on payment of damages. . . .

Two points must be stressed. In the first place the goods must be specified or ascertained. We have already seen that goods are specific if they are identified and agreed upon at the time of the contract.[24] Although the term "ascertained" is not defined in the Act it probably refers to goods which are identified *after* the making of the contract.[25] Thus if a consumer merely orders "a deep freeze" or "a heated trolley" and the seller, who is out of stock, fails to obtain one, the remedy of specific performance would not be available.[26] Secondly, the remedy of specific performance is, and has always been, a discretionary remedy and a court will not grant it if damages would be an adequate remedy. In the vast majority of consumer contracts the buyer can get similar goods elsewhere and any loss can be compensated by an award of damages. Accordingly, specific performance would not be granted. It follows that the scope of the remedy, in practical terms, is extremely limited.

In the case of a contract for services (*e.g.* building, cleaning or repairing) the remedy is even less appropriate[27] and it is difficult to think of any case in which it will be granted.

---

[23] *Post*, p. 11.

[24] s.61, *ante*, p. 84.

[25] See Atkin L.J. in *Re Wait* [1927] 1 Ch. 606. See also n. 24, p. 87.

[26] *Ibid.*

[27] The courts will not grant specific performance if this requires constant supervision of the defendant's work (see, *e.g. Ryan* v. *Mutual Tontine Westminster Chambers Ass.* [1893] 1 Ch. 116).

(2) Can I have the goods repaired or replaced?

In considering this problem there is a vast difference between law and practice. If, for example, a car, television set or a lawnmower proves to be defective, the consumer will usually take it to the seller and ask for it to be repaired or replaced. In practice the seller (or the manufacturer in guarantee cases) will endeavour to repair it. Alternatively, the seller may take the goods back and give the consumer a replacement or a credit note; in the case of a car, however, it is very rare for the car to be taken back. All this is a matter of business practice; *there is no legal right to have the goods repaired or replaced.* The Law Commission Report[28] does not put forward any proposals to change the law on this point.

What happens if the buyer's expensive dishwasher breaks down and the seller tells him "we can't replace the defective part because this particular model has been discontinued"? The Report referred to above confirms that the retailer is under no legal duty to keep a stock of spare parts and servicing facilities and does not recommend that the retailer should be placed under such a duty.[29] However, such an obligation is being gradually adopted on a voluntary basis (see, *e.g.* the electrical Codes of Practice).[30]

(3) Can I get my money back?

When a consumer makes a contract for the purchase of goods or services he is under a basic obligation to pay the contract price. Thus, if he has booked a holiday at a seaside hotel, he cannot simply cancel his booking. If he does so then, as a matter of strict law, the hotel can forfeit his deposit, and can even sue him for damages if they have suffered additional loss by reason of his cancellation and have been unable to mitigate the loss by reletting the room.

There may, however, be cases where the consumer is relieved of his basic duty to pay the price; in these cases he can recover the price (or a deposit) if he has already paid it. This will be so in at least three cases:

(a) where the contract is rescinded for misrepresentation[31];
(b) where specific goods perish before the risk has passed to the buyer[32];
(c) where a contract for the sale of goods is discharged as a result of the supplier's breach.

Discharge by breach

If one party breaks a contractual term (express or implied) the

---

[28] *Sale and Supply of Goods*, Law Com. No. 160 (1987).
[29] *Op. cit.* para. 3.66. Nor does a manufacturer have such a duty.
[30] *Post*, p. 170.
[31] *Ante*, p. 96.
[32] *Ante*, p. 89.

innocent party can claim damages. In some cases he can go further and claim that the entire contract has been discharged by the breach. Once that happens the innocent party can regard himself as excused from further performance and can also claim damages in respect of the past breach. His right to get his money back, however, is only available if the contract so provides or if there has been a total failure of consideration.

In deciding whether a contract has been discharged by breach we must start by looking at the general law and then at the special rules which apply to the sale of goods and (probably) to analogous contracts. Under the general law, a contract is discharged by a breach if the innocent party has been deprived of substantially the whole benefit which it was intended that he should obtain from the contract.[33] In other words the question is not "how was this term classified when the contract was made?" but—much more sensibly—"what effect did the breach have on the innocent party?" Even if the breach was a repudiatory breach, the innocent party may well have received *some* benefit under the contract and therefore has no right to recover money paid by him—although he will have a claim for damages which could well be equal to, or greater than, the amount of payments made.

Sales of goods

If we now turn to sale of goods we find the matter complicated by the condition/warranty classification. By section 61(1) of the 1979 Act a warranty is defined as:

> an agreement with reference to goods which are the subject-matter of a contract of sale, but collateral to the main purpose of such contract, the breach of which gives rise to a claim for damages but not to a right to reject the goods and treat the contract as repudiated.

In contrast, section 11(3) states that:

> Whether a stipulation in a contract of sale is a condition, the breach of which may give rise to a right to treat the contract as repudiated, or a warranty . . . depends in each case on the construction of such contract.

This wording, with its emphasis on "the construction of the contract" appears to leave no scope for the flexibility shown by the *Hong Kong* case (*supra*), where the remedies available to the innocent party depend on the severity and consequences of the breach. (We use the words "appear to leave" because neither the courts nor the Law Commission seem to have considered the word "may" in the above

---

[33] *Per* Diplock L.J. in *Hong Kong Fir Shipping Co. Ltd.* v. *Kawasaki* [1962] 2 Q.B. 26, 66.

definition—this might enable the *Hong Kong* principle to apply after all). Nevertheless in the case of *express* terms the courts have succeeded[34] in breaking out of the statutory straitjacket by holding that a clause could be neither a condition nor a warranty but an "intermediate stipulation" or "innominate term" to which the *Hong Kong* principles apply. Nevertheless there is no scope for such flexibility in the case of the statutory *implied* terms and, as we have seen in Chapters 2–4, the most important of the implied terms are classified as conditions. It remains to add that a buyer who rejects the goods for breach of condition can recover the price paid because there has been a total failure of consideration (see s.54).

Other supply contracts

In the case of hire-purchase, hire and other contracts for the supply of goods the relevant statutes[35] use the condition/warranty terminology but do not define it. It is possible therefore (but unlikely) that a court would feel free to construe the words in a more flexible way. The case law makes it clear that a breach relating to fitness for purpose, etc., does not necessarily amount to a total failure of consideration. Accordingly the innocent party has no direct cause of action to recover payments made but instead he must seek to recover them indirectly by means of an action for damages.[36]

Finally in contracts for services the statutory obligations as to care and skill, time for performance and price are referred to by the neutral word "term."[37] It is clear therefore that the flexible *Hong Kong* test will apply to them.

The Law Commission

The Law Commission Report recommends[38] that in a sale of goods contract where the buyer does *not* deal as consumer, his remedy for breach of the conditions implied by sections 13 to 15[39] should be limited to damages where the breach is so slight that it would be unreasonable for him to reject. This runs counter to the provisional view in their Working Paper when they considered that this might lead to commercial uncertainty. In contrast, in relation to consumers the Report recommends[40] that the present law be retained:

> The regime which applies must be a simple one. Such is the present law. In legal theory the consumer has the absolute right to reject for any defect.

---

[34] *Cehave* v. *Bremer* [1976] Q.B. 44 (C.A.).
[35] Supply of Goods (Implied Terms) Act 1973 for hire-purchase and the Supply of Goods and Services Act 1982 for the other types of contract.
[36] See Law Commission Working Paper No. 85, para. 2.41–2.43 and cases there cited.
[37] Supply of Goods and Services Act 1982, ss.13–15.
[38] *Op. cit.*, para. 4.21.
[39] Section 15 relates to a sale by sample.
[40] *Op. cit.*, para. 4.14.

Loss of right to reject—sale of goods

Section 11(4) of the 1979 Act cuts down the buyer's rights if the goods (or part) have been accepted. Section 11(4) reads as follows:

> Where a contract of sale is not severable and the buyer has accepted the goods or part of them . . . the breach of any condition to be fulfilled by the seller can only be treated as a breach of warranty, and not as a ground for rejecting the goods and treating the contract as repudiated, unless there is an express or implied term of the contract to that effect.

When is a contract severable?

The opening words of the subsection refer to a contract which is "severable." Thus, if a consumer made a contract with a supplier for the delivery of a 12-part encyclopaedia, one part to be delivered each month and to be *separately paid for*, this would be a severable contract. The result would be that the acceptance of one instalment would not prevent the buyer from rejecting a later one on the grounds that, for example, a number of pages were blank.

A further question then arises; does a breach with regard to one or more instalments amount to a repudiation of the entire contract or is it merely a severable breach? In other words, can a buyer who rejects instalment number two be compelled to accept the remaining ten instalments? There is no clear cut answer to this question; by section 31(2):

> it is a question in each case depending on the terms of the contract and the circumstances of the case.

In this example the buyer might well be able to refuse further instalments if, for example, the set as a whole is useless without the missing part. This raises a further unsettled point; if a seller tenders a defective instalment which is lawfully rejected, can he put the matter right by delivering a non-defective instalment? On principle, the answer ought to be "yes"—provided that he is not in breach of an essential time clause.

What is acceptance?

In the overwhelming majority of consumer sales the contract will be non-severable so that the buyer will lose the right to reject when he accepts the goods or any part thereof.[41] As already stated in Chapter 2 this is one of the two most difficult areas of this branch of the law—the other being the definition of "merchantable quality." The statutory provisions are contained in sections 34 and 35(1) of the 1979 Act. Section 34 gives buyers the right to examine the goods:

---

[41] But the right to damages remains untouched. See *post*, p. 111.

(1) Where the goods are delivered to the buyer and he has not previously examined them he is not deemed to have accepted them until he has had a reasonable opportunity of examining them for the purpose of ascertaining whether they are in conformity with the contract.

(2) Unless otherwise agreed, when the seller tenders delivery of the goods to the buyer, he is bound, on request, to afford the buyer a reasonable opportunity of examining the goods for the purpose of ascertaining whether they are in conformity with the contract.

This section is clearly of considerable importance to consumers. It would apply, for example, to a purchase by mail order; it would also apply to a purchase of a cooker or washing machine where the consumer had merely examined a demonstration model. In practice, the goods themselves are usually delivered in a large closed box and the consumer is required to sign a form stating that the contents are satisfactory. Some consumers take the precaution of adding the words "contents unexamined" above their signature, but even if this is not done it is felt that a court would look at the realities of the situation and would hold that the signature would not, of itself, prevent rejection of the cooker or washing machine if it was not of merchantable quality.

Let us now turn to section 35(1). It reads as follows:

The buyer is deemed to have accepted the goods when he intimates to the seller that he has accepted them or (except where section 34 above otherwise provides) when the goods have been delivered to him and he does any act in relation to them which is inconsistent with the ownership of the seller, or when after the lapse of a reasonable time, he retains the goods without intimating to the seller that he has rejected them.

Thus section 35 specifies three types of "acceptance."

(i) **Intimation of acceptance.** There has been no reported case on this topic; it is felt that there must be conduct on the part of the buyer which makes it clear to the seller that the goods have been accepted. One example might be a letter asking the seller to carry out modifications. On the other hand, a form signed by the consumer stating "I accept these goods" would probably not be conclusive.

(ii) **Act after delivery inconsistent with the seller's ownership.** The leading cases are concerned with commercial contracts under which a delivery to a sub-buyer has destroyed the right to reject.[42] The underlying principle appears to be an inability to restore the goods to the seller. Thus, if a consumer receives a large consignment of wood and starts sawing it up in order to build a shed, the act of cutting it up would destroy his right to reject if he then discovers that, for example, the wood does not answer the contract description. Another grey area

---

[42] See, *e.g. Ruben* v. *Faire Bros.* [1949] 1 K.B. 254 as an illustration of this point.

concerns negligent damage. What happens if the buyer of a defective suit stains it with ink when he wears it for the first time? If the stain is indelible it could affect his right of rejection, since it would prevent him from returning the goods in their original form.

It must, however, be remembered that the words in brackets, which were first introduced in 1967, could affect the position. Under the statutory wording an act done by the buyer before he has had a reasonable opportunity for examination will not necessarily destroy the right to reject; it is possible that some of the earlier cases[43] might now be decided differently.

(iii) **Retention beyond a reasonable time.** This is the most contentious type of acceptance in the consumer context. The main bone of contention is whether "a reasonable time" begins to run only after the buyer has *discovered* the defect (or other breach of contract) or at some earlier stage. This is of crucial importance if the goods contain a latent defect which will not show up until some months or even years of use have elapsed.

Suppose that a carpet wears through or a bed collapses after only a year or two of normal use. What if the bearings of a washing machine or the motor of a lawn mower break down after 18 months? Even though it can be shown that the goods must have been unmerchantable at the date of delivery—this is evidenced by their subsequent failure to be durable enough—can the buyer still reject the goods? The consumer's answer would be "Of course! How can the right to reject for breach of condition be lost before the consumer can realise that there has been a breach?" The legal answer, however, may well be otherwise. The misunderstanding arises from confusing "acceptance" in section 35 with affirmation, waiver, laches, etc., which operate at common law or in equity to bar rescission[44] only if the plaintiff treats the contract as continuing *after* discovery of the breach or misrepresentation.

It must be remembered that we are dealing with a commercial statute which has to do service in consumer transactions too. "The general legal proposition that there should, wherever possible, be finality in commercial transactions" was stressed by Rougier J. in *Bernstein* v. *Pamson Motors (Golders Green) Ltd.*[45]

> B bought a new Nissan Laurel from P for £8,000. It was delivered on December 7, 1984. B was ill over Christmas and unable to use it. On January 3 with 140 miles on the odometer the car broke down with a seized camshaft. Next day B wrote to P rejecting the car on the grounds

---

[43] *Ibid.*
[44] *Long* v. *Lloyd* [1958] 2 All E.R. 402.
[45] [1987] 2 All E.R. 220.

that it was not merchantable. P resisted B's claim on the grounds that (1) the car was merchantable and (2) anyway it was too late to reject the car as B had accepted it. P repaired the car under the manufacturer's warranty. B sued for rescission and damages.[46]

Giving judgment for B on the first point (the car was unmerchantable) and for P on the second (it was too late to reject) Rougier J. upheld P's submission that "once a buyer has had the goods for a reasonable time, *not*, be it noted, related to the opportunity to discover any particular defect, he is deemed to have accepted them."
He went on to say:

"In my judgment, the nature of the particular defect, discovered *ex post facto*, and the speed with which it might have been discovered, are irrelevant to the concept of reasonable time in s.35 as drafted. That section seems to me to be directed solely to what is a reasonable practical interval in commercial terms between a buyer receiving the goods and his ability to send them back, taking into consideration from his point of view the nature of the goods and their function, and from the point of view of the seller the commercial desirability of being able to close his ledger reasonably soon after the transaction is complete. The complexity of the intended function of the goods is clearly of prime consideration here. What is a reasonable time in relation to a bicycle would hardly suffice for a nuclear submarine."[47]

Applying those principles to the facts, Rougier J. held that three weeks (discounting the period of illness) was a reasonable time for a new car:

"Reasonable time means reasonable time to examine and try out the goods in general terms."[48]

The decision seems a harsh one and some commentators regard it as suspect on the basis that an appeal was settled out of court on terms which acknowledged that the right to reject had not been lost (see (1987) 137 N.L.J. 962). Nevertheless, it must be admitted that the alternative view (*i.e.* that the buyer has a continuing right to reject until he discovers the defect) has one fundamental weakness—it would enable a buyer to reject and *recover his full price* even though he had used the goods for a considerable time. The Law Commission considered the problem extensively in their Report[49] and reached the conclusion that the present rule should continue; for no one had suggested, and no other common law system provided, a better answer.

[46] The action was really fought between the AA, backing B, and Nissan, backing P.
[47] At p. 230.
[48] *Ibid.*
[49] *Op. cit.*, paras. 5.14 to 5.19.

Considerable room for judicial maneouvre exists because "what is a reasonable time is a question of fact."[50] This gives flexibility, although as three weeks was reasonable for a complex piece of machinery (a new car), an even shorter period might be reasonable for simple products like a pen, pie or pair of pants.

It is easy to concentrate so fiercely on the loss of the right to reject that damages are forgotten. In the *Bernstein* case the car was repaired free of charge. In addition damages were awarded: £33 for the taxi fare home and wasted tank of petrol, £50 for five days' loss of use until a hire car was made available and £150 "for a totally spoilt day, comprising nothing but vexation."

We forecast that the law is unlikely to remain in its current state for many years. A vocal consumer lobby, with the Consumers' Association and National Consumer Council in its van, is pressing for a "continuing right to reject." It can be strongly argued that irrespective of the need for commercial finality the problems of consumers require separate solutions. We suggest that a compromise solution would be to legislate for special fixed periods for those particular types of goods which give rise to the most complaints, *e.g.* three months for cars.[51] The list could be gradually extended by statutory instrument as and when a class of product caused special problems. All other products would be governed by s.35 as it stands.

The next point concerns the effect of complaints. Let us suppose that an expensive camera fails to work. The consumer will usually ask the supplier (or manufacturer) to repair it. What happens if the defect persists after (say) 10 attempts to repair it? Alternatively, what happens if a large number of different defects manifest themselves after purchase? The buyer is certainly entitled to wait for a time to see if the defects can be put right. Thus in *Lee* v. *York Coach and Marine Ltd.*[52] the critical factor which destroyed the right to reject was the delay of six months after the final repair. Nevertheless, if the defect does persist for more than a few weeks there must come a time when the buyer must make up his mind—"do I want to keep the goods or not?" Although the point is not covered by authority it is highly unlikely that a judge would allow rejection once that time has passed. Accordingly, the buyer should make it clear at the outset that he will reject the goods if the defects are not rectified.[53]

Absence of title

If the supplier of goods has no right to sell, the consumer can recover

---

[50] s.59.
[51] See Law Com. No. 160, paras. 5.17, 5.18.
[52] *Ante*.
[53] As happened in the hire-purchase case *Farnworth Finance Facilities* v. *Attryde, post*, p. 109.

the price on the basis of total failure of consideration. His right to do this is not lost by "acceptance"—as Atkin L.J. pointed out in *Rowland v. Divall*.[54] He will, however, lose his right to get his money back if the defect in title is put right before he purports to reject.[55] This is reasonable enough—it would obviously be wrong to allow a claim based on "total failure of consideration" if the buyer has received substantially what he paid for, *i.e.* the property in the goods.

Law Commission proposals

In their Report No. 160 it is proposed that:

1. No consumer should lose the right to reject until he has had a reasonable opportunity of examination, unless a reasonable time has elapsed.[56]
2. A request for cure, and an attempt by or under an arrangement with the seller to cure the defect, should not destroy the right to reject.[57]

Loss of right to reject—other supply contracts

There is nothing in the Consumer Credit Act 1974 nor in the Supply of Goods (Implied Terms) Act 1973 nor in the Supply of Goods and Services Act 1982 regulating the remedies of the consumer. The position is governed by the common law principles of waiver or affirmation which, unlike acceptance, operate only when the consumer becomes *aware* of the defect in the goods. The cases at common law show a fairly broad approach. In *Farnworth Finance Facilities* v. *Attryde*[58]:

Mr. Attryde took a new motor cycle on hire-purchase terms on July 11, 1964. There were a very large number of defects and finally on November 23 he purported to reject it and claimed the return of all payments.

Counsel for the defendants argued that by driving the motor cycle for 4,000 miles Mr. Attryde had affirmed the contract so as to lose his right to reject. The Court of Appeal rejected this argument. In the words of Lord Denning M.R.[59]:

Affirmation is a matter of election. A man only affirms a contract when he knows of the defects and by his conduct elects to go on with the contract despite them. In this case Mr. Attryde complained from the beginning of

---

[54] [1923] 2 K.B. 500 and see, *ante*, p. 23.
[55] *Butterworth* v. *Kingsway Motors* [1954] 1 W.L.R. 1286.
[56] Paras. 5.20 to 5.25.
[57] Para. 5.29.
[58] [1970] 1 W.L.R. 1053.
[59] p. 1059.

the defects and sent the machine back for them to be remedied. He did not elect to accept it unless they were remedied. But the defects were never satisfactorily remedied. When the rear chain broke it was the last straw.

As already stated, there is nothing in hire-purchase law comparable to section 11(4) of the Sale of Goods Act. The Law Commission acknowledge that the right to reject is more readily available than in a sale and recommend that this regime, which is more favourable to customers than the sale of goods regime, should not be disturbed.[60]

The rules as to conditional sale agreements (*post*, p. 299) are similar to those for hire-purchase and in *Rogers* v. *Parish (Scarborough) Ltd.* (*ante*, p. 109) the buyer was allowed to reject after using the car for six months and driving 5,500 miles. It must be noted, however, that the seller's counsel did not raise the matter and one wonders what would have happened if he had done so.

Can the buyer reject part?

What happens if some of the goods are merchantable while others are not? We have seen that under a non-severable contract the buyer has a straight choice—to keep all the goods or to reject them; by accepting part his right to reject is lost.[61]

This rule is, however, modified by section 30 which gives the buyer additional rights in three cases. The effect of section 30 can be summarised as follows:

(a) If the seller supplies *too many* goods, the buyer can (i) reject all the goods or (ii) reject the surplus or (iii) keep all the goods and pay for them at the contract rate.

(b) If the seller tenders *too little*, the buyer can (i) reject the goods or (ii) keep them and pay at the contract rate.

(c) If the seller tenders the contract goods *mixed* with goods of a different description, the buyer can (i) reject all the goods or (ii) reject the goods not answering the description. There is no statutory right to keep the latter goods, but the courts might treat the delivery as an offer to sell them. If the buyer accepted this offer, he would be liable to pay a reasonable price.[62] Alternatively if the buyer did not initially accept the offer, he might be able to take advantage of section 1 of the Unsolicited Goods and Services Act 1971 which was considered in Chapter 6.

The Law Commission Report considers it to be anomalous that where the seller's breach is to deliver goods of the correct description

---

[60] Report No. 160, paras. 5.43 to 5.46.
[61] s.11(4), *ante*, p. 104.
[62] s.8.

mixed with goods of a different *description*, the buyer may accept the former and reject the latt er, but that this right of partial rejection does not apply where they are *defective*. They therefore recommend that the right of partial rejection be extended to all cases where the goods do not conform with the contract requirements.[63]

Practical considerations

There will, in many cases, be practical barriers to repudiation in cases where the price has already been paid. Section 36 of the 1979 Act provides that the buyer can send the seller a notice of rejection; if the property and risk have passed to the buyer the effect of the notice is to re-transfer them to the seller. In practice, however, the seller is likely to dispute the buyer's right to reject. This can mean that the buyer will have neither his money nor the use of the goods until his right to reject has been upheld by a court and until the judgment for the return of the price has been satisfied.

(4) Can I get compensation?

The consumer is always entitled to damages if the other party has broken a term of the contract, express or implied, and the consumer has suffered loss. It is irrelevant whether the term is a condition, warranty or intermediate stipulation. When we turn to the difficult question of quantifying the claim we must consider two closely related problems, namely (a) for what items of loss is the defendant liable? and (b) on what principles should the compensation be assessed?

For what loss is the defendant liable?

The general principles governing remoteness of damage were laid down more than 100 years ago in *Hadley* v. *Baxendale*[64] and more recently by the House of Lords in *Koufos* v. *Czarnikow Ltd. (The Heron II)*.[65] The defendant is clearly liable for damage arising naturally from the breach (normal loss—first rule). He is also liable for other damage which can fairly and reasonably have been within the contemplation of both parties, at the time they made the contract, as the probable result of the breach of it (unusual loss—second rule). It has recently been held that where the general *type* or kind of damage was within the contemplation of the parties, the defendant is liable even though the precise *extent* of the damage, or the precise form of the damage, was outside his contemplation.[66]

---

[63] *Op. cit.*, paras. 6.6 to 6.11 and 6.22.
[64] (1854) 9 Exch. 341, 354.
[65] [1969] 1 A.C. 350.
[66] *Parsons (Livestock) Ltd.* v. *Uttley Ingham & Co.* [1978] 1 Q.B. 791 (sale and construc-tion of hopper for feeding nuts to pigs—ventilator left unopened—nuts became mouldy—pigs died—supplier of hopper liable). See also *Vacwell* v. *B.D.H. Chemicals* [1971] 1 Q.B. 88.

Mitigation

Another basic rule is that of mitigation—the injured party must take reasonable steps to mitigate his loss. Thus, to take an obvious example, a buyer of a defective product could not sue the seller for the cost of having it repaired by a third party if the seller had previously offered to repair it free of charge or presumably if a free repair (parts *and* labour) was available under a manufacturer's guarantee.

General principles of compensation

If the damage is not too remote under the rules set out above, the general principle is that damages should, so far as possible, place the injured party in the same position as if the contract had been performed properly.

Non-delivery

In the case of sale of goods the buyer may have an action for damages against the seller (a) if the seller fails to deliver or (b) if the seller breaks a condition or warranty. In all these cases the general principles laid down in *Hadley* v. *Baxendale*[67] appear in statutory form; thus section 51(2) which deals with non-delivery provides that:

> The measure of damages is the estimated loss directly and naturally resulting, in the ordinary course of events, from the seller's breach of contract.

As an example of this, section 51(3) provides that:

> Where there is an available market for the goods in question the measure of damages is prima facie ... the difference between the contract price and the market or current price of the goods at the time or times when they ought to have been delivered, or (if no time was fixed) at the time of refusal to deliver.

Let us suppose that John agrees to buy a new Ford Escort car from a dealer for £8,000. The contract provides that the car must be delivered by May 1 but the dealer fails to deliver. By that date the price of Ford Escorts has increased by £500. If John has to pay an extra £500 to buy one from another dealer, this sum will prima facie be his damages under section 51(3).

The second rule of *Hadley* v. *Baxendale*, damage within the reasonable contemplation of the parties, is preserved by section 54 which reads:

> Nothing in this Act affects the right of the buyer or the seller to recover interest or special damages in any case where by law interest or special damages may be recoverable. . . .

---

[67] *Ante*, p. 111.

Thus, if, as a result of the non-delivery of the car, John loses a valuable business contract, that would be "special damages" and the defaulting dealer will only be liable for it if it was brought to his attention before the agreement was made.

Damages for breach of warranty

In this situation damages arising naturally are covered by section 53(2) while "contemplated" damages are covered by section 54.[68] Where the warranty relates to quality the damages are prima facie the difference between the actual value of the defective goods and their value if they had answered the warranty.[69] It is clear, however, that damages are not necessarily confined to that amount. Thus, for example, damages for personal injury or death can be recovered on a sale of a defective toy.[70] Then, if a defective car is "off the road" for repair, the buyer will be able to recover from the seller not only the cost of repair but also the cost of hiring a substitute car[71] during this period. The magazine *Which?* has cited a case where a buyer of a leaking caravan spent large sums of money on petrol on numerous journeys to have it repaired. He also planned to have a caravan holiday but was compelled to move into a guest house when the defects reappeared. He successfully recovered both the cost of petrol and the boarding house expenses in county court proceedings.

If the seller is in breach of the condition of "right to sell,"[72] the damages recoverable by the buyer can include not merely the price paid but also the cost of necessary repairs.[73]

The principles set out above apply equally where the seller is in breach of a condition which the buyer elects to treat, or is compelled to treat, as a breach of warranty.

Mental distress

A novel head of damages which no legal adviser should forget in a consumer dispute is mental distress, upset, disappointment and injured feelings. The seminal case on this topic was *Jarvis* v. *Swan Tours*[74] and holiday contracts continue to be a fruitful area for this type of loss.[75] Damages have also been awarded in proceedings for negligence against a solicitor who failed to obtain a non-molestation injunction for a client.[76]

---

[68] *Ante,* p. 112.
[69] s.53(3) and see *Lee* v. *York (Coach and Marine) Ltd., ante,* p. 49.
[70] *Godley* v. *Perry* [1960] 1 W.L.R. 9.
[71] See *Bernstein* v. *Pamson Motors, ante,* p. 106.
[72] *Ante,* p. 22.
[73] *Mason* v. *Burningham* [1949] 2 K.B. 545.
[74] [1973] 1 Q.B. 233. The facts are given *post,* p. 259.
[75] For further examples, see *post,* p. 114.
[76] *Heywood* v. *Wellers* [1976] Q.B. 446.

The first sale of goods case was *Jackson* v. *Chrysler Acceptances*.[77] This has been followed recently by two other car cases where the damages were by no means nominal.[78]

Even so, the courts seem likely to approach this area cautiously, as can be gleaned from the remarks of Staughton L.J. in *Hayes* v. *Dodd*[79] where the Court of Appeal disallowed this head of damage in a business dispute:

> "Damages for mental distress in contract are, as a matter of policy, limited to certain classes of case. I would broadly follow the classification provided by Dillon LJ in *Bliss* v. *South East Thames Regional Health Authority* [1987] ICR 700 at 718:
>> '... where the contract which has been broken was itself a contract to provide peace of mind or freedom from distress ...'
> It may be that the class is somewhat wider than that. But it should not, in my judgment, include any case where the object of the contract was not comfort or pleasure, or the relief of discomfort, but simply carrying on a commercial activity with a view to profit."

Hire-purchase

The principles set out above are equally relevant to hire-purchase transactions. Thus in *Yeoman Credit Ltd.* v. *Apps*[80] the hirer of a car which took one and a half hours to do three or four miles successfully sued for damages. The damages were assessed at the difference between what the car should have been worth and what it was actually worth; on that basis the hirer recovered all his payments, less a very small allowance for use.

Holiday contracts

If the customer finds, on arrival at his resort, that his room has been double booked, or that the hotel does not exist, he can claim the cost of having to stay at an equivalent hotel plus (as already stated) damages for mental distress. If the hotel exists but does not have the promised facilities, the remedy will be damages. In appropriate cases damages can include losses suffered by members of the plaintiff's family.[81]

An interesting recent case is *Spencer* v. *Cosmos Air Holidays*[82]

---

[77] [1978] R.T.R. 474. A consumer told a dealer that he wanted a car for a holiday. The car was defective. The county court judge awarded (*inter alia*) £75 for a spoilt holiday. Although the award was varied on appeal there was no suggestion that such damages could not be recovered.

[78] *Bernstein* v. *Pamson Motors, ante*, p. 113: £150 for spoilt day. *UCB Leasing* v. *Holtom* [1987] R.T.R. 362 (C.A.): £500 for distress where hire car had three complete electrical failures in four months.

[79] [1990] 2 All E.R. 815, 824.

[80] [1962] 2 Q.B. 508.

[81] *Jackson* v. *Horizon Holidays* [1975] 1 W.L.R. 1468 (C.A.). For the facts, see *post*, p. 259.

[82] *The Times*, December 6, 1989.

The plaintiff booked two weeks' holiday in Spain with the defendants for £266. After about a week the hotelier wrongfully ejected her and her two female companions. They spent two nights sleeping on the beach before the defendants found them alternative, inferior accommodation at a less pleasing resort.

The Court of Appeal awarded her £1,000 for her distress, misery and humiliation, reducing by half the award by the trial judge.

Cleaners

If a cleaner negligently ruins or loses a blanket, a carpet or a suit, the damages will be based on the cost of acquiring a replacement, but this will be subject to a discount for age and use.

Builders

If a builder, decorator or plumber does a job badly, the damages would include not only the money paid to another firm to have it put right but also damages for the resulting inconvenience.[83] If the work is done extremely badly, the consumer may be entitled to refuse to pay anything at all.[84]

3. REMEDIES IN TORT

Perhaps the most likely case of a tort claim would be where the consumer has a claim against the manufacturer for negligence or under the Consumer Protection Act 1987. In personal injury cases the damages would include loss of actual and future earnings, medical expenses, pain and suffering and loss of amenities. For further details readers are referred to the standard textbooks on tort and to *McGregor on Damages*.

In a case where the same facts give rise to liability in both contract and tort the rules as to damages are being brought very close together.[85]

---

[83] See, *e.g. Batty* v. *Metropolitan Realisations* [1978] Q.B. 554.
[84] See, *e.g. Bolton* v. *Mahadeva* [1972] 1 W.L.R. 1009.
[85] *Parsons (Livestock) Ltd.* v. *Uttley Ingham & Co.*, *ante*, p. 111.

CHAPTER EIGHT

"THEY SAY THAT I HAVE SIGNED AWAY MY RIGHTS"

Exemption clauses have been widely used in standard form contracts in the past 50 years or so and have come in for severe criticism from the courts and other bodies. The courts have developed certain techniques to control the legal effect of these clauses. Unfortunately the control exercised by the courts has been unsatisfactory because, with the exception of Lord Denning M.R., they have felt themselves unable to break out of the straitjacket of freedom of contract. Accordingly, the use of exemption clauses has been increasingly controlled by statute and the overwhelming majority of these clauses are now controlled by the Unfair Contract Terms Act 1977.

Examples

The first three examples are taken from Law Commission Working Paper No. 39, pp. 74–88.

(1) The shipowner shall be exempt from all liability in respect of any detention, delay, overcarriage, loss, expenses, damage, sickness or injury of whatever kind, whenever and wherever occurring and however and by whomsoever caused of or to any passenger or of or to any person or child travelling with him or her or in his or her care or of or to any baggage, property, goods, effects, articles, matters or things belonging or carried by, with or for any passenger or any such person or child.

(2) [The ferry company] shall not be liable for the death or any injury, damage, loss, delay or accident ... wheresoever, whensoever and howsoever caused and whether by negligence of their servants or agents or by unseaworthiness of the vessel.

(3) The contractors shall not under any circumstances be liable for any loss or damage caused by or resulting from or in connection with fire, howsoever caused.

(4) All cars parked at owner's risk.

(5) In the case of loss or damage the liability of the company is limited to the value of the garment.

(6) All claims within seven days.

Justification

In deciding on the price of his product a supplier is bound to consider

117

the question of loss apportionment. He can also cut down very substantially on administration overheads by having standard form contracts (thus avoiding the need to negotiate each contract separately) and by avoiding litigation. A survey carried out by Yates in *Exclusion Clauses in Contracts* contains the following passage (2nd ed., p. 25):

> The desire to avoid court proceedings in the event of a dispute was also a reason advanced for using exemption clauses which, it was often felt, gave each party a clearer indication of where they stood. ... Distrust of lawyers' and more especially judges' ability to understand the businessman's problems was very marked.

Criticism

When due allowance has been made for the points set out above there is no doubt that exemption clauses are open to abuse. The following passage is taken from the Law Commission's Second Report on Exemption Clauses No. 69, para. 11, on which the Unfair Contract Terms Act 1977 was based:

> We are in no doubt that in many cases they operate against the public interest and that the prevailing judicial attitude of suspicion, or indeed of hostility, to such clauses is well founded. All too often they are introduced in ways which result in the party affected by them remaining ignorant of their presence or import until it is too late. That party, even if he knows of the exemption clause, will often be unable to appreciate what he may lose by accepting it. In any case he may not have sufficient bargaining strength to refuse to accept it. The result is that the risk of carelessness or of failure to achieve satisfactory standards of performance is thrown on to the party who is not responsible for it or who is unable to guard against it. Moreover, by excluding liability for such carelessness or failure the economic pressures to maintain high standards of performance are reduced.

Scheme of this chapter

It is proposed to start by examining the attitude of the courts to exemption clauses and then to consider the statutory controls imposed by the Unfair Contract Terms Act. The broad scope of the Act has made the former topic far less important and accordingly it will be examined fairly briefly. A short reference to other legislation will be made at the end of this chapter.

1. JUDICIAL CONTROL OF EXEMPTION CLAUSES

The reasons for judicial hostility to exemption clauses have already been mentioned: ignorance, non-negotiation and inequality of bargaining power. Perhaps the first of these points is the strongest. After all, the law of contract is, or should be, about agreement. If the consumer were asked "do you know that you have signed away your right to complain if the cleaners lose the carpet?" or "do you know that you will receive no compensation at all if the carriers damage your furniture?" it is unlikely that his reply could be printed in this book; at all events it is likely to include the word "no." When he made the contract he would reasonably have expected that the work would be done with reasonable care, and that he would receive compensation if this was not so. His expectations may have been increased by a glowing advertisement in a newspaper or magazine or on television. Accordingly exemption clauses, which are often inconsistent with his reasonable expectations, are closely scrutinised by the courts.

The courts have to decide two basic problems, namely:

(1) was the clause duly incorporated into the contract, and
(2) does it, on its true construction, cover the event which has occurred?

(1) Incorporation[1]

The general contractual principles relating to incorporation have been well established for a considerable time. Thus:

(a) *Signed document*

If the contractual document is signed, this operates as an incorporation of all the terms which appear on that document or which are referred to in it.[2] The signer will not be bound, however, if he signed the document without negligence and it turns out to be a document of a fundamentally different kind from the document which he thought that he was signing.[3]

(b) *Unsigned document or notice*

If the consumer has not signed a contractual document, a clause will only be incorporated if reasonable steps were taken before contract to bring it to his notice. The following cases illustrate how this principle has been applied.

(i) In the case of *Thompson* v. *L.M.S. Railway*[4] a lady bought a railway excursion ticket containing the words "For conditions see back." The back of the ticket referred to conditions in the railway timetables which were available for purchase. Had Mrs. Thompson

---

[1] For a recent summary of the rules see the judgment of Boreham J. in *John Snow & Son Ltd.* v. *Woodcroft Ltd.* [1985] B.C.L.C. 48.
[2] The leading case is *L'Estrange* v. *Graucob* [1934] 2 K.B. 394.
[3] *Saunders* v. *Anglia Building Society* [1971] A.C. 1039, in which the House of Lords emphasised that this so-called "*non est factum*" defence must be confined within narrow limits.
[4] [1930] 1 K.B. 41.

obtained and read it (by which time she would certainly have missed her train) she would have seen an exclusion clause excluding liability for negligence. The Court of Appeal held that the exemption clause had been incorporated into the contract.

(ii) The case of *Chapelton* v. *Barry U.D.C.*[5] concerned an exclusion clause on a deckchair receipt. It was held that there was no incorporation; this was not the type of document on which the consumer could reasonably expect to find conditions and therefore the local authority had not taken sufficient steps to bring the clause to the consumer's attention.

(iii) In *Olley* v. *Marlborough Court Hotel*[6] a consumer booked a hotel room. After he had done so he saw an exemption notice in the bedroom. It was held that there was no incorporation since the clause had been introduced too late. The position might have been different if the notice was prominently displayed at the reception desk or if the customer had stayed at the hotel on previous occasions. In the latter case the notice might have been incorporated on the basis of a previous course of dealing. Nevertheless, this principle, which can readily be implied in commercial contracts,[7] is very rarely applied in consumer contracts.[8]

(iv) *Thornton* v. *Shoe Lane Parking Co. Ltd.*[9] is perhaps the best modern example of how the basic rules of "contract" are being adapted, in a realistic way, to standard form consumer transactions.

> Mr. Thornton went to park his car at a new multistorey car park—he had not been there before. When he arrived opposite the ticket machine a ticket popped out, the light turned from red to green and he went through and parked his car. The ticket referred to conditions displayed on the premises. These conditions (*inter alia*) excluded liability for personal injuries caused by negligence. There was an accident caused partly by the defendants' negligence and Mr. Thornton was injured.

The Court of Appeal held that the defendants had not taken reasonable steps to bring this particular clause to the notice of Mr. Thornton. In the words of Lord Denning M.R. at p. 170:

> "It is so wide and destructive of rights that the court should not hold any man bound by it unless it is drawn to his attention in the most explicit way. ... In order to give sufficient notice, it would need to be printed in red ink with a red hand pointing to it—or something equally startling."

Megaw L.J. gave an equally vivid example when he said at p. 173:

[5] [1940] 1 K.B. 532. In any case it was post-contractual and so ineffective.
[6] [1949] 1 K.B. 532.
[7] *Spurling* v. *Bradshaw* [1956] 1 W.L.R. 461.
[8] See, *e.g. McCutcheon* v. *David MacBrayne Ltd.* [1964] 1 W.L.R. 125 (H.L.), a notable case, if only because of the appearance in it of a Mr. McSporran!
[9] [1971] 2 Q.B. 163.

"It does not take much imagination to picture the indignation of the defendants if their potential customers . . . were one after the other to get out of their cars leaving the cars blocking the entrance to the garages in order to search for, find and peruse the notices! Yet unless the defendants genuinely intended that potential customers should do just that it would be fiction, if not farce, to treat those customers as persons who have been given a fair opportunity, before the contracts are made, of discovering the conditions by which they are to be bound."

Lord Denning M.R. went so far as to hold that the contract was made when the customer dropped his money into the machine, with the result that the conditions on the ticket were introduced too late.[10] The trouble with this approach is that in many cases the customer does *not* put money into the slot—he merely collects a ticket and pays later. Nevertheless both Lord Denning M.R. and Sir Gordon Willmer were influenced by the finality of a contract made with a machine. To quote again from Lord Denning:

"The customer pays his money and gets a ticket. He cannot refuse it. He cannot get his money back. He may protest to the machine, even swear at it. But it will remain unmoved. He is committed beyond recall."

These interesting problems may never be decided because it may be unnecessary to do so. If the facts of *Thornton* were to recur, a clause excluding liability for death or personal injury resulting from negligence would in any event be void[11] and accordingly the question of incorporation would have no practical importance. The point might, however, remain relevant if the customer suffered damage to his property. In that case the exemption clause would be valid if reasonable[12] and accordingly the customer might well raise the argument of "no incorporation" as his first line of attack.

(v) In *Interfoto Picture Library Ltd.* v. *Stiletto Visual Programmes Ltd.*[13] (a non-consumer case) the Court of Appeal had to consider the situation where one clause in a set of conditions was particularly onerous.

SVP, an advertising agency, telephoned IPL, a photographic library, requesting photographs of the 1950s for a presentation for a client. IPL sent by hand 47 transparencies in a bag with a delivery note stating that they must be returned within 14 days.

Across the bottom of the note were printed nine conditions in four columns, under the fairly prominent heading "CONDITIONS." Condition 2 stated that all transparencies must be returned within 14 days and that "A holding fee of £5.00 plus VAT per day will be charged for each

---

[10] *Cf. Olley* v. *Marlborough Court Hotel, ante*, p. 120.
[11] Unfair Contract Terms Act 1977, s.2(1): *post*, p. 129.
[12] *Ibid.* s.2(2).
[13] [1988] 1 All E.R. 348.

transparency which is retained by you longer than the said period of 14 days. . . ."

SVP accepted delivery, but did not use them and by an oversight kept them for 28 days. When IPL sent an invoice for £3,783.50, SVP refused to pay, for most libraries charged less than 50p per day.

Hitherto the general approach in the "ticket cases" had been to ask whether the supplier has taken reasonable steps to bring the conditions *as a whole* to the notice of the consumer. However, Lord Denning M.R. had signposted a different route with his "red ink—red hand" approach in *Thornton* v. *Shoe Lane Parking Ltd.*[14] Following that route the Court of Appeal held in the *Interfoto* case that condition 2, imposing an exorbitant holding fee, was not part of the contract. Dillon L.J. stated the principle thus[15]:

> "It is in my judgment a logical development of the common law into modern conditions that it should be held, as it was in *Thornton* v. *Shoe Lane Parking Ltd.*, that, if one condition in a set of printed conditions is particularly onerous or unusual, the party seeking to enforce it must show that that particular condition was fairly brought to the attention of the other party."

Bingham L.J., agreeing that "the plaintiffs did not do what was necessary to draw this unreasonable and extortionate clause fairly to their attention," seemed to be of the view that a more general principle of fairness was being applied[16]:

> "The tendency of the English authorities has, I think, been to look at the nature of the transaction in question and the character of the parties to it; to consider what notice the party alleged to be bound was given of the particular condition said to bind him; and to resolve whether in all the circumstances it is fair to hold him bound by the condition in question. This may yield a result not very different from the civil law principle of good faith, at any rate so far as the formation of the contract is concerned."

The actual decision (treating the clause as unduly onerous merely because other libraries charged less) is certainly debatable but, subject to this, three final points can be made. First, the clause was not an exemption clause[17] and it will be interesting to see how far the courts will use this "non-incorporation" tool to protect consumers in areas where Parliament has chosen not to do so. Secondly, we have already

---

[14] *Ante*, p. 120. See also his dictum to similar effect in *J. Spurling Ltd.* v. *Bradshaw* [1956] 1 W.L.R. 461, 466, and the comments of Bramwell and Mellish L.JJ. in *Parker* v. *South Eastern Rly. Co.* (1877) 2 C.P.D. 416.

[15] At p. 352.

[16] At p. 357.

[17] The Unfair Contract Terms Act 1977 could not be used to control the clause for that very reason—see *post*, p. 128.

seen how non-incorporation can be used to outflank the Unfair Contract Terms Act (*ante*, p. 119). Finally, it remains to be seen how far the principle discussed in *Interfoto* (and particularly the fairness point raised by Bingham L.J.) can be called in aid by someone who has *signed* a contract—even though up to now the principle of bringing the conditions to the notice of the consumer has not been relevant in this situation. In other words, *L'Estrange* v. *Graucob*[18] may not be an impassable barrier.

(2) Does the clause cover the event which has occurred?

Even if the clause has been incorporated into the contract it is not automatically effective. The courts have evolved a number of techniques to counter their effect. These techniques may still be relevant in some cases but it must be strongly emphasised that times have changed and, with the arrival of the Unfair Contract Terms Act 1977, the courts will be less concerned with these matters (see *post*, p. 126).

(a) *Privity*

After earlier doubts the House of Lords have held that an exemption clause in a contract between A and B could not protect C, even if C was an employee or contractor employed by B to perform the contract.[19] It seems, however, that this can be outflanked by having a clause whereby a party contracts, as agent for his employees, etc., that they shall have the benefit of the clause. As a matter of strict legal analysis this can create a separate contract between the employees and the other party and the performance of the main contract will provide the consideration for it.[20]

(b) *Strict construction and the contra proferentem rule*

A party seeking the protection of an exemption clause must show that the wording is clear enough to cover the alleged breach. This is well illustrated by three cases involving sale of goods.

In *Wallis, Son and Wells* v. *Pratt and Haynes*[21] a commercial contract for the sale of seed excluded "all warranties." The seller supplied seed of a different description and the buyer claimed damages. The House of Lords held that the seller had broken a *condition* and that a clause referring only to *warranties* did not protect him. The mere fact that the buyer, in ignorance of the breach, had "accepted" the goods, and was

---

[18] *Ante*, p. 119.
[19] *Scruttons* v. *Midland Silicones Ltd.* [1962] A.C. 446.
[20] *New Zealand Shipping Co. Ltd.* v. *Satterthwaite & Co. Ltd.* [1975] A.C. 154 (P.C.).
[21] [1911] A.C. 394. See also *Southern Water Authority* v. *Carey* [1985] 2 All E.R. 1077 where the same result was reached by a different route.

therefore compelled to treat the breach as a breach of warranty,[22] was immaterial.

In *Andrews Bros. (Bournemouth) Ltd.* v. *Singer & Co. Ltd.*[23] the seller sold a "new Singer car" with a clause excluding "implied conditions and warranties." The seller supplied a car which was not new. The Court of Appeal held that he had broken an *express* condition and accordingly a clause which merely referred to *implied* conditions did not protect him.

In *Nichol* v. *Godts*[24] the sellers agreed to supply rape oil "warranted only equal to sample." Sellers supplied a mixture of rape oil and hemp oil which matched the sample. It was held that the exclusion clause did not protect them from their overriding duty to supply rape oil in accordance with the description.

The rule of strict construction leads on naturally to the so-called "*contra proferentem*" rule which provides that an ambiguity must be construed against the party who wishes to rely on the clause. Thus if a plaintiff has two distinct claims against the defendant (one in contract and one in tort for negligence) an exemption clause may well be construed so as to cover only the former and not the latter.[25] Even words like "the company will not be liable for damage caused by fire" may merely operate as a warning that the company will only be liable if negligent.[26] It follows that clear words are required to cover liability for negligence, for example, "howsoever caused" or "whether or not due to negligence."

(c) *Inconsistent oral promise*

An exemption clause will be overridden by an oral promise which is inconsistent with it. Thus in *Mendelssohn* v. *Normand*[27] a suitcase was stolen from a car which the plaintiff had parked at the defendants' car park. An employee of the defendants promised the plaintiff that he would lock the car, but he failed to do so. The Court of Appeal held that a clause excluding "loss or damage howsoever caused" was ineffective.

(d) *Misrepresentation*

The courts will not allow a party to rely on an exemption clause if he has misrepresented its effect to the consumer.[28] On the other hand, the

---

[22] *Ante*, p. 104.
[23] [1934] 1 K.B. 17.
[24] (1854) 10 Exch. 191.
[25] See, *e.g. White* v. *John Warwick* [1953] 1 W.L.R. 1285 and more recently *The Zinnia* [1984] 2 LL.L.R. 211.
[26] *Hollier* v. *Rambler Motors (AMC) Ltd.* [1972] 2 Q.B. 71.
[27] [1970] 1 Q.B. 177. See also *J. Evans & Son (Portsmouth) Ltd.* v. *Andrea Merzario Ltd.* [1976] 1 W.L.R. 1078 (C.A.).
[28] *Curtis* v. *Chemical Cleaning and Dyeing Co.* [1951] 1 K.B. 805 (C.A.).

consumer may find himself faced with a clause which says that "no employee of the company has any authority to add to or vary these terms." Such a clause is legally binding.[29]

(e) *Fundamental breach*

In a number of cases decided before the Unfair Contract Terms Act 1977 the courts sought to relieve the consumer from the harsh effects of an exemption clause by holding that it did not cover the breach of a fundamental term[30] or a fundamental breach.[31] The legal reasoning for this doctrine was highly dubious. The House of Lords has twice rejected it[32] and reaffirmed the basic rule that the scope of an exemption clause is always a question of construction and that there is no rule of law preventing the exclusion of a fundamental breach. In a recent case the House of Lords has warned against the danger of reintroducing the doctrine under another name.[33]

(f) *The new approach*

The most recent cases herald a new approach to the construction of exemption clauses; in future the courts will be less willing to adopt a policy of judicial control of exemption clauses because the need for it has gone. Thus in a case decided on the previous law (but with knowledge that the 1977 Act had been passed) Lord Diplock said this:

> "My Lords the reports are full of cases in which what would appear to be very strained constructions have been placed upon exclusion clauses, mainly in what today would be called consumer contracts or contracts of adhesion. As Lord Wilberforce has pointed out, any need for this kind of distortion of the English language has been banished by Parliament, having made these kinds of contract subject to the Unfair Contract Terms Act."[34]

Quite apart from this, it seems that a clause limiting damages to a fixed amount (a "limitation clause") will not be construed as strictly as a full exclusion clause.[35] It must be said, however, that the reasoning is not convincing.[36]

---

[29] *Overbrooke Estates Ltd.* v. *Glencombe Properties Ltd.* [1974] 1 W.L.R. 1335 (a case on auction particulars).

[30] "Something narrower than a condition—something which underlies the whole contract:" *per* Devlin J. (as he then was) in *Smeaton Hanscomb & Co. Ltd.* v. *Setty (Sassoon) Sons & Co.* [1953] 1 W.L.R. 1468, 1470.

[31] See, *e.g. Karsales (Harrow) Ltd.* v. *Wallis* [1956] 1 W.L.R. 936.

[32] *Suisse Atlantique* v. *N.V. Rotterdamsche Kolen Centrale* [1967] 1 A.C. 361; *Photo Production* v. *Securicor Transport* [1980] A.C. 827.

[33] *George Mitchell (Chesterhall) Ltd.* v. *Finney Lock Seeds Ltd.* [1983] 3 W.L.R. 163.

[34] *Photo Production Ltd.* v. *Securicor Transport* [1980] A.C. 827, 851.

[35] *Ailsa Craig Fishing Co. Ltd.* v. *Malvern Fishing Co. and Securicor (Scotland)* [1983] 1 W.L.R. 964—a House of Lords decision on appeal from Scotland.

[36] *Ibid.* p. 966 (Lord Wilberforce) and p. 970 (Lord Fraser).

2. Unfair Contract Terms Act 1977

The Act is largely based on the Law Commission's Second Report on Exemption Clauses, but it differs from the Law Commission's Draft Bill in several material respects.

Scope of the Act

The Act operates in five overlapping areas, namely:

(a) negligence;
(b) contractual obligations;
(c) terms implied in contracts for the sale of goods, hire-purchase and certain analogous contracts;
(d) guarantees and indemnities;
(e) misrepresentation.

Before considering these areas it is necessary to mention some preliminary points.

Preliminary matters

(1) The Act does not create new duties—it merely controls clauses which cut down a duty which would otherwise exist or which exclude or modify the remedies available on breach of that duty.

> Let us suppose that Richard parks his car in a car park and keeps the key. There is a large notice at the entrance "The company is not liable for any loss or damage to vehicle or contents, whether or not due to negligence of the company or its servants or agents." When Richard comes back to collect his car it cannot be found.

The notice set out above would be controlled by section 2 of the Act[37] and would be subject to the reasonableness test. This, however, is likely to be completely irrelevant; the company can avoid liability on the more basic ground that the transaction was a mere licence and not a bailment and therefore they owed Richard no duty of care. That was the position before the Act[38] and, as already stated, the Act does not create new duties.

(2) The name of the Act is misleading—it is both too narrow and too wide. It is too narrow because it only refers to "contract"; the Act also applies to negligence both at common law and under the Occupiers' Liability Act 1957. It is too wide because it does not control all "unfair terms"; it merely controls exemption clauses and notices.

[37] See *post*, p. 130.
[38] *Ashby* v. *Tolhurst* [1937] 2 K.B. 242.

(3) With very minor exceptions the key provisions of the Act (sections 2–7) only apply to "business liability." By section 1(3) this means:

> liability for breach of obligations or duties arising—
> (a) from things done or to be done by a person in the course of a business (whether his own business or another's); or
> (b) from the occupation of premises used for business purposes of the occupier.

When we turn to section 14 we find that the term "business" includes a profession and the activities of any government department or local or public authority.

The term "business" crops up at various points in this book. Thus we have already come across it in connection with (a) supply of goods— implied conditions of quality and fitness,[39] and (b) unsolicited goods and services.[40] We shall meet it again later in this chapter when considering the phrase "deals as consumer."[41] It is also critical for certain provisions of the Consumer Credit Act, for example, non-commercial agreements[42] and the licensing provisions.[43] There are bound to be borderline cases. Is a landlord carrying on a "business" when he lets a block of flats? Is a charity "bazaar" a business? The tax cases show that the key factors include the frequency of the transaction, the manner of operation and the profit motive. It is felt that, on these criteria, a charity bazaar would not be a business, whereas a landlord might well be carrying on a business—especially if he provided services for the tenants.

Reverting now to section 1(3) the question arises as to whether the Act would apply to the premises of a professional man who worked from his home. The answer is "yes," because the Act does not require the premises to be used *exclusively* for business purposes. The point is rather academic since the home is unlikely to be plastered with exclusion notices.

(4) Sections 2–4 do not apply to certain contracts listed in Schedule 1. For the consumer the two most important are (a) contracts of insurance and (b) any contract so far as it relates to the creation, transfer or termination of an interest in land. The words "so far as" are important. If, for example, a landlord of a block of flats remains the occupier of the common staircase, a notice stating that "visitors enter these premises at their own risk" would be controlled: thus if the landlord negligently allows the staircase to fall into disrepair, he would be liable in damages to an injured visitor under the Occupier's Liability

[39] *Ante*, p. 44.
[40] *Ante*, p. 80.
[41] *Post*, p. 131.
[42] *Post*, p. 305.
[43] *Post*, p. 314.

Act 1957, s.2(2), and the exemption notice would be void by the Act of 1977, section 2(1) (*post*, p. 130).

In relation to insurance the industry successfully lobbied the Government to exclude insurance policies from the Act and in return they issued their Statements of Practice covering life and non-life insurance respectively.

(5) The Act repeatedly refers to a clause which "excludes or restricts liability." This clearly covers a clause that "no liability is accepted for any loss or damage howsoever caused" or "liability shall be limited to the cost of replacing the appliance and all liability for consequential loss is excluded." Then when we turn to section 13(1) we find that:

> To the extent that this Part of this Act prevents the exclusion or restriction of any liability it also prevents
> (a) making the liability or its enforcement subject to restrictive or onerous conditions;
> (b) excluding or restricting any right or remedy in respect of the liability, or subjecting a person to any prejudice in consequence of his pursuing any such right or remedy;
> (c) excluding or restricting rules of evidence or procedure.

Thus the following would be caught:

(a) "all claims within seven days"
(b) "before starting proceedings the customer must pay £1,000 into a joint bank account"
(c) "no rejection"
(d) "if you sue us we will see that you get no further supplies"
(e) "the report by our engineer shall be conclusive."

Section 13(1) then concludes with these words:

> and (to that extent) sections 2 and 5 to 7 also prevent excluding or restricting liability by reference to terms and notices which exclude or restrict the relevant obligation or duty.

What does this mean? How can the Act control a clause which prevents a duty from arising? What is "the relevant obligation or duty?" In the earlier editions of this book we suggested that the answer is to adopt the approach of Lord Denning M.R. in *Karsales (Harrow) Ltd.* v. *Wallis*[44] and look at the contract or activity apart from the clause. If, for example, it is a contract giving rise to a condition of reasonable fitness or a duty of reasonable care, the Act would control a clause or notice providing that "no condition of fitness is implied herein" or "the occupier shall be under no duty of care." The House of Lords has

[44] [1956] 1 W.L.R. 936.

recently confirmed in *Smith* v. *Eric S. Bush*[45] that this is the correct interpretation. Affirming the decision of the Court of Appeal[46] that the disclaimers did not prevent the surveyors having a duty of care Lord Jauncey commented on the concluding words in section 13(1) as follows[47]:

"These words are unambiguous and are entirely appropriate to cover a disclaimer which prevents a duty coming into existence."

Lord Griffiths adopted a "but for" test[48]:

"They indicate that the existence of the common law duty to take reasonable care . . . is to be judged by considering whether it would exist 'but for' the notice excluding liability."

Two final points can be made on this topic. First, an agreement in writing to submit present or future disputes to arbitration is *not* a clause "excluding or restricting liability."[49] Secondly, it is thought that the Act does not apply to a genuine "liquidated damages" clause, nor to a genuine settlement out of court ("I accept this sum [or credit note] in full and final settlement of all claims").

(6) The common law rules as to incorporation, privity and construction mentioned earlier in this chapter remain unaffected, although, as already stated,[50] they will become of far less practical importance. There may, of course, be cases where the common law rules will still be relevant. Thus if the exemption clause is controlled by the reasonableness test[51] this gives the court a wide discretion; so if the consumer can prove non-incorporation, this will of itself defeat the exemption clause and the question of discretion will not arise.

The five areas affected by the Act

(a) *Negligence*

Section 1(1) defines negligence as the breach:

(a) of any obligation, arising from the express or implied terms of a contract, to take reasonable care or exercise reasonable skill in the performance of the contract;
(b) of any common law duty to take reasonable care or exercise reasonable skill (but not any stricter duty);

---

[45] [1989] 2 All E.R. 514. The facts are given *ante*, p. 33. A similar construction was adopted by Slade L.J. in *Phillips Products Ltd.* v. *Hyland* [1987] 1 W.L.R. 659 (C.A.).
[46] [1987] 3 All E.R. 179.
[47] At p. 543.
[48] At p. 530.
[49] s.13(2).
[50] *Ante*, p. 123.
[51] *Post*, p. 139.

(c) of the common duty of care imposed by the Occupiers' Liability Act 1957. ....

In practice the most important example of (a) is to be found in section 13 of the Supply of Goods and Services Act 1982 (ante, p. 90).

We can now consider section 2—one of the most important sections of the Act. It reads as follows:

(1) A person cannot by reference to any contract term or to a notice given to persons generally or to particular persons exclude or restrict his liability for death or personal injury resulting from negligence.
(2) In the case of other loss or damage, a person cannot so exclude or restrict his liability except in so far as the term or notice satisfies the requirement of reasonableness.
(3) Where a contract term or notice purports to exclude or restrict liability for negligence a person's agreement to or awareness of it is not of itself to be taken as indicating his voluntary acceptance of any risk.

The scope of section 2 is wide. Examples include architects, surveyors, builders, carriers, cleaners, dancehalls, cinemas, garages, decorators and holiday tour operators. In all these cases—and there are many more—an exemption clause or notice will be totally void in cases of *death or personal injury*.

If the negligence results in damage to *property* or economic loss, the clause or notice will only be effective if it satisfies the reasonableness test.[52] No distinction is made between contracts with consumers and contracts with businesses—in either case the test is the same.[53]

(b) *Contractual obligations*

The other really far-reaching provision in the Act—and one bristling with problems—is section 3. It reads as follows:

(1) This section applies as between contracting parties where one of them deals as consumer or on the other's written standard terms[54] of business.
(2) As against that party, the other cannot by reference to any contract term—
    (a) when himself in breach of contract, exclude or restrict any liability of his in respect of the breach; or
    (b) claim to be entitled—
        (i) to render a contractual performance substantially different from that which was reasonably expected of him, or
        (ii) in respect of the whole or any part of his contractual obligations, to render no performance at all,
except in so far as (in the cases mentioned above in this subsection) the contract term satisfies the requirement of reasonableness.

[52] s.11, *post*, p. 139.
[53] *Cf.* ss.3, 4, 5, 6 and 7, where the distinction is crucial.
[54] See article in [1983] J.B.L. 226.

This section is based on the recommendation of the Law Commission in their Second Report on Exemption Clauses[55] and is discussed on pages 52–62 of that Report. It applies to a contract (1) between a businessman and a person dealing as consumer or (2) between two businessmen where it is made on the written standard terms of business of one of them. Thus in the consumer situation there is no distinction between a standard form contract and a negotiated contract.

Deals as consumer. The term "deals as consumer" is defined in section 12 as follows:

(1) A party to a contract "deals as consumer" in relation to another party if—
    (*a*) he neither makes the contract in the course of a business nor holds himself out as doing so; and
    (*b*) the other party does make the contract in the course of a business; and
    (*c*) in the case of a contract governed by the law of sale of goods or hire-purchase, or by section 7 of this Act, the goods passing under or in pursuance of the contract are of a type ordinarily supplied for private use or consumption.
(2) But on a sale by auction or competitive tender the buyer is not in any circumstances to be regarded as dealing as consumer.
(3) Subject to this, it is for those claiming that a party does not deal as consumer to prove that he does not.

In most cases it is easy to see whether these factors are present, as the definition is aimed at the everyday consumer situation where (a) the customer is a private consumer; (b) the supplier is in business; and (c) if the contract concerns goods (rather than services) they are ordinary consumer goods.

So if a private individual buys a camera from a shop, acquires a car on hire-purchase from a finance company, has central heating installed in his house by British Gas or books a holiday with a tour operator, in each case he "deals as consumer."

Equally obviously a manufacturing company does not deal as consumer where it buys machinery for its factory, leases cars for its sales force or uses a security company to provide guards for its premises. Taking the three factors in order we see that a customer will *not* be dealing as consumer where:

(a) the customer is a business[56] customer; or
(b) the supplier is a private person (although exemption clauses are rare here, except perhaps "sold as seen" on a used car);
(c) the goods are not ordinarily supplied for private use, *e.g.* a van

---

[55] Law Commission Report No. 69.
[56] No sale by auction or competitive tender is a consumer dealing, even though the buyer is a private person: s.12(2).

or coach, to be converted into a touring home. This part of the definition may give rise to problems, *e.g.* in the case of DIY materials. Are wiring, cisterns, cement, cement mixers and other builder's tools of that type? Here—and in the difficult areas discussed below—section 12(3) should swing the balance in favour of the consumer, for it is for the supplier to prove that a consumer does *not* deal as such.

There are two main areas of difficulty, both concerned with the precise meaning of "in the course of a business" in section 12(1)(*a*) and (*b*). First, suppose a solicitor, accountant or other professional person buys a car through his business, but to be used for mixed business and private use. Secondly, assume that a retailer or estate agent buys a carpet or chair for his office—a rare event. In none of these cases are the goods part of their stock-in-trade, but in every case the goods are ordered through the business and doubtless tax allowances are claimed. Are the goods bought "in the course of a business"? On a straightforward reading of the words, particularly in view of use of the indefinite article, the answer is "yes." The Act does not require the business to deal in goods of the relevant type. Surprisingly the Court of Appeal has recently decided that cases of this type will be classed as consumer transactions.

In *R & B Customs Brokers Co. Ltd.* v. *United Dominions Trust*[57]:

> R & B, shipping brokers, was a private company whose only directors and shareholders were a married couple. R & B bought a Colt Shogun for personal and company use from UDT under a conditional sale agreement. (R & B had previously acquired one or two other vehicles on credit terms.) They both signed the agreement on behalf of the company. It contained an exemption clause excluding (*inter alia*) the implied condition as to fitness for particular purpose. The vehicle leaked badly in breach of the Sale of Goods Act 1979, s.14(3). When UDT sought to rely on the exclusion clause, R & B argued that it was void under the UCTA, s.6(2), as R & B was "dealing as consumer."

The Court of Appeal gave judgment for R & B. On first impression the court was convinced by the argument put forward above that the company bought in the course of a business.[58] In the end, however, the court was persuaded that there should be consistency of meaning for the same words in different statutes dealing with consumer protection and that they should follow the guidance given by the House of Lords in *Davies* v. *Sumner*,[59] a case on the Trade Descriptions Act 1968. The court did not overlook the point that the techniques of construction of

---

[57] [1988] 1 All E.R. 847.
[58] *Ibid.* at p. 857, *per* Neill L.J.
[59] See *post*, p. 199, for the facts and discussion. Dillon and Neill L.JJ. cited with approval the words of Lord Keith set out there.

criminal and civil Acts are different; the judgment of Dillon L.J. underlines the court's approach most clearly[60]:

> Under the Trade Descriptions Act 1968 any person who in the course of a trade or business applies a false trade description to goods is, subject to the provisions of that Act, guilty of an offence. It is a penal Act, whereas the 1977 Act is not, and it is accordingly submitted that decisions on the construction of the 1968 Act cannot assist on the construction of s.12 of the 1977 Act. Also the legislative purposes of the two Acts are not the same. The primary purpose of the 1968 Act is consumer protection, and the course of business referred to is the course of business of the alleged wrongdoer. But the provisions as to dealing as a consumer in the 1977 Act are concerned with differentiating between two classes of innocent contracting parties (those who deal as consumers and those who do not) for whom differing degrees of protection against unfair contract terms are afforded by the 1977 Act. Despite these distinctions, however, it would, in my judgment, be unreal and unsatisfactory to conclude that the fairly ordinary words "in the course of business" bear a significantly different meaning in, on the one hand, the 1968 Act and, on the other hand, s.12 of the 1977 Act. In particular, I would be very reluctant to conclude that these words bear a significantly wider meaning in s.12 than in the 1968 Act.

So when is a purchase by a business customer outside section 12? The answer is that it must be an *integral part of the business carried on* (see below). This will be so if (a) it is a one-off adventure in the nature of a trade or (b) a regular pattern of purchases has emerged. So presumably a firm of solicitors buying a typewriter or word processor or a firm of accountants buying a micro computer would be "dealing as consumer" unless a regular pattern of such purchases could be shown. Referring to the words of Lord Keith in *Davies* v. *Sumner*[61] and of Lord Parker C.J. in *Havering L.B.C.* v. *Stevenson*,[62] Dillon L.J. said[63]:

> In the 1977 Act also, the words "in the course of business" are not used in what Lord Keith called "the broader sense." I also find helpful the phrase used by Lord Parker C.J. and quoted by Lord Keith, "an integral part of the business carried on." The reconciliation between that phrase and the need for some degree of regularity is, as I see it, as follows: there are some transactions which are clearly integral parts of the businesses concerned, and these should be held to have been carried out in the course of those businesses; this would cover, apart from much else, the instance of a one-off adventure in the nature of trade where the transaction itself would constitute a trade or business. There are other transactions, however, such as the purchase of the car in the present case, which are at the highest

---

[60] *Ibid.* at p. 853. See also Neill L.J. at p. 859.
[61] See above.
[62] See below: another Trade Descriptions Act case.
[63] *Ibid.* at p. 854.

only incidental to the carrying on of the relevant business; here a degree of regularity is required before it can be said that they are an integral part of the business carried on and so entered into in the course of that business.

One final comment of Dillon L.J. is worthy of note—that if the husband had personally bought the car for domestic and business use, it would have been difficult to argue that he was not dealing as consumer; so it would be anomalous to reach a different result just because it was bought by a company for such use by its two directors: "It could well be appropriate to pierce the corporate veil and look at the realities of the situation."[64]

While we should applaud this interpretation by the Court of Appeal on the grounds that it assists the consumer, the quirky and unexpected effect on the supplier seems to have been overlooked. The use of such a written exemption clause is a *criminal* offence.[65] Yet how can a supplier know whether the customer has regularly bought such goods in the past or whether they are an essential part of the business? Such a careful examination of the extrinsic circumstances of the sale would be impracticable.

The trader's solution to this danger is perhaps to be found in the wording of the defendants' exemption clause in the *R & B Customs Brokers* case: "If the buyer deals as consumer within section 12 of the Unfair Contract Terms Act 1977 . . . the buyer's statutory rights are not affected" by the following clause. Thus the trader gets it both ways, but leaves the buyer in doubt as to whether or not he is protected by the 1977 Act.

Returning to section 3 itself, let us assume that the client does deal as consumer. In that case section 3 applies the reasonableness test in three cases. The first case is where the trader is in breach of contract and the clause excludes or restricts his liability (for example, liability limited to £100). The second case is where the trader relies on a clause giving him the right to render a contractual performance substantially different from that which was reasonably expected of him. This would apply to a condition on a theatre ticket whereby "the management reserve the right to alter the performance of any member of the cast." In the case of holidays the section would apply to a clause like the one in *Anglo-Continental Holidays Ltd.* v. *Typaldos Lines (London) Ltd.*[66] "Steamers, Sailing Dates, Rates and Itineraries are subject to change without notice." The final case covered by section 3 is where a contractual term gives the trader the right to offer no performance at all. It

---

[64] *Ibid.* at p. 855.
[65] Consumer Transactions (Restrictions on Statements) Order 1976, *post*, p. 274. On the other hand the *R & B* construction would help the supplier if it were applied to *him* because the conditions of merchantable quality and fitness (*ante*, pp. 44 and 53) would not then be implied.
[66] [1967] 2 Lloyd's Rep. 61.

would seem that this provision is wide enough to cover the so-called "force majeure" clause which is very common in practice. It may provide that "the seller shall not be liable for non-delivery if delay is caused by strikes, lockouts or other acts beyond the seller's control." Even a clause giving the right of cancellation might be caught by this provision.[67]

One final comment may be made: if a trader tenders a performance substantially different from that "reasonably expected of him", can the clause which allows him to do so ever be reasonable? The question of reasonableness is considered later[68] but it might be reasonable if it formed part of an arm's-length business contract between two traders where the trader attacking the clause had exactly the same provision in his own standard terms.

(c) Implied terms

Sale of goods. In Chapters 2, 3 and 4 we examined the terms implied by sections 12–14 of the Sale of Goods Act 1979. Until 1973 the parties had complete freedom to exclude these obligations, because section 55, as it appeared in the original Sale of Goods Act 1893, provided that "where any right, duty or liability would arise under a contract of sale by operation of law it can be modified or varied by express agreement or by the course of dealing between the parties or by usage if the usage be such as to bind both parties to the contract." This provision was radically altered by the Supply of Goods (Implied Terms) Act 1973 and the controls introduced by that Act are substantially re-enacted by section 6 of the Unfair Contract Terms Act. There are three basic rules:

(i) The conditions and warranties in section 12 (right to sell) can *never* be excluded.

(ii) Where the buyer deals as consumer (*ante*, p. 131) the conditions under sections 13 (description), 14 (quality and fitness) and 15[69] can never be excluded. Hence they are often called the consumer's "inalienable rights."[70]

(iii) Where the buyer does not deal as consumer, a clause excluding or restricting the obligations referred to in (ii) above will only be valid if it satisfies the test of reasonableness.

Despite section 6 a limited amount of "contracting out" is permitted by the sections themselves. Thus it will be recalled that under section

---

[67] See Law Commission Report No. 69, para. 146.
[68] *Post*, p. 139.
[69] This relates to sales by sample.
[70] Such an exemption clause, if written, is a criminal offence: *post*, p. 274.

12 the seller can agree to transfer only such title as he himself has, while section 14(2) allows the seller to avoid liability for merchantable quality in relation to particular defects by drawing the buyer's attention to those defects before the contract is made.

Private sales. As an exception to the general rule section 6 also applies where the seller is *not* acting in the course of a business.[71] This is unlikely to be of great practical importance because private sales are unlikely to contain exemption clauses and because, in relation to quality and fitness, there will nothing to exclude.[72] Thus the significance of this provision is limited to attempts to exclude liability under sections 13 and 15.

Hire-purchase. The terms implied into a hire-purchase agreement are virtually identical to those set out above[73] and section 6 of the 1977 Act controls them in exactly the same way as it does for sale of goods.

Other supply contracts.

(1) *Title.* It will be recalled that under a contract of hire the owner does not give an undertaking that he has a "right to sell."[74] An exemption clause controlling the more limited form of title undertaking in hire cases is controlled by the reasonableness test and is not subject to an outright ban.[75] Subject to this, the controls are virtually identical to those for sale and hire-purchase.[76]

(2) *Description, quality, fitness, sample.* It will also be recalled that the implied terms are virtually identical to those implied in sale and hire-purchase cases.[77] Similarly, the controls on exemption clauses contained in section 7 of the 1977 Act are virtually identical to those in section 6—the exemption clause is void where the buyer "deals as consumer" and it is controlled by the reasonableness test in other cases.

If a consumer has a complaint relating to a "work and materials" contract (*e.g.* repairs to a car) it will be necessary to find out what was wrong. If the *materials* themselves were defective, there may be strict liability and an exemption clause would be void under section 7. If, however, the complaint relates to the *work* itself, the supplier will only be liable if negligent and a clause excluding this liability will be subject

---

[71] See s.6(4).
[72] *Ante*, p. 42.
[73] *Ante*, pp. 24, 40 and 55 and *post*, p. 345.
[74] *Ante*, p. 24.
[75] Act of 1977, s.7(4).
[76] *Ibid.* s.7(3A).
[77] See Supply of Goods and Services Act 1982, *ante*, pp. 24, 40 and 55.

to the "reasonableness" test under section 2(2) (or totally void if the negligence causes personal injury or death).

(d) *Guarantees and indemnities*

(i) **Indemnities.** Perhaps one of the most unreasonable clauses imaginable was formerly used by a ferry company. It said in effect "if we (the company) incur liability to a third party in carrying your car, you (the consumer) must indemnify us—even if the liability was entirely due to our negligence." Not surprisingly such clauses are now controlled—perhaps the only surprising thing is that they are not subject to an outright ban. Section 4(1) provides that:

> A person dealing as consumer cannot by reference to any contract term be made to indemnify another person (whether a party to the contract or not) in respect of liability that may be incurred by the other for negligence or breach of contract, except in so far as the contract term satisfies the requirement of reasonableness.

The section is expressed to apply not only where the liability is to a third party but also where the liability is to the consumer himself. This could give rise to a conflict between section 4 and other provisions of the Act. To take an extreme case let us suppose that goods are supplied subject to the following condition: "the buyer agrees that if the goods are unmerchantable the buyer will indemnify the seller against any damages and costs payable under any judgment obtained by the buyer against the seller." This would be an attempt to exclude the non-excludable condition of merchantable quality[78] and would be totally void under section 6 (read with the definition of exemption clause in section 13). It would be extraordinary if the clause were saved by section 4.

(ii) **Guarantees.** As already stated,[79] it was common practice for a manufacturer's guarantee to exclude negligence liability. The result was that the consumer, who thought that he was gaining valuable rights, was in effect giving up valuable rights in return for something which might well be far less valuable. Lord Denning M.R. severely criticised such clauses in *Adams* v. *Richardson*.[80] In ringing tones he declared that "If he wished to excuse himself from liability he should say so plainly. Instead of heading it boldly 'GUARANTEE' he should head it 'NON-GUARANTEE'; for that is what it is."

Fortunately, this type of problem should now be a thing of the past in respect of the supply of goods because section 5 of the 1977 Act nullifies a large number of such clauses. By section 5(1):

---

[78] *Ante*, p. 135.
[79] *Ante*, p. 61.
[80] [1969] 1 W.L.R. 1645, 1649.

In the case of goods of a type ordinarily supplied for private use or
consumption, where loss or damage—
- (a) arises from the goods proving defective while in consumer use; and
- (b) results from the negligence of a person concerned in the manufac-
    ture or distribution of the goods,

liability for the loss or damage cannot be excluded or restricted by
reference to any contract term or notice contained in or operating by
reference to a guarantee of the goods.

It will be appreciated that this provision neatly sidesteps the
question of whether a guarantee is a contract; even if it is not a contract
the purported exclusion notice will be ineffective to exclude liability
for negligence.

Two further points should be noted. First, goods are "in consumer
use" when a person is using them, or has them in his possession for use,
otherwise than exclusively for the purpose of a business.[81] Thus if the
buyer of a car and his wife are injured while the car is being used on a
combined business-and-pleasure journey, section 5 would control a
clause in the guarantee excluding liability for the manufacturer's negligence. Presumably, if the negligence resulted in damage to property,
the "outright ban" in section 5 would override the section 2 "reasonableness" test. Secondly, the section does not apply as between the
parties to a contract under or in pursuance of which possession or
ownership of the goods passed.[82] In such cases the consumer would
have the benefit of section 2 in relation to negligence and sections 6 and
7 in relation to the implied terms.

(e) *Misrepresentation*

Exemption clauses relating to misrepresentation have been controlled since the passing of section 3 of the Misrepresentation Act
1967. Section 3 is redrafted by section 8 of the Unfair Contract Terms
Act so that it now reads as follows:

If a contract contains a term which would exclude or restrict—
- (a) any liability to which a party to a contract may be subject by reason
    of any misrepresentation made by him before the contract was
    made; or
- (b) any remedy available to another party to the contract by reason of
    such a misrepresentation,

the term shall be of no effect except in so far as it satisfies the requirement
of reasonableness as stated in section 11(1) of the Unfair Contract Terms
Act 1977; and it is for those claiming that the term satisfies that requirement to show that it does.

The first point to notice here is that the law is to be found in section 3

---

[81] s.5(2)(a). See the example given by Neill L.J. in *R & B Customs Brokers Co. Ltd.* v.
U.D.T. (*ante*, p. 132) at p. 858.
[82] s.5(3).

of the Misrepresentation Act 1967 (as amended) and not in the Unfair Contract Terms Act. It follows that the section applies to all contracts (including those excluded from the Unfair Contract Terms Act) and it is not confined to "business liability."

What type of clauses are caught by section 3? Some cases are obvious: "The purchaser shall have no right to rescind this agreement." or "All liability for misrepresentation is excluded." On the other hand a clause stating that "no employee of the company has any authority to make representations on the company's behalf" might be effective.[83] Finally, the contract might state that "although every care has been taken the vendors do not warrant the accuracy of these particulars and the purchaser shall not rely on them." If such a clause were upheld it would severely limit the scope of section 3. It seems that if the other party does rely on the incorrect particulars there will be a misrepresentation and the clause will be treated as an exemption clause to which section 3 applies.[84]

The reasonableness test

Sections 2, 3, 4, 6, 7 and 8 all refer to the reasonableness test. The concept is not a new one; it has applied to misrepresentation since 1967 and it has applied to the implied terms of sale of goods and hire-purchase since 1973. Section 11 draws a distinction between contractual clauses and non-contractual notices. In the case of contract the person claiming that the term is reasonable must prove that:

> the term shall have been a fair and reasonable one to be included having regard to the circumstances which were, or ought reasonably to have been, known to or in the contemplation of the parties when the contract was made.[85]

Thus the critical date is the date of the contract. For example, a limitation of damages clause which was reasonable at the date of the contract will be upheld even though by the time of the hearing it has become hopelessly inadequate by reason of inflation or by reason of the plaintiff's loss being far greater than expected.

Two more preliminary points are significant. First, the question is whether the clause is reasonable in relation to *this particular contract*[86]; so what may be reasonable between a supplier and one customer may be unreasonable as against another, *e.g.* because there may be equality of bargaining power in the one case and not in the other. This poses insuperable problems for the draftsman of standard form contracts in

---

[83] See *Overbrooke Estates Ltd.* v. *Glencombe Properties Ltd.* [1974] 1 W.L.R. 1335.
[84] *Cremdean Properties Ltd.* v. *Nash* (1977) 244 E.G. 547 (C.A.).
[85] s.11(1).
[86] See Slade L.J. in *Phillips Products Ltd.* v. *Hyland* [1987] 2 All E.R. 620, 628.

that there is no such thing as a clause which is fair and reasonable in itself.

Secondly, the burden of proving reasonableness lies on the supplier; if the factors are evenly balanced, the customer wins the day.[87] This point equally applies to non-contractual notices and disclaimers where the party relying on the notice (*e.g.* a building society surveyor with a potential liability to a house buyer in the tort of negligence) must show that:

> it should be fair and reasonable to allow reliance on it, having regard to all the circumstances obtaining when the liability arose or (but for the notice) would have arisen.[88]

The role of the courts

The concept of reasonableness appears in many areas of the law, including unfair dismissal, matrimonial finance, negligence claims and housing. In relation to the Unfair Contract Terms Act Lord Bridge has emphasised that more than one view is possible. His Lordship dealt with the matter as follows:

> "The court must entertain a whole range of considerations, put them in the scales on one side or the other and decide at the end of the day on which side the balance comes down. There will sometimes be room for a legitimate difference of judicial opinion as to what the answer should be and where it will be impossible to say that one view is demonstrably wrong and the other demonstrably right. It must follow in my view that when asked to review such a decision the appeal court should treat the decision with the utmost respect and refuse to interfere unless it is satisfied that it proceeded upon some erroneous principle or was plainly and obviously wrong."[89]

Guidelines

In any case involving the reasonableness test the court has a wide discretion and must consider all the relevant circumstances; presumably if the matter comes to court the defendant should be advised to plead the facts on which he relies to support his claim of reasonableness. Schedule 2 contains a non-exhaustive list of guidelines. They apply only to contracts controlled by sections 6 and 7, *i.e.* to supplies of *goods* where the plaintiff's claim relies on the *statutory implied* terms.[90] They are as follows:

---

[87] *Ibid.* See s.11(5).
[88] s.11(3).
[89] *George Mitchell (Chesterhall) Ltd.* v. *Finney Lock Seeds Ltd.* [1983] 3 A.C. 803, 816. The case was actually decided on an earlier Act but this does not reduce its importance in the present context.
[90] Where the customer is "dealing as consumer," any exemption clause is void in respect of such terms: *ante*, p. 135.

"Guidelines" for Application of Reasonableness Test

The matters to which regard is to be had in particular for the purposes of sections 6(3), 7(3) and (4), 20 and 21 are any of the following which appear to be relevant—

(a) the strength of the bargaining positions of the parties relative to each other, taking into account (among other things) alternative means by which the customer's requirements could have been met;

(b) whether the customer received an inducement to agree to the term, or in accepting it had an opportunity of entering into a similar contract with other persons, but without having to accept a similar term;

(c) whether the customer knew or ought reasonably to have known of the existence and extent of the term (having regard, among other things, to any custom of the trade and any previous course of dealing between the parties);

(d) where the term excludes or restricts any relevant liability if some condition is not complied with, whether it was reasonable at the time of the contract to expect that compliance with that condition would be practicable;

(e) whether the goods were manufactured, processed or adapted to the special order of the customer.

The first three are of greatest importance. Their broad effect is that if a business buyer, large enough to have bargaining power and with a choice of potential suppliers with whom to negotiate terms, enters into a disadvantageous contract with his eyes open, the court is unlikely to rush to his assistance. The buyer has made a bad bargain and is stuck with it. In contrast if the buyer is a small business, perhaps dealing with a monopoly or with a supplier who belongs to a trade association whose members all adopt standard terms, and does not notice or cannot understand the exemption clause, then the court will probably strike down the clause. He had no real choice—it was a "take it or leave it situation."[91]

No specific guidelines are laid down by the Act in other cases, *e.g.* contracts for *services*, breach of *express* terms. However, by analogy the courts are applying similar guidelines with particular emphasis on the first three criteria—bargaining power, choice and knowledge. Lord Wilberforce stressed the significance of the first factor in the pre-Act case of *Photo Production Ltd.* v. *Securicor Transport*[92]:

"After this Act, in commercial matters generally, when the parties are not of unequal bargaining power, and when risks are normally borne by insurance, not only is the case for judicial intervention undemonstrated,

---

[91] See Slade L.J. in *Phillips Products Ltd.* v. *Hyland* at p. 629 (clause was one of 43 clauses of plant hire company's terms—used by all members of trade association—not fair and reasonable).

[92] [1980] A.C. 827. The respondents' employee purposely set fire to a factory which he was supposed to be guarding!

but there is everything to be said, and this seems to have been Parliament's intention, for leaving the parties free to apportion the risks as they think fit and for respecting their decisions."

The size of print would also be relevant,[93] and a clause is unlikely to be upheld if it is out of line with a Code of Practice adopted by the trader's trade association.[94] The continued use of immensely wide exemption clauses could influence the court in a case involving the reasonableness test. It may be that a clause that "the seller can cancel this agreement in the event of strikes, etc." should now be redrafted so as to give a mutual right to rescind. It is also possible that the contract will specify the factors on which the trader relies in support of his claim of reasonableness. Perhaps we may see the emergence of a dual price contract, £X with full responsibility or £Y without it. We may also see "split clauses"—different clauses dealing with consequential loss, limitation of liability and time limits for claims.

Limitation of damages clauses

A number of small traders (including travel agents) felt very uneasy about the possibility of having to meet very large claims and accordingly Lord Hailsham introduced a new clause which is now section 11(4). It reads:

> Where by reference to a contract term or notice a person seeks to restrict liability to a specified sum of money, and the question arises (under this or any other Act) whether the term or notice satisfies the requirement of reasonableness, regard shall be had in particular ... to—
> (a) the resources which he could expect to be available to him for the purpose of meeting the liability should it arise; and
> (b) how far it was open to him to cover himself by insurance.

This provision, if it is ever litigated, is bound to cause problems. Do the "resources" of a sole trader or partner include his private assets? How far afield does he have to search to find insurance? What happens if the premium would destroy or seriously reduce the commercial viability of the transaction? In spite of such difficulties it seems likely that the courts will view more sympathetically a limitation clause whereby the supplier accepts some liability than an exclusion clause where the supplier in cavalier fashion refuses to contribute at all to the consumer's loss.[95]

The emerging case law

The Act was passed to give added protection to consumers who are

---

[93] In *The Zinnia* [1984] 2 LL.L.R. 211, Staughton J. was minded to strike down the clause on the grounds of (a) size of print and (b) complexity of language. Unfortunately counsel for the party attacking the clause did not raise this point!

[94] *Post*, p. 150.

[95] See *Ailsa Craig Fishing Co.* v. *Malvern Fishing Co., ante*, p. 125, n. 35.

nearly always in a weak bargaining position. The early cases confirm that the Act is having its desired effect[96]; indeed the writers are not aware of a single post-Act consumer case in which an exemption clause has been upheld as reasonable. The following cases show the attitude of the courts.

The first is the latest and most important in that the House of Lords has now given valuable guidance on the operation of the reasonableness test in a consumer context.

Smith v. *Bush*.[97] We have already discussed the first point in this case, namely, whether the surveyors owed a duty of care in tort to the house buyers. To this question the House of Lords unanimously answered "yes."

We now turn to the second point—were the surveyors able to prove that their exemption clauses satisfied the reasonableness test? Again the House of Lords answered the question in favour of the consumers: "no." The judgments of Lords Griffiths and Templeman deserve careful examination. Although Lord Griffiths admitted that it is impossible to draw up an exhaustive list of relevant factors for the court to take into account when applying the reasonableness test, the following extract is crucial for the legal adviser, since he states that these matters should "always be considered"[98]:

"(1) Were the parties of equal bargaining power? If the court is dealing with a one-off situation between parties of equal bargaining power the requirement of reasonableness would be more easily discharged than in a case such as the present where the disclaimer is imposed on the purchaser who has no effective power to object.
(2) In the case of advice, would it have been reasonably practicable to obtain the advice from an alternative source taking into account considerations of costs and time? . . .
(3) How difficult is the task being undertaken for which liability is being excluded? When a very difficult or dangerous undertaking is involved there may be a high risk of failure which would certainly be a pointer towards the reasonableness of excluding liability as a condition of doing the work. A valuation, on the other hand, should present no difficulty if the work is undertaken with reasonable skill and care. . . .
(4) What are the practical consequences of the decision on the question of reasonableness? This must involve the sums of money potentially at stake and the ability of the parties to bear the loss involved, which, in its turn, raises the question of insurance. There was once a time when it was considered improper even to mention the possible existence of insurance cover in a lawsuit. But those days are long past. Everyone knows that all prudent professional men carry insurance, and the

---

[96] The lack of case law strongly suggests that many traders are more prepared to settle out of court than to subject their clauses to the searchlight of the "reasonableness" test.
[97] [1990] 1 A.C. 831, *ante*, p. 32.
[98] At p. 858.

availability and cost of insurance must be a relevant factor when considering which of two parties should be required to bear the risk of a loss."

The effect of this decision is that an exemption clause will not protect a surveyor "in respect of a dwelling house of modest value." The position may well be different where other types of property are valued "such as industrial property, large blocks of flats or very expensive houses,"[99] where it may be reasonable for the mortgagee's surveyor to exclude or limit his liability to the buyer/mortgagor.

Spencer v. *Cosmos Air Holidays*.[1] We discussed this case earlier in relation to damages for distress. The agreement contained a clause whereby the defendants excluded responsibility "for any injury, death, loss or damage which is caused by any negligence of the management or employees of an independent contractor." Without amplifying their reasons the Court of Appeal brushed the clause aside. In the words of Farquharson L.J.:

"It does not bear upon the case at all and does not affect the plaintiff's contractual rights against the defendants—namely, to enjoy 14 days' holiday in the hotel she had chosen."

Walker v. *Boyle*.[2] During negotiations for the sale of V's house V told P that there was no boundary dispute. This was an innocent misrepresentation which induced P to buy. On discovering the facts P refused to proceed whereupon V claimed specific performance in reliance on Condition 17 of the National Conditions of Sale, which provided that "no misdescription can annul the sale." P claimed that the clause was unreasonable. His claim was upheld. Even though the clause was in the National Conditions of Sale it was not the product of negotiation between the parties or their representatives.

South Western General Property Co. v. *Marton*.[3] Property was described in auction particulars as "long leasehold building land." The particulars failed to disclose major restrictions on development and the buyer would never have bought the property if he had known of this. The particulars provided that the statements were made without responsibility and were statements of opinion only and that it was up to intending purchasers to satisfy themselves as to their accuracy. Croom-Johnson J. held that the clause failed to pass the reasonableness test. His Lordship laid great stress on the vital importance of the matter for

[99] *Per* Lord Griffiths, at p. 859.
[1] *The Times*, December 6, 1989 (C.A.), *ante*, pp. 114–115.
[2] [1982] 1 W.L.R. 495.
[3] (1982) 263 E.G. 1090.

the buyer. He also pointed out that many prospective buyers attended auctions at short notice and would obviously have no opportunity to check out the particulars.

Waldron-Kelly v. *British Railways Board.*[4] The defendants agreed to carry the plaintiff's suitcase on "owner's risk" terms. It disappeared. The Board sought to limit their liability by a clause which referred only to the weight of the suitcase (£27) and not to its value (£320). The learned county court judge held that the clause failed to pass the reasonableness test.

Woodman v. *Photo Trade Processing Ltd.*[5] Mr. Woodman took photographs of a friend's wedding. The shop to which he brought the film for development displayed a notice limiting liability to the cost of the film. The film came back ruined and Mr. Woodman (with the support of the Consumers' Association) claimed that the clause was unreasonable. The learned county court judge upheld his claim and awarded £75 for disappointment.

The message from these cases comes through loud and clear—the standard form, non-negotiated consumer exemption clause has had its day. In none of the above cases was there any negotiation; in none of them was the clause expressly brought to the consumer's notice. In only one of them (*Waldron-Kelly*) did the consumer have anything in the nature of a choice. Indeed the most significant feature of the *Woodman* case was the fact that, in the opinion of the learned judge, it should have been possible for the processing industry to offer their customers a choice—£X with limited liability or £Y with greater liability.[6] The Act may therefore mark a return to basic principles of contract law by destroying the fiction that a party has "agreed" to a term if (1) he did not know it was there, (2) even if he had known, he would not have understood it and (3) even if he would have understood it, he would never have agreed to it without modification.

3. Other Controls

Although the Unfair Contract Terms Act 1977 is by far the most important example of statutory control of exemption clauses there are many other statutory controls. One of these, section 3 of the Misrepresentation Act 1967, has already been mentioned. There are also a number of other Acts relating to the carriage of passengers by public

---

[4] [1981] 3 Cur. Law 33.
[5] *Times Business News*, June 20, 1981; *Which?*, July 1981.
[6] The so-called "two-tier system."

service vehicle, rail and air (see particularly the Carriage by Air Act 1961). Other examples include the Occupiers' Liability Act 1957, the Defective Premises Act 1972, the Road Traffic Act 1972, the Consumer Credit Act 1974 and the Solicitors Act 1974. For a summary of the statutory controls readers are referred to *Chitty on Contracts*, Vol. I, paras. 1022–1028.

4. THE EEC DIMENSION

The effect of the European Community will be felt within a year or so in this area and attention is drawn to the draft EC Directive on Unfair Terms in Consumer Contracts considered in Chapter 24.

Chapter Nine

"HOW DO I ENFORCE MY RIGHTS?"

In the previous chapters we have considered the consumer's rights and remedies and attempts to exclude them or to cut them down. We come now to the all-important question—how can the rights be enforced? The lawyer tends to think immediately of court proceedings but in this branch of the law the courts should only be used as a last resort—if only because the cost of proceedings may exceed the amount in dispute.

Scheme of this chapter

A short introduction will be followed by an examination of the codes of practice prepared in consultation with the Office of Fair Trading—one of the most important developments in the consumer field in recent years. This will be followed by a section dealing with county court proceedings and arbitration, including some comments on legal aid and assistance.

1. HOW TO START

The obvious first step is to contact the supplier. If the client himself does not receive satisfaction he might call in to see his solicitor, Citizen's Advice Bureau, Consumer Advice Centre or the Trading Standards Department (Consumer Protection Department) of the local authority. A letter sent to the head office, or to the managing director, might produce results. Alternatively, a member of the staff of the Trading Standards Department might make a telephone call or visit the shop to see what the shop has to say. These Departments are anxious to adopt a neutral role—to play the part of conciliator rather than advocate. They do, of course, compile lists of complaints[1] and forward them from time to time to the Office of Fair Trading.

If the shopkeeper himself is not co-operative the next step might be to contact his trade association. This is especially relevant if he is a member of a trade association with a code of practice approved by the O.F.T. This is considered below.

Mention must also be made of the press, both local and national, radio and television. Many of these bodies have someone dealing with

---

[1] See table on pp. 155–158 for an analysis.

consumer matters and if they are satisfied that the consumer has had a raw deal they will print or publish a story about it. Needless to say they will take great care to get their facts right because damages for defamation can be very high.

2. CODES OF PRACTICE

A. *Introduction*

One method of improving standards of business practice across the board is to introduce legislation (with criminal sanctions) on such matters as trade descriptions and safety.[2] A second method is to use subordinate legislation under Part II of the Fair Trading Act 1973 to correct particular abuses.[3] A third method is to leave it to the different sectors of commerce to put their own houses in order by the introduction of voluntary codes of practice by the various trade associations. The development of voluntary codes can be regarded as the most significant contribution which the Fair Trading Act 1973 has made to the protection of individual consumers and accordingly it may be useful to examine this topic in some detail.

Section 124(3) of the Fair Trading Act places a duty upon the Director General to encourage associations "to prepare, and to disseminate to their members, codes of practice for guidance in safeguarding and promoting the interests of consumers." To date 28 codes have been negotiated with the O.F.T. including cars, electrical appliances, travel agents, shoes, laundries and cleaners, mail order trading and furniture. A complete list of the codes is given in the following table; the names of the sponsoring trade associations and the relevant addresses are set out in Appendix 2.[4]

Operative from	Code
1974	AMDEA (Association of Manufacturers of Domestic Electrical Appliances): Principles for Domestic Electrical Appliance Servicing.
1975	ABTA (Association of British Travel Agents): Codes of Conduct.
1975	Electricity Boards in England and Wales: Domestic Electrical Appliance Servicing.
1975	VBRA (Vehicle Builders and Repairers Association): Code of Practice for Vehicle Body Repair (Motor Car and Caravan Sector).
1975	Scottish Electricity Boards: Domestic Electrical Appliance Servicing.

---

[2] See *post*, pp. 193 *et seq.*
[3] *Post*, pp. 269 *et seq.*
[4] *Post*, p. 415.

1976   RMI (Retail Motor Industry Federation Ltd.):
             SMTA (Scottish Motor Trade Association):
             SMMT (Society of Motor Manufacturers & Traders):
             Code of Practice for the Motor Industry.

1976   NAMSR (National Association of Multiple Shoe Repairers):
             Society of Master Shoe Repairers:
             Code of Practice for Shoe Repairs.

1976   TSA (Textile Services Association Ltd.):
             Code of Practice for Domestic Laundry and Cleaning Services.

1976   FDF (Footwear Distributors Federation):
             Code of Practice for Footwear.

1976   RETRA (Radio, Electrical and Television Retailers' Association (RETRA) Ltd.):
             Code of Practice for the Selling and Servicing of Electrical and Electronic
             Appliances.

1977   MOPA (Mail Order Publishers' Authority):
             Code of Practice.

1978   Furniture Industry Code of Practice.

1978   MOTA (Mail Order Traders' Association):
             Catalogue Mail Order Code of Practice.

1979   N.A.F.D. (National Association of Funeral Directors):
             Code of Practice on Funerals.

1979   Photographic Industry Code of Practice.

1979   Post Office:
             Code of Practice for Postal Services.

1980   DSA (Direct Selling Association Ltd.):
             Direct Selling Code of Practice.

1981   GGF (Glass and Glazing Federation):
             Code of Ethical Practice.

1984   Motorcycle Code.

1987   FHA (Finance Houses Association):
             Code of Practice.

1988   CCTA (Consumer Credit Trade Association):
             Code of Practice.

1988   NCCF (National Consumer Credit Federation):
             Code of Practice.

1988   CCA (Consumer Credit Association of the United Kingdom):
             Code of Practice.

1989   LPFA (London Personal Finance Association Ltd.):
             Code of Practice.

1989   British Holiday and Home Parks Association Ltd.:
             National Caravan Council:
             Code of Practice for Letting Holiday Caravans.
             Code of Practice for Selling and Siting Holiday Caravans.

1989   SMMT (Society of Motor Manufacturers and Traders):
             Code of Practice for Mechanical Breakdown Insurance Schemes.

1989   BDMA (British Direct Marketing Association Ltd.):
             Direct Marketing Code of Practice.

Advantages?

Whether voluntary codes are to be preferred to legislation is a matter of debate. The advantage from the point of view of industry is that traders are allowed to police themselves, but this in turn may be disadvantageous to the consumer. It is clear from the results of monitoring exercises undertaken by the O.F.T. that, predictably, not every member of a trade association honours its code and, more surprisingly, not every trade association checks to ensure that its members follow the code.[5]

Another serious disadvantage of relying on voluntary methods is that, even if all members of an association comply with their obligations, the rogues in the trade may well not be members. This is particularly true of the motor trade. The Director General must then turn to other weapons in his armoury, *e.g.* seeking an assurance under Part III of the Fair Trading Act 1973[6] or refusing a credit brokerage licence under the Consumer Credit Act 1974.[7]

However, some advantages can be cited. (1) Legislation would necessarily be of a general nature and inappropriate for setting precise standards for a particular industry, for example, pre-delivery inspections of cars or service calls within three days for electrical appliances. (2) Businessmen are more likely to comply with their own optional rules than with statutory obligations imposed against their will. (3) Codes can be improved by re-negotiation; for example, the A.B.T.A. Code was amended after a year to include surcharges and overbooking, both common causes of complaint. (4) Codes go beyond the existing law, in recommending practices which impose on suppliers obligations or restrictions not otherwise attaching to them, and thus consumers' rights are enhanced; for example, the laundry code bans all exemption clauses.[8] (5) The opportunity for conciliation and arbitration affords a cheap and quick mode of resolving disputes instead of taking action in the courts.[9]

Sanctions for non-compliance

An increasingly important question is how codes of practice should be enforced. We have seen that by no means all members of a trade association adhere to the recommended practices. The most obvious

---

[5] On monitoring and other aspects of codes see Woodroffe, "Government Monitored Codes of Practice in the United Kingdom," (1984) 7 *Journal of Consumer Policy* 171; Cranston, *Consumers and the Law* (2nd ed.), pp. 31–42.

[6] *Post*, p. 282.

[7] *Post*, p. 313.

[8] *Post*, p. 168. For further examples, see Woodroffe, n. 5.

[9] For an assessment of trade arbitrations, see *Simple Justice*, National Consumer Council (1979), especially pp. 71–82.

way is for the trade association itself to deal with recalcitrant members. Some associations have very wide powers, including fines and expulsion, and are prepared to use them, as can be seen from the activities of the Retail Motor Industry Federation and the Association of British Travel Agents. In contrast sponsors of the Footwear Code and the Society of Motor Manufacturers and Traders can do little more than apply the "club" threat of social ostracism by their peers.

It has been suggested, optimistically in our view, that an individual consumer may enforce a code against a member of a trade association by claiming that a breach of contract occurs when a trader fails to comply with a practice, on the basis that the contract includes an implied term that the trader will comply with the code. In view of the limitations placed by the courts on implied terms such a plea is unlikely to succeed.[10] Of course, it is possible for a consumer to incorporate a code expressly when making the contract, but it would be unrealistic to expect all but the most enthusiastic and well-informed consumers to remember to refer to the point in their conversation when taking a pair of shoes for repair or a car for servicing. In contrast, the criminal law may provide a more hopeful route following the 1980 decision in *Shropshire County Council Trading Standards Department* v. *Telford (Vehicles) Ltd.*: a motor dealer was convicted by the Wrekin Magistrates' Court of an offence under section 14 of the Trade Descriptions Act 1968 for failing to comply with the Motor Industry Code of Practice although stating that he subscribed to the code.[11]

On the assumption the self-regulation is not as effective a method of controlling business suppliers as it should be, two solutions have been canvassed to give teeth to the codes. The less ambitious proposal is to amend section 34 of the Fair Trading Act 1973[12] so as to extend the definition of "unfair" beyond contravention of criminal and civil duties to include non-compliance with a code of practice endorsed by the O.F.T. The virtue of such a change would be that the codes would then be made to apply to *all* members of a particular trade, not merely those who choose to join a trade association.

A much more far-reaching proposal, embracing the extension of section 34, is to impose on traders a statutory "duty to trade fairly." A suggestion to this effect was put forward by Sir Gordon Borrie, the Director General of Fair Trading, in a lecture[13] discussing the self-regulatory system of advertising control:

"The duty not to publish misleading advertisements could be seen as a

---

[10] The narrow "business efficacy" test in *The Moorcock* (1889) 14 P.D. 64. See *Cheshire, Fifoot and Furmston's Law of Contract* (11th ed.), p. 137.
[11] Unreported. See Lawson, *The Supply of Goods and Services Act 1982*, p. 131.
[12] *Post*, p. 283.
[13] Published in "Laws and Codes for Consumers," [1980] J.B.L. 315, 324.

precursor to a more general statutory duty to trade fairly in consumer transactions, a duty which would not be enforceable apart from sectoral or general retail codes of practice giving it practical expression. Such codes could be prepared by the D.G.F.T. after consultation with relevant trade associations and the codes would need to be given some form of ministerial or parliamentary approval before becoming effective. Under Part III of the Fair Trading Act, persistent breaches of the new statutory duty could result in the D.G.F.T. requiring assurances or court orders and, of course, the new statutory duty would be applicable to all traders and not just those who belong to the relevant trade associations. It would be for consideration whether the statutory duty should also be enforceable: (i) by local authorities, or by the D.G.F.T. in respect of individual breaches, and (ii) by an individual seeking damages against a trader. In both cases the court would presumably need to look at the codes for guidance when interpreting the duty."

The Office of Fair Trading floated the idea in March 1982 in "Home Improvements: a discussion paper" and followed this up in 1986 with a discussion paper "A General Duty to Trade Fairly." However, it is no surprise to discover that such a bold approach was not welcomed by industry in a period of free market economy. Indeed the Government's policy at the time can be discerned from the titles of two White Papers—"Lifting the Burden" and "Building Business ... not Barriers."[14] In the end the Director General reluctantly admitted in "Trading Malpractices"[15] that "the original proposals were over-ambitious in aiming in one provision both to raise trading standards generally and to improve the prospects for consumer redress" and came down in favour of a complete overhaul of Part III of the Fair Trading Act 1973.

Conciliation

All the codes provide conciliation procedures and most provide arbitration as a last resort. Generally conciliation procedures conform to the same pattern (suggested in Part 1 of this chapter). A dissatisfied customer should first bring his complaint to the attention of the manager, partner, proprietor or director of the business. If the complaint is not resolved, then it may be appropriate to seek the help of a trading standards officer, Consumer Advice Centre or Citizens' Advice Bureau. If the complaint relates to new goods, the customer may agree to the manufacturer being brought in. Where the dispute is still not settled and the trader is a member of a trade association, the customer should ask the association to conciliate. No charge is made for this service. However, it should be remembered that the association may appear to the consumer, rightly or wrongly, to lack impartiality and to be prejudiced in favour of its own member. If only for this reason an

---

[14] Cmnd. 9571 (1985) and Cmnd. 9794 (1986) respectively.
[15] O.F.T. (July 1990), para. 1.5. The arguments for and against the general duty appear on p. 21.

opportunity to put the matter before a truly independent arbitrator is valuable where conciliation fails.

Arbitration

Where a code provides for arbitration, the customer is required to pay a fee of under £40, often refundable where the claim is upheld: this is the limit of his liability where the arbitration is on the basis of "documents only." The fee does not cover the full cost of arbitration, the balance being borne by the trade association. The arbitrator will usually be appointed by the Chartered Institute of Arbitrators. Normally the arbitration will be "documents only." The expense of attended oral arbitrations is so great that they are discouraged both by the associations and by the Director General, for the purpose of writing arbitration procedures into the codes is to provide an inexpensive and quick adjudication of the dispute.

To discover how well these arrangements for settling consumer disputes were working the O.F.T. undertook a review in 1980 and published the conclusions in December 1981 in "Redress procedures under Codes of Practice."[16] The main conclusions of the report are that arbitration should be on a documents-only basis, as litigants desiring an attended hearing may always resort to the County Court arbitration scheme; that in view of the concern expressed about the slow progress of both the conciliation and arbitration stages, targets should be set of a maximum of three months for the conciliation stage dealt with by the trade associations and 12 weeks for the arbitration stage if undertaken by the Institute of Arbitrators (28 days for the claimant to submit details of the claim, 28 days for the respondent to reply and 28 days for the arbitrator to deliver his decision); that arbitrators should always give reasons for their decisions; and that a standard scale of arbitration fees be introduced. As a result a new "model" arbitration scheme was developed by the Institute in consultation with the O.F.T. who in September 1983 made it known that the Institute would be contacting various trade associations with a view to amending their arbitration arrangements accordingly.

Publicity

It is not enough to introduce legislation and codes of practice to bolster the consumer in his perpetual confrontation with the business world. Such rights are useless unless he knows of them and can exercise them. To ensure that as far as possible the consumer is made aware of his rights the Director General is empowered by section 124(1) to

[16] A recent N.C.C. report on research into arbitration schemes, *Out of Court*, is discussed by Goriely in (1991) N.L.J. 535.

arrange for the publication "of such information and advice as it may appear to him to be expedient to give to consumers" in so far as the matters fall within his duties under section 2(1).[17] From its inception the O.F.T. has enthusiastically exercised this power. Numerous pamphlets and posters are available free of charge to inform the consumer and trader of their respective rights and obligations in respect of goods or services.

It is difficult to know whether the effect of consumer legislation and the codes has been to improve the quality of goods and services. The statistics given in the Director General's Annual Reports show a fairly steady level of complaints running at about 600,000 a year for the last dozen years. For example, there were 591,000 complaints in 1976–77 and 623,000 in 1988–89, an increase of five per cent. However, the Annual Report for 1990 reveals that roughly 700,000 complaints were received by trading standards departments and Citizens Advice Bureaux in 1989–90; whether this marked upward trend will continue remains to be seen. What is significant is that "research indicated that only about one per cent. of people who felt they had a reason to complain about goods or services" sought the help of these agencies.[18] Clearly the reported figures are merely the tip of the iceberg.

The main culprits have regularly been motor vehicles, furniture and floor coverings, household appliances and electronic equipment, and clothing and footwear, with motor vehicles usually taking the gold or silver medal. One area giving an increasingly major headache to consumers, particularly in view of the large sums of money usually at risk, is home improvements (including double glazing); it will be interesting to see whether it has overtaken clothing and footwear in 1989–90 to take fourth place in this unenviable "top of the pops."

The tables on the following four pages analyse consumer complaints for the year ending September 30, 1989. They are taken from the 1989 Annual Report of the Director General of Fair Trading.

---

[17] *cf.* the Consumer Credit Act 1974, s.4, which imposes a *duty* on the Director to disseminate information and advice about the operation of the Act and the credit facilities available to the public.

[18] O.F.T. Press Release June 27, 1991. The 1990 Annual Report was published a few days before this book went to press and so its details and tables could not be included.

Consumer complaints recorded by Trading Standards Departments and advice agencies for year ending September 30, 1989

| | *Trading practices* | | | | | | | | | | |
	1	2	3	4	5	6	7	8	9	Total	Group total
Group A: House, fittings and appliances											
AA House construction	1,204	204	886	364	48	139	121	39	1	3,006	
AB Home maintenance, repairs, improvements	18,232	4,234	6,955	5,676	358	799	1,791	499	41	38,585	
AC Double glazing products and installation	8,167	1,896	3,525	3,554	292	533	248	103	21	18,339	
AD Furniture (other than upholstered or nursery) etc.	10,326	3,330	3,687	2,461	202	509	434	573	113	21,635	
AE Upholstered furniture	12,186	2,168	2,552	4,326	169	377	209	909	110	23,006	
AF Carpets and other floor coverings	9,797	1,310	2,255	2,568	134	310	298	54	40	16,766	
AG Radio, TV, other electrical recreational goods	22,034	3,574	6,978	7,998	824	894	792	638	182	43,914	
AH Major appliances	22,386	2,274	6,027	6,544	573	726	725	2,610	157	42,022	
AJ Repairs to domestic appliances and equipment	4,085	2,058	1,319	2,336	35	317	661	56	18	10,885	
											218,158
Group B: Other household requirements											
BA Food and drink	7,636	653	14,269	320	51	191	2,898	7,628	73	33,719	
BB Domestic solid and liquid fuel	449	79	595	53	9	26	86	93	—	1,390	
BC Gas	709	158	603	252	157	118	382	93	9	2,481	
BD Electricity	514	92	728	195	181	168	607	37	10	2,532	
BE Water	210	31	203	63	55	34	126	49	1	772	
BF Postal services	166	114	141	46	4	31	33	7	10	552	
BG Telecommunications	1,242	212	973	399	136	143	608	17	11	3,741	
BH Laundry and dry cleaning	4,371	465	576	760	18	161	81	15	3	6,450	
BJ DIY materials and tools	1,738	275	1,615	346	15	87	363	276	13	4,728	
BK Textiles and soft furnishings	3,103	569	1,349	644	32	123	164	168	53	6,205	
BL Other household goods/services	6,350	1,450	4,123	1,334	80	378	855	1,514	179	16,263	
											78,833

(cont.)

					Trading practices							Group total
		1	2	3	4	5	6	7	8	9	Total	
Group C: Personal goods and services												
CA	Clothing and clothing fabrics	21,456	2,245	9,616	5,721	216	1,703	958	554	737	43,206	
CB	Footwear	9,275	383	1,792	2,254	29	323	220	101	62	14,439	
CC	Footwear repair	290	52	70	81	8	10	13	3	1	528	
CD	Pharmaceutical products, medical services, etc.	2,785	307	1,413	588	22	126	372	250	47	5,910	
CE	Toilet articles, perfumery, hairdressing	1,965	198	1,515	252	18	72	213	526	32	4,791	
CF	Jewellery, silverware, clocks and watches	6,791	1,488	2,590	1,840	38	415	317	51	183	13,713	
CG	Prams and other nursery furniture	3,391	249	651	895	29	75	71	1,140	31	6,532	
CH	Tobacco and smokers' requisites	276	49	299	58	1	28	85	116	1	913	
CJ	Other personal goods and services	8,430	3,048	12,071	1,262	260	879	1,153	841	569	28,513	
												118,545
Group D: Other services												
DA	Banking	460	88	516	138	336	165	145	15	6	1,869	
DB	Hire and credit—unsecured	512	176	2,201	499	6,582	385	428	63	97	10,943	
DC	Credit secured by a first mortgage	82	16	253	32	395	28	31	1	3	841	
DD	Other secured credit	171	28	369	39	1,083	48	50	5	6	1,799	
DE	Ancillary credit business	295	78	983	208	2,548	186	128	15	51	4,492	
DF	Life insurance	288	118	559	114	35	152	90	6	4	1,366	
DG	Non-life insurance (including holiday insurance)	1,627	1,053	3,309	1,092	185	1,286	893	27	15	9,487	
DH	Other financial services	277	121	791	64	295	119	121	10	11	1,809	
DJ	Legal services	356	96	524	69	59	54	163	14	8	1,343	
DK	Estate agency	290	84	860	63	38	120	148	2	2	1,607	
												35,556 (cont.)

				Trading practices						Total	Group total
		1	2	3	4	5	6	7	8	9	Total	

Group E: Transport

		1	2	3	4	5	6	7	8	9	Total	Group total
EA	Rail (including U/ground), bus and coach travel	452	115	308	91	9	72	86	28	6	1,167	
EB	Air travel	200	142	299	70	6	66	64	4	1	852	
EC	Other public transport (including taxis and ferries)	317	112	286	44	5	42	124	16	1	947	
ED	New motor cars	4,461	359	2,142	1,128	448	230	216	72	5	9,061	
EE	Secondhand cars	31,415	1,707	18,113	6,656	1,049	1,038	621	895	29	61,523	
EF	Car repair and servicing	8,068	936	2,505	2,127	37	342	940	108	5	15,068	
EG	Motorcycles and motorcycle repairs	2,145	161	614	465	62	67	91	90	12	3,707	
EH	Bicycles and bicycle repairs	1,697	130	364	439	18	53	55	292	20	3,068	
EJ	Other vehicles and repairs	1,530	183	616	339	22	61	103	206	7	3,067	
EK	Petrol and oil	1,033	97	2,550	69	14	39	478	459	—	4,739	
EL	Other vehicle running costs	4,468	684	2,353	944	36	324	469	508	45	9,831	113,030

Group F: Leisure

		1	2	3	4	5	6	7	8	9	Total	Group total
FA	Package holidays in the UK (including travel)	755	172	829	120	10	105	99	15	5	2,110	
FB	Package holidays overseas (including travel)	2,583	774	3,647	460	46	426	420	47	13	8,416	
FC	Travel agents	217	183	397	81	12	63	64	6	1	1,024	
FD	Holiday caravans renting and caravan sites	661	64	383	132	21	109	63	14	1	1,448	
FE	Time-sharing in the UK and overseas	495	81	2,810	83	100	159	41	39	8	3,816	
FF	Sports goods, toys, games and camping equipment	4,099	927	1,914	731	43	158	259	4,703	180	13,014	
FG	Books, newspapers and magazines	573	528	2,025	213	91	149	282	64	382	4,307	
FH	Entertainment, catering and accommodation	1,256	450	2,744	215	66	300	441	396	30	5,898	
FJ	Other recreational goods and services	6,393	2,369	5,808	1,335	83	387	540	1,113	364	18,392	58,425

Goods and services: Group	A	B	C	D	E	F	Total
Citizens Advice Bureaux	13,678	3,073	6,040	3,812	5,537	2,389	34,529
Local Authorities	203,204	75,071	111,757	31,504	106,580	55,644	583,760
Other	1,276	689	748	240	913	392	4,258
Total	218,158	78,833	118,545	35,556	113,030	58,425	622,547

Trading practices

1 Defective goods or substandard service
2 Non-delivery of goods and delay or non-completion of services
3 Selling techniques; misleading claims, representations or advertisements (price, quality etc.); presentation of goods or services (availability, labelling, packaging); lack of information
4 Difficulty in getting faults put right
5 Credit practices
6 Unfair terms and conditions including attempts to restrict liability
7 Price complaints not falling in 3 or 4 and complaints about 'value' not falling in 1 or 3
8 Health or safety
9 Mail order/prepayments

B. *Particular codes*

Caravans

There are two codes drawn up in 1989 by the British Holiday and Home Parks Association Ltd. and the National Caravan Council. One relates to letting and the other to selling and siting holiday caravans, *i.e.* permanently sited on a park licensed for recreational use (not mobile homes).

Letting Code

The Code of Practice for Letting Holiday Caravans is binding on members of the two trade associations mentioned above whether they let caravans owned by themselves (as park owners) or as agents for individual owners. The main provisions are these:

(i) **Caravan park.** Facilities must be well maintained with staff available during all reasonable hours.

(ii) **Caravans.** They must be in good condition with equipment functioning properly. They should be thoroughly cleaned between hirings. Breakages should be replaced and gas supplies maintained.

(iii) **Information.** The owner must send to enquirers detailed information on park facilities, caravan type and equipment (the appendix to the code gives a suggested list), and the charges, including additional charges for swimming pools, insurance, etc.

(iv) **Disclaimers.** If they are void under the Unfair Contract Terms Act 1977, they are prohibited; otherwise they are apparently permissible. Thus a disclaimer relating to damage or loss of property caused by negligence may be introduced into the contract.

(v) **Complaints.** The four-step procedure is adopted with free conciliation and low cost, documents-only arbitration.

Selling and Siting Code

The Code of Practice for Selling and Siting Holiday Caravans is to protect the caravan owner in his dealings with the park owner.

(i) **Sale of caravan.** If a prospective buyer will have to sub-let his caravan as a condition of the purchase, he must be given detailed information before making a binding contract.

(ii) **Written agreement.** On the first purchase of a caravan the buyer must be offered a written agreement to occupy a pitch for at least five years, renewable annually for another five years provided the caravan is in good condition. A long list is set out of the contents of the agreement, including the right of the caravan owner to assign the pitch to a buyer of the caravan: such resale of caravans is specially provided for.

(iii) **Complaints.** The procedures are the same as in the Letting Code.

Cars

There are three codes:

> Code of Practice for the Motor Industry
> VBRA Code of Practice for Vehicle Body Repair
> Mechanical Breakdown Insurance.

The Motor Industry Code[19]

This Code was drawn up by the RMI, SMTA and SMMT. It governs the conduct of manufacturers, importers, distributors and retail dealers. It covers the supply of new and used cars, petrol, parts and accessories, and servicing and repair. Its main provisions are set out below.

(i) **New cars.** Dealers should carry out the pre-delivery inspection required by the manufacturer and give a copy of the P.D.I. check list to the customer. Order forms must make clear the total price payable to put the car on the road and their conditions must be fair and reasonable.

(ii) **Manufacturers' warranties.** The dealer should draw the terms of the warranty to the attention of the consumer. It must state that it does not adversely affect the consumer's remedies against the seller.[20] Transfer to subsequent owners should be allowed. The consumer may take the car to any franchised dealer for rectification work. An extension of the warranty period may be given when the car has been off the road for an extended period or if faults worked upon during the warranty period recur later.

(iii) **Used cars.** Dealers are reminded of their obligations under the Sale of Goods Act 1979, *e.g.* merchantable quality. Guarantees should not purport to take away the consumer's rights and should state that

---

[19] Revised in 1981. Reproduced in Appendix 1, *post*, p. 383.
[20] This is a statutory requirement under the Consumer Transactions (Restrictions on Statements) Order 1976: see p. 277.

they are in addition to his statutory rights.[21] Copies of information provided by previous owners about the car's history should be passed on, *e.g.* service records. Advice is given about odometers and the form of disclaimer to be used; the dealer should not quote the recorded mileage, unless satisfied that it is accurate. (These aspects are of great practical importance under the Trade Descriptions Act 1968.)[22]

One major effect of the 1981 revision of the code was to strengthen the requirements about pre-sales inspections. The dealer should inspect the car before sale in accordance with an approved checklist, which should be completed and displayed in a prominent place in the car[23]; a copy should be given to the customer. (This is generally known as a PSIR—pre-sales information report). Unfortunately only a minority of RMI members complied with this procedure, prompting the Director General of Fair Trading to make the following remarks in his 1982 Annual Report:

> "It seems to me in this instance that self-regulation is *not* an effective substitute for law and that if, as I believe, there is a strong case for consumers to be given a more detailed written description of a used car at the point of sale than is common now, it must be done by law and therefore be enforceable against *all* used car dealers. Yet again, it is a matter of 'horses for courses' and legal regulation, not self-regulation, is the appropriate 'horse' in this race. I am fortified in my view by support from the Motor Agents' Association [now RMI] and the Institute of Trading Standards Administration. The consumer needs more protection in this area of activity and I hope that, on further consideration, the Minister of State for Consumer Affairs will make the displaying of a PSIR a legal requirement."

As yet hope, like virtue, is its own reward.

(iv) **Servicing.** A distinction is drawn between quotations and estimates. Although the words "estimate" and "quotation" generally have no well-settled legal meaning, the code clarifies their use in this context: "an estimate is a considered approximation of the likely cost involved whereas a quotation constitutes a firm price for which the work will be done." A firm quotation should be given for a major repair. Where estimates are given, it should be made clear that they are only estimates. In either case the VAT position must be clarified. If a charge is to be made for the estimate, for example, to cover dismantling, the consumer should be notified in advance. No attempt should be made to exclude liability for loss or damage to cars or contents[24] which must be adequately protected and insured. Repairs must be guaranteed for a specific mileage or period.

[21] See n. 19.
[22] *Post*, p. 208.
[23] Such a system operates in a number of states of the U.S.A., *e.g.* Wisconsin.
[24] Such a clause would be controlled by the Unfair Contract Terms Act 1977, ss.2 and 3: see *ante*, p. 130.

(v) **Complaints.** The following procedure is laid down:

(a) First refer the complaint to the dealer, addressing it to a senior executive, director, partner or proprietor.

(b) If it relates to a new car warranty and the dealer does not resolve the matter, contact the manufacturer direct.

(c) If no satisfactory solution is reached, write to the relevant trade association provided the dealer is a member:
new car warranty claim—SMMT
dealer in Scotland—SMTA
dealer in the rest of the United Kingdom—RMI.

Although the code imposes no time limits except a "reasonable time," the RMI have prescribed their own limit by requiring complaints to be made in writing within three months of the complaint arising. It is arguable that the operation of this bar is itself in breach of the code. In any case, three months is too short a period, bearing in mind the weeks of discussion and correspondence which may elapse before the consumer loses patience with the dealer and considers alternative steps.

(d) The trade association will try to effect a settlement between the consumer and its member.

(e) If conciliation fails, the association will arrange for arbitration. The arbitration will normally be "documents only"—the cost of oral arbitration is prohibitive. A written award is made which is enforceable in the courts.

(f) Consumers must be advised that they may sue in the courts instead of choosing arbitration. However, as arbitration is cheap and reasonably quick, it is preferable in the usual, run-of-the-mill case involving comparatively small sums.

(vi) **Monitoring.** The trade associations are required to analyse all complaints about the code or other matters referred to them for conciliation or arbitration. The Office of Fair Trading has also carried out several exercises to monitor the working of the code, the most recent being undertaken in 1986.

Body repairs[25]

The VBRA Code of Practice for Vehicle Body Repair is, as its title discloses, much more limited in its scope than the Motor Industry Code. In cases where the garage is a member of both the RMI and VBRA, the consumer will have the benefit of both codes where a body repair is involved.

---

[25] Revised 1989.

In many respects it is similar to the Motor Industry Code. It deals with estimates. Guarantees must last for at least 12 months or 12,000 miles, whichever occurs first, and be transferable to later owners.

The complaints procedure follows the pattern outlined earlier. First complain to the trader, who should readily give access to senior management. Next seek the advice of a trading standards officer, C.A.B., Consumer Advice Centre, etc. Then proceed to use the VBRA Conciliation Service under which the complaint may be referred to an independent examiner appointed by the Institute of Automotive Engineer Assessors. No fee is payable for conciliation. If a member has ceased trading and cannot comply with a settlement recommended under the Conciliation Service, the association will pay up from its "Contingency Fund" established for the purpose.

As a last resort arbitration is available. It is normally on a "documents only" basis.

Mechanical breakdown insurance

The latest of the codes relating to vehicles was drawn up by the SMMT in 1989: The Code of Practice for Mechanical Breakdown Insurance Schemes.

(i) **Insurers.** All schemes must be underwritten by an authorised insurer or Lloyds.

(ii) **Policy.** The policy must be written as a direct contract between the consumer and the insurer (in some schemes it has been difficult to work out against whom the consumer's rights lie). The documentation given to the consumer must set out the contractual position in a clearly displayed panel.

(iii) **Assignment.** The policy should be transferable to a subsequent owner, if the insurer approves: the latter point weakens this aspect.

(iv) **Claims.** Consumers must be informed of the result of their claims within seven days, if possible. Of course, quick payment is another matter!

(v) **Complaints.** Conciliation is provided by the SMMT. However, after that the consumer will have to turn to the relevant insurance body, depending on the type of insurer, *e.g.* the Lloyd's Consumer Enquiries Department. Ultimately the Insurance Ombudsman or Personal Insurance Arbitration Service may be called to arbitrate. The code's appendix gives details of the various insurance bodies.

Credit

There are five Codes of Practice relating to credit which were adopted between 1987 and 1989. They contain virtually identical provisions and so will be explained together. They regulate the business operations of the following associations:

Finance Houses Association
Consumer Credit Trade Association
National Consumer Credit Federation
Consumer Credit Association of the U.K.
London Personal Finance Association.

In broad terms the codes require the associations' numerous members to comply with legislation and to conduct their businesses with integrity. The following obligations are noteworthy at a time when thousands of debtors are finding it difficult to cope with their financial commitments.

(i) *Plain English*

In pursuance of the desirable trend of wording documents so that they are readily intelligible, all communications and agreements should be in plain English.

(ii) *Credit brokers*

A member must satisfy itself that credit-brokers have integrity and competence. Clearly it is in the interest of creditors to vet such intermediaries carefully, if only as a matter of self-interest, *e.g.* in view of their possible liability under section 75 of the Consumer Credit Act 1974.[26]

(iii) *Ability to repay*

A frequent criticism of moneylenders is that they tempt the improvident into borrowing more than they can afford. The codes state that members must not pressurise customers into loans which they may find difficult to repay. Before granting credit they should take "all reasonable steps . . . to discover the existing commitments of the consumer." Particular care should be taken in relation to young applicants.

(iv) *Complaints*

Conciliation is available as a first resort, after the chief executive of the member has considered the complaint. Then the usual documents only arbitration comes into play.

Direct marketing

Two codes cover the various activities described as "direct marketing":

---

[26] *Post*, pp. 342–343.

The Association of Mail Order Publishers Code of Practice (MOPA Code).
The BDMA Direct Marketing Code of Practice.

The MOPA code is the earlier dating from 1977. In 1989 these Associations jointly drew up a code, but adopted a separate version for each as there are some minor differences to suit the individual constitutions of the two bodies.

As the meaning of "direct marketing" is not self-evident we give the explanation set out in Annex 2 of each code:

> **Marketing** comprises the whole range of activities in providing the public with goods and services. **Direct Marketing** has the same broad function except that it requires the existence and maintenance of a database of information to record names of customers, actual and potential; and to provide the means for continuing direct communication with the customer. It may take place where the buyer responds to the seller's advertisement in a newspaper, on television or on the radio, or by postal advertising; it may take place when the seller contacts the buyer—direct selling; it may take place when the buyer contacts the seller and places an order by post; it may take place where the advertiser makes use of a mailing list.

This includes mail order selling as the name of the MOPA code indicates. This code is the narrower in scope in that it is confined to the supply of books and records, *e.g.* by book clubs, the Reader's Digest.
Two other codes should be borne in mind in this area of activity:

> The MOTA Code relating to *mail order* catalogue trading[27];
> The DSA Code relating to *party plan* selling.[28]

Both are discussed below.

As the MOPA and BDMA codes are so similar, we shall deal with them together and pick out just a few features of these lengthy, 46-page documents.

(i) *Samples*

Samples of goods, including bespoke or made-to-measure goods, should be available for public inspection.

(ii) *Free gifts and prizes*

In view of the prevalence of these inducements, special rules are set out concerning free gifts, premiums, prize draws and competitions: the last two items have special appendices devoted to them.

---

[27] *Post*, p. 174.
[28] *Post*, p. 166.

(iii) *On approval*

If goods are offered on "free" approval or trial, return postage and carriage must be refunded.

(iv) *Prepayments*

The name and address of the member must be given. Orders must normally be despatched within 28 days of receipt of order.

(v) *Club schemes*

There are special rules for club schemes (*e.g.* book clubs) and for a continuing series with an open-ended commitment.

(vi) *Collectables*

Advertisements for facsimiles of swords, antique guns, etc., or other "collectibles" (*sic*), where emphasis is placed on their scarcity or aesthetic quality, are dealt with in an appendix.

(vii) *Telephone selling*

Guidelines on telephone marketing appear in an appendix.

(viii) *Complaints*

The BDMA has its own free conciliation service, but no arbitration scheme. The MOPA code is supervised and monitored by the Mail Order Publishers' Authority (MOPA) under an independent chairman, not by the Association itself. MOPA has a free conciliation scheme and arrangements for arbitration by the Chartered Institute of Arbitrators.

Direct selling

The Direct Selling Code of Practice was drawn up in 1980 by the Direct Selling Association in consultation with the Office of Fair Trading after an O.F.T. study had identified consumer problems arising out of party plan selling. It has only two pages.

(i) *Liability insurance*

Suppliers should have adequate public liability and product liability insurance and indemnify the hostesses against any claims arising out of such parties.

(ii) *Cancellation and deposits*

Members should not insist on payment in full when the order is placed. Customers are given a 14-day cancellation period; any deposit is then to be refunded. However, the customers may now be in a better position by reason of the Consumer Protection (Cancellation of Contracts Concluded away from Business Premises) Regulations 1987.[29]

(iii) *Copies*

A copy of the order should be given to the customer when it is placed. Copies of the code should be available for inspection.

(iv) *Complaints*

There is an unusual complaints procedure which is an improvement on the usual conciliation procedure, although no arbitration scheme is included. Initially a complaint will be referred to the Association. If it is not resolved by the chief executive of the member company within 21 days, it passes to the Association's Code Administrator, a post created especially for this purpose. Unlike arbitration, however, if the customer is dissatisfied with the Administrator's decision, it is still open to him to seek redress in the county court. Failure by a member to comply with his decision could lead to expulsion from the DSA.

Double glazing

The home improvement sector has figured prominently in consumer complaints in recent years. Double glazing contractors appear to have been one of the main causes of dissatisfaction.[30] The Office of Fair Trading has identified the main problems as high-pressure salesmanship, delays in installation, unexpected price increases, lost deposits and poor workmanship. Accordingly a Code of Ethical Practice was introduced by the Glass and Glazing Federation in November 1981.[31]

(i) *Cancellation*

Whether or not credit is involved, a customer may cancel a contract. The code points out that the statutory rights must be notified to the customer: here again the 1987 Regulations should be considered.[32]

(ii) *Price*

If after placing an order a survey by the contractor reveals that additional work is required, thus increasing the price, the customer may cancel the contract with a refund of the deposit.

---

[29] See *ante*, p. 81.
[30] See table on p. 155.
[31] Revised 1988.
[32] See n. 28.

(iii) *Deposits*

A supplier taking deposits must be covered by the G.G.F. Deposit Indemnity Fund. If a member cannot carry out work for which a deposit has been taken, the G.G.F. will arrange for the work to be completed at a fair price or refund the deposit. This covers deposits up to £2,500.

(iv) *Quotations*

A written quotation should be given to a customer where the contract is negotiated away from business premises.

(v) *Quality and guarantees*

The material should conform to relevant B.S.I. and G.G.F. standards. The guarantee period should be clearly stated, although the code does not specify a minimum period.

(vi) *Delivery dates*

These provisions are not of much benefit to consumers. Although suppliers should quote a completion date, it is not to be of the essence of the contract unless otherwise agreed. If it is not met, the customer can give notice making time of the essence and the code itself provides that six weeks' notice "would be reasonable." (The customer could do this in any case, and at common law reasonable notice might be even shorter.[33]) At the end of the six weeks' period the customer may cancel "without penalty to the householder." Of course the customer should not be liable to the supplier, for the supplier himself has broken the contract by failure to complete on time! These rights must be set out in customers' contracts.

(vii) *Complaints*

The code has the normal complaints procedure including conciliation and low cost, documents only arbitration run by the Chartered Institute of Arbitrators.

Dry cleaners and laundries

The Code of Practice for Domestic Laundry and Cleaning Services was drawn up by the Textile Services Association which represents more than 75 per cent. of such traders in the United Kingdom.

(i) *Exclusion clauses*

Members will not exclude or limit their liability for negligence.[34]

---

[33] *Ante*, p. 92.
[34] See *ante*, n. 24.

They will reprocess free of charge any article which has been processed unsatisfactorily due to their fault. Where loss or damage is caused by fire or burglary, even though the trader is not negligent, compensation will be paid unless the customer has his own insurance cover; this goes beyond the supplier's legal liability for negligence.

(ii) *Prices*

A list of prices for standard articles should be displayed.

(iii) *Delay*

Where an article has been mislaid and not returned within a reasonable time, a reduction in the charge is recommended to compensate for the customer's inconvenience.

(iv) *Complaints*

The TSA has a Customer Advisory Service to whom unresolved complaints should be referred in writing. If the TSA considers that a laboratory test is necessary, this will be made free of charge; otherwise a fee is payable. Arbitration is not available.

Electrical goods

There are four codes:

RETRA Code of Practice for the Selling and Servicing of Electrical and Electronic Appliances.[35]
AMDEA Principles for Domestic Electrical Appliance Servicing.
Domestic Electrical Appliance Servicing by Electricity Boards.
Domestic Electrical Appliance Servicing by Scottish Electricity Boards.[36]

In the trade such goods fall into two categories: "white goods," *i.e.* domestic appliances, such as washing machines, refrigerators, cookers and toasters; and "brown goods" such as radios, televisions and stereo systems. All the codes cover white goods; only the RETRA code includes brown goods as well.

RETRA Selling and Servicing Code

RETRA is an association of retailers and represents thousands of shops. The code covers both the sale of goods and their servicing and repair. The following are some of its more important provisions.

---

[35] Reproduced *post*, p. 405.
[36] The last three codes were revised in 1984 to take account of recommendations made by the O.F.T.—see Bee Line Special No. 8 (1980), *Monitoring the Electrical Codes.*

(i) **Sale of goods.** Prices should be clearly indicated. Refunds are encouraged even where a customer has simply changed his mind and has no right to his money back. Where a retailer receives a deposit, he should indicate the delivery period and, if delivery is not made in time, offer the customer a refund.

A guarantee of new goods must be given, covering parts and labour for a minimum period of a year. This is additional to the buyer's rights under the Sale of Goods Act 1979 and under any manufacturer's guarantee. If the retailer cannot effect a repair within 15 working days from the date of notification of the defect, he should normally lend a similar item or, if this is impracticable, extend the guarantee period. Where a customer moves away, the guarantee should be transferred on request to a local retailer.

(ii) **Repairs and servicing.** The retailer should accept for repair goods sold by him but not necessarily other goods (*e.g.* bought from a rival discount shop?). Customers will be told the minimum service charge when they ask for service. Estimates should be offered in the case of major repairs. The code points out that quotations when accepted constitute a contract binding upon both parties. Customers are encouraged to return faulty goods to the workshop, which should be so organised as to be able to complete 80 per cent. of all repairs within five working days.

Where they request a visit, this should be made within three working days; if the repair cannot be effected then, it should normally be completed within a further 15 working days. (One is tempted to ask whether the association's aim of providing prompt and efficient after-sales service is fulfilled when it may take three weeks to repair such essential equipment as a washing machine or spin drier.) The retailer will guarantee repairs on products outside the normal guarantee period for three months for parts and labour.

(iii) **Life expectancy.** The code states that "most electronic equipment can be expected to last about seven years and in certain cases this period may be longer." Presumably "electronic equipment" means brown goods. It is arguable that this provides a guide as to the meaning of "merchantable quality" in this context, *i.e.* that the retailer will be liable if the goods prove to be beyond economic repair within that period.

No guide is given in respect of the life expectancy of domestic appliances. However, a table is included of the availability of functional parts after the date when production of the appliance ceases, which at least gives an indication of the durability of the appliances in the list. "Functional parts" are electrical and mechanical parts which are essential to the continued operation and safety of the appliance.

Small appliances.	5–8 years
Cleaners, direct acting space heaters, refrigerators and freezers, spin and tumble driers and wash boilers.	8 years
Cookers, dishwashers, washing machines.	10 years
Thermal storage space heating.	15 years

(iv) **Complaints.** The now familiar sequence is suggested. First, complain to the retailer or service agent. Next try the C.A.B., trading standards officer or Consumer Advice Centre. Finally, complain in writing to the Secretary of RETRA under its Conciliation Service. If he cannot resolve the dispute, it may be referred to the RETRA Conciliation Panel. No fee is payable. However, arbitration is not available. If conciliation is unsuccessful, the customer will have to resort to the courts.

AMDEA Servicing Code[37]

AMDEA is an association of manufacturers. The code covers only white goods. Its aim is to ensure that users of domestic appliances receive the same high standard of service whatever the source of the product and whether the service is provided directly by the manufacturer or indirectly by electricity boards, major retailers or specialised servicing organisations.

Its provisions are similar to the RETRA code, but there are some detailed differences, *e.g.* guarantees. The main improvements made in 1984 were: (1) the first home repair visit should be made within three working days "wherever possible"; (2) the customer should be notified of minimum charges at the outset and be given a written quotation on request; (3) repairs should be guaranteed for 12 months (except "small appliances," three months only)—previously no period was specified.

It improves on the RETRA code in one respect, namely by offering independent arbitration, not merely conciliation, for a "nominal fee." It is on a documents only basis. It covers only claims relating to the appliance itself and its servicing, not claims for personal injuries.

The Electricity Boards Codes[38]

There are two similar codes, the Electricity Boards Code, which covers England and Wales, and the Scottish Electricity Boards Code.

---

[37] See *ante*, n. 36.
[38] See *ante*, n. 36.

Each is concerned only with the servicing of domestic appliances; this is an odd limitation of their after-sales responsibilities in view of their sales including brown as well as white goods.

The codes have almost identical provisions to those in the AMDEA code except that all guarantees are for 12 months.

The aims of the codes are the same: (1) to offer service within an average of three working days at a reasonable cost; (2) to carry adequate stocks of spare parts and to ensure that functional parts are available throughout the reasonable life of the product; (3) to resolve complaints and to provide conciliation and simple arbitration.

The complaints procedure is as follows:

(i) Complain to the local manager of the Board's shop.
(ii) Next write to the manager of the Area Electricity Board.
(iii) Conciliation is the third stage. The independent Electricity Consultative Councils perform this role. There is one for each Area Board.
(iv) Finally independent arbitration may be sought.

Funerals

This is the ultimate and inevitable service provided for us all. The Code of Practice on Funerals was prepared by the National Association of Funeral Directors whose member firms are responsible for 80 per cent. of all funerals in the United Kingdom. The majority of complaints in this area concern charges. Complaints about the quality and workmanship of the product are increasingly rare, as cremations have gained popularity compared with burials in spite of the pollution problems.[39]

(i) *Advertising*

It should always be in good taste. (Presumably to guarantee the product "for life" would seem out of place!)

(ii) *Information*

Guidance should be given on registration of death and on social security benefits. A price list or leaflet should be available covering the range of services offered, including a "basic funeral,"[40] the elements of which are explained in the code.

(iii) *Estimates*

A written estimate should be given to the client as soon as is

---

[39] For an amusing (?) case on incomplete performance see *Vigers* v. *Cook* [1919] 2 K.B. 475: the agreed fee was not payable, as the priest refused to allow the coffin into his chapel for the burial service because of the smell and leakage from the decomposed body.

[40] The Code was revised in 1990 to change the "basic funeral."

practicable before the day of the funeral. The invoice should separate charges for the funeral from disbursements.

(iv) *Complaints*

The familiar procedure applies, including conciliation and low-cost arbitration.

Furniture

The Voluntary Code of Practice for Furniture was prepared by the following trade associations:

Branded Furniture Society
British Furniture Manufacturers Federated Associations
British Shops and Stores Association
National Bed Federation Ltd.

The code covers new household furniture: it does not include contract, garden or office furniture. The theme of the code is familiar.

(i) *Advertising*

Advertising must be clear and honest: misleading price offers are prohibited.

(ii) *Prices*

Prices charged are normally to be those ruling when the goods are offered for sale: if the retailer proposes to charge the price ruling at the delivery date, he must tell the customer so.[41]

(iii) *Delivery and deposits*

Delivery dates should be quoted in writing when deposits are taken, except when delivery should take place within one month. If a specific delivery date is not met, any deposit will be refunded on request.

(iv) *Labels*

A labelling system informs buyers of the basic construction of the furniture, the materials used and the finish; for example, solid wood, wood veneer or plastic laminate.

(v) *Complaints*

The usual procedure (in this and other codes usually called a "four-step" procedure) is adopted:

---

[41] This is the position at common law.

    (a) Contact the retailer, where "senior management must demon-
strate a high degree of interest and involvement in customer
problems"!

    (b) Seek help from a local consumer adviser.

    (c) Use the trade associations' conciliation service by writing to the
British Shops & Stores Association. Where an independent
examiner needs to be appointed to inspect the goods, a charge is
payable.

    (d) Finally independent arbitration is available, normally on a
"documents only" basis.

(vi) *Glossary*

The code contains a useful eight-page glossary of descriptive terms
for furniture and bedding, for example, antique, melamine-faced, zip
and link, latex foam, hair pad, glide and other terms of art.

Mail order[42]

This code was adopted by the Mail Order Traders Association in
1978. The MOTA code is concerned with buying goods from mail
order catalogues from such organisations as Great Universal Stores
and Littlewoods. The following are the main provisions.

(i) *Prices*

Prices must be V.A.T.-inclusive and it should be made clear
whether postage and packing are included.

(ii) *Cancellation*

Unless otherwise stated, goods should be dispatched "on approval"
giving the customer the right of cancellation within a period of at least
14 days after receipt of the goods. A full refund should then be made
promptly of the "purchase price," which presumably does not include
postage and packing.

(iii) *Damage in transit*

Where goods are damaged in transit the customer will receive a
replacement, if available, or otherwise a full refund, including carriage
costs.

(iv) *Delivery*

If a quoted delivery date is not met, the customer has a right to
cancel the order and obtain a full refund.

---

[42] The MOPA code also covers mail order, *inter alia: ante*, p. 165.

(v) *Complaints*

The usual four-step procedure is adopted, including conciliation and low-cost arbitration.

Motor cycles

This code was prepared by the RMI, SMTA, Motorcycle Retailers Association and Motor Cycle Association. It came into effect in October 1984.

Not surprisingly, bearing in mind some of its sponsoring associations, it bears a close resemblance to the Motor Industry Code.[43] Thus it deals with the sale of new and used motor cycles and spare parts as well as their servicing and repair. In view of the similarity we do not propose to spell out in detail its provisions, covering such matters as manufacturers' warranties, checklists and mileages on used motor cycles, quotations and estimates, and the availability of spare parts.

In two respects, however, this code differs from the car code. First, it deals specifically with delayed delivery and recommends that where a delivery date of a vehicle is given and not met, the buyer should be offered a refund. As regards repairs, it requires dealers to give an indication of the time to be taken, where possible, and to notify customers of the reason for any undue delay; in this respect the code goes beyond the dealers' legal duties.

Secondly, the code takes account of the fact that many buyers of motor cycles are young. It advises dealers to try to persuade first-time riders to choose a sensible type of vehicle and to undertake formal training. Where a minor cannot obtain his parents' consent to the purchase, dealers should promptly refund any deposit.

As usual under the codes, free conciliation is available together with arbitration procedures.

Photography

The Code of Practice for the Photographic Industry covers a wide range of sales and services relating to photography—the sale and repair of cameras and other photographic equipment, film processing and professional photographers. Eight trade associations[44] subscribe to the code. In view of the disparate activities covered by the code we shall highlight only its main points.

Sales of equipment

The retailer. Prices should be V.A.T.-inclusive. When a deposit is

---

[43] *Ante*, p. 160.
[44] See list in Appendix 2, *post*, p. 415.

taken on an order, the price will be the price at that date unless the contrary is made clear, and the delivery period should be made known in writing. (This suggests, wrongly, that when no deposit is taken on an order, retailers are at liberty to increase the price on delivery.)

Second-hand equipment should be given an adequate pre-sales inspection before sale and a suitable guarantee should be provided commensurate with the price and condition of the goods—a weak provision of doubtful value.

Manufacturers and importers. They will provide a guarantee covering parts and labour but no period is recommended. It should be transferable to new owners.

Repairs

Retailers. They should tell the customer how long a repair will take and give the consumer a written estimate (if the cost is known) or otherwise offer to obtain an estimate.

Manufacturers, importers and independent repairers. Repairs should normally be effected within 21 days. Manufacturers and importers should keep stocks of spares for a minimum period of five years following the last sale to the trade and for 10 years "for expensive equipment." A written guarantee should be given covering parts and labour, but again no period is recommended.

Film processing

The retailer should display his prices and give the name and address of the processing laboratory if requested. There is an ambiguous provision relating to compensation for films lost or damaged: "The consumer may be informed of the reasonable compensation offered." Presumably this means that the consumer should always be entitled to reasonable compensation, although he need not necessarily be informed of this right. This part of the code would be clearer, if it stated specifically that suppliers should not attempt to exclude or limit liability.

Where the customer has informed the retailer that a film has exceptional value or importance, the retailer should advise the laboratory, as "there may be a special service combined with higher prices." This provision was an important factor in *Woodman* v. *Photo Trade Processing*[45] in deciding whether the defendants' limitation clause was reasonable. Judge Clarke pointed out that it was not necessary for the defendants to set up their own special service of a higher quality at

[45] *Ante*, p. 145.

extra cost, but at least they should have informed their customers that such a service was available from other specialised laboratories:

> "In the light of the Code of Practice I reach the conclusion that some such form of two-tier system is not only reasonable but practicable."

Professional photography

The photographer should ensure that clients understand his fee structure and give them a statement of the completion date for the work. In contrast with the repairer it is clearly stated that he should not restrict his legal liability.

Complaints

Conciliation is undertaken by the appropriate trade association. An arbitration scheme is operated under the aegis of the Chartered Institute of Arbitrators, on a documents only basis.

Post Office

The Code of Practice for Postal Services was one of the two codes of practice introduced by the Post Office in 1979. The code is concerned with two matters—compensation and complaints.

(i) Compensation

If a letter or parcel is damaged or lost in the post, maximum compensation of £25 for ordinary mail and recorded delivery may be paid. As regards registered mail, customers have a legal right to compensation for lost or damaged packets, unless the Post Office can show that it was not negligent; here compensation increases in stages depending on the fee paid. For overseas post there are different types of service with different levels of compensation.

Compensation is assessed on the basis of the market value of the items lost. It does not cover consequential loss, although sympathetic consideration is given to requests for a refund of costs incurred in making enquiries about packets.

(ii) Complaints

Complaints are made in the first instance to the Customer Service Unit. The hierarchy is then the District Manager, the Post Office Users' National Council and, finally, a complaints panel drawn from members of the Chartered Institute of Arbitrators.

Shoes

There are two codes:

FDF Voluntary Code of Practice for Footwear.
Code of Practice for Shoe Repairs.

Sales

The Code of Practice for Footwear was drawn up by the Footwear Distributors Federation and sponsored by the FDF and five other associations concerned with the manufacture, distribution and retailing of footwear.[46] Its more significant features are these:

(i) **Prices.** These must be V.A.T.-inclusive. Reductions must be on the retailer's previous price or the manufacturer's recommended price. Deposits are returnable within seven days of an unmet delivery date.

(ii) **Exclusions.** Notices appearing to limit customers' rights are banned; for example, "No goods exchanged."[47]

(iii) **Fitting.** Measuring facilities should be available where children's shoes are sold.

(iv) **Labels.** The materials used in the uppers and soles and the country of origin must be marked on the shoes or labels.

(v) **Complaints.** There are no conciliation or arbitration procedures. However, an independent report may be obtained from the Footwear Testing Centre for a fee of a few pounds.

Perhaps the most important question is whether adherence to the code should be obligatory on all members of the sponsoring associations as is the case with all the other codes. As it is, if a member subscribing to the code fails to comply, he can be removed from the *scheme*, not from membership. Thus if he finds the code too burdensome, he shrugs it off. What disincentive is there to such an irresponsible attitude?

Repairs

Members of the National Association of Multiple Shoe Repairers and the Society of Master Shoe Repairers are governed by the Code of Practice for Shoe Repairs. It applies not only to their repair services but also to their sales: in the latter case its guidance is almost identical to the FDF code discussed above.

Its repairing provisions are similar to the Laundry Code explained earlier (they came into operation within two months of each other). In

---

[46] See list in Appendix 2, *post*, p. 415.
[47] This notice is not void, and so not illegal: *post*, p. 277.

the case of a complaint the associations are prepared to conciliate and to obtain an independent test report, apparently free of charge, but arbitration is not available.

Travel

The ABTA Code of Practice consists of two Codes of Conduct—the Tour Operators' Code and the Travel Agents' Code. It was first introduced in January 1975, but was amended a year later to take account of criticisms by the O.F.T. with regard to surcharges and overbooking. The latest 1990 revision makes further improvements in respect of surcharges and liability. All ABTA members (about 800 tour operators and 3,000 travel agents) are bound by the code.

Tour Operators' Code[48]

(i) **Brochures.** Considerable detail is set out in the code and in an appendix "Standards on Brochures" on the information required in brochures. For example, they must mention the arbitration scheme.

(ii) **Liability.** Times have changed significantly for the better. Gone are the days of disclaimers. Instead the code positively states that in respect of foreign inclusive holidays the contract must include a term "accepting responsibility for acts and/or omissions of their employees, agents, sub-contractors and suppliers."

(iii) **Cancellation and alteration.** Problems have often been caused by holidays being cancelled or rearranged by the tour operator at the last minute. Now a cancellation must not be made after the date when the balance of the price becomes due; but if the tour operator does cancel so late, he must pay compensation on "a rising scale . . . , *i.e.* the nearer to departure, the higher." If it occurs before that date, customers must be informed as soon as possible and offered a choice between a comparable alternative holiday and a full refund. Exceptionally it may be necessary to cancel as a result of force majeure as in the recent Gulf War: again a choice should be offered of an alternative holiday or a refund.

There are comparable provisions relating to material alterations to holiday arrangements. That is as it should be; for what is the difference to a customer with a holiday booked in Acapulco between cancelling it and offering him a holiday in Rhyl? In either case the holiday in Mexico is cancelled, either specifically or by a unilateral variation.[49]

---

[48] Reproduced, *post*, p. 393.
[49] Clauses excusing the tour operator in such cases would now be open to attack, if not reasonable, under the Unfair Contract Terms Act 1977, s.3.

(iv) **Overbooking.** Cancellation and alteration caused by overbooking of hotels, which may be the fault of the tour operator or the hotel management, are dealt with by separate provisions of the code. Where this occurrence is beyond the control of the tour operator, the code imposes different obligations depending on whether or not he knows of the overbooking before the departure of the customer. (1) If he is aware at that stage, he must immediately inform the customer and offer an alternative holiday or full refund as above. (2) If it is discovered only on arrival, the customer must be offered alternative accommodation plus "disturbance" compensation where the location or facilities are inferior.

The code proceeds on the basis that the tour operator has complied with the code by taking all reasonable steps to ensure that arrangements are not cancelled or altered, *i.e.* he can show that the overbooking is beyond his control. Presumably if he is at fault, the customer will be treated at least as generously.

(v) **Surcharges.** Surcharges resulting from fluctations in fuel costs or rates of exchange have been a major cause of discontent amongst holidaymakers. The code was strengthened in 1976 to prohibit such surcharges, unless made more than 30 days before departure. In 1988 a separate document, "Standards on Surcharges," was added to the code. Tour operators must now absorb increased costs up to two per cent. of the holiday price. If they exceed 12 per cent., the customer may cancel and obtain a refund.

(vi) **Building works.** Resorts which turn out to be more like a massive building site than a place for a holiday have been a common problem. The code requires the tour operator to notify customers when he becomes aware of building works which may "seriously impair the enjoyment of the holiday" and to offer them an alternative or their money back.

(vii) **Bonds.** The code notifies customers of the ABTA Scheme of Protection in Appendix 1. All tour operators must provide bonds or guarantees. If they become insolvent, ABTA will reimburse advance payments on prospective holidays and, where a holiday is in progress, try to arrange for the holiday to continue and return travel. This is of vital importance to consumers in the current economic climate with holiday companies failing all too frequently. Unfortunately this has proved so costly that ABTA may well cease to operate this scheme, and also curtail its conciliation role.[50]

If the customer has paid by credit card and so can claim against the

---

[50] See *The Times*, May 26, 1991.

credit card company under section 75 of the Consumer Credit Act,[51] ABTA may require the customer to pursue that claim first. This has caused problems, as some card companies take the opposite stance, wrongly in our view, by insisting on the customer claiming under the ABTA scheme first.

(viii) **Conciliation and arbitration.** ABTA will conciliate where there is a breakdown in communication or serious disagreement. Arbitration is available for disputes not settled by conciliation. Its availability should be included as a term of the contract in booking conditions so that customers are aware of this facility. It covers claims up to £1,500 per person or £7,500 per booking form.

"Documents only" arbitration is the norm. Originally attended hearings were available with the disincentive of the prospect of paying unlimited costs, but they were rare and expensive. Accordingly the O.F.T. recommended that attended hearings be withdrawn from the scheme[52]; this change took place in 1982.

Travel Agents' Code

The code relating to the conduct of travel agents covers such matters as ensuring that counter staff "carefully study travel brochures" to provide accurate information to customers (yet how often is the customer simply given an armful of glossy brochures and left to work out for himself which operator offers the best terms for children, off-peak holidays, etc.?); passing on immediately alterations to travel arrangements; advising on insurance, visas and health requirements; and generally acting as intermediaries in negotiations and disputes between the tour operators and the customers. So presumably it is now unheard of for an agent, having booked a holiday and earned his commission, to wash his hands of the matter and to tell the customer to go direct to the tour operator/supplier in case of difficulty!

The code also brings travel agents within the conciliation and arbitration procedures.

Disciplinary procedures

The ABTA Codes of Conduct give the association the power to investigate infringements of the codes and to impose penalties ranging from a reprimand to a fine or even termination of membership.

Relationship between the parties

The Law Commission Second Report on Exemption Clauses[53]

---

[51] See *post*, p. 342.
[52] A general recommendation to the same effect was made in *Redress procedures under Codes of Practice* (O.F.T., 1981).
[53] Law Commission Report No. 69 (1975), para. 126.

touches on an interesting and difficult question—the precise legal relationship between the customer and the other organisations involved in providing his holiday (the travel agent, the tour operator, the hotel and the airline).

It is suggested that generally the position is as follows. The customer makes only one contract with one legal entity—the tour operator.[54] This is effected via the travel agent who acts on behalf of the tour operator, not the customer. As the agent is known to be acting for a named principal, he will incur no personal responsibility to the customer on the contract.

The contracts for accommodation and transportation are made by the tour operator on his own account: only he is responsible to the hotelier and airline for these costs, even though the services will be supplied by them to the tour operator's customer. Clearly the tour operator is under an implied obligation to his customer to pay the necessary sums to the carrier and hotelier to enable the customer to travel and to stay at his chosen resort without additional payment; if he fails to do so, so that the carrier or hotelier refuse to provide their services to the customer unless the customer himself pays for them direct, the tour operator will have broken his contract with the customer and be liable in damages for such additional charges. Of course, if he does not provide the promised accommodation and facilities, he will be liable for breach of contract too,[55] as well as risking a prosecution under the Trade Descriptions Act 1968.[56]

Although the travel agent is not a party to the main holiday contract, he may incur liability to the customer in other ways. If he makes untrue statements to the customer about the subject-matter of the contract, for example, hotel amenities, he may be liable (1) in tort for deceit[57] or negligence[58] or (2) for breach of an implied warranty of authority if the statement is outside his actual or ostensible authority. Further, he may be in breach of a collateral contract between himself and the customer—a contract collateral to the main contract between the tour operator and the customer. Such rights against the travel agent are unlikely to be needed unless the tour operator is unable to meet his responsibilities under the main contract, e.g. because he is bankrupt or in liquidation.

EC Directive

The consumer's position will be considerably strengthened when legislation is passed to comply with the EC Directive on Package

---

[54] See Lord Scarman in *Wings Ltd.* v. *Ellis* [1984] 3 All E.R. 577, 586.
[55] See the cases cited *ante*, pp. 113–114.
[56] *Post*, p. 228.
[57] *Ante*, p. 96.
[58] *Ante*, p. 32.

Travel, Package Holidays and Package Tours (90/314/EEC). This was adopted by the EC Council in June 1990 and should be brought into force by the end of 1992.

Most of its provisions can already be found in the ABTA Code of Practice, which no doubt was revised recently to take account of the initiatives in Brussels. We shall comment on its main provisions, particularly where they improve the consumer's position.

Package. The Directive does not apply to travel or accommodation individually, *e.g.* a flight. Article 2 makes it clear that generally there must be a combination of these two elements to form a "package."

Organiser and retailer. These terms are used to identify the tour operator and travel agent.

Information. Article 3 contains a long list of information to be included in brochures, *e.g.* type of accommodation, itinerary, price and deposit. This is supplemented by Article 4 which requires the organiser or retailer to explain (*inter alia*) passport and visa requirements, and before the journey starts to provide information on transport connections and local representatives. The contract must contain the elements set out in the Annex to the Directive.

Prices. Article 4 also deals with price revisions. Prices are fixed unless the contract "states precisely how the revised price is to be calculated." Even so they are permitted only to allow for variations in transport costs, taxes or exchange rates. No increase can be made during 20 days before departure.

Cancellation and alteration. There are ABTA-like provisions entitling the consumer to cancel or to accept an alternative package, with compensation if appropriate, *e.g.* if the organiser "is constrained to alter significantly any of the essential terms"; force majeure excuses the organiser.

Liability for sub-contractors. The Directive takes the line in Article 5 that the organiser "is liable to the consumer for the proper performance of the obligations arising from the contract, irrespective of whether such obligations are to be performed by that organiser and/or retailer or by other suppliers of services." As explained above, this is already the legal position in the United Kingdom, but it does no harm for the Directive to spell this out. Unfortunately the Article goes on to permit limitation clauses which "shall not be unreasonable." This is the same as the U.K. position under section 3 of the Unfair Contract Terms Act 1977, but worse than under the ABTA Code which outlaws disclaimers.

One point for the consumer to watch is that complaints must be speedy—"on the spot" to the supplier of the services (*e.g.* hotel or airline) *and* in writing "at the earliest opportunity" to the organiser or retailer.

Assignment. One valuable new right is that the consumer may transfer his booking to a third party. However, Article 4(3) confines this possibility to a case where "the consumer is prevented from proceeding with the package." Will this cover only force majeure circumstances, *e.g.* illness? It would appear so.

Insolvency. We have already drawn attention to the problem of insolvency, which has underlined the value of booking a holiday with an ABTA tour operator to take advantage of its Scheme of Protection. Of course, not all businesses are members of ABTA. Further, it seems that because of its severe financial difficulties caused by the failure of many travel businesses in late 1990 and early 1991, ABTA's role will be substantially curtailed in respect of both its bonding scheme and its conciliation service.

Article 7 requires the organiser to prove that there is "security" for refunds or repatriation in the event of insolvency. How will the U.K. Government enact this provision? It may be that a licensing system will be introduced, supervised by the Civil Aviation Authority—the D.T.I. is still considering this matter. It seems likely that the CAA will take over the bonding activities of ABTA.

3. Arbitration

Cheap, quick, informal

Until 1971 the consumer, faced with a supplier who was not prepared to meet his proper obligations, had no choice but to abandon his complaint unless he was determined enough to launch himself upon the uncertain seas of litigation. The prospect of such action caused the consumer considerable anxiety for three principal reasons. First, it was likely to be expensive because of the level of legal fees. Secondly—and a related point—although he could save legal fees by conducting the case himself, he was put off playing the role of the litigant in person by the formality and complexity of court proceedings. Thirdly, he knew litigation to be a long-winded affair and was unhappy at having the doubtful outcome hanging over him like the sword of Damocles for years on end. Whatever the validity of these reasons—and many within the legal profession would say that they bear little resemblance to the realities of the situation—the layman saw access to his legal rights guarded by a Cerberus whose three heads were expense, delay and formality.

These disadvantages were particularly identified in the 1960s and fully discussed in "Justice out of Reach," the crucial report by the Consumer Council published in 1970. The report proposed a nation-wide system of small claims courts, drawing partly upon experience in North America. (It is salutary to recall that the county courts were set up in 1846 to provide the sort of forum being ardently espoused a century and a quarter later.) The nearest we have come so far to such a system incorporating the triple desiderata of cheapness, speed and informality are the voluntary small claims arbitration schemes intro-duced in Manchester (1971) and Westminster (1973) and the county court arbitration scheme inaugurated in 1973.[59] The Manchester and Westminster schemes, however, ceased in 1979 when financial support was withdrawn by the local authorities then funding them: a sad end to a successful experiment.[60]

The consumer adviser must remember, however, that many of the codes of practice discussed in the previous section provide for low cost, documents only arbitration arranged by the relevant trade association.

Consumer Arbitration Agreements Act 1988

The codes of practice approved by the O.F.T. do not compel con-sumers to take advantage of an arbitration scheme, if available, and point out that the complainant is free to take the alternative route of suing in the courts. This contrasts with the type of clause common in commercial contracts which makes arbitration a condition precedent to action in the courts (the so-called "*Scott* v. *Avery*"[61] clause).

One consumer area identified by the Consumers' Association where problems frequently arose was furniture removals. The British Furni-ture Removals Association's standard terms included a *Scott* v. *Avery* clause and members often insisted on arbitration of disputes with consumers, in spite of the high fees payable. The Consumers' Associa-tion successfully lobbied for law reform and the 1988 Act was passed as a Private Member's Bill.

The main thrust of the Act is that by section 1 an agreement with a consumer that "future differences . . . are to be referred to arbitration cannot be enforced." The definition of "consumer" in section 3 closely follows the definition in section 12 of the Unfair Contract Terms Act 1977.[62]

If the claim exceeds the "small claims limit" of £1,000, section 4 empowers the court to disapply section 1, but "the court must be satisfied that it is not detrimental to the interests of the consumer" to

---

[59] *Post*, p. 187.
[60] Details of these schemes are given in the 1st edition of this book, pp. 145–149.
[61] (1856) 5 H.L.C. 811.
[62] *Ante*, p. 131.

order arbitration. In view of the emphasis of these words it is unlikely that the courts will deny a consumer his desire to go to court instead of arbitration.

4. Proceedings in the County Court

If no settlement can be reached it may be necessary to take proceedings in the county court. The vital question to consider is whether the cost, trouble and anxiety of litigation will, in the end, be justified.

Legal advice and assistance (the "Green Form" scheme)

Under the Legal Aid Act 1988 the consumer may be entitled to assistance from a solicitor and counsel if he qualifies financially. The ceiling for assistance is raised once or twice a year to reflect changes in earnings and inflation; by section 8 of the Act the consumer will qualify if:

   (a) his "disposable income" (as defined) does not exceed £135 per week, or
   (b) he is in receipt of income support, and
   (c) in either case his "disposable capital" (as defined) does not exceed £935.

If his disposable income exceeds £64 per week he may have to pay a contribution towards the costs.[63]

The scope of this form of assistance is limited in two respects. First of all, the effect of section 8(5) is that this form of assistance does not cover the institution or conduct of any proceedings before a court or tribunal. Secondly, by section 10 the cost of the assistance is limited to two hours' work unless this limit is increased by the Area Committee in any particular case. Thus the scheme could be useful for writing letters, negotiating settlements and giving general advice on such matters as how to draw the particulars of claim. The actual conduct of the proceedings would, however, have to be conducted by the client in person unless he can obtain a legal aid certificate for proceedings or is prepared to instruct the solicitor at his own expense.

Legal aid

Section 14 of the 1988 Act enables legal aid to be granted for the conduct of civil proceedings where the client has a "disposable income" (as defined) not exceeding £6,350; it may, however, be refused if he has disposable capital exceeding £6,310 and it appears

---

[63] See s.9(6).

that he can proceed without legal aid. Once again he may have to pay a contribution if his disposable income and/or capital exceed a specified amount.[64] There is also a general power to refuse legal aid if (*inter alia*) it appears unreasonable that he should receive it in the particular circumstances of the case.[65] As part of the policy of excluding solicitors in "compulsory arbitration" cases[66] The Law Society has stated that legal aid will not be granted in such cases.[67]

Costs and the statutory charge

Even if it is granted to a consumer it may not be very beneficial. If a person is granted legal aid for proceedings he or she will select a solicitor from a panel. The client may have to pay a contribution to the legal aid fund (see above). If the claim succeeds then:

(a) the defendant will be ordered to pay a sum of money (for example, damages or return of price) to the plaintiff;

(b) the defendant *may* have to pay the plaintiff's taxed costs (but this is discretionary and is nearly always less than the plaintiff's true costs)[68];

(c) the plaintiff's solicitor will be paid out of the legal aid fund.

Suppose that the plaintiff recovers damages of £550 and no costs. Let us also assume that his contribution was £100 and that the legal aid fund pay his solicitor £400 for his costs and disbursements. The legal aid fund have now made a "loss" of £300 on the case and to that extent section 16(6) gives them a first charge on any property recovered or preserved in the proceedings. So at the end of the day, the litigation will have benefited the consumer by a mere £150.

County court arbitration

The above figures strongly point towards "do-it-yourself" claims, but clearly the litigant in person will feel out of his depth on such matters as pleading, particulars, discovery, pre-trial reviews and, above all, the hearing in open court. As already stated, a solicitor may be able to help behind the scenes under the "Green Form" scheme. There is a booklet to assist the litigant in person—published by the Office of the Lord Chancellor and available free from the court.[69]

The so-called "Small Claims Court" or county court arbitration

---

[64] See s.16.

[65] See s.15(2).

[66] See below.

[67] Sweet & Maxwell Legal Aid Handbook 1990, p. 4. Legal aid is now administered by the Legal Aid Board.

[68] For an explanation of the different bases of costs, see O'Hare and Hill, *Civil Litigation* (5th ed.).

[69] *Small Claims in the County Court.*

procedure is found in C.C.R., Ord. 19, r. 2. Where the amount claimed does not exceed £1,000, the proceedings will be automatically referred for arbitration (rather than trial) if a defence to the claim is filed. Where the claim exceeds £1,000, the plaintiff can ask for arbitration in his particulars of claim. The district judge will sit as arbitrator.[70]

The object of the arbitration procedure is to remove some of the terrors of litigation for the litigant in person. This is reflected in Order 19, r. 5, which provides the following "terms of reference":

(1) The arbitrator shall appoint a date for the preliminary consideration of the dispute and ways of resolving it, unless the size or nature of the claim or other circumstances make such a course undesirable or unnecessary.

(2) At or after the preliminary appointment, if there is one, the arbitrator shall fix a date for the dispute to be heard (unless the parties consent to his deciding it on the statements and documents submitted to him) and shall give such directions regarding the steps to be taken before and at the hearing as may appear to him to be necessary or desirable. Where the district judge is the arbitrator, he shall have the same powers on the preliminary appointment as he has under Order 17 on a pre-trial review.

(3) Any hearing shall be informal and the strict rules of evidence shall not apply.

(4) At the hearing the arbitrator may adopt any method of procedure which he may consider to be convenient and to afford a fair and equal opportunity to each party to present his case.

(5) If any party does not appear at the arbitration, the arbitrator may make an award on hearing any other party to the proceedings who may be present.

(6) Where an award has been given in the absence of a party, the arbitrator shall have power, on the party's application, to set the award aside and to order a fresh hearing as if the award were a judgment and the application were made pursuant to Order 37, rule 2.

(7) With the consent of the parties and at any time before giving his decision and either before or after the hearing, the arbitrator may consult any expert or call for an expert report on any matter in dispute or invite an expert to attend the hearing as assessor.

(8) Subject to the provisions of Order 19, rule 6, in respect of claims involving £1,000 or less, the costs of the action up to and including the entry of judgment shall be in the discretion of the arbitrator to be exercised in the same manner as the discretion of the court under the provisions of the County Court Rules.

Apart from procedural terrors (which the above rules are designed to assuage) the other great fear of the litigant in person is that of legal costs—and in particular the burden of having to pay the costs of his opponent if he loses. To deal with this problem Order 19, r. 6, pro-

---

[70] There are some exceptions where the district judge (formerly called the Registrar) may order a full trial. He can also in appropriate cases rescind the reference to arbitration (C.C.R., Ord. 19, r.4).

vides that no costs shall be awarded as between party and party in "compulsory arbitration" cases except (1) the costs stated on the summons, (2) the costs of enforcing the award and (3) such costs as are certified by the arbitrator as having been incurred through the unreasonable conduct of the other party.

How widely is it used?

A survey on small claims arbitration carried out by the Birmingham University Institute of Judicial Administration showed that between 1974 and 1977 the number of arbitrations rose from 5,911 to 10,017. Nearly two-thirds were in respect of goods and services, and rather surprisingly, firms were defendants in only 24 per cent. of the cases. In 1989 the figure reached almost 50,000, of which about a quarter were consumer disputes. This clearly suggests that the scheme is not being extensively used for its primary purpose, *i.e.* encouraging litigants in person to bring their claims against business suppliers to the county court.

The figures contrast with the huge number of consumer complaints reaching the Office of Fair Trading[71] and illustrate the point made at the beginning of this chapter—that the county court is treated as a last resort. The reluctance of the dissatisfied consumer to take advantage of the informal arbitration procedure can be explained on the basis that it is still necessary to take the step—for some, unnerving—of entering the county court itself. One obvious solution is to create a distinct system of Small Claims Courts, housed in separate buildings like the industrial tribunals. Such a far-reaching and expensive reform is unlikely to receive Government support in the present economic climate. A compromise suggested in 1979 by the National Consumer Council in their valuable report "Simple Justice" is a small claims division of the county court, but even this modest proposal, requiring no additional buildings, has not been adopted.

The best to be expected at the moment is a review of the rules of court relating to arbitration announced by the Lord Chancellor at a conference on "Consumer Redress" organised by the O.F.T. in January 1991. It is proposed to dispose of simple cases at a single hearing without the preliminary hearing and to give the district judge an interventionist role by his sole questioning of the parties and witnesses. It is to be hoped that these changes, implemented perhaps in 1992, will help consumers conducting their own cases.

[71] See table, *ante*, pp. 155–158.

Part II

THE CONSUMER AND THE CRIMINAL LAW

CHAPTER TEN

INTRODUCTION

In Part I we have examined the consumer's position as far as the civil law is concerned. We saw that it is not enough for him to show that he has a right of action, for example, for breach of contract or negligence. His main problem is how to enforce that right. It is evident from the figures given at the end of Chapter 9 that the proportion of complainants who are prepared to sue to enforce their rights is small. This encourages traders to assume that they can adopt careless and sloppy practices with impunity. If they can get away with providing shoddy goods and incompetent service, traders will be enticed into lowering their standards by the prospect of increased profitability. Not only is this clearly contrary to the interests of consumers; it is equally unfair to the honest trader who endeavours to maintain high standards and at the same time to compete with the rogues operating in the same line of business.

In pursuing its twofold aim—to protect consumers and to ensure that honest traders are able to make a living on equal terms without the need to resort to the malpractices of their dishonest competitors—Parliament has increasingly turned to the sanctions of criminal law in its search for control. This approach has the significant advantage for the consumer that the expensive and time-consuming process of disciplining the rogue is entrusted to public officials who in recent legislation usually have a duty to enforce its provisions. If the provisions of the criminal law enable the consumer to obtain full compensation,[1] it will be unnecessary for him to rely on the rights explained in Part I: they will be superfluous.

The full range of criminal controls is very extensive. The following examples show some of their ambit.

(1) The Food Safety Act 1990[2] controls the quality of food. Section 14 prohibits the sale of "any food which is not of the nature or substance or quality demanded by the purchaser," for example, containing maggots, mould or metal.

(2) The Weights and Measures Act 1985 empowers trading

---

[1] Chap. 13, *post*, p. 257.
[2] Repealing most of the Food Act 1984.

standards inspectors to test weighing and measuring equipment, and also makes it an offence to deliver short weight when goods are sold by weight, number or other measurement.[3]

(3) The Trade Descriptions Act 1968 controls business activities at large in so far as they involve descriptions of goods or services. Criminal sanctions are imposed for non-compliance.[4]

(4) The Fair Trading Act 1973, Part II, enables orders to be made outlawing general trade practices which adversely affect the economic interests of consumers, for example, the use of certain exemption clauses invalidated by the Unfair Contract Terms Act 1977. A trader who contravenes one of these orders commits a criminal offence.[5]

(5) The Consumer Credit Act 1974 creates a large number of criminal offences (*e.g.* carrying on a consumer credit business without a licence).[6]

(6) The Consumer Protection Act 1987 creates a general safety requirement and enables regulations to be made prohibiting the supply of unsafe goods. It is an offence to fail to comply.[7]

In Part II we propose first in Chapter 11 to look in detail at the Act which has given rise in recent years to more consumer complaints than all the other criminal legislation put together—the Trade Descriptions Act 1968—and then to proceed to Part III of the Consumer Protection Act 1987 which controls misleading prices in place of the repealed section 11 of the 1968 Act. Next in Chapter 12 we survey those statutory provisions which protect the consumer against unsafe goods, now to be found in Part II of the 1987 Act. Finally in Chapter 13 we consider the important question of compensation for the victims of criminal offences. How can they obtain financial redress for any loss which they may have suffered as a result of the convicted person's failure to comply with his statutory obligations under the criminal law? Two aspects are examined—orders for compensation under the Powers of Criminal Courts Act 1973 and the right to bring civil proceedings for breach of statutory duty.

---

[3] For an explanation of the food and drugs and weights and measures legislation, see Harvey, *The Law of Consumer Protection and Fair Trading* (3rd ed.), Chap. 13.
[4] See Chap. 11, p. 195.
[5] See Chap. 14, p. 267.
[6] See Chap. 17, p. 313.
[7] See Chap. 12, p. 243.

CHAPTER ELEVEN

"THE DESCRIPTION MISLED ME"

1. INTRODUCTION

Scheme of this chapter

This chapter is primarily concerned with the Trade Descriptions Act 1968 and the two types of criminal offence to which it gives rise—misdescriptions of goods and of services.

Originally the 1968 Act also contained the provisions relating to misleading prices, but they are now separately controlled by the Consumer Protection Act 1987, Part III, and discussed at the end of the chapter.

In the Review of the Trade Descriptions Act 1968 published in 1976 the Director General of Fair Trading stated that "by and large, the Act has achieved what its authors and Parliament intended it to do: encourage high standards of truthfulness in describing goods and services."[1] Although the Review contains numerous recommendations to strengthen the Act, the Director General emphasised that "widely as the Act had been drawn, it was never intended to be a panacea for all consumer ills."[2]

Clearly it did not prove to be so, as was evidenced by the Director General's Annual Report for 1977.[3] Consumer complaints notified to the Office of Fair Trading numbered well over half a million in 1977, an increase of 26 per cent. on the previous 12 months. (The Report was unclear whether the increase was "due to a general rise in the level of consumer dissatisfaction, a greater readiness by consumers to seek aid from the enforcement and advisory bodies, or a combination of both.") The analysis of consumer complaints by criminal legislation contained in the Report showed that by far the largest single category continued to be complaints under the 1968 Act. A comparison with the figures given in the latest Annual Report shows that the position has not improved in the intervening period. Complaints still exceed half a million per year[4] and trade descriptions offences still figure prominently among the convictions obtained under consumer protection legislation.

[1] Cmnd. 6628, para. 1.
[2] *Ibid.* para. 2.
[3] H.C. Paper No. 228, Session 1977/78, App. 1.
[4] See *ante*, p. 155, for recent statistics.

Background to the Act

As early as 1423 an Act was passed regulating the marking of silver plate. Others dealt with the marking of gold and other precious metals, cutlery and linen. The first statute to cover goods in general was the Merchandise Marks Act 1862 which was replaced in 1887 by an Act of the same name. This was added to by later statutes culminating in the Merchandise Marks Act 1953.

Apart from these statutes dealing specifically with marking, there are related Acts dealing with other aspects of the supply of goods. For example, the Weights and Measures Act 1985, replacing earlier legislation, as its name implies, is particularly concerned with the *quantity* of goods being sold, *e.g.* coal and petrol, and with ensuring that weighing and measuring equipment is accurate, *e.g.* petrol pumps, whereas the Trade Descriptions Act 1968 is also concerned with *quality*. There is one major similarity between the two Acts, namely, that their provisions are enforced by trading standards officers[5] (formerly known as inspectors of weights and measures) employed by local authorities but responsible at ministerial level to the Department of Trade and Industry (as to which see *ante*, p. 3). Whilst it is true that the above legislation has the effect of protecting the consumer, most of the legislation, like that relating to patents and trade marks, was passed with the intention of protecting one trader or manufacturer against unfair competition from another who would otherwise be tempted to make business use of the goodwill attaching to a particular mark or brand-name.

The position with regard to trade descriptions generally was looked into about 30 years ago by the Committee on Consumer Protection, generally known as the Molony Committee, which published its Final Report in 1962.[6] It paid particular attention to the working of the Merchandise Marks Acts and highlighted a number of defects:

(a) Consolidation was desirable in view of the law being contained in a multiplicity of Acts.

(b) The Acts were limited in their scope since they were relevant only where a description had been "applied" to goods, *i.e.* where goods had been physically marked with labels, dies, blocks, etc. Thus oral statements[7] and many advertisements were not covered.

(c) Whatever the merits of the Acts, they were not generally enforced. The Acts of 1891 and 1894 gave the Board of Trade and Ministry of Agriculture, Fisheries and Food respectively

---

[5] See *post*, p. 227.
[6] Cmnd. 1781.
[7] But see now 1968 Act, s.4(2), *post*, p. 201.

the *power* to enforce the regulations; the Local Government Act 1933 gave a similar power to local authorities, and an individual could bring a private prosecution. Yet nobody was under a *duty* to enforce them. The Committee found that only about a dozen prosecutions were brought each year by the Board of Trade, though a larger number were brought by local authorities.

These defects were cured by the passing of the Trade Descriptions Act 1968.

Purpose and ambit

The beginning of the preamble to the Act sets out its essential purpose and scope:

> An Act to replace the Merchandise Marks Act 1887 to 1953 by fresh provisions prohibiting misdescriptions of goods, services, accommodation and facilities provided in the course of trade; to prohibit false or misleading indications as to the price of goods . . .

The preamble discloses the two main offences[8]:

(a) applying a false trade description to *goods* or supplying goods with such a description[9];
(b) making a false statement as to the provision of *services*, accommodation or facilities.[10]

Before considering these offences in detail, two important general features of the Act need to be grasped. First, the Act operates in the criminal area only: it does not give any direct civil remedy to the misguided consumer.[11] Secondly, it applies only to suppliers in the course of a trade or business, *i.e.* not to private suppliers.[12] However, it is irrelevant whether or not the recipient of the goods or services is a private consumer or a trader: the Act protects all and sundry—domestic consumers, sole traders, partnerships and corporations.

In the course of a trade or business

As mentioned above, the Act applies to business suppliers only. Section 1[13] includes an express limitation to persons "in the course of a

---

[8] s.11 created a third offence and controlled misleading *prices*, but has now been repealed: see *post*, p. 231.
[9] s.1.
[10] s.14.
[11] See *post*, p. 264. For the possibility of a compensation order see *post*, p. 258.
[12] The by-pass provision (s.23) is an exception. See p. 224.
[13] *Post*, p. 200.

trade or business" and section 14[14] has an almost identical limitation to persons "in the course of any trade or business": presumably the two expressions have the same meaning.

A question giving rise to some slight doubt is whether the professions fall within the scope of the Act. Unlike the Fair Trading Act 1973, s.137, and the Consumer Credit Act 1974, s.189, no definition of "business" is given so as to make it clear that professional practice is included. It seems probable that the professions are covered in the light of the *obiter dicta* of the Divisional Court in *R.* v. *Breeze*,[15] a case on section 14 concerning an architectural student describing himself as an architect. The point was left open because the defendant was convicted on the basis that, as he lacked the necessary professional qualification, it did not lie in his mouth to say that he was engaging in a professional activity. Here again the Review recommends a clarifying amendment.

Clearly the Act applies where the essence of the business is the supply of the goods or services in question. Yet the Act is wider. Provided the transaction occurs in the course of *a* business, it may be caught even though it does not form part of the primary activities of the business. Thus in *Havering L.B.C.* v. *Stevenson*[16]:

> The defendant ran a car hire business. When the cars were about two years old, his practice was to sell them and to use the proceeds to buy new cars. He sold a car with a false description as to the mileage. When prosecuted he argued that the sale was outside section 1, since he did not carry on the business of a car dealer. The Divisional Court was unmoved. When a car hire business as part of its normal practice buys and sells cars, the sale of a car and the related application of a trade description is an integral part of (and thus in the course of) the car hire business.

A more difficult question is posed where the sale or other transaction is an isolated occurrence or is not part of the trader's normal practice. Suppose that an electrician inaccurately describes the mileage on his van when selling it to purchase a new one, an infrequent event. Or perhaps a solicitor, refurbishing his office, misdescribes an old desk in an advertisement as "used by Lord Chief Justice Widgery when an articled clerk." Clearly the transaction involves an asset of the business, for which no doubt tax allowances have been claimed. At first sight the transaction falls within the wide wording of section 1(1) as the phrase "a trade or business" is not in terms limited to businesses which normally deal in goods of the type in question. The House of Lords, however, adopted a narrow interpretation of the provision in the recent case of *Davies* v. *Sumner*[17]:

[14] *Post*, p. 214.
[15] [1973] 1 W.L.R. 994.
[16] [1970] 1 W.L.R. 1375.
[17] [1984] 3 All E.R. 831.

The defendant was a self-employed courier whose whole activity lay in transporting films and other material round Wales for Harlech Television. In June 1980 he bought a new Ford car; he had previously hired a car for a few months. In July 1981 he offered the car in part exchange for a new car and was given an allowance on the basis of the mileage of 18,100 shown on the odometer. The defendant failed to disclose that the true mileage was 118,100, as the odometer had gone right round the clock. He was convicted by the Clwyd Justices of having applied a false description to the car in that he represented that it had travelled the lower mileage. His appeal on the grounds that the description was not applied "in the course of á trade or business" was allowed by the Divisional Court and the prosecutor's appeal to the House of Lords was dismissed.

Lord Keith, with whose judgment the other members of the court agreed, accepted that in a sense any disposal of a chattel held for the purposes of a business might be said to be in the course of that business, whether it was acquired for resale, for consumption or as a capital asset. However, section 1(1) is not intended to cast such a wide net. Lord Keith, accepting that the *Havering* case was correctly decided, distinguished it from the present case on a number of grounds[18]:

> "The expression 'in the course of a trade or business' in the context of an Act having consumer protection as its primary purpose conveys the concept of some degree of regularity, and it is to be observed that the long title of the Act refers to 'misdescriptions of goods, services, accommodation and facilities provided in the course of trade.' Lord Parker C.J. in the *Havering* case clearly considered that the expression was not used in the broadest sense.
> The reason why the transaction there in issue was caught was that in his view it was 'an integral part of the business carried on as a car hire firm.' That would not cover the sporadic selling of pieces of equipment which were no longer required for the purposes of a business. The vital feature of the *Havering* case appears to have been, in Lord Parker's view, that the respondent's business *as part of its normal practice* bought and disposed of cars.
> The need for some degree of regularity does not, however, involve that a one-off adventure in the nature of trade, carried through with a view to profit, would not fall within section 1(1) because such a transaction would itself constitute a trade."[19]

There were other differences too. In the present case the defendant might well revert to hiring a car as he had previously done; the outcome would apparently have been different had the prosecution been able to establish that as part of his normal practice the defendant had bought and disposed of cars at regular intervals. Again in the

---

[18] *Ibid.* p. 833.
[19] *Quaere* whether *Blakemore* v. *Bellamy* [1983] R.T.R. 303 (D.C.) is still good law. (Postman's hobby of buying, refurbishing and selling numerous cars. No significant profit. Not "trade or business").

Havering case the defendant had exploited his stock-in-trade (the hire cars), whereas the defendant here was merely using his car as a piece of equipment in providing his courier service.

From the point of view of the consumer the House of Lords restrictive interpretation is disappointing. Had the draftsman of the 1968 Act wished to limit its application to the supply of goods in a business which normally deals in goods of that type, it would not have been difficult to find an appropriate formula. For example, the wording of section 14(2) of the Sale of Goods Act 1893 was limited in this way before it was amended in 1973 to widen its scope. The decision can be justified on the basis that here we are dealing with criminal legislation where a narrow interpretation in favour of the defendant is appropriate, but surprisingly the Court of Appeal recently followed *Davies* v. *Sumner* in a civil case on the interpretation of the same expression in section 12 of the Unfair Contract Terms Act 1977.[20]

2. Goods

Section 1(1) prohibits false trade descriptions of goods:

> Any person who, in the course of a trade of business—
> (*a*) applies a false trade description to any goods; or
> (*b*) supplies or offers to supply any goods to which a false trade description is applied;
> shall, subject to the provisions of this Act, be guilty of an offence.

Business suppliers

As we saw above, an offence is committed only by a person acting "in the course of a trade or business." The provision does not catch supplies by private persons.[21]

Strict liability

The offences created by section 1 are offences of strict liability. Although charges under these provisions often involve an element of dishonesty, as was pointed out by the Divisional Court in *Alec Norman Garages Ltd.* v. *Phillips*,[22] it is not necessary for the prosecution to prove dishonesty.

Two offences

Section 1 covers two different offences: first, the application of a

---

[20] *R & B Customs Brokers Co. Ltd.* v. *United Dominions Trust* [1988] 1 All E.R. 847. For a full discussion, see *ante*, p. 132.
[21] *Ante*, p. 197.
[22] [1985] R.T.R. 164.

false trade description to goods; secondly, the supply of goods to which such a description has already been applied. Thus the first offence would be committed by a manufacturer incorrectly labelling goods, while the second offence would occur when a retailer displays or sells those same goods.

Applying a false trade description: section 1(1)(a)

The first of the offences occurs when a person "applies a false trade description to any goods." A wide meaning is given by section 4 to the word "applies":

(1) A person applies a trade description to goods if he—

    (a) affixes or annexes it to or in any manner marks it on or incorporates it with—
        (i) the goods themselves, or
        (ii) anything in, on or with which the goods are supplied; or
    (b) places the goods in, on or with anything which the trade description has been affixed or annexed to, marked on or incorporated with, or places any such thing with the goods; or
    (c) uses the trade description in any manner likely to be taken as referring to the goods.

(2) An oral statement may amount to the use of a trade description.

(3) Where goods are supplied in pursuance of a request in which a trade description is used and the circumstances are such as to make it reasonable to infer that the goods are supplied as goods corresponding to that trade description, the person supplying the goods shall be deemed to have applied that trade description to the goods.

It covers:

(i) markings on the goods themselves, e.g. labels;
(ii) markings on anything in which the goods are supplied, e.g. packaging[23];
(iii) markings on anything in which the goods are placed, e.g. display units, vending machines, point-of-sale material;
(iv) oral statements, specifically mentioned in section 4(2).

The inclusion of oral descriptions is one of the major differences between the 1968 Act and the Merchandise Marks Acts which were limited to the physical application of descriptions to goods.[24] This

---

[23] In the unreported "*Astral*" case (1981) A & F Pears Ltd. was convicted of a s.1 offence for selling jars of face cream 30 per cent. larger in volume than their contents which were correctly given as 54 grams on their labels. Presumably the goods described themselves by their packaging. For a critical analysis, see Woodroffe, "*False Bottoms, Thick Skins*," 79 L.S.Gaz. 62.
[24] See *Coppen* v. *Moore (No. 1)* [1898] 2 Q.B. 300.

extension of the law was effected against the recommendation of the Molony Committee whose reasons for the preservation of the status quo are set out in paragraph 659 of their Report.

Descriptions used by the customer in his request for goods, when it is reasonable to infer that the goods are supplied as goods corresponding to that description, are deemed to have been applied by the supplier.[25] Thus if a customer asks a men's outfitters for a cotton shirt and is supplied with a polyester shirt, the shopkeeper applies the description "cotton" to the shirt even if he says nothing and the shirt is not labelled.

In most cases the trader has quite clearly described the goods and thus applied a description to them. However, "applies" was given a much wider meaning by the Divisional Court in *Tarleton Engineering Co. Ltd.* v. *Nattrass*[26]:

> A dealer sold a car with a false odometer reading. He had not altered the odometer himself. He did not know it was false nor did he repeat the reading or vouch for it. Held, he had applied a false trade description to the car.

It is difficult to justify such a wide interpretation of any of the expressions used in section 4. It might have been preferable to bring a prosecution under section 1(1)(*b*) on the grounds that the trader had supplied the car with a false trade description.

Nevertheless it now seems to be settled beyond doubt that a person "applies" a description to goods, even in the absence of a written or oral statement, if he fails to take steps to correct a misunderstanding which is induced by a description borne by the goods themselves. Thus in *Davies* v. *Sumner*[27] the defendant applied a false description to the car, in that "he represented that it had travelled 18,100 miles when the true mileage was 118,100 miles," by merely standing by and not disclosing the truth.

Supplying goods with a false trade description: section 1(1)(*b*)

The second of the two offences contained in section 1 is committed when a person "supplies or offers to supply any goods to which a false trade description is applied." The offence is most likely to occur where a retailer sells goods with a description applied by a manufacturer, importer or another distributor earlier in the commercial chain.

Offer to supply

To resolve the problem that, where goods are in a shop window, on a

---

[25] s.4(3). See *R.* v. *Ford Motor Co.* [1974] 1 W.L.R. 1220: description in order form completed by supplier. See *post*, p. 213.

[26] [1973] 1 W.L.R. 1261. *Cf. Newham L.B.C.* v. *Singh* [1988] R.T.R. 359 (D.C.): dealers not aware of alteration—no offence.

[27] *Ante*, p. 199, *per* Lord Keith of Kinkel at p. 832.

supermarket shelf or put up at an auction,[28] no offer for sale is made in a contractual sense by the prospective supplier—there is only an invitation to treat to customers who then make an offer to buy—section 6 provides that "a person exposing goods for supply or having goods in his possession for supply shall be deemed to offer to supply them."

Knowledge

It appears from *Cottee* v. *Douglas Seaton (Used Cars) Ltd.*[29] that a supplier does not commit this offence if he neither applied the description to the goods himself nor knew or had means of knowing that this had been done by another. However, where a supplier knows that a description has been applied, even though he does not know that it is false, he is liable, *e.g.* selling a car with an inaccurate odometer.

The facts of the *Cottee* case were as follows:

> Dealer A patched up the bodywork of a car which he sold to dealer B. The repair was so skilfully done that B did not discover it. B sold it to C. Held, B had not committed an offence under section 1(1)(*b*) as he was unaware of the defect. Knowledge that a trade description was applied was essential. Accordingly, A was acquitted of an offence under section 23[30] which depended upon the commission of an offence by B.

In short, knowledge of the *existence* of the description is a prerequisite, but not knowledge of its *falsity*.

Time of application

No offence is committed under section 1 where the description is applied to goods *after* they have been supplied. Thus in *Hall* v. *Wickens*[31] the Divisional Court upheld the acquittal of a motor dealer who had falsely described a car as not being in need of repair 40 days after supplying it to a customer. The description must precede or be contemporaneous with the supply of goods.

Meaning of trade description

Section 2(1) defines a trade description as "an indication" of any of the matters exhaustively listed in its 10 paragraphs and amplified in section 2(2) and (3).

---

[28] Shop window—*Fisher* v. *Bell* [1961] 1 Q.B. 394. Supermarket—*Pharmaceutical Society of G.B.* v. *Boots Cash Chemists (Southern)* [1952] 2 Q.B. 795. Auction—*Payne* v. *Cave* (1789) 3 Term Rep. 148.

[29] [1972] 1 W.L.R. 1408. The "description" in this case consisted of the covering up of the defect by A.

[30] See *post*, p. 225. B could have relied on the s.24(3) defence: *post*, p. 224.

[31] [1972] 1 W.L.R. 1418. *Cf. R.* v. *Haesler* [1973] Crim. L.R. 586.

(1) A trade description is an indication, direct or indirect, and by whatever means given, of any of the following matters with respect to any goods or parts of goods, that is to say—

(a) quantity, size or gauge;
(b) method of manufacture, production, processing or reconditioning;
(c) composition[32];
(d) fitness for purpose, strength, performance, behaviour or accuracy;
(e) any physical characteristics not included in the preceding paragraphs;
(f) testing by any person and results thereof;
(g) approval by any person or conformity with a type approved by any person;
(h) place or date of manufacture, production, processing or reconditioning;
(i) person by whom manufactured, produced, processed or reconditioned;
(j) other history, including previous ownership or use.

(2) The matters specified in subsection (1) of this section shall be taken—

(a) in relation to any animal, to include sex, breed or cross, fertility and soundness;
(b) in relation to any semen, to include the identity and characteristics of the animal from which it was taken and measure of dilution.

(3) In this section "quantity" includes length, width, height, area, volume, capacity, weight and number.

There are special provisions relating to seeds, agriculture and food and drugs.[33]

Examples

The following examples may assist readers; the lettering follows that in section 2(1):

(a) size of shoes, shirts, dresses or other clothing;
(b) Axminster or Wilton carpet;
(c) shirt labelled "65% polyester, 35% cotton";
(d) "top speed 102 mph, 28 mpg";
(e) car equipped with "five-tone horn playing 'Colonel Bogey' ";
(f) "tested by the Road Research Laboratory";
(g) tennis racket "as used by McEnroe"[34];

---

[32] "Composition" includes the way in which components are arranged: *Queensway Discount Warehouses Ltd.* v. *Burke* (1986) 150 J.P. 17 (D.C.) (furniture in newspaper advertisement—picture showed it ready assembled but it was not).
[33] s.2(4) and (5).
[34] See also s.3(4).

(h) 1978 Lamborghini;

(i) "tuned by High Performance Motors Ltd.";

(j) "only one private owner[35]; 46,000 miles."

Review recommendations

The Review considered the suggestion of replacing the list in section 2 with a general offence of misdescribing goods or services with the object of catching the misdescription of any feature not included in the list. However, such a suggestion was rejected on the grounds that "it seems a good principle when creating criminal offences that the offence is defined as precisely as possible."[36] To block a number of loopholes some possible additions to the list in section 2(1) were canvassed, *e.g.* the standing, importance or capabilities of a distributor or wholesaler (only manufacturers are currently covered); the contents or authorship of printed or recorded matter.[37]

Definition orders

Difficulties can arise where a term is used which has a special meaning and is not meant as a literal description of the goods, *e.g.* "Dover Sole" not from Dover or "Bombay Duck" which is neither duck nor from Bombay. The problem was discussed in a case under the Merchandise Marks Acts, *Lemy* v. *Watson*,[38] in which it was held to be a false trade description to describe brisling as "Norwegian sardines." Darling J. used as an illustration the "Holy Roman Empire"—a description of an institution which was neither holy nor Roman nor an Empire.[39]

To alleviate this problem section 7 gives the Department of Trade and Industry power to make definition orders assigning definite meanings to expressions used as part of a trade description.

Is it false?

Let us assume that (a) there is a trade description within the meaning of section 2; (b) the defendant has either applied it or supplied goods to which it has been applied within section 1(1); and (c) the defendant has done so in the course of a trade or business. The next question to consider is whether the trade description is a *false* trade description.

---

[35] See *R.* v. *Inner London Justices, ex p. Wandsworth L.B.C.* [1983] R.T.R. 425 (D.C.): "One owner" car sold by leasing company after leasing to five successive hirers. Acquittal quashed. "One owner" means that the car has been controlled and maintained by only one person.

[36] Para. 121.

[37] Paras. 123–132.

[38] [1915] 3 K.B. 731.

[39] See also *Kat* v. *Diment* [1951] 1 K.B. 34 (non-brewed vinegar).

Section 3(1) states simply and clearly that "a false trade description is a trade description which is false to a material degree." These last four words were considered by the Divisional Court in *Donnelly* v. *Rowlands*[40]:

> Rowlands was a Welsh dairy farmer and milk retailer. He bottled his milk in various types of bottles, some of which were embossed Express, C.W.S., Northern and Goodwins. The foil cap on every bottle was embossed with the words "Untreated milk. Produced from T.T. cows. Rowlands" and the name of his farm. A prosecution was brought by an Inspector of Milk Vessels Recovery Limited (not by a trading standards officer) under section 1(1)(*b*). The justices decided that no offence had been committed on the basis that, as the description on the foil cap was accurate, the false description on the bottle was not false "to a material degree." The Divisional Court dismissed an appeal by the prosecutor.

The court, while agreeing that it was possible to approach the problem by looking at the description as a whole on both the bottle and the cap, took a different line. In their view the trade description was not false to any degree at all. The words on the foil cap were an accurate trade description of the milk; the words on the bottle did not refer to the milk but merely conveyed that the bottle belonged to the company whose name was embossed.[41]

The meaning of "false trade description" is extended by section 3(2) and (3):

> (2) A trade description which, though not false, is misleading, that is to say, likely to be taken for such an indication of any of the matters specified in section 2 of this Act as would be false to a material degree, shall be deemed to be a false trade description.
> (3) Anything which, though not a trade description, is likely to be taken for an indication of any of those matters and, as such an indication, would be false to a material degree, shall be deemed to be a false trade description.

The latter subsection was considered by the Divisional Court in *Holloway* v. *Cross*,[42] another of the numerous cases relating to clocked cars:

> A motor dealer bought a car with an odometer reading 716 miles, although unknown to him the true mileage was over 70,000 miles. He told an interested customer that he would make inquiries as to the true mileage. Later he told the customer that in his opinion it was probably about 45,000 miles and wrote on the invoice "recorded mileage 716,

---

[40] [1970] 1 W.L.R. 1600.
[41] *Cf. Stone* v. *Burn* [1911] 1 K.B. 927 where an offence was committed under the Merchandise Marks Acts when Bass beer was sold in another brewer's bottles with Bass labels.
[42] [1981] 1 All E.R. 1012.

estimated mileage 45,000 miles." He was convicted of offences under section 1(1)(*a*) and (*b*) by the Chatham Justices who considered that, as the estimate was an opinion, it was not "an indication" falling within section 2(1)(*j*) but was within the extension to the concept of a false trade description provided by section 3(3); the disparity between the actual and estimated mileages was sufficiently large to render the estimate false to a material degree.

Donaldson L.J. thought it debatable that the estimate was not caught by section 2(1). In any case the dealer's estimate was likely to be taken by the buyer as an indication of the history of the vehicle and amounted to a false description within section 3(3). The dealer's appeal against conviction was dismissed.

Advertisements

The Act does not create a separate offence relating to advertisements incorporating a false description. However, this is not to say that manufacturers or retailers may include false descriptions in their publicity material with impunity; they run the risk of committing offences under section 1(1)(*a*) and (*b*). The importance of section 5 of the Act, which is concerned solely with advertisements, is its relation to the section 1 offences and also to section 4 which, as we have seen, defines the ways in which a trade description may be applied.

It is to be remembered that section 4(1)(*c*) states that a person applies a trade description to goods if he "uses the trade description in any manner likely to be taken as referring to the goods." Section 5 provides an answer when one is trying to ascertain whether an advertisement relates to those goods which are the subject-matter of proceedings: it states that where a trade description is used in an advertisement in relation to any class of goods, the description "shall be taken as referring to all goods of the class, whether or not in existence at the time the advertisement is published."[43] Factors to be taken into account in deciding whether a customer would think of his goods as belonging to the relevant class are the form and content of the advertisement and the time, place, manner and frequency of its publication.

Example

A manufacturer launches a national television advertising campaign in relation to certain goods. A retailer supplies goods of that type with knowledge of the advertisement. The retailer commits an offence under section 1(1)(*b*) if the advertisement includes false information. If the goods are accompanied by point-of-sale material which also includes a false trade description, the retailer will in addition commit an offence

[43] s.5(2).

under section 1(1)(*a*), for he will have applied the description within the meaning of section 4(1)(*b*) by placing such material with the goods.

It should be noted that the meaning of "advertisement" is defined in section 39, the interpretation section, as including a catalogue, circular and price list.

Disclaimers and odometers

The Review reveals that the most prevalent offence dealt with by enforcement authorities involves tampering with odometers (or milometers) to understate the true mileage.[44] Accordingly, it is proposed to look particularly at this type of offence. Further, as the cases involving disclaimers are, in the main, concerned with false odometer readings, this area will be considered at the same time.

The first question is whether a false odometer reading can in law be a false trade description. Counsel's submission that it cannot be so was described as "bold but hopeless" by Lawton L.J. in *R.* v. *Hammertons Cars Ltd.*[45] The Divisional Court decided that an odometer reading is an indication of the use which the car has had and is "other history, including previous ownership or use" within section 2(1)(*j*).[46]

Effect of disclaimer

An important limitation on the use of disclaimers is that they may assist defendants only where a section 1(1)(*b*) "supplier" offence is charged. The common law doctrine of disclaimer has no application where the defendant himself is the culprit who "applies" the description. Thus in *Newman* v. *Hackney L.B.C.*[47] a motor dealer turned back an odometer from 46,328 to 21,000 and then stuck a disclaimer over it; this later action did not prevent the commission of an offence under section 1(1)(*a*).

In *R.* v. *Hammertons Cars Ltd.* the Divisional Court also considered the effect of a disclaimer and the related problem of the burden of proof. Does a disclaimer prevent a trade description being applied or does it prevent a trade description which has been applied from being false? The court considered it unwise and likely to cause confusion as to the burden of proof to try to divide the evidence into that which establishes that a trade description has been applied and that which is

---

[44] Para. 160.

[45] [1976] 1 W.L.R. 1243, 1246.

[46] But a statement in an MOT certificate as to mileage, etc., is not an indication of the vehicle's history: *Corfield* v. *Sevenways Garage Ltd.* [1985] R.T.R. 109 (D.C.). Such a statement as to year of manufacture may be: *R.* v. *Coventry City Justices, ex p. Farrand* [1988] R.T.R. 273 (D.C.).

[47] [1982] R.T.R. 296 (D.C.). Approved by Court of Appeal in *R.* v. *Southwood* [1987] 1 W.L.R. 1361.

said to be a disclaimer of that description. Lawton L.J. stated that the right question for the court at the end of the case was, "Has the prosecution proved that the defendant supplied goods to which a false trade description was applied?"[48]

Disclaimer in time?

To be effective a disclaimer must be introduced by the trader before he "supplies" the goods, the word used in section 1(1)(b). It is tempting to apply by analogy the contractual rules relating to the incorporation of terms and to take the view that, if a disclaimer is introduced after the contract has been made, it is entirely ineffective. However, the test is not a contractual one. Clearly if the disclaimer is sufficiently brought to the attention of the customer at an early stage during the negotiations, it will be successful. Equally clearly a disclaimer after the buyer has taken possession of the goods will fail, for a disclaimer must be made before the goods are supplied.

The most difficult problem occurs where the trader endeavours at the moment of delivery to disclaim responsibility by telling the buyer only then that the odometer reading is unreliable. Supply and delivery are not to be equated, as can be seen from the judgment of Lawton L.J. in *R.* v. *Hammertons Cars Ltd.* Such an oral statement at the delivery stage may not be enough to displace the impression given by the odometer reading which may linger on in the buyer's mind. "The issue for the court of trial is whether when the purchaser takes possession of the goods he gets them with a false trade description applied to them."[49] So while it is possible for a trader to disclaim when making delivery, he will have great difficulty by delaying so late in persuading a court that a false trade description has not been applied.

It is to be noted that a disclaimer can be implied from a previous course of dealing or because of an understanding between the parties, at least when both of them are experienced car dealers.[50]

General tests

A number of tests have been propounded in the cases to assist in deciding whether in a particular case a disclaimer is effective. In *Norman* v. *Bennett* Lord Widgery C.J. stated that the disclaimer must be "as bold, precise and compelling as the trade description itself" and "must equal the trade description in the extent to which it is likely to get home to anyone interested in receiving the goods."[51] Lawton L.J.'s

---

[48] [1976] 1 W.L.R. 1243, 1246. See also *Tarleton Engineering Co. Ltd.* v. *Nattrass* [1973] 1 W.L.R. 1261.
[49] *Ibid.* p. 1248, *per* Lawton L.J.
[50] *Norman* v. *Bennett* [1974] 1 W.L.R. 1229.
[51] *Ibid.* p. 1232.

instruction to dealers who do not want prospective purchasers to take any notice of odometer readings is that "they must take positive and effective steps to ensure that the customer understands that the milometer reading is meaningless."[52] Lord Widgery C.J. returned to the problem in *Waltham Forest London Borough Council* v. *T.G. Wheatley (Central Garage) Ltd. (No. 2)*[53] when he said, "The purpose of the disclaimer is for it to sit beside, as it were, the false trade description and cancel the other out as soon as its first impression can be made on the purchaser."[54]

All these tests come to the same thing. At the moment of delivery at the latest the buyer must be fully aware that he should place no reliance at all on the odometer reading which has been effectively neutralised or cancelled by the disclaimer, be it oral or contained in a notice, agreement or other document.

Particular disclaimers

Oral. For two reasons an oral disclaimer is least likely to be effective. First, there is the evidential problem of proving what the salesman said. Secondly, a casual remark in the course of negotiations will hardly satisfy the general criteria mentioned above. In *R.* v. *Hammertons Cars Ltd.*:

> Car dealers sold two cars to a customer. The odometers showed 25,600 miles and 25,300 miles, whereas the true mileages were 53,714 miles and 34,000 respectively. At the time of delivery the buyers were given a printed document headed "SPECIFIC GUARANTEE OF USED MOTOR VEHICLE." At the bottom of the document in small print under the heading "MILEAGE AND DATE" appeared: "any estimate or opinion of the mileage . . . which the Suppliers may have given to the Customer during negotiations . . . was given according to their best information and belief. (The suppliers are not answerable for the mileage shown on the vehicle's milometer)." The salesman also gave evidence that he had clearly given the purchasers to understand that the mileage as shown on the odometer was not guaranteed but his evidence was rejected by the jury. Held, the dealers had committed an offence under section 1(1)(*b*). A casual remark in the course of oral negotiations or small print in a contractual document are unlikely to be sufficient disclaimers.

Documents. As has just been seen, disclaimers in small print will not protect the dealer. Presumably, disclaimers printed boldly in documents read by the buyer before the goods are supplied will suffice. However, here again a distinction must be drawn between the contractual rules relating to the incorporation of terms, *e.g.* exemption

---

[52] *R.* v. *Hammertons Cars Ltd.* [1976] 1 W.L.R. 1243, 1248.
[53] [1978] R.T.R. 333.
[54] *Ibid.* p. 339.

clauses, and the present situation. In view of the statement of Lord Widgery C.J. in *Norman* v. *Bennett*[55] that the disclaimer "must be effectively brought to the notice" of the customer, it seems that the dealer will not be able to rely on the fact that the customer happened to sign the relevant document. Thus to have the desired neutralising effect the clause must be both boldly printed and brought clearly to the attention of the customer.

Notices. In a number of cases dealers have attempted to rely on disclaimers in notices on their premises. Thus in *Zawadski* v. *Sleigh*[56]:

> Dealers auctioned three cars with false odometer readings. Disclaimers as to the mileage of the cars appeared both in the auction entry forms and in notices in the auction premises. A Divisional Court held that the general notices were insufficient to be disclaimers.

Similarly, in *Waltham Forest L.B.C.* v. *T.G. Wheatley (Central Garage) Ltd.*[57] a notice in the dealer's office was held to be an insufficient disclaimer. One difficulty is that prospective buyers looking at vehicles on the forecourt or in the showroom may not enter the dealer's office and so will not have an opportunity of seeing the notice. Even so the dealer is offering to supply the goods within the meaning of section 1(1)(*b*). It may be that prominent notices placed in close proximity to the relevant goods are apt to neutralise the odometer reading. Clearly the safest method to adopt is to place the disclaimer notice next to or over the odometer so that it does "sit beside the false description." If, in addition, there is a written contract with a boldly printed clause to the same effect and both the clause and the notice are pointed out to customers, then with this belt and braces technique the dealer is unlikely to run the risk of committing an offence.

A case where a rogue dealer deserved to escape liability, if ingenuity were the criterion, is *Corfield* v. *Starr*[58]:

> A motor dealer purchased a car for resale and substituted an odometer showing a misleadingly low mileage. He attached a notice to the dashboard stating, "With deep regret due to Customer's Protection Act we can no longer verify that the mileage shown on this vehicle is correct." The Divisional Court allowed the prosecutor's appeal against acquittal, as the notice with its reference to the non-existent Act was misleading and fell far short of disclaiming the unmistakable representation given by the odometer.

Zeroing. One practice adopted by some motor dealers is to zero the

---

[55] *Ante*, n. 50.
[56] [1975] R.T.R. 113.
[57] [1978] R.T.R. 333.
[58] [1981] R.T.R. 380.

odometer. Clearly the reading is then false. Has the trader applied a false trade description and committed an offence? Doubtless the trader would argue that it is not false to a material degree, as it can mislead no one. His position is more secure if he uses a disclaimer too, as in *Lill Holdings* v. *White*[59]:

> The defendants zeroed an odometer reading 59,000 miles, attached a disclaimer and sold it to A. A resold it to B, who resold to C with a reading of some 5,000 miles. The Divisional Court allowed the defendants' appeal against conviction under section 23,[60] as they had not been guilty of any "act or default."

Code of Practice. The Code of Practice for the Motor Industry[61] no longer recommends a particular form of disclaimer. Instead it points out in paragraph 3.9 that "any disclaimer used must be as bold, precise and compelling as the car's mileage reading itself and as effectively brought to the prospective customer's attention." It also draws attention in paragraph 3.8 to the need to verify recorded mileages with the previous owners.

Defences

Even where a prima facie offence has been committed because the disclaimer fails in its purpose, the defendant may be able to take advantage of the defences available under section 24(1). These are discussed later.[62] The only point to be made at this stage is that in *Simmons* v. *Potter*[63] the Divisional Court held that a car dealer who had not published a disclaimer had failed to take an obvious precaution and therefore could not rely on the statutory defence. It appears then to be advantageous for dealers to use disclaimers. On the one hand they may well prevent an offence being committed in the first place. On the other hand even if they fail in that primary objective, a dealer's attempt to disclaim responsibility may itself enable him more readily to call in aid the section 24 defence.

Illustrative cases on section 1

In all the following cases a prima facie offence was committed under section 1, although in some of them the defendant was able to rely on the section 24 defence.

Beckett v. *Kingston Bros. (Butchers) Ltd.*[64]

Butchers sold a turkey labelled "Norfolk King Turkey." It had in

---

[59] [1979] R.T.R. 120.
[60] See *post*, p. 225, for the "by-pass" provision.
[61] See Appendix 1, *post*, p. 383.
[62] p. 220.
[63] [1975] Crim.L.R. 354.
[64] [1970] 1 Q.B. 606.

fact come from Denmark. It was held to be an offence under section 1(1)(*b*).

British Gas Corporation v. Lubbock[65]

In response to her inquiry at a corporation showroom about a Parkinson cooker, a customer was given a brochure which stated "ignition is by the hand-held battery torch supplied with the cooker." She ordered a cooker which was supplied without a torch. It was held that the brochure referred to a "package" of goods which included the torch. The description in the brochure was an indication as to "composition" under section 2(1)(*c*); alternatively, an indication of "physical characteristics not included in the preceding paragraphs" under section 2(1)(*e*). An offence was committed under section 1(1)(*a*). (Presumably there was also an offence under section 1(1)(*b*), as the appellants supplied the goods as well as applying the description.)

Sherratt v. Geralds The American Jewellers Ltd.[66]

The jewellers sold a watch described as a "diver's watch" and engraved "waterproof." The purchaser tested the watch by immersing it in a bowl of water; it filled with water and stopped. Held, an offence under section 1(1)(*b*).

Fletcher v. Budgen[67]

A private seller wished to sell his car to a car dealer. The dealer said that there was no possibility of repairing the car; repairs would not make the car safe; and the only possible course of action was for the car to be scrapped. So the car was sold to him for £2. The dealer spent £56 repairing it and then advertised it at a price of £135. It was held to be an offence under section 1(1)(*a*), the description falling within section 2(1)(*e*). The Act applied even though the description was applied by a prospective trade *buyer*, the reverse of the normal situation.

R. v. Ford Motor Co.[68]

Fords supplied a "new" car to a dealer who resold it to a customer. It had been damaged after leaving their factory and while in the hands of their forwarding agents, and properly repaired at a cost of £50. Fords were charged under section 1(1)(*b*) (and also under section 23 because of the dealer's section 1(1)(*b*) offence). The Court of Appeal held that no offence was committed. The description "new" is not false where

---

[65] [1974] 1 W.L.R. 37.
[66] (1970) 114 S.J. 147.
[67] [1974] 1 W.L.R. 1056.
[68] [1974] 1 W.L.R. 1220.

the damage is superficial, or limited to parts which can be simply replaced by new parts, and is perfectly repaired so that the car is as good as new.

Leather funwear[69]

Suppliers described goods as "exciting leather funwear." The goods supplied—bra, panties, catsuit—were made of plastic. Held, an offence under section 1. (One is tempted to ask whether an offence would have been committed had the clothing been made of leather but proved to be neither exciting nor fun to wear.)

3. SERVICES

An area not covered by the Merchandise Marks Act nor by the Molony Report is services. This novel extension of criminal liability from goods to services doubtless accounts for a more tentative approach in section 14. The offence of making false or misleading statements about services is not an offence of strict liability, as can be seen from the wording of section 14(1):

> It shall be an offence for any person in the course of any trade or business—
> (a) to make a statement which he knows to be false; or
> (b) recklessly to make a statement which is false;
> as to any of the following matters, that is to say—
> (i) the provision in the course of any trade or business of any services, accommodation or facilities;
> (ii) the nature of any services, accommodation or facilities provided in the course of any trade or business;
> (iii) the time at which, manner in which or persons by whom any services, accommodation or facilities are so provided;
> (iv) the examination, approval or evaluation by any person of any services, accommodation or facilities so provided; or
> (v) the location or amenities of any accommodation so provided.

Like section 1 the Act applies only to the provision of services in the course of trade or business. As has been seen, it is likely that this expression includes services rendered by members of the professions.[70] Again like section 1 this section includes oral as well as written statements.

However, although a statement made after the supply of goods has been completed is not an offence under section 1,[71] section 14 has a wider application, as is shown by *Breed* v. *Cluett*.[72]

---

[69] *The Times*, June 14, 1973.
[70] *R.* v. *Breeze* [1973] 1 W.L.R. 994. *Ante*, p. 198.
[71] *Hall* v. *Wickens Motors (Gloucester) Ltd.* [1972] 1 W.L.R. 1418, *ante*, p. 203.
[72] [1970] 2 Q.B. 459.

A builder built a bungalow, sold it and afterwards falsely stated that it was covered by an N.H.B.R.C. 10 years' guarantee. The Divisional Court held that such a statement could be a statement as to the provision of services within section 14.

The distinction between this case and the later section 1 decision in *Hall's* case[73] is that the provision of services may involve continuing obligations and, had there been an N.H.B.R.C. guarantee, the builder could have been called upon to provide services during the guarantee period.

Recklessly

Another distinction between this offence and the section 1 offences is that section 14 is not an offence of strict liability. Section 14 requires that the person making the false statement knows it to be false or makes it recklessly. A reckless statement is defined by section 14(2)(*b*) as "a statement made regardless of whether it is true or false ... whether or not the person making it had reasons for believing that it might be false." Lord Parker C.J. in *Sunair Holidays Limited* v. *Dodd*[74] stated *obiter* that the Act imported the common law definition of "reckless."

> Travel agents in their brochure described accommodation offered at a hotel as "all twin-bedded rooms with private bath, shower, w.c. and terrace." They had a contract with the hotel to provide such accommodation. Two couples booked holidays with them on this basis, but on arrival were given rooms without terraces. It was held by the Divisional Court that no offence had been committed. At the time the statement was made the accommodation existed and the statement was perfectly true. Nothing which happened afterwards could alter the accuracy of the description when it was made. Further, the definition of reckless does not include negligence.

However, a different view was taken by the Divisional Court in *M.F.I. Warehouses* v. *Nattrass*[75]:

> A mail order company advertised goods "on 14 days free approval" and "carriage free." These offers were intended to cover only some of the goods in the advertisement but appeared to relate to all of them. The company's conviction for recklessly making false statements as to the provision of facilities was upheld on appeal. The court considered that the chairman of the company had given insufficient care to his perusal of the advertisement so that the company had been reckless as to its contents.

While this case to an extent throws doubt on the dictum of Lord

[73] *Ante*, p. 203.
[74] [1970] 1 W.L.R. 1037.
[75] [1973] 1 W.L.R. 307.

Parker and appears to give a wider meaning to the words "recklessly," the main point of *Sunair Holidays Limited* v. *Dodd* still stands. No offence is committed merely because the trader fails to provide services which accord with the description. Provided the services or accommodation existed when the statement was made and provided that he then had an intention of providing them,[76] the statement is not false and no offence occurs.

It is important to distinguish the two related points. First one asks the question, "Is the statement false?" If the answer is "no," as in *Sunair Holidays Limited* v. *Dodd*, then one need not proceed further: there is no offence. If the answer is "yes," then one goes on to ask, "Did the trader know that the statement was false when he made it or make it recklessly?" If the answer to either alternative is "yes," an offence has occurred.

Knows to be false

In *Wings Ltd.* v. *Ellis*[77] the House of Lords were called upon to consider the wording of section 14(1)(*a*), namely, "to make a statement which he knows to be false." The certified question for the opinion of the court was "Whether a Defendant may properly be convicted of an offence under section 14(1)(*a*) of the Trade Descriptions Act 1968 where he has no knowledge of the falsity of the statement at the time of its publication but knew of the falsity at the time when the statement was read by the complainant." The case is one of the many cases relating to tour operators.

> The respondents published a brochure in May 1981 describing the Sea-shells Hotel, Sri Lanka, as having air conditioning in the bedrooms. This was untrue, but the respondents at the time believed it to be true. In June 1981 on discovering the error the respondents took steps to prevent potential customers from reading the false statement. Even so in January 1982 a customer read a copy of the brochure in its original form and booked a holiday on the strength of it. The respondents argued success-fully in the Divisional Court[78] that no offence was committed because, when the brochure was published, they did not know that the statement was false and, when it was read by the customer, they honestly believed that a member of the public would read it in its corrected and accurate form so that they did not knowingly make a false statement.

The House of Lords, allowing the prosecutor's appeal, answered the question as follows (*per* Lord Scarman)[79]:

> "A statement which was false was made by the respondent company in the

---

[76] "The state of a man's mind is as much a fact as the state of his digestion": *per* Bowen L.J. in *Edgington* v. *Fitzmaurice* (1885) 29 Ch.D. 459, 483.
[77] [1984] 3 All E.R. 577.
[78] [1984] 1 All E.R. 1046.
[79] [1984] 3 All E.R. 577, 591.

course of its business when it was read by Mr. Wade, an interested member of the public doing business with the respondent company on the basis of the statement. The offence was committed on that occasion because the respondent company then knew that it was false to state that the hotel accommodation was air-conditioned. The fact that the respondent was unaware of the falsity of the statement when it was published as part of the brochure in May 1981 is irrelevant."

In reaching this conclusion the court interpreted the words according to their literal and natural meaning. As Lord Scarman pointed out, "The subsection says not that it is an offence knowingly to make the statement but that it is an offence to make the statement."[80] There is therefore an important difference between section 14(1)(*b*), under which an offence is committed only if the trader recklessly makes a statement, and section 14(1)(*a*) where an offence may be committed even though the statement is not *made* knowingly. In his judgment Lord Scarman succinctly explains the current state of the law together with the policy reasons behind it.[81]

"The respondent submits that the essence of the offence is knowingly making a false statement. The appellant submits that it suffices to prove that the statement was made on a person's behalf in the course of his business and that its content was false to the knowledge of the person carrying on the business.

My Lords, I accept the appellant's construction as correct. First, it advances the legislative purpose embodied in the Act, in that it strikes directly against the false statement irrespective of the reason for, or explanation of, its falsity. It involves, of course, construing the offence as one of strict liability to the extent that the offence can be committed unknowingly, that is, without knowledge of the act of statement; but this is consistent with the social purpose of a statute in the class to which the Act belongs."

Lord Scarman's reference to "strict liability" needs to be read carefully; earlier he describes it as an offence of "semi-strict liability."[82] The court decided that there is no need for the prosecution to prove fraud, intent or *mens rea* and "to that extent" the offence is one of strict liability. This contrasts with section 1 where an offence may be committed by a person who does not even know that his description is false.[83] It is clear from comments in all the judgments that the respondents might have been better advised to admit the offence and then to put forward their efforts to correct the erroneous information as a defence under section 24.[84]

[80] *Ibid.* p. 590.
[81] *Ibid.* p. 589.
[82] *Ibid.* p. 585.
[83] *Ante*, p. 203.
[84] *Post*, p. 220. See also *Yugotours* v. *Wadsley* [1988] Crim.L.R. 623 (D.C.).

When is a statement made?

A second question to be answered in *Wings Ltd.* v. *Ellis* was what was meant by the word "make" in section 14(1). The question is particularly important in relation to brochures issued by tour operators and others where millions may be published and read by different members of the public over a period of many months. Are the statements in the brochures "made" when the brochure is published, when read by members of the public or in other circumstances? In *R.* v. *Thomson Holidays Ltd.*[85] the Court of Appeal decided that a statement is made only when communicated to someone, *e.g.* by reading. Although approving the decision in *Thomson* as correct, the House of Lords has not accepted the Court of Appeal's reasoning. A statement may be made although not communicated to anyone. Lord Hailsham explained the breadth of the meaning of the word in his judgment[86]:

> "When, in the course of a trade or business, a brochure containing a false statement is issued in large numbers through a chain of distribution involving several stages, and intended to be read and used at all or some of the stages, it does not follow that it is only "made" at its ultimate destination. It may be "made" when it is posted in bulk, when the information is passed on by telephone or in smaller batches by post, and when it is read by the ultimate recipient, provided that at each stage what happens is in accordance with the original intention of the issuing house."

Future services

A decision showing that promises about the provision of services in the future are not caught by section 14 is *Beckett* v. *Cohen*[87]:

> The defendant agreed to build a garage like the neighbours' within 10 days but did not do so. The Divisional Court held that section 14 did not apply to statements unrelated to existing facts which amounted to a promise as to the future, because these could not be true or false when made. (The court was prepared to accept for the purpose of the case that building a garage was within section 14).

This interpretation of the section erodes very substantially the protection afforded to consumers. Even so, as has been seen, if accommodation is advertised which at the time of publication of the holiday brochure does not exist, then an offence can be committed. This is well illustrated by *R.* v. *Clarksons Holidays Ltd.*[88] where the brochures stated that Clarksons' hotels were chosen for their cleanliness, good food and efficiency of service, and included a picture of a large modern

---

[85] [1974] Q.B. 592. The facts are given on p. 228.
[86] [1984] 3 All E.R. 577, 582.
[87] [1972] 1 W.L.R. 1593.
[88] [1972] Crim.L.R. 653.

hotel with a swimming pool. This turned out to be an artist's impression: the hotel, which was still in the course of construction, was not finished by the time the holidaymakers arrived and was never intended to be ready by then.

Similarly in *British Airways Board* v. *Taylor*[89] the appellants would have been liable for a statement as to the future, had the statement been made by the Board and not by their predecessors B.O.A.C. The facts were as follows:

> The case arose out of the common airline practice of overbooking to take account of "no show" passengers who fail to take up reservations; occasionally this results in passengers being transferred to another flight. Here a passenger received a letter confirming his reservation but in the event no seat was available on the flight. The House of Lords held that the statement in the letter was false, as at that time B.O.A.C. fully intended to off-load passengers if too many arrived for the flight.

Facilities and prices

Section 11 (now repealed) was concerned only with prices of *goods*. This gap has now been filled by section 20 of the Consumer Protection Act 1987 which covers "goods, services, accommodation or facilities."[90] However in the intervening 20 years ingenious, but mostly unsuccessful, attempts were made to squeeze the price of services into section 14 by a broad interpretation of the word "facilities" in section 14(1)(*b*). A number of decisions of the Divisional Court show that the provision is to be construed strictly.[91]

Thus in *Newell* v. *Hicks*[92] Robert Goff L.J. pointed out, "Although the word 'facility' is used widely in commercial circles to describe almost anything available commercially, when the word appears in a criminal statute it is wrong to stretch its meaning in that way."

> Motor dealers advertised a video cassette recorder "Absolutely free with every X-registration Renault" ordered within a specified period. The trade-in allowance of old vehicles, however, was reduced where customers wished to take up the offer.

The Divisional Court held that the statement fell outside section 14 because (1) the offer of a free recorder was a statement about the supply of goods, and (2) section 14(1) did not cover a false statement about the price at which services or facilities were provided.

---

[89] [1976] 1 All E.R. 65.
[90] See *post*, p. 233.
[91] *e.g. Westminster City Council* v. *Ray Alan Manshops* [1982] 1 W.L.R. 383 (D.C.): permanent "closing down" sale—no offence.
[92] [1984] R.T.R. 135.

Yet this case is not authority for the proposition that section 14 has no application merely because the supplier's statement relates to and is ancillary to goods. Thus the section has been held to cover a three months' guarantee of a second-hand car[93] and a statement that the purchaser of a moped would receive a year's insurance.[94]

In the event, as stated above, many of these problems have been solved by the Consumer Protection Act 1987, Part III.

Review recommendations

Amongst the many recommendations made by the Review with regard to section 14 is one designed to close the gap relating to the provision of future services by the creation of a new offence, namely that of supplying any services, accommodation or facilities to which a false description has been applied.[95]

Buildings

The Review also recommended[96] that the Act be extended to cover house sales. This reform has recently been effected by the Property Misdescriptions Act 1991—a Private Member's Bill advocated by the Consumers' Association. It received the Royal Assent on June 28, 1991.

4. DEFENCES

As has been seen, liability for offences under section 1 is strict, whereas the offence under section 14 is committed only if the trader knows the statement to be false or makes it recklessly. However, certain defences are available. Section 24(1) applies to both types of offence. Section 24(3) assists only in the case of prosecution under section 1(1)(b). Section 25 is confined to the publication of advertisements.

The general defence

The defence provided by section 24(1) may be used by a defendant when charged with an offence under section 14 in relation to services or under section 1(1)(b) for supplying goods with a false trade description. However, the Court of Appeal decided in *R.* v. *Southwood*[97] that it is not available in respect of a charge under section 1(1)(a) where the

---

[93] *Bambury* v. *Hounslow L.B.C.* [1971] R.T.R. 1.
[94] *Kinchin* v. *Ashton Park Scooters* (1984) 148 J.P.N. 459. But statements about the provision of clothing were not within s.14.
[95] Para. 106.
[96] Para. 90.
[97] [1987] R.T.R. 273. Nor is a disclaimer effective: *ante*, p. 208.

defendant *applied* the description himself. Section 24(1) reads as follows:

> In any proceedings for an offence under this Act it shall, subject to subsection (2) of this section, be a defence for the person charged to prove—
>
> (*a*) that the commission of the offence was due to a mistake or to reliance on information supplied to him or to the act or default of another person, an accident or some other cause beyond his control; and
>
> (*b*) that he took all reasonable precautions and exercised all due diligence to avoid the commission of such an offence by himself or any person under his control.

It may be split into five defences. The defendant must prove that the commission of the offence was due to any one of the following causes:

(i) a mistake;
(ii) reliance on information supplied to him;
(iii) the act or default of another person;
(iv) an accident;
(v) some other cause beyond his control.

As Lord Templeman pointed out in *Wings Ltd.* v. *Ellis*,[98] where the company failed to invoke section 24, "Good intentions and mistake do not by themselves constitute a defence. The accused must plead and prove the circumstances specified in section 24."

Mistake

As far as mistake is concerned this is available only where the mistake is of the defendant himself; it cannot be used where someone else's mistake is involved (*e.g.* an employer pleading the mistake of an employee).[99]

Act or default of another person

The defence most frequently relied upon is that the offence was due to the "act or default of another person," for example, an odometer run back by a previous owner. When an employer is charged, he may rely on the default of an employee. When the Act first came into force, there were those who thought that the defence could be used only where the employee was in a junior position but it appeared to have been quickly settled that even where the "person" was a branch manager, the defence was still available.[1]

---

[98] [1984] 3 All E.R. 577, 594. See *ante*, p. 216, for the facts.
[99] *Birkenhead & District Co-operative Society Ltd.* v. *Roberts* [1970] 1 W.L.R. 1497.
[1] *Beckett* v. *Kingston Bros. (Butchers)*, *ante*, p. 212.

However, when the employer is a company, it is necessary to distinguish between those employees who are the *alter ego* of the company, when their defaults are the company's defaults, and those employees who are not thus identified with the company which can then claim that the defaults are those of "another person." The difficulty was fully discussed by the House of Lords in *Tesco Supermarkets* v. *Nattrass*,[2] a case involving section 11 (now repealed):

> Soap powder was advertised in a supermarket "Radiant 1 shilling off giant size 2/11d." This was intended to apply only to "flash packs" which were marked "1 shilling off recommended price." As the supermarket had run out of these packs, ordinary packs were on display. A customer was charged the full price of 3/11d for one of these.

Their Lordships held that where the person charged is a limited company, the only persons who can be identified with the controlling mind and will of the company are the board of directors, the managing director and any other superior officer[3] to whom the board has delegated full discretion to act independently from the board. Thus, though a general manager may be the company's *alter ego*, the supermarket manager was not. Accordingly, since the offence was caused by his failure to ensure that sufficient flash-packs were available, Tesco were able to rely on his default.

To establish this defence the defendant must not merely produce the list of staff who might have been at fault; he must at least try to identify the actual person responsible by carefully investigating the circumstances to discover how the offences occurred.[4] Further, to rely on this defence section 24(2) requires the defendant at least seven clear days before the hearing to serve on the prosecutor a written notice giving such information as he has to identify the other person.[5] The reason for this provision is to enable the prosecution to consider whether to proceed directly against the other person either for one of the main offences or under the by-pass provision in section 23.[6]

Due diligence

It is not enough to the defendant to prove one of the five defences in section 24(1)(*a*). He must also show "that he took all reasonable precautions and exercised all due diligence to avoid the commission of such an offence by himself or any person under his control."[7] These

---

[2] [1972] A.C. 153.
[3] By s.20 such officers may be prosecuted too, where the offence has been committed with their consent or connivance.
[4] *McGuire* v. *Sittingbourne Co-operative Society Ltd.* [1976] Crim.L.R. 268.
[5] See *Birkenhead & District Co-operative Society Ltd.* v. *Roberts, ante*, n. 99.
[6] See p. 224.
[7] s.24(1)(*b*).

factors have generally been considered by the courts in relation to the default defence, particularly with regard to its application in the areas of vicarious liability, odometers and sampling.

Vicarious liability

Where an employer is charged with an offence because of the conduct of an'employee and endeavours to rid himself of this vicarious liability by showing that the offence was due to the act or default of the employee, broadly the employer will be acquitted if he can show that he is personally blameless. Obviously, when this defence is used somebody is to blame. The question is whether the offence occurred in spite of the precautions and diligence of the employer. In the *Tesco* case the House of Lords rejected the argument that the employer has to show that he and all the persons to whom he has delegated responsibility are blameless: the company was held to have satisfied the requirements of section 24(1)(*b*) by having a chain of command with a careful system of control and supervision, even though one of the cogs in this machine, the supermarket manager, had failed to carry out his responsibilities properly.

Odometers

The second area where due diligence is of special significance relates to false odometer readings. Sometimes a car dealer honestly—not all car dealers are rogues—supplies a vehicle with an odometer which unknown to him has been tampered with by an earlier owner. Assuming that he can prove that the offence was due to reliance on information supplied, or the default of another person, the question arises whether he can also prove that he took precautions and was diligent. This normally involves checking with the person from whom he bought the vehicle and, if he has the registration document, with previous owners to verify the mileage.[8] However, in *Naish* v. *Gore*[9] the Divisional Court said that it was impossible to lay down as a general principle that a dealer selling second-hand cars must have the log book and check with previous owners. In that case the defence was available to a dealer who bought from somebody with whom he had been doing business for years and resold the car before receiving the log book from his seller. Nevertheless, Lord Widgery C.J. warned that justices "should be very quick and alert to consider whether there are further proper precautions which might have been taken."

Sampling

The last dictum should be borne in mind by suppliers dealing with

---

[8] *Richmond upon Thames L.B.C.* v. *Motor Sales (Hounslow) Ltd.* [1971] R.T.R. 116. See also *Wandsworth L.B.C.* v. *Bentley* [1980] R.T.R. 429 (D.C.).
[9] [1971] 3 All E.R. 737. See also *Crook* v. *Howells Garages* [1980] R.T.R. 434 (D.C.).

large quantities of goods and relying on sampling to show that they have been taking reasonable precautions and been duly diligent. In *Rotherham Metropolitan B.C.* v. *Raysun (U.K.) Ltd.*[10]:

> The defendants, large-scale importers of Far East products, imported once a year about 100,000 packets of children's wax crayons from Hong Kong. Their agents there had samples analysed and had to send back only adverse reports: none were received. The defendants tested in England a single packet. They sold the crayons as "poisonless." The black crayons contained excessive amounts of toxic material.

The Divisional Court rejected their defence under section 24(1). They had not checked that the Hong Kong analyses were in fact taking place and their sample in England was "very moderate." "By itself," said Woolf L.J., "it did not indicate the taking of a standard of care required by the statutory provisions."

Supplier's defence

In *Naish* v. *Gore* the dealer also relied on the defence in section 24(3). This is confined to the offence of supplying goods with a false trade description under section 1(1)(*b*). The defence is:

> In any proceedings for an offence under this Act of supplying or offering to supply goods to which a false trade description is applied it shall be a defence for the person charged to prove that he did not know, and could not with reasonable diligence have ascertained, that the goods did not conform to the description or that the description had been applied to the goods.

The comments made above with regard to "diligence" in section 24(1) appear to be relevant here also, as the use of the adjective "reasonable" rather than "due" is not intended to affect or reduce the standard of diligence.[11] For example, in *Simmons* v. *Ravenhill*,[12] another "clocked car" case, the defence failed because in view of the vehicle's low mileage (19,000) the dealer should have made inquiries with the previous owner. The Divisional Court stated, however, that generally it would be unreasonable to expect a dealer to check the whole pedigree back through all its owners.

The by-pass provision

Although the so-called "by-pass provision" in section 23 is not a

[10] *The Times*, April 27, 1988. See also *Amos* v. *Melcon (Frozen Foods)* (1985) 149 J.P. 712 (D.C.): "rump steak" was really silverside of beef—insufficient evidence of sampling—no defence.

[11] This interpretation, suggested in earlier editions of this book, has been given by the Divisional Court in *Texas Homecare* v. *Stockport M.B.C.* [1987] Crim.L.R. 709.

[12] [1983] Crim.L.R. 749 (D.C.). See also *Richmond upon Thames L.B.C.* v. *Motor Sales (Hounslow) Ltd.*, *ante*, p. 223.

defence, it is appropriate to deal with it at this point in view of its close interaction with the defence in section 24(1). Section 23 states:

> Where the commission by any person of an offence under this Act is due to the act or default of some other person that other person shall be guilty of the offence, and a person may be charged with and convicted of the offence by virtue of this section whether or not proceedings are taken against the first-mentioned person.

Thus where A commits an offence, but the real culprit is B, B may be prosecuted for the offence committed by A. It is irrelevant whether or not proceedings have been taken against A. The corollary is that if no offence is committed by A, B cannot be prosecuted under section 23.[13]

Example

B, a car dealer, runs an odometer back. He sells the car to another dealer A. A sells the car to a customer. On the assumption that A has committed an offence under section 1(1)(*b*), B can be prosecuted under section 23 because A's offence is due to the "act or default" of B.

In this example it can be seen that the prosecution need not resort to section 23 in order to charge B; for B has committed an offence under section 1(1)(*a*) by applying a false trade description. The example is not unrealistic. Quite frequently local authorities have taken themselves into unnecessarily deep water by using the by-pass provision instead of prosecuting directly for one of the main offences.[14] However, section 23 is not entirely superfluous. It can result in an offence being committed by a private person who cannot otherwise be charged, because he is not acting "in the course of a trade or business." Thus even if B were a private seller, he could be charged under section 23.[15]

Interaction with default defence

Earlier, the interaction between section 23 and section 24(1) was mentioned. In the example if A is charged under section 1(1)(*b*) he may plead the section 24(1) defence, *i.e.* that the offence was due to the "act or default of another person," namely B. This creates an apparently unbreakable circle. B is liable under section 23 only if A has committed the offence. So if A when prosecuted under section 1 successfully relies on section 24 due to B's default, B when prosecuted under section 23 can apparently argue that he has committed no offence in the absence of an offence by A. It would seem perverse that

---

[13] *Cottee* v. *Douglas Seaton (Used Cars) Ltd.* [1972] 1 W.L.R. 1408.
[14] *Ibid.* The facts appear on p. 203.
[15] *Olgeirsson* v. *Kitching* [1986] 1 W.L.R. 304 (D.C.).

the real culprit B should escape with impunity merely because his guilt provides the innocent A with a defence.

This iniquitous circle was broken by the robust interpretation given to section 23 by the Divisional Court in *Coupe* v. *Guyett*.[16] The court stated that where A's sole defence is the section 24 defence, A can be regarded as having "committed" the offence for the purposes of section 23, *i.e.* for the purposes of a prosecution against B. Thus B (the real culprit) can be convicted under section 23 even though A is acquitted as a result of the section 24 defence. If, however, A has some other defence (*e.g.* absence of knowledge in a section 14 case) the prosecution will *not* be able to charge B under section 23, although they might well be able to charge him under one of the principal charging sections.

Review recommendation

We have already seen that the by-pass provision can result in a successful prosecution against a private person. The Review recommends that, while the possibility of such proceedings should be retained, it should be possible only where the private individual has deliberately falsified a trade description. Accordingly, their recommendation is that section 23 be amended so that the prosecution must show *mens rea* on the part of the individual in any case, be it section 1 or 14.[17]

Advertisements

Section 25 affords a special defence in the case of advertisements. In any proceedings for an offence relating to the publication of an advertisement the defendant is free from liability if he can prove that (a) the advertisement was received and published in the course of a business involving such publication, and (b) he did not know and had no reason to know that the publication would amount to an offence under the Act. The defence protects not only the publishers themselves, *e.g.* of newspapers and magazines, but also those who arrange for the publication of advertisements, *e.g.* advertising agencies.

5. ENFORCEMENT

One of the major defects of the Merchandise Marks Acts was the absence of anybody with a duty to enforce their provisions. The Molony Committee when considering who would be most suitable to police any replacing legislation suggested a number of solutions,

---

[16] [1973] 1 W.L.R. 669.
[17] Para. 38.

including enforcement centrally by the Board of Trade, but finally came down strongly in favour of enforcement at local level. Section 26(1) clearly places the obligation of prosecution on trading standards officers in the following unequivocal terms: "It shall be the duty of every local weights and measures authority to enforce within their area the provisions of this Act." The Minister may require such authorities to report to him and, if a complaint is received that any authority is not properly discharging its duties, he may institute a local inquiry whose report must be published.[18]

To assist the inspectors in carrying out their duties the Act gives them the power to check compliance with the Act by purchasing goods or securing the provision of services, accommodation or facilities.[19] One can picture the more zealous inspectors as a matter of duty reluctantly sunning themselves on the beaches of Barbados in order to check that the amenities and location of hotels in travel brochures are not falsely described!

Section 28 of the Act enables them to enter premises to make spot checks and, if reasonable cause for suspicion of an offence exists, to require production[20] of the books and documents of the business.

Before instituting proceedings the local authority must give notice to the Department of Trade and Industry. Such liaison helps to prevent numerous prosecutions in different areas for the same offence, for example, for goods or services advertised and supplied nationally. However, multiple prosecutions do sometimes occur.[21]

A prosecution must be brought within three years of the commission of an offence or one year from its discovery, whichever is the earlier.[22]

Finally, it should be observed that, although generally prosecutions are brought by local authorities, it is open to a member of the public to bring a private prosecution for an offence.

6. PENALTIES

The only sanctions under the Act for its contravention are of a criminal nature—fines or imprisonment. The Act affords the aggrieved consumer no separate civil remedy at all[23] (but see Chapter 13 where compensation orders are discussed). Yet clearly the threat of criminal proceedings brought at public expense is a much greater deterrent to the dishonest trader than the possibility of a civil action by a private individual at his own expense.

---

[18] s.26.
[19] s.27.
[20] "Produce" does not mean "hand over and allow to take away": *Barge* v. *British Gas Corp.* (1983) 81 L.G.R. 53 (D.C.).
[21] *e.g.* the travel brochures in *R.* v. *Thomson Holidays Ltd., post,* p. 228.
[22] s.19(1). But see also s.19(2) and s.19(4).
[23] See *post,* p. 228.

If proceedings are brought summarily, a fine not exceeding £2,000[24] may be levied in respect of each offence. If the defendant is convicted on indictment, not only may the fine be unlimited but imprisonment of up to two years may be imposed—both penalties may be meted out.[25] In a number of cases defendants have been fined substantial sums of £1,000 or more.[26] Occasionally prison sentences are imposed but the Divisional Court stated in *R. v. Haesler*[27] that imprisonment is normally reserved for cases involving dishonesty. Generally heavy fines and prison sentences seem to be a privilege of car dealers.[28]

It will be appreciated that multiple prosecutions may be brought in different areas in respect of the same false trade description with a new fine on each conviction. In *R. v. Thomson Holidays Ltd.*[29]:

> Tour operators published a brochure containing a false statement. They were convicted in one area of an offence under section 14. When prosecuted by a different local authority in respect of the same false statement the defendants pleaded *autrefois convict* in respect of the previous conviction.[30] The Court of Appeal held that every time someone read one of the brochures a false statement was made, for it was made when communicated to the reader.[31] Accordingly, a new offence was committed on each occasion and the plea was unsuccessful. Theoretically millions of prosecutions could be brought in respect of a single error in the printed brochures.

The advantage of multiple prosecutions from the point of view of the consumer is that, if he wishes to seek compensation under the Powers of Criminal Courts Acts 1973, he will require the defendant to be convicted. Thus different consumers seeking compensation in different areas would each look for separate convictions.[32]

7. CIVIL REMEDIES

We have seen that the Act is essentially one which creates criminal offences to protect consumers, but gives no right to bring a civil action. Consumers are left to pursue their civil remedies in the ordinary way, for example, for breach of contract or misrepresentation where appropriate. It will be appreciated that not every set of facts giving rise to an

---

[24] Originally £400 (s.18). Increased to £2,000 by S.I. 1984 No. 447.
[25] s.18.
[26] See *R. v. Hammertons Cars Ltd.* [1976] 1 W.L.R. 1243.
[27] [1973] Crim.L.R. 586.
[28] See *R. v. Hewitt, The Times*, June 21, 1991 (C.A.): two months imprisonment and fine of £500 on each of eight counts of "clocking".
[29] [1974] Q.B. 592.
[30] This is a rule that a defendant cannot be charged more than once for the same offence.
[31] Although the House of Lords approved this decision in *Wings Ltd.* v. *Ellis*, they gave a wider meaning to "make a statement": see *ante*, p. 218.
[32] See p. 259.

offence under the Act will necessarily result in a civil remedy being available. Conversely a consumer may well have a civil remedy even where no offence has been committed (as, for example, where the trader lacks the necessary knowledge in section 14 cases or where section 24 applies).

A separate but related question is whether, assuming there to be a contractual right available to the consumer, the contract is vitiated or the right of action lost because of the statutory contravention. As far as the supply of goods is concerned this question is answered by section 35 which states, "A contract for the supply of any goods shall not be void or unenforceable by reason only of a contravention of any provision of this Act." Clearly when the contract involves the supply of goods whether by way of sale, hire-purchase, rental or in any other way, the rights of both the supplier and the consumer are unaffected. Strangely, section 35 is not wide enough to cover contracts for the supply of services (the Review recommends in para. 256 that section 35 should be amended to cover such contracts). However, it seems unlikely that such contracts are invalidated by the commission of an offence under the Act. This is an example of what is usually described as "incidental illegality," *i.e.* illegality which has no effect on the contract. In any case the consumer's rights would not be affected, as he would not be *in pari delicto* with the guilty supplier.

As regards civil remedies the consumer is slightly worse off as a result of the 1968 Act. The Act repealed section 17 of the Merchandise Marks Acts 1887, whereby a seller was deemed to warrant the accuracy of any trade description, but in practice this warranty was very seldom used.

Finally, two points need to be made with regard to civil remedies and compensation for the consumer. First, a conviction under the Act may be used as evidence in a later civil action by virtue of the Civil Evidence Act 1968. Secondly, compensation may be claimed under the Powers of Criminal Courts Act 1973 as a consequence of the conviction.[33]

8. Prices: Consumer Protection Act 1987, Part III

Background

> "Recommended price £210, our price £170"
> "Normal price £78, sale price £52"
> "£8 off recommended price"
> "Elsewhere £50, our price £28"
> "Worth £80, our price £60"

The public and consumer bodies have for many years been concerned at the difficulty in distinguishing between genuine reductions

---

[33] *Post*, p. 258.

and false comparative price claims. The Molony Committee recommended[34] that the problem should be tackled by including in the definition of trade description "the former or usual price of any goods." However, instead of following this approach the 1968 Act endeavoured to deal with the mischief with separate price provisions contained in section 11. Section 11 created three offences: (i) false comparisons with a recommended price; (ii) false comparisons with the trader's own previous price; (iii) an indication that the price is less than that actually being charged.

Recommended prices

The first offence caused little difficulty inasmuch as it was obvious and easy to prove from manufacturers' lists whether or not an offence had been committed. However, the Act had no deterrent effect on the practice—indeed it probably led to its expansion—of manufacturers of setting unrealistically high recommended prices (so-called "sky prices") to enable retailers to offer an apparent bargain to their customers. The practice is particularly rife in the area of furniture and electrical goods where discount houses proliferate. The Review discusses the difficulties and some possible solutions, including the prohibition of recommended retail prices, but in the end the Director General throws up his hands in despair stating that he "can put forward no suggestions for controlling this practice within the framework of the 1968 Act."[35]

However, concurrently with the preparation of the Review, the Office of Fair Trading was considering the control of this and other price problems under the Fair Trading Act 1973. Their proposals were published in 1975 in the paper entitled "Bargain Offer Claims—A Consultative Document." Although ultimately an attack was made on some forms of bargain offers by the Price Marking (Bargain Offers) Order 1979, recommended prices were not generally prohibited.

Previous prices

The second offence was similar to the first offence except that the false indication related to the price at which the supplier previously offered the goods. The purpose of this provision was to attack the practice of buying in goods especially for sales and pretending that those goods were previously offered at a higher price in order to persuade bargain hunters that a bargain was in fact being offered. The practice is not confined to sales periods but is most rife at such times.

Overcharging

The third offence was expressed in very wide terms and covered

---

[34] Para. 636.
[35] Para. 210.

situations where the customer was charged a higher price than he would have expected to pay in view of the indications as to price given to him by the supplier.[36]

Price Marking (Bargain Offers) Order 1979

In the event section 11 of the 1968 Act proved inadequate for its task and many loopholes were enthusiastically used by suppliers. For some years the O.F.T. had been examining bargain offer claims and their effects on consumers. The Director General's original intention was to refer the matter to the C.P.A.C. under Part II of the Fair Trading Act 1973,[37] but it appeared that it might be difficult to provide evidence that the practice adversely affects the economic interests of consumers. Comparatively few complaints are made about bargain offers either because consumers do not realise that they have been misled or because they are chary of revealing that they have been duped and that the bargain which they obtained was not such a good deal after all.

Accordingly, early in 1978 the Director General made his first recommendations to the Secretary of State under section 2(3) of the 1973 Act. This provision enables the Director General to by-pass the C.P.A.C. and to make recommendations "as to any action which in the opinion of the Director it would be expedient for the Secretary of State or any other Minister to take in relation to any of the matters in respect of which the Director has any such duties," *e.g.* his duties under section 2(1). The Secretary of State used a regulation-making power under the Prices Act 1974 to introduce the Price Marking (Bargain Offers) Order 1979.[38]

The Order was complex and not a model of clarity, although not as completely impossible to interpret, to comply with or to enforce as many of its critics suggested. It well illustrates the difficult task of attempting by detailed regulations to block up numerous distinct business malpractices. Such a specific approach was a challenge to entrepreneurs and their legal advisers to invent new practices and slogans which technically did not fall foul of the Order—hardly a valuable use of commercial time and ingenuity. In the event the severe criticism of the Order from both sides of the fence—business suppliers and trading standards departments—resulted in the replacement of both the Order and section 11 of the 1968 Act with primary legislation.

Services

Apart from the complexity of the law, which even so failed to control the malpractices adequately, there was one major gap in the regulatory

---

[36] See the *Tesco* case, *ante*, p. 269.
[37] *Post*, p. 222.
[38] S.I. 1979 No. 364, as amended by S.I. 1979 No. 633.

regime, namely services. Section 11 of the 1968 Act affected only the price of goods. For that reason enforcement authorities tried to control misleading prices relating to services by using section 14, but, as we have seen, the courts were unwilling to interpret the meaning of "facilities" to embrace prices.[39]

Although the Bargain Offers Order covered services too, it was limited in its scope. In his Review of the Order published in 1981[40] the Director General of Fair Trading proposed as one of the options for reform a general prohibition against false or misleading statements about the price of goods or services. After considerable delay this was the route chosen by the Government.

Scheme of the 1987 Act

The purposes of Part III of the Consumer Protection Act 1987 is to adopt a much more flexible approach than the previous legislation in the hope that this will cope with the constantly changing commercial practices and marketing techniques of the modern world. This more general approach can be found in the main offence created by section 20(1) of giving a misleading price indication. The offence covers "any goods, services, accommodation or facilities." This broad approach is not unique in the field of consumer protection. Indeed, it can be found elsewhere in the 1987 Act in that section 10 introduced the "general safety requirement" as an umbrella to cover areas not dealt with in specific regulations.[41] Similarly Part III has a general umbrella offence. This is complemented by section 26 giving power to make regulations which will be activated when particular practices require specific provisions.

A major criticism of the Bargain Offers Order was that traders alleged that it was incomprehensible so that they did not know how to comply with it. Whether or not that was true, clearly it is desirable that legislation should be easily understandable both by those in business and by the enforcement authorities. With this in mind, section 25 enables a code of practice to be approved by the Secretary of State and such a code is already in place.

The two offences

Section 20 contains two offences:

(1) Subject to the following provisions of this Part, a person shall be guilty of an offence if, in the course of any business of his, he gives (by any means whatever) to any consumers an indication which is misleading as to the price

---

[39] *Ante*, p. 219.
[40] "Review of the Price Marking (Bargain Offers) Order 1979" O.F.T., 1981.
[41] *Post*, p. 249.

at which any goods, services, accommodation or facilities are available (whether generally or from particular persons).

(2) Subject as aforesaid, a person shall be guilty of an offence if—

- (a) in the course of any business of his, he has given an indication to any consumers which, after it was given, has become misleading as mentioned in subsection (1) above; and
- (b) some or all of those consumers might reasonably be expected to rely on the indication at a time after it has become misleading; and
- (c) he fails to take all such steps as are reasonable to prevent those consumers from relying on the indication.

The first offence appears in section 20(1); this is the main offence on which we shall concentrate our discussion. The second offence in section 20(2) is concerned with a price indication which is correct when given, but *later* becomes misleading. This is aimed at the sort of problems that have arisen in the package holiday industry which we discussed earlier in relation to section 14 of the 1968 Act.[42] In those cases the misdescription related to a misdescription of the facilities or accommodation themselves; section 20(2) covers misleading prices in those areas as well as in relation to goods.

Business of his

There is a similarity between these two offences and the offences under sections 1 and 14 of the 1968 Act[43] in that they cannot be committed by a private person: both offences require the misleading price indication to be given "in the course of any business of his." However, there is an important distinction between these new offences and those under the 1968 Act. The additional words "of his" have the effect of taking employees outside the ambit of the 1987 Act. In practice it has been unusual for junior employees to be prosecuted even under the 1968 Act.

However, section 40(2) creates a danger for "any director, manager, secretary or other similar officer" of a body corporate, since proceedings may be brought against them personally where the company is guilty of an offence which was committed with their consent or connivance or as attributable to their neglect.[44]

Two definitions

Consumer

No offence is committed unless the indication is given "to any

---

[42] *Ante*, p. 215.
[43] *Ante*, pp. 197 and 214.
[44] *Cf.* 1968 Act, s.20, *ante*, p. 222.

consumers." Again, this can be contrasted with the 1968 Act where it is irrelevant whether the recipient of the misleading information is a private consumer or a trader. Indeed, trading standards officers frequently put the view that the 1968 Act is intended mainly to protect the honest trader against the rogue trader rather than to protect consumers at large. The new price provisions are clearly aimed at consumer protection.

"Consumer" is defined by section 20(6) as follows:

(a) in relation to any goods, means any person who might wish to be supplied with the goods for his own private use or consumption;
(b) in relation to any services or facilities, means any person who might wish to be provided with the services or facilities otherwise than for the purposes of any business of his; and
(c) in relation to any accommodation, means any person who might wish to occupy the accommodation otherwise than for the purposes of any business of his.

The subsection clearly brings out the scope of Part III in that it separately mentions (a) goods, (b) services or facilities and (c) accommodation. In any of these cases a consumer is someone who "might wish" to be supplied, etc.; an offence may be committed even though no actual supply takes place. So if in a supermarket the prices on the goods themselves and on the shelf edge differ, a prosecution may be brought.

Price

Prices are also defined in section 20(6) to mean:

(a) the aggregate of sums required to be paid by a consumer for or otherwise in respect of the supply of the goods or the provision of the services, accommodation or facilities; or
(b) except in section 21 below, any method which will be or has been applied for the purpose of determining that aggregate.

It follows that if a trader merely gives an estimate as a rough guide to the likely charge to be made, he does not give an indication as to price; for at that stage no one can tell what the consumer will be *required* to pay when the work has been done. In contrast, a firm quotation by which the supplier makes an offer for the supply of goods, etc., will be caught.

Indication

Both offences require the supplier to "give an indication." It does not matter how the indication is given, as section 20(1) expressly states "by any means whatever." So it obviously covers prices on goods, on shelf edges, in holiday brochures and on estate agents' photographs and also indications by word of mouth.

Presumably it also covers bar-coding. An increasingly common problem is that goods are not priced individually, so that the consumer relies on the price on the shelf and then assumes that the laser at the checkout reads out the same price from the bar-code. A number of supermarkets, some with famous names, have been prosecuted successfully under the old prices legislation because of discrepancies between the shelf price and the checkout price, usually because the computers at head office feeding the information to the tills have been altered without staff at the local supermarket altering the shelf prices too.

The word "indication" was also used in section 11 of the 1968 Act and was considered by the Divisional Court in *Doble* v. *David Greig Limited*.[45]

> Bottles of Ribena in a self-service store were priced at 5s. 9d. and bore a manufacturer's label "the deposit on this bottle is 4d. refundable on return." At the checkout was a notice reading "In the interests of hygiene we do not accept the return of any empty bottles. No deposit is charged by us at the time of purchase." Customers paid 5s. 9d. a bottle but were refused 4d. refund. This was held to be an offence under section 11(2).

The Divisional Court took the view that the word "indication" was designedly wider than some such word as "representation" and was chosen in order to protect customers. "Section 11(2) was looking at the customers and the effect on them of whatever was said, done or displayed" (Ashworth J.) and "was intended to extend over conduct or signs of many different kinds" (Melford Stevenson J.). On the facts there was an indication likely to be taken as an indication that the purchaser who paid 5s. 9d. would be given 4d. on returning the bottle. The store had argued that the counter-indication displayed at the check-out point had the effect of disabusing the customer of a false impression which he might have obtained at the shelves. The court decided that the offence was committed when the Ribena was placed on the shelf with the false indication.

Misleading

Having looked at two elements of misleading price indications ("price" and "indication") we now turn to the meaning of "misleading." This is widely defined by the Act. Section 21(1) gives the main part of the definition:

> For the purposes of section 20 above an indication given to any consumers is misleading as to a price if what is conveyed by the indication, or what those consumers might reasonably be expected to infer from the indication or any omission from it, includes any of the following, that is to say—

[45] [1972] 1 W.L.R. 703.

(a) that the price is less than in fact it is;

(b) that the applicability of the price does not depend on facts or circumstances on which its applicability does in fact depend;

(c) that the price covers matters in respect of which an additional charge is in fact made;

(d) that a person who in fact has no such expectation—

    (i) expects the price to be increased or reduced (whether or not at a particular time or by a particular amount); or

    (ii) expects the price, or the price as increased or reduced, to be maintained (whether or not for a particular period); or

(e) that the facts or circumstances by reference to which the consumers might reasonably be expected to judge the validity of any relevant comparison made or implied by the indication are not what in fact they are.

Similar provisions appear in section 20(2) where the misleading indication is as to the *method* of determining a price.

It is important to observe that the list of factors (a) to (e) is an exhaustive list in that an indication is misleading "if what is conveyed . . . includes any of the following. . . ." So although the offences at first sight seem very wide, they are limited by this list of factors. If the list had been worded so as to make it clear that it was illustrative only and through marketing ingenuity a supplier were able to invent a scheme falling outside section 21, the courts could have turned to the all-embracing words of section 20. This is not the case.

A further point is that the test to be applied on the effect on consumers is not entirely objective. Although the first factor for the court to consider is "what is conveyed by the indication," the subsection goes on to ask "what those consumers might reasonably be expected to infer from the indication." So presumably the court should take into account the effect of the indication on the particular consumers—*those consumers* who receive the indication.

Examples

The following are examples of the five factors set out in section 21(1).

(a) shelf price £1.40, price charged at checkout £1.48;

(b) a discount on goods, apparently generally available, given only to cash customers, not to those paying by credit card;

(c) additional charges for delivery, postage and packing or fitting, when these appear to be included in the stated price;

(d) a sale stating that the price of goods will be increased after the sale, when there is no such intention to increase prices; a similar problem arises with introductory offers;

(e) flat pack book shelves at £60 compared with ready-assembled book shelves at £95, when the latter are not available or do not sell at the stated price.

Price comparisons

Two final points should be noted. First, the practices expected to be followed by traders, particularly in respect of the price comparisons mentioned in (e), are set out in the Code of Practice discussed below.[46] Secondly, section 21(3) deals specifically with price comparisons.

Services and facilities

We have already mentioned[47] that because section 11 of the 1968 Act applied only to goods, trading standards officers tried to fit mis-statements about prices into section 14 of that Act, but achieved only limited success. Such verbal gymnastics will no longer be necessary as Part III covers these areas too. Section 21(1) shows the breadth of meaning of the words "services or facilities" by explaining, perhaps unnecessarily, that references to these words are "references to any services or facilities whatever." More helpfully the subsection contains a non-exhaustive list of some areas covered by these words to put their inclusion beyond doubt. They are:

(a) credit, banking or insurance services;
(b) the purchase or sale of foreign currency;
(c) the supply of electricity;
(d) the provision of off-street car parks;
(e) arrangements for keeping caravans on land unless occupied as the person's main residence.

The Code of Practice deals briefly with credit and insurance. Regulations under section 26 are imminent in respect of bureaux de change and are under discussion in relation to the resale by landlords of electricity and gas.[48]

Accommodation

Section 23 deals with the provision of "accommodation or facilities." It seems that facilities are mentioned both in section 22 in conjunction with services and in section 23 in conjunction with accommodation to make it clear that they are included in both contexts. It should be remembered that the words "services, accommodation or facilities" appear in section 14 of the 1968 Act and presumably the meaning given to those words in that legislation will be followed in interpreting the

[46] *Post*, p. 239.
[47] *Ante*, p. 219.
[48] *Post*, p. 240.

same words in this context. Package holidays offered by tour operators have provided a fruitful source of prosecution under the 1968 Act and will doubtless provide frequent causes for investigation by trading standards officers under the 1987 Act too.

Sales of new homes

A relatively new problem encountered by consumers has been the effect of falling house prices resulting from high rates of interest, particularly during 1990. The result has been the rare sight of property developers cutting the prices of their new houses and flats. There has been a suspicion that these advertised reductions may not be genuine. The Government was shrewd enough to cater for these unusual circumstances when drafting section 23. Although section 23(1) excludes from the Act "the creation or disposal of an interest in land," such a transaction is caught where:

(a) the person who is to create or dispose of the interest will do so in the course of any business of his; and

(b) the interest to be created or disposed of is a relevant interest in a new dwelling and is to be created or disposed of for the purpose of enabling that dwelling to be occupied as a residence, or one of the residences, of the person acquiring the interest.

It can be seen from this wording that the Act does not affect the sale by an ordinary house-owner, or a sale by a property developer or other businessman of a shop, office, factory or other business premises. This provision is aimed at the problem mentioned above—the sale by a builder or developer of a new house or flat to be occupied by the buyer as his residence. The definition of "new dwelling" in section 23(3) makes it clear that both new constructions and the conversion of old buildings into flats are covered unless the individual unit has previously been occupied as a residence. Section 23(3) also defines "relevant interest" to take outside the Act leases which were originally granted for 21 years or less or have such a short period left to run. If evidence were needed that alleged price reductions on new houses is a problem for consumers, such evidence can be provided by the fact that one of the first prosecutions under Part III related to this area.

> Taylors Estate Agents, part of Hambro Countrywide, placed a newspaper advertisement stating that the price of a four-bedroom house in Oxfordshire had dropped from £194,950 to £164,950. The property had never been offered at the higher price. Its highest asking price had been £185,000. The defendants were fined £800.[49]

Not surprisingly the Act applies even where, as part of the land

---

[49] New L.J., January 18, 1991.

transaction, goods or services are also provided, *e.g.* carpets or kitchen equipment.[50] Finally, the Code of Practice will need to be borne in mind by builders as Part 4 is devoted to the sale of new homes.

Code of Practice

We have referred already on a number of occasions to the Code of Practice. Its full title is "Code of Practice for Traders on Price Indications." It was introduced in November 1988 under powers given to the Secretary of State under section 25(1) to approve a code for two purposes:

(a) to give practical guidance on the requirements of section 20; and
(b) to promote desirable practices as to the way in which price indications should be given.

There was considerable debate during the passage of the Bill of the effect on traders of compliance or non-compliance with the Code. Some argued that where the trader complied with the Code, he should have a complete defence. Arguments were also put forward for the reverse side of the coin, namely, that failure to comply with the Code would of itself be an offence. Such proposals were heavily criticised by the so-called "Concordat" comprising consumer bodies, trading standards representatives and the Retail Consortium. As a result, the proposals were amended and the position now is as stated in section 25(2).

> A contravention of a code of practice approved under this section shall not of itself give rise to any criminal or civil liability, but in any proceedings against any person for an offence under section 20(1) or (2) above—
> (a) any contravention by that person of such a code may be relied on in relation to any matter for the purpose of establishing that that person committed the offence or of negativing any defence; and
> (b) compliance by that person with such a code may be relied on in relation to any matter for the purpose of showing that the commission of the offence by that person has not been established or that that person has a defence.

The Code turns out to be rather like the Highway Code in that if a trader contravenes it, the prosecution can rely on that fact to establish the commission of an offence, whereas if the trader complies with the Code he can use that fact as a defence. It is very detailed with pictorial illustrations and other examples showing traders what to do and what not to do. It falls into four parts:

[50] s.23(2).

Part 1. Price comparisons
Part 2. Actual price to the consumer
Part 3. Price indications which become misleading after they have
         been given
Part 4. Sale of new homes.

A Review Committee has been set up by the DTI to monitor the working of the Code and also to consider whether regulations are desirable in particular areas to give more bite to the control of malpractices. The Concordat has been rather sceptical of the Code of Practice approach and keen for regulations to be introduced in five areas: misleading indications in comparison with recommended retail prices; comparisons with a trader's own previous price and the related 28-day rule; introductory offers; claims as to "worth" and "value"; and the substantiation of certain price indications. However, at the moment it seems most unlikely that the Government will give way to these pressures.

Regulations

The power to make regulations is given to the Secretary of State by section 26. So far no regulations have been made. The first relates to differential pricing in respect of the payment for transactions by cash or other methods, *e.g.* credit cards.[51] Draft regulations affecting bureaux de change were circulated for consultation in 1989 and again in a simplified form in February 1991, and should be in place soon. For the moment no progress is being made with regulations relating to the resale of electricity and gas by landlords. In summary, it appears that this tool is one which will be used sparingly by the Secretary of State.

Defences

There are a number of defences in the Act. Part III contains some defences specific to section 20. Section 39 contains a more general defence relating to offences prosecuted under both Part II[52] and Part III of the Act.

Specific defences

Four defences of limited scope are provided by the four subsections of section 24. The first three apply to offences under both subsections of section 20. The fourth defence relates to section 20(1) only. A brief comment will be made on each subsection.

---

[51] Price Indications (Method of Payment) Regulations 1991, S.I. 1991 No. 199.
[52] Part II is concerned with product safety: *post*, p. 245.

(1) Here the defendant must show that his acts or omissions were authorised by section 26 regulations.
(2) This defence is to protect the media in respect of editorial comments. Where the price indication is in a book, newspaper, film or broadcast, there is no offence if the indication was not in an advertisement.
(3) This subsection provides a defence for publishers and advertising agents who have no reason to suspect that advertisements passing through their hands are illegal.
(4) This relates to recommended prices. It protects the business which recommends the price if the goods, services, etc., are provided by a third party and the offence results from the unexpected failure by the third party to follow the recommendation.

Due diligence defence

The defence provided by section 39, which relates to offences committed under Parts II and III of the 1987 Act, is like the familiar "due diligence" defence found in other consumer protection statutes. However, they are not exactly the same. Section 39(1) reads as follows:

> Subject to the following provisions of this section, in proceedings against any person for an offence to which this section applies it shall be a defence for that person to show that he took all reasonable steps and exercised all due diligence to avoid committing the offence.

This is very similar to section 24(1) of the Trade Descriptions Act 1968[53] in that it requires the defendant to show that he took all reasonable "steps"—a wider word than "precautions" in the 1968 Act—and exercised all due diligence to avoid the commission of an offence. However, there is no equivalent to section 24(1)(a), *i.e.* here the defendant does not also have to show that the offence was due to one of a number of specific reasons, *e.g.* "the act or default of another person." Nevertheless in practice it is likely that the defendant will produce evidence to similar effect.

If he does point the finger of blame in another direction by alleging that the offence was due to the act or default of or information given by another, he must give information to the prosecution to identify that other person at least seven days before the hearing to preserve the defence.[54] Further, in the case of information given by another, he must also show that it was reasonable for him to rely on and believe the information bearing in mind any steps he could take to verify it.[55]

[53] *Ante*, p. 221.
[54] s.39(2) and (3).
[55] s.39(4).

The by-pass provision

Another similarity with the 1968 Act is the inclusion of a by-pass provision comparable with section 23 of the 1968 Act.[56] It appears in section 40(1):

> Where the commission by any person of an offence to which section 39 above applies is due to an act or default committed by some other person in the course of any business of his, the other person shall be guilty of the offence and may be proceeded against and punished by virtue of this subsection whether or not proceedings are taken against the first-mentioned person.

However, there is one major difference—a private person cannot be prosecuted under section 40. This is because the words "in the course of any business of his" have been added.

This was a change we noted earlier when discussing section 20 which also has the effect of preventing a prosecution of employees. For this reason it is anticipated that employers may be more ready to blame employees knowing that the employees themselves are not thereby endangered.

Enforcement and penalties

We have already discussed these topics in relation to trade descriptions.[57] The provisions in the 1987 Act are very similar with regard to enforcement which is once again the duty of trading standards departments. In view of the similarity, we think that no further comment is necessary except to direct attention to Part IV of the Act where the relevant provisions may be found.

However, there is one major difference with regard to penalties—the sanction of imprisonment is not available to the courts.[58]

[56] *Ante*, p. 224.
[57] *Ante*, pp. 226 and 227.
[58] See s.20(4). *Cf.* Part II, *post*, p. 254.

CHAPTER TWELVE

"THE GOODS AREN'T SAFE"

1. INTRODUCTION

In Chapter 5 we considered Part I of the Consumer Protection Act 1987 which imposes *civil* liability on *producers* of unsafe goods. In this chapter we turn to Part II of the 1987 Act which imposes *criminal* sanctions on *suppliers* of unsafe consumer goods. First Part II of the 1987 Act will be placed in its historical context by briefly reviewing its legislative predecessors.

We have seen in earlier chapters that some consumer protection legislation is concerned as much with shoddy goods as with unsafe goods; no distinction is drawn. This is true of both civil and criminal statutes, *e.g.* the Sale of Goods Act 1979 and the Trade Descriptions Act 1968.

However, in many statutes a different approach is adopted where death or personal injury is concerned: provisions are likely to be more stringent or restrictive than in cases where only financial or economic loss results. Thus, under the Unfair Contract Terms Act 1977, section 2, a clause excluding liability for negligence is void in the case of death or personal injury, but valid if reasonable in the case of other loss or damage, *e.g.* damage to property.[1] In other "consumer" areas the same emphasis is placed on ensuring that the individual receives compensation for death or injury, but not for damage to property. For example, the Health and Safety at Work, etc. Act 1974, section 6, restricts its control with regard to articles for use at work to ensuring that they are safe and without risk to health and safety when properly used.

There is no doubt that concern for safety at home should be as serious as concern for safety in the work place. The Foreword to "Consumer Safety. A Consultative Document"[2] provides ample evidence.

> About 7,000 people in Great Britain die each year from accidents in the home, over a tenth of them from fires. This is comparable to the number killed on the roads. In addition over 100,000 receive hospital in-patient

---

[1] *Ante*, p. 130.
[2] Cmnd. 6398, 1976.

treatment for home accident injuries. No central statistics are kept for those not admitted to hospital, but it is estimated that in England and Wales 650,000 receive out-patient care in hospitals and 500,000 attend their general practitioner for treatment.

Apart from the toll of human suffering which these figures represent, there are substantial economic costs, both direct—through damage to property, as in the case of the 50,000 or so fires in the home each year—and indirect—e.g. the cost of medical treatment and hours lost from work.

Home accidents occur at all ages: research has indicated that 30 per cent of victims treated in hospital are children under five, 16 per cent are aged 5 to 14, and 41 per cent aged 15 to 64. Over 65's are involved in some 13 per cent of such accidents, though this age group accounts for two-thirds of all the deaths so caused.

This Consultative Document is concerned with ways of reducing the cost and suffering caused by home accidents. It considers how information, publicity and education on causes of home accidents and means of avoiding them can be improved; and in particular it discusses how the law can best ensure that goods which reach consumers are as safe to use as the public may reasonably expect.

As the last paragraph states, the Green Paper paid particular attention to the way in which the law could be improved with a view to ensuring that goods used by the consumer are safe. At that time this branch of the law was regulated by the Consumer Protection Acts 1961 and 1971. Several of the proposals contained in the paper for improving the legal protective framework were incorporated in the Consumer Safety Act 1978.

Consumer Safety Act 1978

Its main purpose was to prevent dangerous goods reaching the market or, if they have done so, to prohibit their sale. The most important changes effected by the Act were these:

(1) It gave any Secretary of State much more flexible powers to make regulations to ensure that goods are safe and to prohibit the supply of unsafe goods.[3]

(2) It enabled quick action to be taken to ban the supply of dangerous goods by the use of "prohibition orders" and "prohibition notices."[4]

(3) It provided power by the service of a "notice to warn" to require manufacturers and distributors of goods, which were found to be dangerous only after they had been sold, to publish notices warning the public of the danger.[5]

[3] s.1.
[4] s.3(1). Prohibition orders are no longer available: *post*, p. 253.
[5] *Ibid.*

(4) It imposed an enforcement duty on local authorities.[6]

All these improvements are retained in the 1987 Act.

Consumer Safety (Amendment) Act 1986

Less than six years after the 1978 Act came into force the Government published a White Paper, "The Safety of Goods,"[7] setting out the Government's conclusions with regard to the effectiveness of the consumer products safety legislation. It contained proposals for amending the 1978 Act with a view to strengthening its provisions. One example mentioned in the White Paper illustrated the difficulties. In 1981 over a hundred types of electrical hair curling brushes were imported in large numbers, mostly from the Far East. They failed to satisfy the requirements of regulations on matters such as insulation, but this hazard did not become apparent until they had reached the shops and were in use. It proved to be an expensive, time-consuming exercise to track down the unsafe appliances and have them removed from sale. In the interval, a death or serious injury could easily have occurred.

The purpose of the recommendations was to introduce preventative measures to assist in identifying and halting the supply of unsafe goods before they reach the shops; to enable enforcement officers to suspend the supply of apparently unsafe goods; and to introduce a general safety duty on all suppliers.

The 1986 Act added the first two of those new weapons to the armoury of the enforcement authorities. They both reappear in the 1987 Act:

(1) Customs officers were given power to detain imported goods for two days and to pass on information to trading standards officers, who would thus be given time to activate their other procedures.

(2) Trading standards officers were empowered to serve suspension notices to prohibit supplies of goods for up to six months; and to apply to the court for an order that goods be forfeited and destroyed. Related compensation provisions were also enacted.

2. CONSUMER PROTECTION ACT 1987, PART II

The suggestion that there should be a general statutory duty on suppliers to supply safe consumer goods was first put forward in the

---

[6] s.5(1).
[7] Cmnd. 9302, 1984.

consultative document "Consumer Safety."[8] The absence of this duty on suppliers of consumer goods contrasted with the duty on suppliers of articles for use at work imposed by section 6 of the Health and Safety at Work, etc. Act 1974. The Government's policy is clearly stated in para. 34 of the White Paper[9]:

> The Government accepts that there is a case for widening the scope of the Act to place a general obligation on the suppliers of consumer goods to achieve an acceptable standard of safety where it is reasonable to expect them to anticipate and reduce risks arising from those goods. This would induce a greater sense of responsibility on the part of those suppliers who currently regard themselves as unaffected by legislation (and who may not be adequately deterred by the common law duty of care). At the same time it would provide wider scope for swift remedial action by enforcement authorities in the case of newly identified dangerous products.

This "general safety requirement" (GSR) is the novel feature of the 1987 Act. Otherwise the 1987 Act is in the main a consolidating statute bringing together in Part II the provisions of the 1978 and 1986 Acts.

The regulatory regime now consists of a series of measures which we shall consider in the following order:

(1) The GSR creates a general offence of supplying consumer goods which are not reasonably safe.
(2) Safety regulations impose specific requirements in relation to a particular type of product.
(3) Prohibition notices, notices to warn and suspension notices provide back-up powers to control particular traders dealing in unsafe goods.

As a preliminary, though, it is necessary to look at some key words defined in the Act.

Key definitions

The definitions are found in various places. Those definitions relating to the Act as a whole are found in sections 45 and 46 (some of these have already been discussed in Chapter 5 in relation to Part I); those relating only to Part II appear in section 19; and a few of more limited importance are given in the relevant section itself.

Safe

This is the core of Part II—it is essentially concerned with safe and unsafe goods, not with shoddy goods of poor quality (this is true of Part I too). Section 19(1) gives this meaning:

---

[8] Cmnd. 6398, 1976.
[9] *Ante*, n. 7.

"safe," in relation to any goods, means such that there is no risk, or no risk apart from one reduced to a minimum, that any of the following will (whether immediately or after a definite or indefinite period) cause the death of, or any personal injury to, any person whatsoever, that is to say—
  (a) the goods;
  (b) the keeping, use or consumption of the goods[10];
  (c) the assembly of any of the goods which are, or are to be, supplied unassembled;
  (d) any emission or leakage from the goods or, as a result of the keeping, use or consumption of the goods, from anything else; or
  (e) reliance on the accuracy of any measurement, calculation or other reading made by or by means of the goods,
and "safer and "unsafe" shall be construed accordingly.

It can be seen that goods do not have to be absolutely safe, but the risk at worst must be "reduced to a minimum." This is a commonsense approach, since otherwise some products would be outlawed, *e.g.* motor vehicles, lawn mowers.

It is enough to refer to some of the regulations made under the 1961 and 1978 Acts[11] to find examples of unsafe goods: unstable carry-cot stands or prams; anorak hoods causing strangulation; explosive oil heaters or lamps; dummies which choke; toys with sharp edges or spikes or loose doll's eyes; inflammable nightdresses and foam furniture.

Electrical appliances provide frequent examples; here faulty insulation brings with it the hazard of electrocution—electric blankets, hair curling brushes, vacuum cleaners, electric razors, and illuminated, gold novelty gondolas (presumably even people with such appalling taste should not reap the penalty of death).

The importance of (b) lies in making regulations relating to the effectiveness of safety equipment, *e.g.* life jackets, buoyancy rafts, fire extinguishers; for the risk arises not from the product itself but from the fact that, when circumstances occur in which the equipment is in "use," it is found at that late, critical stage to be unsuitable and thus to expose the user to risk. The significance of the word "keeping" can be seen in relation to labelling requirements on goods which create a hazard if not safely stored, *e.g.* garden pesticides.

Examples of the other factors in the list may be helpful:

  (c) flat pack furniture;
  (d) household cleaning fluids, pressure cookers, hot water bottles, gas cylinders;
  (e) tyre pressure gauges, speedometers.

---

[10] s.19(2) amplifies this aspect.

[11] These regulations continue in force until replaced by new regulations. s.50(5) permits regulations made under the 1961 Act to be treated as if made under the 1987 Act, if the Minister so orders.

Goods

The definition of "goods' in section 45(1) is very wide:

> "goods" includes substances, growing crops and things comprised in land by virtue of being attached to it and any ship, aircraft or vehicle.

However, safety regulations may not be made in respect of crops, water, food, feeding stuff, fertilisers, mains gas, drugs and medicines.[12] (The same products are excluded from the GSR, as well as aircraft, motor vehicles and tobacco).[13]

Supply

A supply is caught only if made "in the course of carrying on a business (whether or not a business of dealing in the goods in question[14]) and either as principal or agent."[15] So the business supply is covered; the private supply is not.

What types of transaction are "supplies"? The definition provides a detailed answer.

- (i) Sale.
- (ii) Hire or loan.
- (iii) Hire-purchase.

    Section 45(2) provides that in the case of hire, hire-purchase, credit sale or conditional sale agreements, "the supplier" is not the provider of the credit (the "ostensible supplier") but "the effective supplier" who is enabled to provide the goods by virtue of such financial facility.

    Example

    D wishes to acquire on credit terms a car owned by a dealer S. S sells the car to a finance house C. C lets the goods on hire-purchase to D. S is "the supplier" under the 1987 Act. (To use Consumer Credit Act jargon, the credit-broker S (not the creditor C) is the supplier).

- (iv) Work and materials.
- (v) Exchange, *e.g.* for trading stamps.
- (vi) Provision under a statutory function, *e.g.* the N.H.S.
- (vii) Gift, *e.g.* a prize.

---

[12] s.11(7).

[13] s.10(7).

[14] s.46(5). These clarifying words do not appear in the equivalent provision of the 1961 Act. But in *Southwark L.B.C.* v. *Charlesworth* [1983] C.L.Y. 3311 the Divisional Court reached the same conclusions: a shoe repairer who sold an unsafe electric fire through his shop breached the Electrical Equipment (Safety) Regulations 1975.

[15] s.46(1).

General safety requirement (GSR)

This wide-ranging duty imposed on all types of suppliers—not merely manufacturers—is now the linch-pin of the safety legislation. No longer is it necessary to bring in regulations piecemeal when particular products prove to be dangerous. This was the difficulty faced by the enforcement authorities before the 1987 Act, when the closing of various specific loopholes by regulations was no help when tackling another type of unsafe product when it appeared on the market.

The offence

Section 10(1) contains the GSR offence:

> A person shall be guilty of an offence if he—
>
> (a) supplies any consumer goods which fail to comply with the general safety requirement;
> (b) offers or agrees to supply any such goods; or
> (c) exposes or possesses any such goods for supply.

Unlike the safety regulations and the product liability provisions of Part I, it is confined to *consumer* goods, *i.e.* "ordinarily intended for private use or consumption."[16] This is followed by a non-exhaustive list of factors to be taken into account:

> (2) For the purposes of this section consumer goods fail to comply with the general safety requirement if they are not reasonably safe having regard to all the circumstances, including—
>
> (a) the manner in which, and purposes for which, the goods are being or would be marketed, the get-up of the goods, the use of any mark in relation to the goods and any instructions or warnings which are given or would be given with respect to the keeping, use or consumption of the goods;
> (b) any standards of safety published by any person either for goods of a description which applies to the goods in question or for matters relating to goods of that description; and
> (c) the existence of any means by which it would have been reasonable (taking into account the cost, likelihood and extent of any improvement) for the goods to have been made safer.

A few comments can be made on these subsections.

(a) This is very similar to section 3(2)(a) in Part I and the comments made on that provision should be borne in mind here too.[17]

---

[16] s.10(7). The same expression is used in s.5(3)(a) in relation to property damaged by defective goods: *ante*, p. 138. *Cf.* Unfair Contract Terms Act 1977, s.12.
[17] *Ante*, p. 67.

(b) The relevant safety standards are any "published by any person." This goes beyond standards approved under section 10(3)[18] to encompass British Standards, European Standards (*e.g.* CEN and CENELEC) and presumably any recommended in trade journals.

(c) This will pose immense problems in that a cost/benefit analysis will need to be undertaken to assess whether additional manufacturing costs would have been justified to make the goods safer. Against that must be balanced the commercial risk of making some types of goods so safe and therefore so expensive that few could afford to buy them. Motor cruisers and sailing craft are just one area of difficulty.

Defences

There are other general defences elsewhere in the Act,[19] but two groups of provisions in section 10 itself should be discussed here. The first group in section 10(3) are not strictly defences: they provide, in a somewhat roundabout way, that goods comply with the GSR when they meet certain requirements:

> For the purposes of this section consumer goods shall not be regarded as failing to comply with the general safety requirement in respect of—
>
> (a) anything which is shown to be attributable to compliance with any requirement imposed by or under any enactment or with any Community obligation;
>
> (b) any failure to do more in relation to any matter than is required by—
>
> (i) any safety regulations imposing requirements with respect to that matter;
> (ii) any standards of safety approved for the purposes of this subsection by or under any such regulations and imposing requirements with respect to that matter;
> (iii) any provision of any enactment or subordinate legislation imposing such requirements with respect to that matter as are designated for the purposes of this subsection by any such regulations.

"Requirement" is an important word which runs right through this subsection. The question is whether it is *compulsory* for the goods to meet the standards, etc.—not merely desirable because they were recommended, *e.g.* British Standards (BSI).

As regards safety standards, the relevant ones here are those "approved," rather than simply "published" as in section 10(2)(b). The Secretary of State has made regulations giving him power to

---

[18] See below.
[19] *Post*, p. 254.

approve safety standards.[20] Twice a year he publishes a list of approved standards. They already cover such product areas as children's equipment, DIY and household equipment and vehicle accessories.

There are three defences set out in section 10(4):

> In any proceedings against any person for an offence under this section in respect of any goods it shall be a defence for that person to show—
>
> (a) that he reasonably believed that the goods would not be used or consumed in the United Kingdom; or
> (b) that the following conditions are satisfied, that is to say—
>
>> (i) that he supplied the goods, offered or agreed to supply them or, as the case may be, exposed or possessed them for supply in the course of carrying on a retail business; and
>> (ii) that, at the time he supplied the goods or offered or agreed to supply them or exposed or possessed them for supply, he neither knew nor had reasonable grounds for believing that the goods failed to comply with the general safety requirement; or
>
> (c) that the terms on which he supplied the goods or agreed or offered to supply them or, in the case of goods which he exposed or possessed for supply, the terms on which he intended to supply them—
>
>> (i) indicated that the goods were not supplied or to be supplied as new goods; and
>> (ii) provided for, or contemplated, the acquisition of an interest in the goods by the persons supplied or to be supplied.

(a) This defence of exporters is difficult to justify from the consumers' point of view. At first sight it has the unpleasant flavour of discriminating against foreigners—the goods may not be safe enough for the British, but who cares about the rest of the world? In fact the policy is to assist United Kingdom manufacturers in competing with overseas manufacturers who might otherwise be at an advantage in having to meet only their own local, possibly lower, safety standards. The same is true for United Kingdom exporters—they have to pay regard only to the foreign requirements.

(b) The retailers' defence[21] does not extend to other distributors such as wholesalers. Further, they are exonerated only if they reasonably believed the goods to be safe.

(c) The exclusion of secondhand goods from the GSR is unjustifiable, as they are more likely to be dangerous than new goods. In spite of heavy criticism from consumer organisations this defence protects suppliers of used goods.

---

[20] The Approval of Safety Standards Regulations 1987 (S.I. 1987 No. 1911).
[21] See also s.10(5).

Safety regulations

Safety regulations are an old feature of this area of consumer protection. Indeed, regulations under the Acts of 1961–1978 continue in force. The current offences for contravention of safety regulations are to be found in section 12, *e.g.* supplying goods prohibited by regulations. It is section 11 which contains the regulation-making power:

> (1) The Secretary of State may by regulations under this section ("safety regulations") make such provision as he considers appropriate for the purposes of section 10(3) above and for the purpose of securing—
>
>> (a) that goods to which this section applies are safe;
>> (b) that goods to which this section applies which are unsafe, or would be unsafe in the hands of persons of a particular description, are not made available to persons generally or, as the case may be, to persons of that description; and
>> (c) that appropriate information is, and inappropriate information is not, provided in relation to goods to which this section applies.

Thus regulations may cover not only the goods, but also information about them. Further, section 11(1)(b) makes it clear that they may relate to the supply of goods to certain groups only, a doubtful point in earlier legislation, *e.g.* fireworks not to be sold to children.

The possible contents of regulations are illustrated by a list set out in section 11(2). They include provisions relating to:

(i) composition or contents, design, construction, finish or packing;

(ii) standards to be approved, *e.g.* British Standards;

(iii) testing or inspection, *e.g.* manufacturers' quality control procedures to prevent faulty batches of aerosol cans from reaching the market;

(iv) marks, warnings, instructions or other information on goods, *e.g.* warning symbols, first-aid instructions, lists of ingredients in cosmetics; or prohibiting the giving of "inappropriate information," *e.g.* misleading marks or insignia.

The regulations may also prohibit the supply of goods or components which are unsafe or do not satisfy the requirements of the regulations. Thus a permanent ban may be imposed on dangerous products which the Secretary of State considers to be inherently unsafe irrespective of design or construction.

Emergency procedures

Extensive consultation is required by section 11(5) before the making of regulations. As many months may elapse in this way, the 1978 Act contained power for the Minister to make prohibition orders to by-pass the normal regulation-making procedures as a temporary measure in an emergency.[22]

Prohibition orders have now disappeared and been replaced by the expedited procedure set out in section 11(5). The Secretary of State may make regulations without consultation for a 12 months' maximum where "the need to protect the public requires that regulations should be made without delay."

Notices

The Act contains various powers to stop the distribution, or further distribution, of unsafe goods.

Suspension notice[23]

If an enforcement authority reasonably suspects that a trader is supplying goods in contravention of a safety provision, it may serve a "suspension notice" on him. This will prevent him disposing of his stock for a maximum of six months. The authority may have to pay compensation, if there was no contravention after all.[24] A separate, but sometimes related, route is to apply to the court for forfeiture of the goods, which usually involves their destruction.[25] In neither of these cases is a conviction of the trader a prerequisite; only a "contravention" is needed.

Prohibition notice[26]

Like the suspension notice, the "prohibition notice" is aimed at a particular trader. It is served by the Secretary of State and prohibits the supply of unsafe goods. This is a useful follow-up to the local authority's suspension notice.

Notice to warn

Prohibition notices are appropriate where goods are still in the hands of the suppliers. What can be done if the goods have already reached the public and are in daily use? Prior to the Act the most that the Department of Trade and Industry could do was to ask manufacturers to publish a warning or itself to issue a press notice. Responsible manufacturers and importers readily do so. The motor industry is a good example; as soon as any apparent defect reveals itself as a danger, e.g. brakes, the producer gives it widespread publicity and advises owners to take in their vehicles to be checked.

---

[22] See 2nd ed. of this book, pp. 238–240, for an explanation of this procedure.
[23] s.14(1).
[24] s.14(7).
[25] s.16.
[26] s.13(1)(a).

Now it is possible for a "notice to warn" to be served on any trader requiring him to publish a specified warning about unsafe goods at his own expense. So far no such notice has ever been served.

Recall

A major defect in the legislation is that no one has the power to order manufacturers to recall dangerous products.[27] In practice they do recall such goods to avoid being sued under Part I of the Act or for negligence.[28]

Penalties and defences

The penalty for any of the offences is the same—on summary conviction a maximum fine of £2,000 and up to six months' imprisonment.[29]

In addition to the special defences set out in section 10(4)[30] in respect of the GSR, the familiar defence is available that the accused "took all reasonable steps and exercised all due diligence to avoid committing the offence," with the same duty to notify the prosecutor of the identity of any one else who is being blamed.[31] These provisions are discussed elsewhere in relation to Part III.[32]

Enforcement

Although the 1961 Act merely gave a discretionary power to trading standards inspectors, section 27(1) makes it their duty to enforce the provisions creating the offences explained above. Whether with the depleted resources available to them local authorities are managing to cope with their ever-increasing responsibilities—the Consumer Credit Act 1974 is also their problem—is a matter of doubt. Nevertheless this duty is one which they must do their best to fulfil unless the Secretary of State exercises the power given to him by section 27(2) to transfer the duty elsewhere. Sections 28 and 29 give the authorities the usual related powers of purchase, entry and seizure, testing, etc., and section 30 enables a customs officer to detain imported goods for two days.

Civil remedy

In the following chapter breach of statutory duty is examined. The

---

[27] But see EC draft directive on General Product Safety, *post*, p. 378.
[28] *Ante*, p. 76.
[29] *e.g.* s.12(5).
[30] *Ante*, p. 251.
[31] s.39(1) and (2). See *Riley* v. *Webb* [1987] Crim.L.R. 477.
[32] *Ante*, p. 240.

Acts of 1961 to 1987 stand alone among the criminal statutes concerned with consumer protection in expressly affording the victim a civil remedy. Section 41(1) offers the remedy and section 41(4) prevents it being snatched away by invalidating any exclusion clause. Further, any contractual rights of the victim remain untouched.[33] However, this civil remedy applies only to breach of the safety regulations, not of the GSR. In practice, it is rarely, if ever, used.

[33] s.41(3).

CHAPTER THIRTEEN

CRIME AND COMPENSATION

1. INTRODUCTION

(1) Jane buys a used car described as "Immaculate. A really nice little bus." It is clapped out and incapable of self-propulsion. The car dealer repudiates his liability with a few unequivocal words.

(2) James reads a holiday brochure. The tour operator confirms that the hotel facilities are exactly as described, whereupon James books a holiday. When he reaches his destination, he discovers that the hotel bears little resemblance except in name to that shown in the brochure. The tour operator refuses to give compensation.

A commonly held view of the consumer protection lobby is that it is a waste of effort for Parliament and the courts to amend and improve upon the long-standing rights of consumers, *e.g.* under the Sale of Goods Act 1979, and to launch new assaults across a broad front on attempts to rob the consumer of those rights, *e.g.* under the Unfair Contract Terms Act 1977. Thus in both the above examples the consumers clearly have a right of action for breach of contract, but of what benefit are their rights unless machinery exists to enable them to be enforced without difficulty? The immediate need is for reform to be concentrated upon the enforcement of existing rights rather than the creation of new ones.

We discussed in Chapter 9 enforcement under the civil law. We saw that frequently the consumer has no alternative to suing the recalcitrant trader in the county court; for there is often no trade association able or prepared to bring about a settlement of the complaint by conciliation or to discipline the trader for falling below the standards set out in a code of practice. In such circumstances there are clearly considerable advantages to the consumer if he can reap some benefit from the fact that the trader has committed a criminal offence in addition to having broken one of his civil obligations. However, it should be borne in mind that criminal offences are not created for the purpose of providing consumers with compensation, as is pointed out in the Review of the Trade Descriptions Act 1968, para. 281:

> We believe that compensation is primarily a matter for the civil law, and
> that an award of compensation under the Powers of the Criminal Courts

Act should be regarded as a windfall rather than a right which itself justified prosecution under the Act.

It is proposed in this chapter to deal with two aspects of recovery arising out of the criminal law. First, we shall look at the power of the courts on conviction to award compensation under the Powers of Criminal Courts Act 1973. Secondly, we shall consider the circumstances in which it is possible to sue for breach of statutory duty.

2. Powers of Criminal Courts Act 1973

The recommendations of the 1970 Widgery Report with regard to the remedies available under the criminal law for compensating victims of crime were broadly carried into effect by the Criminal Justice Act 1972. The particular provision which now concerns us was replaced by section 35(1) of the Powers of Criminal Courts Act 1973.

In essence it enables the court to order a convicted person to pay compensation for any damage resulting from the offence. The section states:

> A court by or before which a person is convicted of an offence, instead of or in addition to dealing with him in any other way, may, on application or otherwise, make an order (in this Act referred to as "a compensation order") requiring him to pay compensation for any personal injury, loss or damage resulting from that offence or any other offence which is taken into consideration by the court in determining sentence.[1]

This discretionary power is available whenever there has been a conviction in any court, including a magistrates' court. It is especially valuable in cases brought under the Trade Descriptions Act 1968, where the loss may be too small to justify the cost of civil litigation.

Maximum

The amount of compensation where the conviction is on indictment in the Crown Court is unlimited. In the magistrates' court it is limited to £2,000.[2] This limit relates to each offence of which the accused is convicted; so if a supplier is convicted of four offences, the order may reach £8,000.

Special care must be taken when the accused asks for other offences to be taken into consideration for which he has not been prosecuted. No additional sums may be awarded in respect of such t.i.c. offences.[3]

---

[1] As amended by Criminal Justice Act 1982, s.67.
[2] Magistrates' Courts Act 1980, s.40, as amended by S.I. 1984 No. 447.
[3] See H. Street, "Compensation Orders and the Trade Descriptions Act," [1974] Crim. L.R. 345.

Example

A tour operator publishes a brochure containing false statements in contravention of section 14 of the Trade Descriptions Act 1968. Forty people from different parts of the United Kingdom book holidays in reliance on the brochure. The tour operator, when prosecuted in one area, asks for the 39 other offences to be taken into consideration. The magistrates' order for the 40 offences cannot exceed £2,000 in total.

From the point of view of the victims in this example it would be preferable for separate charges to be brought in each area, so that altogether the orders would have a ceiling of £80,000.[4]

Type of loss

The compensation may relate to "any personal injury, loss or damage." Thus claims for breach of contract (as in Examples 1 and 2[5]) or for negligence are covered. Further, the Act is wide enough for an order to be made in respect of loss for which no civil remedy is available: in such a case in the absence of a successful prosecution the victim would be remediless.[6]

This is most important in the case of misleading advertising, where usually the advertisement will not be a term of the contract nor a misrepresentation but mere puff. However, it may result in the commission of a criminal offence, *e.g.* under the Trade Descriptions Act, when compensation for the consumer's loss can be ordered.

Let us consider Example 2 given at the beginning of this chapter. There the statements about the hotel facilities are terms of the contract in view of the express confirmation prior to booking.[7] In the absence of that confirmation it would be more difficult, but not impossible,[8] for James to show that the wording in the brochure was by itself a term or misrepresentation; nevertheless if a conviction were obtained under the Trade Descriptions Act, compensation could be claimed.

There are two exceptions where an order cannot be made[9]: (a) for

---

[4] Multiple prosecutions are discussed in the chapter on Trade Descriptions: see p. 228.
[5] *Ante*, p. 257.
[6] See *R.* v. *Chappel* [1984] Crim.L.R. 574.
[7] See *Jackson* v. *Horizon Holidays Ltd.* [1975] 1 W.L.R. 1468 (C.A.). A four week family holiday in Sri Lanka proved to be a disaster, with very distasteful food apparently cooked in coconut oil, and only a shower and no bath. The holiday price was £1,200. Damages of £1,100 were awarded for breach of contract.
[8] *Jarvis* v. *Swans Tours* [1973] 1 Q.B. 233 (C.A.) is another heart-rending case. The plaintiff, on a fortnight's holiday in the Swiss Alps, spent an entire week surrounded by foreigners who could not speak English! As a further insult instead of Swiss cakes he was served crisps and desiccated nut rolls. (As their Lordships pointed out during the trial, "You don't have to go to Switzerland to get those": Stephenson L.J. "You can get them at Crewe": Edmund Davies L.J.—*The Times* October 19, 1972.) Damages of £125 were awarded, double the cost of the holiday.
[9] s.35(3).

loss suffered by dependants in consequence of the victim's death; (b) for injury, loss or damage due to an accident arising out of the presence of a motor vehicle on a road unless resulting from a Theft Act offence.

Assessment

As the assessment of compensation will commonly be made by lay magistrates, it is inappropriate for the power to be exercised in complicated cases, *e.g.* where the principles of remoteness of damage need to be understood and applied. An order will be made only in straightforward cases. Lawton L.J. explained the court's approach in *R.* v. *Thomson Holidays Ltd.*[10]

> "Parliament, we are sure, never intended to introduce into the criminal law the concepts of causation which apply to the assessment of damages under the law of contract or tort. . . . [The court] must do what it can to make a just order on such information as it has. Whenever the making of an order for compensation is appropriate, the court must ask itself whether loss or damage can fairly be said to have resulted to anyone from the offence for which the accused has been convicted."[11]

The defendants were convicted under section 14 of the Trade Descriptions Act 1968 for making a false statement in their brochure that a hotel had a night club and swimming and paddling pools. Compensation of £50 was awarded to the complainant.

A separate point to bear in mind is that the victim must show that the defendant is liable for the amount claimed. In *R.* v. *Vivian*[12] the Court of Appeal quashed an order in respect of damage to a car alleged to have been done by a thief in a collision, as there was no proof that he was responsible for all the damage: further, the appellant claimed that the sole estimate given for the repairs was excessive. Talbot J. said[13] that the view of the court was that "no order for compensation should be made unless the sum claimed by way of compensation is either agreed or has been proved." This appears to leave a large loophole for defendants and certainly makes it necessary in this type of case for victims to be less perfunctory in preparing claims, *e.g.* by obtaining more than one estimate.

Situations where it would be appropriate to make an order include misdescribed goods, *e.g.* clocked or misdescribed cars (Example 1),[14] where the reduction in value or cost of repair can be easily proved, and

---

[10] [1974] Q.B. 592, 599.
[11] See also *R.* v. *Daly* [1974] 1 All E.R. 290; *R.* v. *Kneeshaw* [1974] 1 All E.R. 896: the machinery is intended "for clear and simple cases" (*per* Lord Widgery C.J.).
[12] [1979] 1 All E.R. 48.
[13] *Ibid.* p. 50.
[14] *Ante*, p. 257.

holiday cases where part of the cost can be refunded to take account of inconvenience and loss of enjoyment (Example 2).

In determining whether to make an order and, if so, for what amount, the court must take into account the defendant's means[15] and generally limits the award to a sum which he can manage to pay over two or three years. Thus in *R.* v. *McIntosh*[16] the Court of Appeal revoked a £90 order against a burglar on the grounds that he had no means and would find it hard to obtain employment on his release from prison because of his wooden leg—surprisingly not an impediment to the nefarious activities of this Long John McSilver in a trade where one would expect agility to be a *sine qua non*! Similarly it is not generally appropriate to make an order where the defendant is sentenced to a significant period of imprisonment, unless he has assets in hand to pay the compensation.[17]

How to apply

No procedure is laid down for making the application for compensation. Generally it is enough for the victim to forewarn the clerk or prosecutor before the trial commences, so that the application may be brought to the notice of the court after conviction and the victim then heard. Alternatively the court may act of its initiative without an application. Although it is customary for the prosecution to pass on a request for compensation, they are not under a duty to conduct an inquiry into the defendant's means.[18]

An order is enforceable in the same ways as a fine.[19] Thus the court may impose a term of imprisonment in default.

Interrelation with civil rights

Generally the trial of the criminal charge will be held some time before any civil proceedings reach that stage. In the subsequent civil proceedings two points must be borne in mind. First, the conviction may be used in evidence.[20] Secondly, when awarding damages the court must take into account sums paid under the order.[21]

If exceptionally the civil proceedings have already come to an end, whether by judgment or settlement, no order can be made even though the victim can still show loss. In *Hammertons Cars Ltd.* v. *London Borough of Redbridge*[22]:

---

[15] s.35(4).
[16] [1973] Crim.L.R. 378.
[17] *R.* v. *McCullough* (1982) 4 Cr.App.R.(S.) 98 (C.A.); *R.* v. *Morgan* (1982) 4 Cr.App.R.(S.) 358 (C.A.).
[18] *R.* v. *Johnstone* (1982) 4 Cr.App.R.(S.) 141.
[19] Magistrates' Courts Act 1980, s.76.
[20] Civil Evidence Act 1968, s.11.
[21] 1973 Act, s.38(2).
[22] [1974] 2 All E.R. 216.

The complainant bought a car described as "in perfect condition." It was not. He settled an action against the sellers on the basis that he paid his own legal costs of £170 and expert's fee of £25. When the sellers were convicted under the Trade Descriptions Act he was awarded £195 compensation by the justices. The dealer successfully appealed against the order to the Divisional Court.

Lord Widgery C.J., doubting whether in any case the section would cover such legal costs, said:

> "It seems to me to be abundantly clear that if the victim brings civil proceedings, and those civil proceedings are brought to an end, then they should be regarded as quite independent of the criminal proceedings and no compensation order should be made in respect of liabilities which arose, or might have arisen, in the civil proceedings."

3. Breach of Statutory Duty

As has been seen earlier, frequently a consumer who has suffered loss will have a remedy flowing directly or indirectly from the civil or criminal law. As far as the civil law is concerned, the remedy may be for breach of contract, *e.g.* against a supplier of goods or services who has not fulfilled obligations imposed upon him by statute or the common law, or in tort for negligence or under the Consumer Protection Act 1987, *e.g.* against a manufacturer. Alternatively or additionally, where the supplier's activities involve a criminal offence resulting in a successful prosecution, the consumer may seek compensation under the Powers of Criminal Courts Act.

However, a hiatus exists where the supplier has not broken a contract with the consumer, maybe because they are not in a contractual relationship; nor has he been negligent; nor does the Consumer Protection Act apply, perhaps because his damage is too small; nor has the consumer recovered compensation, even though the supplier has committed a criminal offence, *e.g.* because no prosecution was brought or, even if it was and a conviction obtained, the justices would not make an order, as perhaps it was too complicated a case. (If, of course, the supplier is not guilty of any offence, the consumer has reached the end of the road.) In such circumstances the consumer's last resort is to try to show that the supplier is liable in tort for breach of statutory duty.[23]

If it were possible for such an action to be brought in every case where a supplier has failed to comply with his statutory duties, the consumer's position would be much more straightforward. In the absence of an award of compensation under the 1973 Act, he would be able to institute civil proceedings on this basis without concerning himself with such questions as privity of contract with the supplier.

However, the courts when construing statutes have been reluctant

---

[23] For a more general treatment of this topic, see the leading works on tort, *e.g. Winfield and Jolowicz on Tort*, Sweet & Maxwell (13th ed.), Chap. 7.

to imply into them civil rights for the victim. The rationale seems to be that the legislation is for the protection of the public generally and is not intended to afford a civil remedy to individual members of the public. The reasoning is unconvincing. To draw an analogy from the contractual principles of offer and acceptance, where an offer is made to the world at large, contracts are formed only with those individuals who accept the offer; similarly where a duty is imposed on suppliers for the benefit of the public at large, it should be possible for those particular members of the public who suffer loss as a result of a breach of that duty to come forward and claim damages in a civil action founded upon that statutory duty.

Yet generally the courts are content to leave consumers to their separate civil rights. Thus in *Square* v. *Model Farm Dairies (Bournemouth) Ltd.*,[24] where the plaintiff alleged that contaminated milk sold in breach of the food legislation had made his family ill with typhoid fever, the Court of Appeal rejected his claim because he had a remedy under the Sale of Goods Act. A comparable case is *Buckley* v. *La Réserve*[25] where an action failed against a restaurant which in contravention of the Food and Drugs Act 1955 sold food unfit for human consumption (the food was snails: legal symmetry would have been attained had the contamination resulted from ginger beer). It is important to note that on the particular facts the plaintiff's civil rights would not have given him a remedy unless he could prove negligence, as he was taken to the restaurant as a guest, and had no contractual claim against the restaurant: nevertheless the court adopted the same stance as in the *Square* case.

Two cases involving defective cars also illustrate the courts' unhelpful attitude to consumers. In *Phillips* v. *Britannia Hygienic Laundry Co.*[26] the plaintiff failed to recover for injuries resulting from the defendants' breach of duties imposed by the antecedents to the present Motor Vehicles (Construction and Use) Regulations. Similarly a seller was not liable to a victim injured by a vehicle which the seller delivered in such a condition that its use on the road was unlawful, although he thereby committed an offence under what is now section 75 of the Road Traffic Act 1988.[27]

The courts' restrictive interpretation leads to this principle in the consumer field: an action for breach of statutory duty has a chance of success only if the statute *expressly* states that a breach of the duty is actionable, *e.g.* the Consumer Protection Act 1987, s.41(1):[28]

---

[24] [1939] 2 K.B. 365.
[25] [1959] Crim.L.R. 451.
[26] [1923] 2 K.B. 832.
[27] *Badham* v. *Lambs Ltd.* [1946] K.B. 45.
[28] *Ante*, p. 255. For another example, see Consumer Credit Act 1974, s.92(3): entry to premises to recover possession of goods or land, *post*, p. 358.

> An obligation imposed by safety regulations shall be a duty owed to any person who may be affected by a contravention of the obligation and, subject to any provision to the contrary in the regulations and to the defences and other incidents applying to actions for breach of statutory duty, a contravention of any such obligation shall be actionable accordingly.

Where a statute states the opposite, the position is equally clear. Where a statute is silent on the point, the presumption is that it gives no civil remedy. Such a presumption is strengthened where the statute expressly preserves other civil remedies, following the reasoning in *Square* v. *Model Farm Dairies (Bournemouth) Ltd.*,[29] for then Parliament is implicitly leaving the public to their general civil rights.

It is on these grounds that we take the view that no action will lie for breach of statutory duty arising out of the Trade Descriptions Act 1968, section 35[30] of which saves civil rights by stating, "A contract for the supply of goods shall not be void or unenforceable by reason only of a contravention of any provision of the Act." That view is fortified by observing that the 1968 Act does not include any provision equivalent to section 17 of the repealed Merchandise Marks Act 1887 whereby a seller was deemed to warrant the accuracy of any trade description. The omission is deliberate and contrary to the recommendation in the Final Report of the Committee on Consumer Protection (Cmnd. 1781) that the provision should remain and "contracting-out" be prohibited. We think it fitting to end with a plea that further consideration be given by the courts and parliamentary reformers to the view expressed in para. 459 of the Report.

> We cannot avoid the conclusion that Section 17 reflects a sound principle, namely that persons trading in goods to which false trade descriptions have been applied should be liable, not merely under the criminal law, but also to meet any civil claim in favour of a purchaser arising from the same circumstances.

[29] *Ante*, p. 263.
[30] *Ante*, p. 229.

Part III

ADMINISTRATIVE CONTROL

The civil and criminal sanctions discussed earlier in this book do a great deal to protect the consumer, but by themselves they are not enough. In particular:

1. Industry is never static for long and the enterprising trader is likely to come up with new business practices. Some of these, while within the law, may be harmful to consumers and swift action may be needed to curtail them.

2. There may be a number of dishonest or inefficient traders who may make large profits, *e.g.* by the delivery of shoddy goods or by practices which infringe the Trade Descriptions Act 1968. They may not be deterred by the occasional fine or award of compensation. What the consumer really needs is a system whereby such traders can be restrained from trading altogether unless they mend their ways.

3. The standards set by the law are minimum standards and the consumer can benefit if traders can be persuaded to undertake additional voluntary obligations.

4. Neither the civil nor the criminal law achieve one of the most important aims of consumer protection—making the consumer aware of his rights.

It is at this point that we meet the third weapon of consumer protection—administrative control. This involves a public body charged with the task of keeping the consumer scene under permanent review. The principal weapons of administrative control are to be found in the Fair Trading Act 1973 and the Consumer Credit Act 1974. The former (which also deals with monopolies, mergers and restrictive practices) is examined in Chapter 14 and the Consumer Credit Act will be dealt with in Chapters 15–23.

Chapter Fourteen

FAIR TRADING

1. Introduction

UNLIKE the Consumer Credit Act 1974, which was substantially based upon the recommendations of the Crowther Committee's Report on Consumer Credit, the Fair Trading Act 1973 appeared out of the blue with no warning or consultation in the form of Green or White Papers.

Most of the Act does not break new ground inasmuch as broadly it consolidates, with some changes and improvements, the pre-existing law relating to competition, *i.e.* monopolies, mergers and restrictive practices. However, it contains five innovations. First, it creates the post of Director General of Fair Trading (Part I). Secondly, it gives to the Director General power to initiate subordinate legislation to protect the consumer by banning undesirable trade practices as and when they appear (Part II). Thirdly, it enables the Director General to bring into line individual rogue traders who regularly flout their legal obligations (Part III). Fourthly, the Director General is under a duty to encourage trade associations to prepare, and to disseminate to their members, voluntary codes of practice (s.124(3)). Finally, the Director General can arrange for publication of information and advice to consumers (s.124(1)). The last two topics have already been considered in Chapter 9[1] and accordingly this chapter will examine the other novel features of the Act mentioned above.

It is true that the Act gives to the consumer no right of action or opportunity to claim compensation, but he can lodge a complaint with the Office of Fair Trading directly or via a trading standards officer or C.A.B. This gives the consumer two benefits: the satisfaction of knowing that his complaint has added to the information kept by the O.F.T. and may have helped to identify and ultimately to outlaw an undesirable trade practice within Part II; and the exhilaration of hoping that a note of his grievance on the file of the particular trader may tip the balance and provide the evidence to show that the trader is persistent in his improper activities and should be brought to book under Part III.[2] (One should not underestimate the importance to the consumer of a chance to vent his feelings to a public official in the

---

[1] *Ante*, pp. 148–154 and see also the Appendices *post*, pp. 383–420.
[2] Or, in appropriate cases, deprived of his licence under the Consumer Credit Act (*post*, p. 315).

expectation, sometimes vain, that some action will ensue whether or not he is able to recover financial redress.)

The Director General

The Director General is appointed by the Secretary of State for Trade and Industry for a term of office not exceeding five years although he may be re-appointed (s.1). The first Director General was Sir John Methven, a solicitor with a local government and industrial background. His successor, now in his third term of office, is Sir Gordon Borrie, a barrister, formerly a member of the Consumer Protection Advisory Committee and Professor of Law at Birmingham University.[3]

The Director General has two general functions relating to consumer protection, which are set out in section 2(1). These duties must be carried out "so far as appears to him to be practicable from time to time." One is active, the other passive. His active rôle is to keep under review the carrying on of commercial activities which relate to the supply of goods or services to consumers and to collect information with respect to such activities and the persons by whom they are carried on. He is to do this with a view to becoming aware of and ascertaining the circumstances relating to practices which may adversely affect the economic interests of consumers—only the economic interests, nothing else.

His other rôle, his passive function, is to receive and collate evidence becoming available to him with respect to such activities. The purpose of this is to build up dossiers of evidence on practices which may adversely affect consumer interests, but in this case the interests may be not only economic but also interests with respect to health, safety or other matters. An example given in the debates on the Act was unsafe child "safety" harnesses. So unless economic interests are affected, the Director General is obliged to do nothing except to wait to see what information comes in to him.

In addition the Director General must assist the Secretary of State when required to do so and can make recommendations to him (s.2(3)), as happened in the case of the Price Marking (Bargain Offers) Order 1979.[4]

The Office of Fair Trading

The O.F.T. is not specifically created by or mentioned in the Act. Section 1(5) enables the Director General to appoint such staff as he

---

[3] For a résumé of his functions by the Director General himself, see the transcript of a lecture to the Bar Association for Commerce, Finance and Industry (1977) 74 L.S.Gaz. 70.
[4] *Ante,* p. 231.

thinks fit—there are over 300 now. The O.F.T. is the Director General and his staff in aggregate. It is a Government department but not all of the staff are civil servants. Its address is Field House, Breams Buildings, London, EC4A 1PR.

Perhaps it might be useful at this point to mention one function which the O.F.T. does not have; *it does not deal with individual complaints* (although it will keep a record of the complaint which may become relevant in a future investigation).

The Consumer Protection Advisory Committee

The C.P.A.C., established under section 3, has between 10 and 15 members appointed by the Secretary of State. It has merely an advisory role. It cannot take any initiative by making proposals for action and exists to consider references to it under section 14 and, if the references are coupled with proposals under section 17, to consider the proposals too. The controlling and directing power lies with the Secretary of State. This is clear from section 12, which states that the Secretary of State may give general directions indicating considerations to which the Director General should have particular regard in determining the order of priority in which matters are to be brought under review under section 2, whether to make a reference to the Committee under Part II, etc.

It has been moribund since 1982 when the Minister for Consumer Affairs announced that he had "decided for the present not to reappoint existing members . . . as their appointments expire or to appoint new members."[5] The last reference to the C.P.A.C. was made in 1977 in respect of VAT-exclusive prices.

2. PART II—ADVERSE CONSUMER TRADE PRACTICES

The essential differences between Parts II and III is that Part II is concerned with undesirable *practices*, whereas Part III is concerned with undesirable *traders*. Thus under Part II it is possible for a statutory order to be made banning certain undesirable trade practices, whereas under Part III the attack is not upon a general practice but upon an individual trader who persistently acts in a way which is unfair to consumers.

The point of Part II is to refer consumer trade practices to the C.P.A.C. so that the C.P.A.C. may consider whether they adversely affect the economic interests of consumers and then report. More importantly it is possible to couple with that reference proposals for action, so that the C.P.A.C. when reporting may give its view on those proposals.

---

[5] Department of Trade Press Notice, September 24, 1982.

Consumer trade practice

There is no complete freedom of choice as to what practices may be referred; the term "consumer trade practice" is exhaustively defined in section 13, *i.e.* any practice carried on in connection with the supply of goods or services to consumers and which relates to one of the six matters specified in paragraphs (a) to (f) of the section:

(a) the terms or conditions of supply, *e.g.* the continued use of void exemption clauses, VAT-exclusive prices;

(b) the manner in which those terms are communicated, *e.g.* the size of print;

(c) promotion, *e.g.* advertisements, labels;

(d) methods of salesmanship, *e.g.* doorstep selling, traders masquerading as private sellers in small ads;

(e) packaging, *e.g.* large containers only half filled but accurately marked with the amount of their contents;

(f) methods of demanding or securing payment, *e.g.* requiring a deposit when an order is placed.

The procedure

A reference under section 14 can be made by the Director General or any Minister. The C.P.A.C. considers "whether a consumer trade practice specified in the reference adversely affects the economic interest of consumers" and reports back. Unless the reference falls within section 17 and includes proposals, that is the end of the matter.

There are some exclusions from section 14. No reference may be made in respect of certain professions, *e.g.* legal, medical, dental, where it appears that a monopoly situation exists[6] nor, without Ministerial consent, in respect of the supply of certain goods or services, *e.g.* gas, electricity, rail, post.[7]

The real punch in Part II lies in section 17, which provides that references by the Director General—by no one else—may include proposals for action by the Secretary of State. The scope of section 17 is narrower than section 14 in that, although the reference must again relate to a consumer trade practice as defined in section 13, the practice must also fall within one of the four paragraphs of section 17(2). It is necessary for the Director General to consider that the practice has or is likely to have the effect:

(a) of misleading consumers as to, or withholding from them adequate information as to, or an adequate record of, their rights and obligations under relevant consumer transactions, or

---

[6] s.15 and Schedule 4.
[7] s.16 and Schedule 5.

(b) of otherwise misleading or confusing consumers with respect to any matter in connection with relevant consumer transactions, or

(c) of subjecting consumers to undue pressure to enter into relevant consumer transactions, or

(d) of causing the terms or conditions, on or subject to which consumers enter into relevant consumer transactions, to be so adverse to them as to be inequitable.

The common flavour of these four recipes is of misleading or confusing consumers or pressurising them to enter into unfair transactions. Schedule 6 to the Act gives half a dozen illustrations, but not exhaustively, of matters falling within the scope of section 17 proposals. The third one is "prohibition of the inclusion in specified consumer transactions of terms or conditions purporting to exclude or limit the liability of a party to such a transaction in respect of specified matters"; this proved to be the substance of the first order under Part II.[8]

The sequence of a section 17 reference is as follows. The reference is made by the Director General who may—but there is no obligation—include proposals for recommending to the Secretary of State that he exercises his powers under the Act. The C.P.A.C. considers the reference and proposals and reports within three months, unless that period is extended by the Secretary of State.[9] In fact all four of the reports to date took six months or more to be published. In its report the C.P.A.C. states whether the practice is adverse and, if so, for which of the reasons mentioned in section 17. Where the practice is adverse, it must also state whether it agrees with the Director General's proposals, would agree with them if they were modified or disagrees with them.[10] Unless the C.P.A.C. disagrees with the proposals, the Secretary of State may make an order by statutory instrument giving effect to the proposals as set out in the reference or as modified by the C.P.A.C. in its report.[11] This order will not be effective until it has been approved by a resolution of each House of Parliament.

Penalties and enforcement

Orders under section 22 are enforced by criminal sanctions only. There is a marked similarity between Part II of this Act and the Trade Descriptions Act 1968 as regards penalties, defences and enforcement. Accordingly, it is not proposed to discuss such provisions in detail in this chapter: readers are referred to Chapter 11.[12]

Briefly, the maximum penalties for contravention of a prohibition are a £2,000 fine on summary conviction; an unlimited fine or two

[8] *Post*, p. 274.
[9] s.20.
[10] s.21.
[11] s.22.
[12] See *ante*, p. 195 *et seq.*

years' imprisonment or both if convicted on indictment.[13] Proceedings may be taken against any director, manager, secretary or other similar officer of a company, where an offence by the company was committed with his consent or connivance or is attributable to his neglect.[14]

Section 25 provides the same five defences, *e.g.* mistake, act or default of another person, etc. Again the defendant must prove the two factors of "reasonable precautions" and "due diligence."

Enforcement is once more by local weights and measures authorities[15] whose officers have power to make test purchases[16] and to enter premises to inspect and to seize goods and documents.[17]

The Act provides no special remedy but does not vitiate any such remedy which may otherwise be available, *e.g.* for breach of contract.[18]

Speedy procedure?

The intention and expectation was that it would be possible to identify new abuses at an early stage, to recommend and quickly to put into effect prohibitive measures and thus to squash the practice before it mushroomed. Indeed, in April 1974 the Director General stated, when announcing the first reference to the C.P.A.C., that he hoped that in six months a statutory order would be made: it actually appeared two and a half years later. Both Director Generals have expressed disappointment with the slow working of Part II. There are many reasons. Sometimes the C.P.A.C. is unable to agree a report within the three months' period (first and fourth references); on other occasions (second and third references) publication of the reports is delayed by the Government while it clarifies its own intentions. Further delays occur when the report passes from the O.F.T. to the Department of Trade and Industry for implementation. It may be significant that, in relation to bargain offers, the Director General chose to sidestep the C.P.A.C. completely by using his power to present the Secretary of State with a recommendation for action.[19] As the last reference was made in 1977, it seems that the Part II machinery has been moth-balled, if not placed in a museum.

However, although the Part II procedure is time-consuming there can be little doubt that it is quicker than waiting for Parliamentary time to legislate on each particular matter. One comparison will suffice. In 1966 a Working Party was established to assist the Law Commission in

[13] s.23, as increased by S.I. 1984 No. 447.
[14] s.132.
[15] s.27.
[16] s.28.
[17] s.29.
[18] s.26.
[19] s.2(3), *ante*, p. 231.

its consideration of exclusion clauses relating to negligence and contracts for the supply of services. This resulted, after the intervening publication of a Working Paper and Report, in the Unfair Contract Terms Act 1977. Perhaps that places in perspective the two and a half years from reference to Order in the case of the first reference, to which we now turn.

Restrictions on statements

"No refunds"
"Money will not be refunded. Credit notes only"
"Sale goods may not be returned"

The first reference to the C.P.A.C. in April 1974 was described in the Director General's Dossier 17/1 as "The Purported Exclusion of Inalienable Rights of Consumers and Failure to Explain their Existence." The reference, the report and the Order embraced the supply of goods by way of sale, hire-purchase and trading stamps. It covers three practices.

C.P.A.C. reference

(1) The first practice is the continuing use of void exemption clauses. The Supply of Goods (Implied Terms) Act 1973 contained provisions which invalidated exemption clauses relating to the statutory implied terms in consumer sale and hire-purchase agreements.[20] However, such clauses, though void, were not illegal. So the practice continued of exhibiting shop notices like the above examples which purport to take away the buyer's right of rejection and money back for breach of condition. Similarly, there was nothing to prevent a car dealer or other seller from incorporating an exclusion clause in his printed sales agreement with the intention that a customer reading the agreement would mistakenly think that the clause was valid and effective and that therefore he had no remedy for defects. Terms of sale printed in price lists and catalogues could be similarly misleading.

(2) The second practice is concerned with written statements furnished by suppliers of goods which purport to set out the rights and obligations of the parties but fail to advise consumers of their inalienable rights, *e.g.* under sections 13–15 of the Sale of Goods Act 1979. Thus a car dealer might give a three months' guarantee on a second-hand car, covering parts but not labour, without revealing to the buyer that, irrespective of the guarantee, the buyer has the benefit of the implied conditions under the 1979 Act.

---

[20] The relevant provisions are now ss.6 and 12 of the Unfair Contract Terms Act 1977. See Chap. 8, *ante*, pp. 131 and 135.

(3) The third practice is similar to the second practice except that the written statements relate to the consumer's rights against *third parties* such as manufacturers. Thus, a shopkeeper may pass on to his customer a manufacturer's guarantee giving the impression that the customer's rights in respect of defects lie only against the manufacturer under the terms of the guarantee without explaining the buyer's statutory rights against the shopkeeper *qua* seller.[21] The Dossier identifies the problem as follows:

> There is apparently a wide-spread belief among consumers that manufacturers are primarily responsible to them *in law* for defects in manufactured goods, (particularly goods which are packed by the manufacturer, so that a retailer may be unaware of the defect); and this belief is often fostered by shop staff, who are naturally eager to preserve the retailer's reputation when faulty goods are identified or returned, by attributing responsibility to the manufacturer. Thus in a situation where goods fail to correspond to their description or are unfit for the purpose made known to the seller, or are of unmerchantable quality or fail to correspond with the sample—or where goods are deficient on more than one of these counts—this aspect of the practice undermines the consumer's proper understanding of his legal position.

The C.P.A.C. published its Report[22] in December 1974. It found that all three practices fell within section 13(*a*) and adversely affected the economic interests of consumers by having the effects specified in section 17(2), namely, of misleading consumers as to their rights under relevant consumer transactions or otherwise confusing them as to the terms of the transaction. They agreed with the Director General's proposals subject to certain modifications narrowing their scope. Those modified proposals were put into effect by the Consumer Transactions (Restrictions on Statements) Order 1976.[23]

The Order

(1) Article 3 banned the first practice. It made it an offence to display at any place where consumer transactions[24] are effected, *e.g.* a shop or car showroom, a notice containing a term invalidated by what is now section 6 of the Unfair Contract Terms Act 1977[25] (Article 3(*a*)). A ban was also imposed on the following items in so far as they relate to consumer transactions and include similar void terms—advertisements, including catalogues and circulars; goods or their containers;

---

[21] See Chap. 5, *ante*, p. 60, for a discussion of guarantees.
[22] H.C. 6 Session 1974/75.
[23] S.I. 1976 No. 1813, as amended by S.I. 1978 No. 127 in consequence of the repeal by the 1977 Act of s.55(3) to (11) of the 1893 Act: no substantive changes result.
[24] The definition of "consumer transaction" in Art. 2(1) gives it the same meaning as "consumer dealing" in the 1977 Act, s.12, *ante*, p. 131.
[25] *Ante*, p. 135 *et seq*.

and documents (Article 3(*b*), (*c*) and (*d*)). However, *oral* statements are not illegal, even though void; this explains why shop assistants adopt the practice of telling customers, particularly at sale time, that they cannot bring goods back if dissatisfied.

Two Divisional Court cases have shed some darkness on the meaning of Article 3(*d*). Article 3 provides that "A person shall not, in the course of a business—

> (d) furnish to a consumer in connection with the carrying out of a consumer transaction or to a person likely, as a consumer, to enter into such a transaction, a document which includes a statement which is a term of that transaction and is void. . . ."

In the first of the two cases, *Hughes* v. *Hall*,[26] the court considered the expression "sold as seen and inspected" in a document furnished to a private customer by a motor dealer. The court decided that an offence had been committed. The court agreed that the clause would not necessarily remove all the consumer's rights and in particular that express obligations might remain. "But in my judgment he would lose some of his rights, even if he might still have other rights. This to my mind is quite sufficient to create an offence under this Act, because anything which has that effect would be voided by section 6(2) of the Unfair Contract Terms Act 1977."[27] The court was of the view that the clause excluded the conditions as to description implied by section 13 of the 1979 Act.

The court reached the opposite conclusion when considering a very similar phrase—"bought as seen"—in the later decision of *Cavendish-Woodhouse Ltd.* v. *Manley*.[28] The court distinguished the earlier decision on a number of questionable grounds. The first related to the fact that the expression appeared in an invoice relating to a suite sold by a furniture store. Ackner L.J. distinguished *Hughes* v. *Hall*, "a puzzling decision," on the grounds that the court was dealing with a "somewhat different phrase in a different trade. I consider that we are entitled to treat it as a decision on its particular facts which we are not obliged to follow." This facile distinction is in our view a distinction without a difference.

An unfortunate aspect of the case was that both parties agreed that the sale was not a sale by description within section 13. "The respondent went into a shop during a sale and he chose the goods which he decided to purchase. They were specific goods which he inspected" (Ackner L.J.). Yet it is well settled that a sale may still be governed by section 13 even though the buyer buys specific goods inspected prior to

[26] [1981] R.T.R. 430.
[27] *Per* Donaldson L.J., *ibid.* at 437.
[28] (1984) 148 J.P. 299.

purchase.[29] The authority of earlier decisions on the point is strengthened by section 13(3), the effect of which is that goods on display may describe themselves.[30] It can hardly be correct that a buyer will have no redress under section 13 if, for example, a suite described on a label as "covered in real leather" proves to be plastic. On the assumption that generally such sales are sales by description, what difference should it make whether the goods are a suite, a shirt or a second-hand car, or whether the words used are "bought" or "sold" as seen?

The crucial question, therefore, was whether the words purported to exclude the implied conditions of merchantable quality and fitness for a particular purpose. On this question of construction, as Ackner L.J. pointed out, "it was well-established that if the statutorily implied terms were to be excluded, very clear language had to be used."[31] It has to be admitted that applying the *contra proferentem* rule the phrase "bought as seen" is not an apt expression to exclude the conditions in sections 14(2) and 14(3), even though an uninformed buyer may wrongly believe that it precludes a claim for defective goods. The court's decision on the meaning was explained by Ackner L.J.:

> "In my judgment all this phrase does is to confirm that the purchaser has seen the goods which he has bought. Accordingly, if thereafter there is a dispute as to the condition of the goods when he purchased them, a factor which can be used as part of the material to resolve that dispute is the fact that it was not a purchase by description. It was a sale of specific goods which he in fact did see and purchased as a result of seeing them."

Thus if the goods had an obvious defect, the seller could use the invoice as evidence of a pre-contractual examination by the buyer and call in aid the proviso in section 14(2)(*b*).[32] As the phrase is not an exemption clause, it is not invalidated by section 6(2)(*a*) of the 1977 Act and so does not give rise to a criminal offence. We can but hope that the courts will consider that this later decision too is "a decision on its particular facts" and refuse to follow it, if another trading standards authority is bold and affluent enough to take a test case to resolve the present dilemma, preferably to the Court of Appeal. Meanwhile it is all very puzzling indeed.

(2) The second practice was outlawed by Article 4. It makes it an offence to supply goods, their container or a document to a consumer with a statement about his rights against the supplier with regard to defects, fitness for purpose or correspondence with description unless there is, "in close proximity" to that statement, another "clear and conspicuous" statement to the effect that the statutory rights of the

[29] *Ante*, p. 37.
[30] *Ibid.*
[31] *Ante*, p. 123.
[32] *Ante*, p. 51.

consumer are not affected. Like Article 3 this applies only where the goods or documents are supplied in a consumer transaction where there is a *contractual relationship* between the supplier and the consumer.

(3) The third practice was prohibited by Article 5. Its requirement is similar to that in Article 4, *i.e.* an obligation on the supplier to give information by drawing the consumer's attention to his statutory rights where the goods, their packaging or a document contain statements setting out the obligations accepted by the supplier. The difference between the two is that Article 5 applies where, although there is no direct consumer transaction between the business supplier and the consumer, the supplier intended or might reasonably have expected his goods to become the subject of a *subsequent* consumer transaction.

The provision applies to a manufacturer's guarantee where the manufacturer realises that the goods will reach a consumer indirectly via a retailer. It is unfortunate that the Order does not lay down any precise form of wording to be adopted by suppliers. A common formula in guarantees is "This does not affect your statutory rights." It is doubtful whether this cryptic message disabuses the shopper in Balham of the misapprehension that an express guarantee replaces the statutory implied terms, however self-explanatory it may be to readers of this book.

No exchange

One practice which is still legal and unaffected by the Order is that of displaying notices stating "Goods may not be *exchanged*." The reason is simply that there is in law no right to claim a replacement, however defective goods may be—the remedies for breach are rejection with a refund and damages. Such a term is not, therefore, invalidated by the 1977 Act and so falls outside the Order. Yet notices of this sort tend to mislead members of the public who are unlikely to see the distinction between refunds and exchanges and may well think that a notice denying one implicitly denies the other. Indeed the Director General proposed that such statements should fall within the Order but this was one of the points on which the C.P.A.C. modified his proposals. Their view was that the Order should be limited to void terms and should not make it illegal to make an accurate statement of law.

Void but legal

Since the reference to the C.P.A.C. was made, the wider statutory attack on exemption clauses made by the Unfair Contract Terms Act 1977 has invalidated further contractual terms and notices, *e.g.* certain exemption clauses in contracts for the hire of goods or in work and materials contracts, and also clauses and notices excluding liability for death or personal injury resulting from negligence.[33] Statements relating to such matters, though void, are not illegal as they are not within the ambit of the 1976 Order. They can still be seen in notices displayed in such places as car parks, car washes and wildlife parks, and in tickets or agreements issued by ferries, car hire companies and home improvement firms. This must be very confusing for consumers. For example, if a consumer buys kitchen units and a split-level oven to fit them himself or to have them fitted by a tradesman, any exemption clause in the sales agreement relating to the statutory implied terms is void and illegal; but if he arranges for the tradesman to supply *and* install the goods—a contract for work and materials governed by the Supply of Goods and Services Act 1982—a similar exemption clause, though still void, is legal. The consumer would be forgiven in the latter case for assuming incorrectly that the exemption clause affects his rights in civil law.

If these practices are to be prohibited under Part II, a separate reference will have to be made to the C.P.A.C. unless the Director General makes use of his power under section 2(3) to make recommendations directly to the Secretary of State.[34] Both of these courses of action seem remote in the present political climate. Meanwhile the Director General is trying to dissuade traders from using such misleading terms by writing to them and their trade associations pointing out the effect of their practices. This persuasion is backed by such comments as "I would remind those traders engaged in consumer credit or hire that when I examine their fitness to obtain or retain a credit licence, I take into account the fairness of their standard contract terms. If these are suspect, it obviously brings their fitness to be licensed into doubt."[35] The O.F.T. claims that this campaign for voluntary self-regulation has been 80 per cent. effective.[36]

Intervention from Brussels, however, to protect consumers may well provide the solution to some of these areas of difficulty. In this context the draft directives on Unfair Contract Terms and on Suppliers of Services, discussed in Chapter 24, are particularly relevant.

Mail order transactions

"Send c.w.o."
"Payment with order POST FREE"
"Send now only £1 per pair including postage"

The second reference made in May 1974 related to "Prepayment in

---

[33] See Chap. 8, *ante*, pp. 150 *et seq.*
[34] *Ante*, p. 231.
[35] O.F.T. Press Release, March 28, 1984.
[36] Bee Line No. 34 (June 1984).

Mail Order Transactions and in Shops."[37] It concerns the practice whereby suppliers require prepayments in full, or a deposit, when goods are ordered without specifying a delivery period or specifying a delivery date which is not met. Such problems are most frequent in mail order businesses where a wide range of goods is available either direct from the manufacturers or from the postal bargain trade, *e.g.* records, binoculars, beds, greenhouses, garages. Difficulties are more likely to arise when ordering from traders advertising in newspapers, magazines and colour supplements, than from the established catalogue firms whose business is conducted mainly on credit. However, the practice is not confined to mail order business. Frequently shops require deposits when taking orders for goods not in stock, *e.g.* furniture. Of course, the civil remedy available to the buyer if goods are not delivered within the specified time or, if none, within a reasonable time is to treat the contract as repudiated and to demand his money back, but if the deposit is not repaid he must resort to civil proceedings.[38]

The Director General's proposals were that mail order catalogues and advertisements should state a delivery period by prescribed wording, *e.g.* "Despatch within . . . days of order or refund"; if the trader did not supply the goods on time, he would have to send a refund to the customer within seven days of receiving a request. Similar proposals were made with regard to shop transactions where the prepayment was £10 or more. The C.P.A.C. in their Report[39] supported the Director General's proposals relating to mail order business only. However, the Secretary of State was unwilling to make traders criminally liable for failing to return money on time and put into effect only one comparatively minor proposal. This is contained in the Mail Order Transactions (Information) Order 1976.[40] It merely requires the name and address of the business to be given where an advertisement, circular or catalogue (other than an advertisement by radio, television or film) invites orders for goods by post where payment is to be made before the goods are despatched.

The effect of this damp squib was slight. Complaints from consumers who had paid in advance continued at a high level, split about equally between mail order and other transactions. In 1979 the O.F.T. published a consultative paper containing proposals for a further reference to the C.P.A.C. in relation to non-mail order transactions, but nothing came of it.[41] The current policy appears to be to leave the problem to be resolved piecemeal by Codes of Practice[42] and by the

---

[37] Dossier 17/2.
[38] See *ante*, p. 101.
[39] H.C. 285 Session 1975/76.
[40] S.I. 1976 No. 1812.
[41] Prepayment in Non-Mail Order Transactions.
[42] See the direct marketing codes, *ante*, p. 166.

power to control individual rogue traders under Part III of the 1973 Act.[43]

Business advertisements

> ELECTRIC FIRE, £4.95. 2-bar coal effect, new.—Tel. White-haven 0000
> GOLF CLUBS, half set, new, £23.50.—Tel. Whitehaven 0000
> SPANISH STYLE GUITAR, full size. Brand new, £7.95.—Tel. Whitehaven 0000

These are three of 10 advertisements placed by one trader in one newspaper on one day. It is not obvious to a reader when seeing them scattered amongst the other small ads that he will be dealing with a trader. There are three obvious disadvantages to a consumer who deals with a trader masquerading as a private person. First, if the goods prove to be defective, the buyer will be advised that, as the seller was not selling in the course of a business, the implied conditions of merchantable quality and fitness for purpose do not apply. Secondly, if he discovers that any of the descriptions used is false, a trading standards officer will be reluctant to take action as the Trade Descriptions Act 1968 catches only descriptions applied in the course of a trade or business. Lastly, because he thinks that he is dealing with a private seller, he is likely to be less suspicious and may think that he is getting a better bargain than if he were dealing with a trader.

The Director General's third reference to the C.P.A.C. in March 1975 covered this consumer trade practice describing it as "Seeking to Sell Goods Without Revealing that they are being Sold in the Course of a Business."[44] The C.P.A.C. Report "Disguised Business Sales" was published in May 1976.[45] It showed the practice to be particularly widespread in relation to second-hand cars, furniture and electrical appliances.

The Director General's proposals were approved by the C.P.A.C. and put into effect by the Business Advertisements (Disclosure) Order 1977.[46] The Order requires business sellers of goods to make it clear in their advertisements directed at consumers that they are traders. The fact may be made apparent by "the contents of the advertisement, its format or size, the place or manner of its publication or otherwise."[47] This can be achieved in a number of ways: by using an obvious business name or company name; by placing an advertisement of a business size

---

[43] *Post*, p. 282.
[44] Dossier 17/3.
[45] H.C. 355 Session 1975/76.
[46] S.I. 1977 No. 1918.
[47] Art. 2(1).

or format; or by adding the word "dealer," "trader" or "trade" at the end of the advertisement. The effect of the Order can be observed by perusing the small ad columns of any newspaper where the last method will be seen to be common practice.

There are two exemptions—sales by auction or tender, and agricultural produce or game produced or taken by the seller himself.

VAT-exclusive prices

"£15.24 VAT extra"
"Recommended retail price £58.50 excluding VAT"

Since the introduction of VAT consumers frequently have been asked to pay more than they anticipated for goods or services. Sometimes, *e.g.* in DIY shops or builders' merchants, goods on display are priced but when the consumer reaches the cash desk VAT is added, although the price shown appeared to be VAT-inclusive. On other occasions as in the above examples an indication is given that VAT is payable in addition to the specified price but neither the amount nor rate of VAT is mentioned. These practices were referred to the C.P.A.C. in 1977 and they duly published their report "VAT-Exclusive Prices. A Report on Practices relating to Advertising, Displaying or otherwise Quoting VAT-Exclusive Prices or Charges."[48]

The Director General identified two practices which he considered should be banned. The first, illustrated by the first of the above examples, is the practice of advertising, displaying or quoting to consumers as the price of goods or services an amount which excludes a sum to be added on account of VAT. The second practice, illustrated by the second of the examples, is that of advertising recommended retail prices which take no account of the VAT amount which the retailer is likely to add when selling to a consumer.

The C.P.A.C. in its report concluded that the first practice, but not the second, adversely affected the economic interests of consumers and went on to consider the Director General's proposals only in respect of the first practice. The main economic detriment to the consumer is the extra amount which he will be called upon to pay, even though sometimes, as a matter of strict contract law, he may only be liable for the lower amount. In some cases it will be too late to withdraw from the transaction, *e.g.* when he has eaten a meal in a restaurant or has had his car serviced and wishes to drive it away. In other cases where withdrawal is possible he may be too embarrassed to argue about the price at the cash desk or unwilling to go to the bother of starting his search again in other shops. Broadly, the C.P.A.C.

---

[48] H.C. 416 Session 1976/77.

agreed with the Director General's proposal that only VAT-inclusive charges should be shown, but in the event no order was forthcoming.[49]

Even so the practice disappeared in many areas of business. Indeed this has been one of the problems of the C.P.A.C. when looking at a practice. The very fact that the trade knows that the practice has been referred to the C.P.A.C. means that it disappears in many quarters. By the time the C.P.A.C. look for evidence of the practice there may be much less than there was when the Director General identified it and referred it to the Committee. Then when the Secretary of State considers the C.P.A.C. report, the practice may have virtually died with the result that it may seem unnecessary to introduce secondary legislation to kill a corpse. Thus the consumer can benefit in a very real sense from the mere fact that the regulatory power exists. We shall meet a similar point when we consider the licensing system under the Consumer Credit Act.[50]

3. Part III—Persistently Unfair Traders

I, Robert James Pickersgill, of Import House, Northallerton Road, Croft on Tees, Nr. Darlington trading as Solaire Electric, hereby give to the Director General of Fair Trading written assurances sought by him pursuant to section 34(1) of the Fair Trading Act 1973:
"That I will use all reasonable precautions and exercise all due diligence to avoid continuing the following courses of conduct or any similar course of conduct in the course of my business, namely—

(1) Committing offences under section 1 of the Trade Descriptions Act 1968 by applying false trade descriptions to goods or by supplying or offering to supply goods to which a false trade description is applied.
(2) Committing offences under section 11(2) of the Trade Descriptions Act 1968 by giving indications likely to be taken as indications that goods offered by me are being offered at a price less than that at which they are in fact being offered.
(3) Committing breaches of contract with consumers by supplying goods:

  (a) which do not correspond with any description by which they are sold as required by subsection (1) of the amended section 13 of the Sale of Goods Act 1893, or
  (b) which are not fit for a particular purpose for which they are being bought as required by subsection (3) of the amended section 14 of that Act.

(4) Failing to return to consumers money to which they are legally entitled, that has been received from them in the course of mail order transactions."

---

[49] The Code of Practice under Part III of the Consumer Protection Act 1987 provides that price indications to private consumers "should include VAT." Part III is discussed *ante*, p. 232.
[50] See *post*, p. 335.

For the purpose of these assurances the word "goods" means lamps intended to emit ultra violet rays and/or to emit infra red rays and any accessory supplied or offered for supply with such a lamp.

This is the historic first assurance given in October 1974 to the Director General under Part III of the 1973 Act. The increasing use of this power to curtail the activities of rogue traders is evidenced by the numbers of assurances obtained—after a slow start with only 36 in all in 1974–76, the average annual rate is about 50.[51] Used car dealers, home improvement firms, sellers of electrical goods and mail order businesses figure most prominently, but the club membership also includes a wide range of other commercial activities, e.g. a correspondence school for freelance writers, a chain of 74 restaurants, a door-to-door salesman of goods said to be made by the blind, and a major computer company.

The first assurance is typical in so far as it covers three improper practices which frequently result in assurances being sought, namely, Trade Descriptions Act offences, breaches of the Sale of Goods Act implied conditions and the non-delivery of goods paid for in advance.

Section 34(1) requires the Director General to try to obtain an assurance where a person has persisted in a course of conduct which

(a) is detrimental to the interests of consumers in the United Kingdom, whether those interests are economic interests or interests in respect of health, safety or other matters, and[52]
(b) in accordance with the following provisions of this section is to be regarded as unfair to consumers.

Business

The section applies only to a person carrying on a business where the conduct occurs in the course of that business. "Business" includes a professional practice and any undertaking which supplies goods or services otherwise than free of charge.[53] Thus private sellers are not caught, whereas charitable institutions are.[54] A firm of solicitors could be asked for an assurance if frequent, justified complaints were made about its negligent conduct of clients' matters.

Persistent

Part III is aimed at the trader who is a rogue in the sense that he repeatedly breaks his civil or criminal obligations and thumbs his nose at dissatisfied customers and trading standards officers alike. Only if

---

[51] Since the introduction of this sanction, 700 assurances, undertakings and orders have been obtained: 1989 Annual Report of the D.G.F.T.
[52] These criteria are similar to those laid down in section 2(1)(b): ante, p. 268.
[53] s.137(2).
[54] Cf. the definition in the Unfair Contract Terms Act 1977, s.14, ante, p. 127.

he has persisted in such a course of conduct may the Director General take action. Evidence is built up from many sources: direct complaints from consumers; complaints passed on by trading standards departments, C.A.Bx., consumer advice centres, etc.; convictions and civil judgments notified by the courts. The Director General must have regard to all such complaints and information in determining the question of persistence.[55]

No criteria are laid down by the Act. Clearly what may amount to persistent conduct in the case of a small trader with one outlet may not be sufficient in the case of a retail chain with dozens of branches: the number of breaches must be weighed against the overall turnover and number of outlets of the business. It seems likely that successful prosecutions and civil actions carry more weight than complaints, however justified, and that a small trader with a half dozen or so judgments and a score of complaints against him may well find himself being required to give an assurance. The message for the consumer is clear: if he fails to have a complaint properly dealt with by a trader, he should complain to the trading standards department and thus add weight to the trader's file—indeed, the suggestion that this is about to happen may accelerate a compromise.

Unfair

Conduct is not to be regarded as unfair unless it is one of the two types specified in the Act; there is no general concept of unfairness to which to resort. First, it may be contravention of an enactment imposing duties, prohibitions or restrictions enforceable by *criminal* proceedings.[56] It seems that some traders are still prepared to flout the provisions of the Trade Descriptions Act or the Food Safety Act on the basis that if they are prosecuted, the fines imposed are outweighed by the profitability of their unfair trading. Another example is offences under Part II Orders.

Secondly, the unfair conduct may consist of breaches of contract or other wrongs enforceable by *civil* proceedings.[57] For example, a trader may be content to sell defective goods confident in the knowledge that very few buyers are likely to go to the trouble and expense of suing him for the few pounds required to repair the goods; even if he is sued, his profits from this form of trading may far exceed the occasional damages awarded against him. In addition to such breaches of section 14(2) and (3) of the Sale of Goods Act 1979, other common courses of conduct are the supply of goods not corresponding with their description in accordance with section 13 of the 1979 Act; the failure to carry

---

[55] s.34(4).
[56] s.34(2).
[57] s.34(3).

out contracts for work and materials with reasonable care and skill; the failure to deliver goods; and the failure to return money for goods or services not supplied.

It is important to notice that there is no need to show that the trader has in fact been prosecuted or sued, as section 34 states that it does not matter whether or not the person has been convicted or the subject of civil proceedings.

Finally, it should be remembered that for years proposals have been under discussion for the possible expansion of section 34 to include non-compliance with a code of practice or even with a general duty to trade fairly.[58] The latest proposals for reform are set out in the O.F.T. report "Trading Malpractices" published in July 1990. The essential change would be to broaden the meaning of "unfair" to include "deceptive or misleading practices" or "unconscionable practices." Both of these general provisions would be supported by an illustrative "black list" of particular malpractices. It would no longer be necessary to prove a breach of existing law to resort to Part III. Perhaps it is too optimistic to expect that the coming of age of the 1973 Act will be immediately celebrated in this way.

Court proceedings

The Director General's first step is to "use his best endeavours" to obtain a satisfactory written assurance from the trader that he will discontinue the course of conduct and will not carry on any similar course of conduct.[59] If the trader gives an assurance, it is given wide publicity and included in the Annual Report. If the trader abides by his assurance the matter rests there.

If the trader fails to observe his assurance or refuses to give one, the Director General may bring proceedings against him before the Restrictive Practices Court.[60] Alternatively, the county court (or sheriff court in Scotland) has jurisdiction except in the case of a company with share capital exceeding £10,000 or except where a question of general application is involved.[61] The court may accept an undertaking or, if it considers that the respondent is likely to continue as before in the absence of an order, may make an order to restrain the continuation of the malpractice.[62] The trader is then faced with the prospect of a fine or imprisonment for contempt of court if he does not comply with the order or undertaking. Thus the end of the road for a trader who fails to honour his civil responsibilities can be imprisonment—this is the ultimate sword of Damocles to deter him under Part III. This happened

[58] See *ante*, p. 151.
[59] s.34(1).
[60] s.35.
[61] s.41.
[62] s.37.

for the first time in August 1984 when a double glazing supplier was committed to prison for 14 days for breach of an undertaking given to the court during earlier contempt proceedings.[63]

It is seldom necessary for the Director General to have recourse to court proceedings. He regards them as a last resort and only a handful of cases occurs each year. For example, in 1978 legal proceedings were instituted against three businesses for refusal to give assurances. In one case the assurances were obtained at the door of the court; in another an undertaking was given by a trader whose place in the history of consumer protection is probably unchallenged with a record 800 complaints about him notified to the O.F.T. Lastly, in the first case of this kind to come before the Restrictive Practices Court, *Director General of Fair Trading* v. *Smiths Bakeries (Westfield) Ltd.*,[64] undertakings were accepted from the company and its director as accessory who had refused to give assurances following 46 convictions under the Food and Drugs Act 1955 over a period of three years.

Accessories

An obvious loop-hole would be for a rogue trader to trade as a company and, when cornered into giving an assurance on behalf of X Ltd., to set up in business with a different identity as Z Ltd. Sections 38 and 39 make this device ineffective by giving the Director General power to seek an assurance, order or undertaking from an "accessory" who has consented to or connived at the company's conduct. An accessory is defined as a director, manager, secretary or other similar officer, or someone with a controlling interest in that he can determine the way in which one-half of the votes can be cast at a general meeting.[65] Thus the above trader, who doubtless will be an accessory of X Ltd., can be required to give a personal assurance which will limit his activities when he puts X Ltd. into liquidation and starts up in the guise of Z Ltd. The power is used frequently.

There are also provisions enabling the court to make an order binding members of a group of "interconnected bodies corporate," *i.e.* broadly a holding company and its subsidiaries.[66]

4. MISLEADING ADVERTISEMENTS

We now turn to the most recent power given to the Director General in the consumer protection area—the power to apply to the court for an injunction to prevent the publication of misleading advertisements. It

[63] 1983 Annual Report of the D.G.F.T., pp. 21 and 57.
[64] *The Times*, May 11, 1978.
[65] s.38(2) and (7).
[66] ss.40 and 137(5).

emanates from the Control of Misleading Advertisement Regulations 1988,[67] which came into force on June 20, 1988. The Regulations were passed in order to implement the 1984 EC Misleading Advertising Directive.[68]

The EC Directive

In 1978 the EC Commission presented to the Council a draft directive on Misleading and Unfair Advertising. The preamble expresses the Commission's view that:

> the laws against misleading and unfair advertising now in force in the Member States differ widely; whereas, since advertising reaches beyond the frontiers of individual Member States, it has a direct effect on the establishment and the functioning of the common market.

The draft directive[69] encountered considerable opposition in view of its extension beyond misleading advertising to unfair advertising, a concept unfamiliar in English law, and its legitimation of comparative advertising ("knocking copy") which is illegal in some Member States. In an effort to reach agreement the Council decided to omit unfair and comparative advertisements. This compromise achieved success in 1984 when the Council adopted the Misleading Advertising Directive.

Member States were supposed to bring forward legislation to comply with the Directive by October 1986. However, the consultations between the D.T.I. and commercial and consumer organisations were protracted. Indeed, the D.T.I.'s consultative document containing its outline proposals was not issued until July 1985. The major area of debate was the relationship between the self-regulatory bodies or "established means of dealing with complaints," as the Directive expresses it, and the courts or "administrative authorities" to which the Government had to give the power to control misleading advertising.

The Government's proposals set out in the consultative paper suggested that the powers should be given to the Director General of Fair Trading rather than to a multiplicity of other public authorities, *e.g.* local authorities. Its attitude to the existing self-regulatory system can be gleaned from the consultative document which stated that the Director General's power was seen "as a reinforcement to the self-regulatory system of control rather than a substitute for it." Commenting in particular on the areas of advertising where the Advertising

---

[67] S.I. 1988 No. 915, made under European Communities Act 1972, s.2(2).

[68] 84/450. OJ 1984 L250/17.

[69] For a discussion of the background to the draft directive and of its provisions, see Freedman, "Proposed EEC Directive on Misleading and Unfair Advertising" in Woodroffe (ed.), *Consumer Law in the EEC*, Chap. III. See also 2nd ed. of this book, pp. 362–364.

Standards Authority provide the main control, the paper stated that "The Government sees the new powers which the Directive require to be introduced essentially as a 'long-stop.' The Government hope that the effect will be to strengthen rather than diminish the authority of the self-regulatory system." It will be seen that this policy was followed when the regulations were made.

Self-regulation

A brief note on the United Kingdom system of self-regulation may help to put in perspective the scope and purpose of the 1988 Regulations.

The Advertising Standards Authority (ASA) was established in 1962 to provide independent supervision of the industry's self-regulatory arrangements through a monitoring programme and investigation of complaints—it receives about 9,000 complaints each year. The main instrument of control is the British Code of Advertising Practice (BCAP) which was published in 1961 and modelled on the 1937 International Code of Advertising Practice. It is kept under continuous review and amendment by the Committee of Advertising Practice (CAP). The Code applies to advertisements in newspapers, magazines, posters, brochures and leaflets for the public, cinema commercials and viewdata services. It should be added that the ASA and CAP also administer the British Code of Sales Promotion Practice.

A separate system operates in relation to broadcasting. The Broadcasting Act 1981 imposed a duty on the Independent Broadcasting Authority (IBA) to draw up a code governing standards and practice in advertising and to secure compliance with the code. The IBA Code of Advertising Standards and Practice governs all advertising on independent television and independent local radio in contrast with BCAP which, we have seen, is concerned mainly with *written* advertisements. Regulations 8 and 9 deal specifically with the IBA.

Finally the Cable Authority, set up under the Cable and Broadcasting Act 1984, regulates advertisements included in licensed cable services. Its operations are dealt with separately in regulations 10 and 11.

Other legislation

It should be remembered that legislative control of misleading advertisements is not exercised only, or even mainly, under powers given by the 1988 Regulations. The Trade Descriptions Act 1968 covers advertisements relating to the supply of goods and services.[70]

---

[70] See Chap. 11.

Misleading price indications are covered by the Consumer Protection Act, Part III.[71] Finally, credit advertisements are caught by the detailed regulations under the Consumer Credit Act 1974.[72]

1988 Regulations

The purpose of the regulations is to enable the Director General to take action in the courts to obtain an injunction to prevent the publication of a misleading advertisement. He cannot obtain compensation or other redress for a complainant. Before considering a complaint the Director General will normally require the complainant to show that "established means" of dealing with such a complaint have already been tried, *e.g.* the ASA.[73] This implements the Government's policy that the Director General shall be a "long-stop."

Advertisement

Article 2 contains a number of definitions. "Advertisement" means:

> any form of representation which is made in connection with a trade, business, craft or profession in order to promote the supply or transfer of goods or services, immovable property, rights or obligations.

The definition is wide enough to cover advertisements relating to land and houses as well as goods and services. In common with most legislation protecting consumers, it does not apply to an advertisement by a private person—it must be in connection with a trade, business, craft or profession.

Misleading

A wide definition of misleading is given in Article 2(2). The question is whether it "deceives or is likely to deceive" the people whom it reaches. Further, it must be likely "to affect their economic behaviour or . . . to injure a competitor."

Injunctions

When considering an advertisement, the Director General must have regard not only to the public interest, but also "the desirability of encouraging the control, by self-regulatory bodies, of advertisements."[74] If he thinks it appropriate, he may bring proceedings for an injunction (including an interlocutory injunction).[75]

[71] See Chap. 11.
[72] See Chap. 17.
[73] Reg. 4(3).
[74] Reg. 4(4).
[75] Reg. 5.

Article 6 deals with the functions of the court. It requires a court before granting an injunction to have regard "to all the interests involved and in particular the public interest." An injunction may be limited to the particular advertisement complained of or may extend to "any advertisement in similar terms or likely to convey a similar expression."[76]

In an important and instructive decision on these regulations Hoffmann J. made some valuable comments on the meaning of "misleading" and on the court's functions under regulation 6. In *Director General of Fair Trading* v. *Tobyward Ltd.*[77]:

> T advertised a product called "SpeedSlim" claiming (1) it could result in permanent weight loss; (2) success was guaranteed; (3) it contained an ingredient representing a medical or scientific breakthrough; (4) it prevented fats entering the blood stream; (5) the user could lose a specific amount of weight in a specified time; and (6) it was 100 per cent. safe. The ASA received complaints and found the advertisements to be contrary to BCAP in that the six claims were misleading. The ASA advised T on how to comply with the code but T took no notice. The ASA referred the breaches to the Director General, who applied for a interlocutory injunction to restrain publication of the misleading advertisements and "any advertisement in similar terms or likely to convey a similar impression."

Hoffmann J. discussing the meaning of misleading in regulation 2(2) said that the requirement that the advertisement is likely to affect the economic behaviour of the persons to whom it is addressed "means in this context no more than that it must make it likely that they will buy the product." Turning to regulation 6 and the exercise of his discretion he thought there were two reasons why he should grant the injunction[78]:

> "First, the regulations contemplate that there will only be intervention by the director when the voluntary system has failed. It is in my judgment desirable and in accordance with the public interest to which I must have regard that the courts should support the principle of self-regulation. I think that advertisers would be more inclined to accept the rulings of their self-regulatory bodies if it were generally known that in cases in which their procedures had been exhausted and the advertiser was still publishing an advertisement which appeared to the court to be prima facie misleading an injunction would ordinarily be granted. . . .
> Second, in my view the interests of consumers require the protection of an injunction pending trial of the action. It does not seem to me that the respondents could complain of any legitimate interference with their business if they were restrained from making claims of the kind to which the director is here taking objection."

The respondents' main objection to the application for an injunction

---

[76] Reg. 6(2).
[77] [1989] 2 All E.R. 266.
[78] *Ibid.* at p. 270, 271.

was the wording of the injunction. They claimed that it was too vague so that it would not be clear to them what they could lawfully do. In granting the injunction in the terms of the Director General's application Hoffmann J. said[79]:

> "In a case like this the formulation of the injunction must avoid extremes on either side. On the one hand it must not be so specific that by a small variation in the terms of the advertisement the advertiser can escape its effect and publish an advertisement which is nevertheless misleading in the same kind of way. On the other hand, it must not be in terms so general that the advertiser does not have a clear idea of what he is not allowed to do."

It is no surprise that the form of the wording was approved, as it followed precisely the words in regulation 6(2). In due course on July 21, 1989, the High Court granted a permanent injunction in the same terms.[80]

Exclusions

Some types of advertisements are excluded from the regulations. As explained above, they do not apply to advertisements on radio, television or cable networks.[81] Secondly, certain advertisements relating to investments or investment business are not covered which broadly are the responsibility of the Securities and Investments Board under the Financial Services Act 1986.[82]

---

[79] *Ibid.* at p. 271.
[80] 1989 Annual Report of D.G.F.T., p. 53. See also *D.G.F.T.* v. *Blinkhorn*, November 7, 1989: *ibid.*
[81] *Ante*, p. 289.
[82] Reg. 3(1).

Part IV

SPECIAL PROTECTION IN CREDIT
TRANSACTIONS

CHAPTER FIFTEEN

THE BACKGROUND TO CONSUMER CREDIT

1. INTRODUCTION

There has been a dramatic increase in consumer credit in the present century—both in this country and in other Western industrialised countries. By far the greatest area is house purchase but there are many others including furniture, electrical appliances, clothing, vehicles, holidays and home repairs and improvements. The scale of consumer credit can be seen from figures published in the Crowther Report on Consumer Credit. In the year 1966 the amount of medium and long-term credit extended totalled £3,692,000,000, (house purchase credit accounted for approximately 45 per cent. of this figure). At the end of the year the total outstanding was £9,684,000,000, of which some 80 per cent. was attributable to houses and flats.

The Crowther Committee clearly realised that:

> The use of consumer credit . . . enables individuals to enjoy the services of consumer durable goods sooner than they otherwise would and in a period of inflation offers them a real prospect of acquiring them more cheaply. Consumers in general are able to obtain a more satisfying 'basket' of goods and services with the same income. Thus consumer credit may be said to enhance consumer satisfaction. Furthermore, some individuals, who lack the self-discipline to save up for the purchase of a durable consumer good but are nevertheless unlikely to break their contract with a creditor, are able to buy a durable consumer good which might otherwise never be theirs.[1]

One need only add that this reason applies, *a fortiori*, to house purchase.

The situation described above has its corresponding dangers and these are two-fold. First, borrowers may be tempted to overstretch their resources—either through bad economic planning or because they do not appreciate the full extent of their obligations. Secondly, some lenders might be tempted to "cash in" on the attractions of consumer credit by inducing borrowers (some of whom may already be under severe financial stress) to sign agreements which are one-sided and impose unduly onerous obligations.

Until the passing of the Consumer Credit Act 1974 the law developed in a fragmentary and piecemeal fashion—following rather than

---

[1] Cmnd. 4596, p. 118.

leading, checking abuses *after* they had come to light rather than laying down ground rules in advance. Thus:

(1) The Bills of Sale Acts 1878–1882 were passed to deal with (*inter alia*) mortgages of personal property where the borrower retained possession.

(2) The Moneylenders Acts 1900–1927 were passed to regulate the activities of certain moneylenders (but not, *e.g.* banks).

(3) The Pawnbrokers Acts 1872–1900 regulated the activities of pawnbrokers.

(4) The Hire-Purchase Act 1965 regulated hire-purchase agreements where the hire-purchase price did not exceed £2,000 and where the hirer was not a body corporate. (This limit was increased to £5,000 in 1978 and increased again to £7,500 in 1983.)

The unsatisfactory nature of this fragmentary approach can be seen by looking at moneylending. If the lender happened to be a bank, the Moneylenders Acts did not apply at all, even though the borrower may have been an inexperienced private individual and the contract may have been a harsh one on the particular facts. On the other hand, if the lender was within the provisions of the Act the full rigours of the Act were applied, even though the borrower was a large public company well able to look after itself. Again, as new forms of credit developed (*e.g.* credit cards) the absence of any regulatory machinery meant that there was virtually no effective control at all. All this was changed by the Consumer Credit Act 1974 which is almost certainly the most comprehensive and sophisticated Act of its kind in the Western world.

The Act is designed to sweep away the piecemeal controls listed above and to replace them with a single code governing all forms of lending. The only pieces of legislation which remain unrepealed are the Bills of Sale Acts 1878–1882—the reason is that the Consumer Credit Act does not regulate mortgages of personal property. A suggestion made by the Crowther Committee that the Government should introduce a Lending and Security Act has not so far been implemented.

2. CONSUMER CREDIT ACT 1974—TEN PRELIMINARY POINTS

The scope and effect of the Consumer Credit Act will be examined in detail in the next eight chapters. In the remainder of this chapter it is proposed to deal with 10 preliminary matters.

(1) The Act contains no definition of the word "consumer." We have already seen that under the Unfair Contract Terms Act 1977 the term "consumer" means a "private consumer" as opposed to a business consumer, and the Fair Trading Act 1973 adopts a similar approach. *The Consumer Credit Act 1974 is not limited in this way.* In the two major types of agreement—consumer credit and consumer hire—the

Act provides control where the debtor or hirer is an "individual" but the definition of this term is not what one might expect. By section 189:

> "individual" includes a partnership or other unincorporated body of persons not consisting entirely of bodies corporate.

So then, the unincorporated trader is protected just as much as the private individual, *e.g.* a firm of solicitors. Conversely, the Act regulates (at least in part) agreements where the creditor or owner is *not* acting in the course of a business.[2]

(2) The Act received the Royal Assent on July 31, 1974, but it took nearly 11 years to bring it fully into force. The Act was brought into force in stages and for many of its provisions the commencement date was May 19, 1985. There were a number of difficult problems as to whether or not a particular provision was retrospective (in the light of the general presumption against this) and these problems had to be solved by considering Schedule 3 and the relevant Commencement Order.

(3) Section 189 adopts the very helpful practice of drawing together all the definitions which appear throughout the Act. Section 189(1) contains no less than 177 definitions. Some are defined in the section itself (*e.g.* the term "individual"[3]). In other cases section 189 refers to the section where the definition is to be found, *e.g.*

> "exempt agreement" means an agreement specified in or under section 16.

It is vitally important to refer constantly to section 189 because words are often used in unexpected ways. Thus, for example, the definition of the word "surety" is wide enough to include the principal debtor (unless the context otherwise requires).

(4) Another helpful innovation (not so far copied by the draftsman of the annual Finance Act) is Schedule 2 which contains 24 worked examples showing the use of the new terminology. Section 188(3), however, provides that:

> In the case of conflict between Schedule 2 and any other provision of this Act that other provision shall prevail.

A learned writer[4] has expressed the view that Example 18 (which relates to multiple agreements) is wrong.

(5) Although the Act is a long one a very large part of the detail is contained in regulations. They cover such matters as the total charge

---

[2] See *post*, p. 305.
[3] See above.
[4] Goode, *Consumer Credit Law*, p. 156.

for credit, regulated and exempt agreements, advertising, documentation and rebates for early settlements.

(6) The control provided by the Act is twofold:

(a) Control of business activity—notably through the licensing system administered by the Director General of Fair Trading.[5]

(b) Control of individual agreements.

(7) The Act provides various civil and criminal sanctions, as well as the administrative sanctions in sections 29 and 32 (non-renewal, suspension and revocation of a licence). The criminal sanctions are usefully collected together in Schedule 1. Section 170(1) provides that:

> A breach of any requirement made (otherwise than by any court) by or under this Act shall incur no civil or criminal sanction as being such a breach except to the extent (if any) expressly provided for under this Act.

Thus section 48 makes it an offence to canvass certain types of agreement (*e.g.* personal loans) off trade premises. If a person borrows money in a case where the lender has contravened section 48, he cannot avoid liability under that contract by pleading that it is illegal. Nor could he bring an action for breach of statutory duty. Such claims or defences are shut out by section 170(1). Presumably the criminal court would still be able to award compensation under section 35 of the Powers of Criminal Courts Act 1973.[6] The section does not affect the power of the court to grant an injunction (s.170(3)).

(8) As one might expect, the statutory rights enjoyed by the debtor, the hirer, a surety or a relative[7] cannot in any way be cut down or fettered by the agreement.[8]

(9) One of the features of the Act is that certain steps can only be taken if the court or the Director General makes an order to that effect. An example of the former is the enforcement of an agreement which has not been properly executed.[9] An example of the latter is the enforcement of an agreement made by a creditor or owner while he was unlicensed. In either case section 173(3) provides that consent of the debtor or hirer "given at that time" shall be as effective as an order. The words "given at that time" presumably refer to the time of enforcement so that a provision for consent in the contract would not be effective. Clearly the court would examine the facts very carefully to ensure that there was a true consent.

(10) It may be useful to end this chapter by setting out a few

[5] See Chap. 17, *post*, p. 312.
[6] *Ante*, p. 258.
[7] As to which see *post*, p. 299.
[8] See s.173(1) and (2).
[9] *Post*, p. 323.

important definitions which will be met from time to time in the next eight chapters.

(a) *Hire-purchase agreement*

This is defined as an agreement under which goods are bailed[10] in return for periodical payments by the bailee and the property in the goods will pass to the bailee if the terms of the agreement are complied with and one or more of the following occur:

(i) the exercise of an option to purchase by the bailee or
(ii) the doing of any other specified act by any party to the agreement or
(iii) the happening of any other specified event.

(b) *Conditional and credit sale agreements*

A *conditional sale* agreement is an agreement for the sale of goods or land under which the purchase price or part of it is payable by instalments and the property in the goods or land is to remain in the seller (notwithstanding that the buyer is to be in possession of the goods or land) until such conditions as to the payment of instalments or likewise as may be specified in the agreement are fulfilled.

If, however, there is a straight sale of goods on credit terms the property will usually pass to the buyer immediately (Sale of Goods Act 1979, s.18, rule 1[11]) and the agreement will be a *credit sale* agreement, *not* a conditional sale agreement.

Thus the crucial difference is whether the property passes to the buyer when the contract is made (credit sale) or at a later stage (conditional sale).

(c) *Relative*

Relative means husband, wife, brother, sister, uncle, aunt, nephew, niece, lineal ancestor or lineal descendant. Relationship by marriage is also included and the reference to "husband or wife" includes a former or a reputed spouse.

(d) *Associate*

The associate of an individual means (i) a relative and (ii) a partner, or the relative of a partner, of that individual.

(e) *"Restricted-use" and "unrestricted-use"*

These terms are defined in section 11 and are largely self-explanatory. If the debtor can physically use the credit in any way he wishes the

---

[10] Goods are "bailed" if one person ("the bailor") transfers possession to another ("the bailee") for a specific purpose.
[11] *Ante*, p. 85.

agreement will be an "unrestricted-use" agreement, even though certain uses would constitute a breach of contract. Thus a loan paid by the lender to the borrower would be an unrestricted-use agreement. On the other hand, a hire-purchase agreement, or a sale on deferred terms, or a loan where the money goes straight from the lender to a third party (*e.g.* the supplier of goods or services) would be a restricted-use agreement. We shall meet the distinction at several points in the following chapters.

CHAPTER SIXTEEN

"WHAT AGREEMENTS ARE CAUGHT BY THE ACT?"

In this chapter and in Chapters 17–23 a reference to "the Act" is a reference to the Consumer Credit Act 1974 (unless otherwise stated) and a reference to a section is to that section in the Act.

We have already seen that the scope of the Act is very wide. In this chapter it is proposed to work through the very intricate provisions of the Act and regulations to find out the precise extent of control. The scheme of this chapter is as follows:

1. Regulated agreements.
2. Partially regulated agreements.
3. Exempt agreements.
4. Linked transactions.

1. REGULATED AGREEMENTS

Most of the statutory controls only apply to a "regulated agreement." In order to find out whether an agreement is regulated it is necessary to proceed in two stages:

(1) Does the agreement come within the definition of "consumer credit agreement" in section 8 or "consumer hire agreement" in section 15? If the answer is "no", the agreement cannot be a regulated agreement.

(2) If the answer to (1) above is "yes", then by sections 8(3) and 15(2) any such agreement *is* a regulated agreement unless it is an exempt agreement. The concept of "exempt agreement," which depends on section 16 and regulations, is dealt with later in this chapter.[1]

(1) Consumer credit agreement

Let us start by listing the many types of agreement which can come within this term. They include:

(a) Hire-Purchase

---

[1] *Post*, p. 306.

   (b) Conditional Sale
   (c) Credit Sale
   (d) Personal Loan
   (e) Overdraft
   (f) Loan secured by land mortgage
   (g) Credit card
   (h) Pledges
   (i) Budget accounts in shops.

Section 8(2) (as amended) defines a consumer credit agreement as an agreement whereby one person (the creditor) provides an individual (the debtor) with credit not exceeding £15,000. Four points are worthy of note:

(i) There must be an "agreement." Thus where a sale is for cash and on delivery of the goods the buyer asks for time to pay, the granting of "credit" would not amount to an "agreement" unless it formed part of a separate bargain—as, for example, where the borrower agrees to pay interest on the outstanding amount.

(ii) The creditor can be an "individual" or a body corporate, but the debtor must be an "individual."[2]

(iii) The Act draws a sharp distinction between the "credit" and the "total charge for credit." The term *credit* includes a cash loan and any form of financial accommodation[3] and clearly refers to the loan, etc., itself. The term "total charge for credit" refers to interest and other charges.[4] Section 9(4) provides that:

> An item entering into the total charge for credit shall not be treated as credit even though time is allowed for payment.

(iv) As an illustration of the above principles section 9(3) defines the "credit" in a hire-purchase agreement as the total price of the goods less (a) the deposit (if any) and (b) the total charge for credit.

Example

A finance house C agrees to let a Porsche car on hire-purchase to D (an individual). The total price is £23,000; this includes a down payment of £5,000 and a total charge for credit of £3,000. When these two items are deducted from the price (£23,000–£8,000) one is left with credit of £15,000. This is, therefore, a consumer credit agreement within section 8(2).

The provisions may be contrasted with the provisions of the Hire-Purchase Act 1965. Under that Act protection was limited to cases

[2] See *ante*, p. 297.
[3] s.9(3).
[4] See *post*, p. 308.

where the hire-purchase *price* did not exceed £7,500. Under the 1974 Act the *price* may be far higher; what matters is the amount of the *credit*.

Fixed and running-account credit

The term "consumer credit agreement" is subdivided into "fixed-sum credit" and "running-account credit"—the distinction is important in deciding whether an agreement is regulated or exempt[5] and for certain other purposes. Section 10(1)(*a*) tells us that:

> running-account credit is a facility under a personal credit agreement whereby the debtor is enabled to receive from time to time (whether in his own person or by another person) from the creditor or a third party cash, goods and services (or any of them) to an amount or value such that, taking into account payments made by or to the credit of the debtor, the credit limit (if any) is not at any time exceeded.

Perhaps the two most common examples are bank overdrafts and budget accounts in shops. It would clearly be possible to take the agreement outside the definition of "consumer credit agreement"[6] by fixing a credit limit in excess of the statutory ceiling or by fixing no credit limit at all. Section 10(3) is designed to block attempts to oust the Act in this way. It provides, in effect, that a running-account will still qualify as a consumer credit agreement if:

(i) the debtor cannot draw more than the "specified amount" (£15,000) at any one time; or

(ii) a term unfavourable to the debtor (*e.g.* raising of the rate of interest) will become operative if the debit balance rises above the "specified amount" or a lower figure; or

(iii) at the time of the agreement it it unlikely that the debit balance will rise above the "specified amount." An example of this provision (Schedule 2, example 7) is where X agrees to provide Y with short-term finance to enable Y to acquire trading stock from time to time; at the time of the contract Y has trading stock worth £1,000 and it is therefore unlikely that he will require credit in excess of £15,000.

Debtor-creditor-supplier (D-C-S) agreements and debtor-creditor (D-C) agreements

These terms are defined in sections 12 and 13. It is necessary to mention them at this point because a knowledge of them is vital when

---

[5] See *post*, p. 307.
[6] *Ante*, p. 302.

considering the all important question of whether the agreement is *regulated* or *exempt*.[7] The distinction between D-C-S and D-C turns on the relationship between the supplier of the credit and the supplier of the land, goods or services. The effect of sections 12 and 13 can be summarised as follows:

(i) If the supplier of the credit and the supplier of the goods, etc., is *the same person* then it is D-C-S. Examples would include hire-purchase, credit sale, and sale of land where the vendor agrees to leave the price outstanding. This can be referred to as "two-party D-C-S."

(ii) If the supplier of credit and the supplier of the goods, etc., are *different* but work together under "*arrangements*" then again it is D-C-S. Thus, a credit card company has "arrangements" with its approved suppliers and a finance company might have "arrangements" with a car dealer whereby they would provide loans to finance sales made by him to customers. In both these cases the credit contract would be a D-C-S agreement. This can be referred to as "three-party D-C-S."

(iii) If there are no such arrangements, the agreement is a D-C agreement. Thus if a customer borrows £1,000 from his bank to pay for central heating or for a holiday or to finance his business, this is a D-C agreement.

(iv) If an agreement is made to refinance an existing indebtedness, whether to the creditor or any other person, then again it is D-C.

As already stated the distinction is critical on the "regulated or exempt" point—we shall see that under a D-C-S agreement the critical factor is the number of instalments, whereas under a D-C agreement the critical factor is the annual percentage rate of charge for credit. The distinction is also important for other purposes, including joint responsibility of supplier and creditor in cancellation cases[8] and under section 75.[9]

(2) Consumer hire agreement

The second type of agreement to which the Act applies is the consumer hire agreement. Clearly, this type of agreement is less important than the consumer credit agreement, but it is worth remembering that it covers not only the domestic hiring of, *e.g.* a television set but also the commercial hiring of, *e.g.* equipment. Section 15 makes it clear that there are six elements:

(a) a bailment of goods
(b) by one person (the owner)

---

[7] *Post*, p. 307.
[8] *Post*, p. 336.
[9] *Post*, p. 342. This is a vital provision in relation to credit cards.

(c) to an individual (the hirer), provided that

(d) it is not hire-purchase, and

(e) it is capable of lasting for more than three months and

(f) it does not require the hirer to make payments[10] in excess of £15,000.

Only the last point calls for comment. In deciding on how much the hirer is *required* to pay one must look at his minimum contractual liability, having regard to any contractual right to terminate. Thus, if a three year hiring (with no break clause) required the hirer to pay a rental of £6,000 per annum, this would bring the total to £18,000 and it would *not* be a consumer hire agreement (see Schedule 2, example 20). The position would be different if, for example, the hirer had a right to terminate, without further payment, at the end of the second year.

2. PARTIALLY REGULATED AGREEMENTS

As already stated, the all important distinction is between *regulated* and *exempt* agreements. Before considering the nature of exempt agreements it might be useful to mention two types of agreement which are regulated in part only.

Non-commercial agreements

By section 189 a non-commercial agreement is an agreement not made by the creditor or owner in the course of a business carried on by him. It is important to notice the words "*a* business." If, for example, a manufacturer made loans to his employees to enable them to buy season tickets or houses, the loans *would* be made in the course of *a* business (even though it was not a consumer credit or consumer hire business) and accordingly it would not be "non-commercial." If, however, the agreement is non-commercial then a number of specific provisions do not apply. The most important area is formalities and cancellation.[11]

Small agreements

A small agreement is defined in section 17 as either;

(a) a regulated consumer credit agreement for credit not exceeding £50,[12] other than a hire-purchase or conditional sale agreement;[13] or

---

[10] Inclusive of VAT: *Apollo Leasing Ltd.* v. *Scott* [1986] Consumer Credit Law Reports 1.

[11] See s.74(1)(*a*) and ss.77–79.

[12] The figure is reduced to £35 if it comes within the Consumer Protection (Cancellation of Contracts Concluded away from Business Premises) Regulations 1987, reg. 9.

[13] See *ante*, p. 299.

(b) a regulated consumer hire agreement which does not require the hirer to make payments exceeding £50.

There is a further condition, namely, that the agreement is unsecured or secured by a guarantee or indemnity only. Not surprisingly, section 17(3) blocks attempts to split up a transaction into a series of small agreements (at one time encyclopaedia salesmen were notorious for this) by providing that in such a case each small agreement shall be treated as a regulated non-small agreement.

Small debtor-creditor-supplier agreements for restricted-use credit are exempt from most of the provisions relating to formalities and cancellation.[14]

3. Exempt Agreements

Having decided that an agreement is a consumer credit or consumer hire agreement, we must now decide whether it is taken out of control by one of the exemptions. These are to be found in section 16 and in the Consumer Credit (Exempt Agreements) Order 1989. The first four of them relate to land.

(1) A debtor-creditor-supplier agreement is exempt if (a) the creditor is a local authority or a body named in the regulations and (b) the agreement finances (i) the purchase of land, or (ii) the provision of dwellings on any land, and in either case is secured by a mortgage of *that* land.[15]

(2) A debtor-creditor agreement is exempt if (a) the lender is a local authority and (b) the agreement is secured by a mortgage of land. It will be apparent that in this case the purpose of the loan is immaterial.[16]

(3) A debtor-creditor agreement is exempt if (a) the lender is a body named in the regulations and (b) the agreement is secured by a mortgage of land and (c) the agreement is to finance the purchase of land, the provision of dwellings or business premises on land and certain ancillary purposes.[17]

The bodies named in the regulations include a large number of insurance companies, friendly societies and charities. Also included are certain public bodies (*e.g.* development corporations), but there the exemption only applies to a more limited class of purpose which is set out opposite to their names in Part II of the Schedule to the regulations.

Building Societies originally enjoyed blanket exemption but with the widening of their powers under the Building Societies Act 1986 this

[14] See *post*, pp. 323 and 334.
[15] s.16(2)(*a*).
[16] Art. 2.
[17] *Ibid.*

was abolished. Instead, any Building Society authorised under that Act will enjoy exemption if and only if the relevant agreement is exempt under the Order. For example, a Building Society loan of £15,000 or less not linked to house purchase, etc., would be regulated.

(4) Even if an agreement to finance the purchase of land is not exempt under (1)–(3) above (*e.g.* because the lender is not one of the specified bodies) a further exemption is to be found in article 3(1)(*b*) which exempts a debtor-creditor-supplier agreement to finance the purchase of land, if the number of payments to be made by the debtor does not exceed four. There are further exemptions covering agreements to finance a premium under a contract of insurance relating to land.

(5) A debtor-creditor-supplier agreement is exempt under article 3(1)(*a*)(i) if (a) it is not hire-purchase or conditional sale and (b) it is for fixed-sum credit and (c) the number of payments to be made by the debtor *in respect of the credit* does not exceed four and (d) they must be paid within 12 months of the date of the agreement. This exempts (*inter alia*) normal trade credit (*e.g.* payment within 30 days of invoice).

(6) A debtor-creditor-supplier agreement is exempt under article 3(1)(*a*)(ii) if (a) it is not hire-purchase or conditional sale and (b) it is for running-account credit and (c) the whole of the credit for a period is repayable by a single payment. This will exempt many budget accounts in shops and certain charge card agreements, *e.g.* American Express and Diners Club.

(7) A further important exemption is to be found in article 4 and relates to debtor-creditor agreements in respect of which the annual percentage rate of the total charge for credit does not exceed the higher of (a) 13 per cent. or (b) 1 per cent. above the highest of any base rates published by the English and Scottish Clearing Banks, being the latest rates in force 28 days before the making of the agreement. Thus, for example, a loan by an employer to an employee would be exempt if the interest rate (*i.e.* the APR as to which see below) does not exceed the statutory ceiling.

In practice, many agreements seek to protect the creditor by including a term in the agreement whereby the debtor's liability fluctuates according to a specified formula (*e.g.* the retail price index or changes in Bank of England minimum lending rate). In deciding whether the "low interest exemption" applies to such a case it is necessary to distinguish sharply between *credit* and *the total charge for credit*. If the *credit* can fluctuate then exemption under regulation 4 is destroyed. On the other hand the fluctuation of the annual *rate* of charge is permissible and this will not destroy the exemption—provided that *at the date of the agreement* the rate did not exceed the statutory ceiling set out above.

Thus if the agreement provided for interest to be paid annually at "1 per cent. above Lloyds Bank base rate for the time being" the agreement will be exempt if at the date of the agreement the base rate did not exceed (a) 12 per cent, or alternatively (b) the highest rate prevailing 28 days before the making of the agreement. An increase in the rate after the date of the agreement will not destroy the exemption.[18]

The total charge for credit

We have already met this term on several occasions and it is now necessary to examine it more closely. It is vitally important for a number of reasons, including the following:

(a) Any sum forming part of the total charge for credit does not form part of the credit[19] and must, therefore, be ignored in deciding whether or not the credit exceeds £15,000.

(b) Under article 4[20] a debtor-creditor agreement is exempt if the annual percentage rate of charge (*post*, p. 309) does not exceed the statutory maximum.

(c) One of the cardinal principles of the Act is to give the debtor information on various matters and one such matter is the "true cost of borrowing."[21] In the United States this is known as "truth in lending." One of the objects of the legislation is to give the debtor an opportunity of "shopping around" and comparing the cost of credit offered by different lenders. It is certainly debatable whether many debtors are likely to take advantage of this facility and it could well be that the effect of this requirement could be counter-productive, in that the extra cost involved will doubtless increase the cost of borrowing and may put the credit beyond the reach of some prospective borrowers.

The total charge for credit is dealt with in the Consumer Credit (Total Charge for Credit) Regulations 1980. The object of these regulations is three-fold, namely (a) to specify what items are to be included, (b) to specify what items are to be excluded, and (c) to require the charge to be calculated as an annual percentage rate.

Items included

Regulation 4 provides that there shall be included (a) the total of the interest payments and (b) other charges at any time payable under the transaction by or on behalf of the debtor or a relative of his, whether to the creditor or to any other person. This would clearly cover the general costs incurred in setting up the agreement—survey fees, legal fees and stamp duty are obvious examples.

Items excluded

The generality of regulation 4 is cut down by regulation 5. Among

[18] See *post*, p. 310.
[19] s.9(3) *ante*, p. 302.
[20] *Ante*, p. 307.
[21] See s.20.

items excluded are the following: (a) sums payable on default, (b) sums which would be payable in any event even if it were a cash transaction (*e.g.* installation charges), (c) sums paid under a maintenance or insurance contract where the debtor had a free choice in the matter and could have made substantially the same arrangements elsewhere, and (d) a life insurance premium in a case where the policy monies are to be used to repay the credit.

Annual percentage rate (APR)

To enable comparisons to be made regulation 7 requires the total charge to be stated as an annual percentage rate reflecting (a) annual compounding and (b) the continuing repayment of credit. If a prospective borrower is told by a finance house that the rate of interest is 12 per cent. this is seriously misleading, because it does not acknowledge that the *outstanding capital is reducing* all the time: the true rate of interest (APR) is about double the flat rate of 12 per cent.

As part of the policy of providing an annual percentage rate, regulation 7 provides a formula for converting a period rate (*e.g.* 10 per cent. per six months) into an annual rate. Conversely, regulation 8 provides a formula whereby the annual rate can be extracted where the whole indebtedness (credit and total charge) is repayable in a single lump sum.

This leaves the question—how can the annual rate be calculated in the case of a land mortgage or hire-purchase agreement where capital and interest are being repaid over several years? The calculation can be a nightmare but fortunately the Government has produced Consumer Credit Tables in 15 volumes. These tables (complete with amendment slips!) can produce the annual percentage rate, provided that the instalments and the repayment periods are equal. Thus, for example, the tables cannot be used if the final hire-purchase instalment is larger than the others because it contains a small extra amount (*e.g.* £1) for the option to purchase.

If the tables cannot be used, the annual rate must be calculated (by trial and error) in accordance with regulation 9. This provides (in effect) that the annual rate is the rate at which the present value of all future repayments equals the amount of the credit.

The above explanation presupposes that all the items are constant and known at the date of the agreement. In practice this may not be so and the regulations recognise this by making certain assumptions. For example, a provision giving the creditor the right to increase the charges (very common in mortgage contracts) must be disregarded.[22] Similarly, there may be a clause for the index linking of the total charge

---

[22] reg. 2(1)(*d*).

for credit; here again it is to be assumed that changes will not occur (regulation 15). If, however, the amount of a particular item is unknown at the date of the agreement and is not covered by the assumptions, then it seems that the exemption for low cost credit[23] cannot be claimed. This could arise where, for example, the creditor's insurance company require the debtor to pay for the installation of a burglar alarm and the cost of this is not known at the date of the agreement.

4. LINKED TRANSACTIONS

Having examined the crucial distinction between regulated and exempt agreements, it is necessary to end this chapter with a brief mention of linked transactions, *i.e.* transactions which are linked to an actual or prospective regulated agreement. The term "linked transaction" is important for a variety of reasons, including withdrawal, cancellation, early settlement and extortionate credit bargains. It is clear from section 19 that an agreement for security will not be a linked agreement but, subject to this, the following are included:

(1) A transaction entered into in compliance with a term of the principal agreement, *e.g.* "the debtor shall insure his life with XYZ insurance company and shall enter into a maintenance contract with Eezikleen Ltd."

(2) A transaction to be financed by a debtor-creditor-supplier agreement; thus where the supplier of a car and the supplier of the credit have "arrangements," the sale of the car is "linked" to the loan contract, so that cancellation of the latter will also cancel the former.[24]

(3) A transaction entered into by the debtor, hirer or a relative at the suggestion of the creditor, owner, an associate of his[25] or a person negotiating the principal agreement. Thus a dealer might say to a prospective borrower "you would have a better chance of getting a loan from the finance company if you took out a life policy." Such tie-ins are now rendered unlawful by the Courts and Legal Services Act 1990, but many building societies offer discounted rates of interest—but with "stings" such as a house or contents insurance.

Regulations have been made[26] whereby certain types of linked agreement are excluded from the provisions of the Act relating to effectiveness,[27] cancellation and early settlement. The excepted classes are:

---

[23] See *ante*, p. 307, n. 7.

[24] s.69(1), *post*, p. 336.

[25] *Ante*, p. 299.

[26] Consumer Credit (Linked Transactions) (Exemptions) Regulations 1983: S.I. 1983 No. 1560.

[27] In general a linked agreement is ineffective until the main agreement is made (s.19(3)).

1. Contracts of insurance
2. Guarantees of goods
3. Agreements for the operation of a deposit and/or current account.

CHAPTER SEVENTEEN

CONTROL OF BUSINESS ACTIVITIES

We have already seen that the Consumer Credit Act controls business activities as well as individual agreements. It is clear that business control is of very great benefit to the consumer. It should help to ensure that the other party to the transaction is a reputable trader and that the consumer is not pressurised into a transaction by misleading advertising or other undesirable business practice. In this chapter it is proposed to consider this aspect of consumer protection under three main headings, namely:

1. Licensing
2. Advertising
3. Canvassing.

1. LICENSING

The licensing system set out in sections 22–24 and 147–150 can be described as the linch pin of the whole Act. For the first time a centrally administered licensing system enables the entire credit industry to be kept under close scrutiny. There is little doubt that the threat of the refusal or revocation of a licence (*i.e.* loss of livelihood) is by far the strongest sanction provided by the Act. It is a perfect example of the administrative control mentioned earlier in this book.[1]

Who needs a licence?

The Act lists seven types of business for which a licence is required, namely:

(a) consumer credit;
(b) consumer hire;
(c) credit brokerage;
(d) debt-counselling;
(e) debt-adjusting;
(f) debt-collecting;
(g) credit reference agency.

---

[1] *Ante*, p. 265.

A number of problems arise. The first one is "what is a business?" The Act merely tells us that it includes a profession or trade; presumably cases from other branches of the law (*e.g.* income tax) can offer some guidance. The key factors include (i) the frequency of the transactions (ii) the manner of operation and (iii) profit motive. The word "frequency" leads on naturally to section 189(2) which provides that:

> A person is not to be treated as carrying on a particular type of business merely because *occasionally* he enters into transactions belonging to a business of that type [italics supplied].

There will clearly be borderline cases. Thus section 189 defines "consumer credit business" by reference to the crucial phrase "regulated agreement" which was considered in Chapter 16. It provides that:

> "consumer credit business" means any business so far as it comprises or relates to the provision of credit under regulated consumer credit agreements.

Let us take an example. Suppose that John sells television sets. Most of his customers pay cash but from time to time he sells a set on credit. Such a sale will be a debtor-creditor-supplier agreement and will be regulated, unless the credit is repayable by four or fewer instalments. Whether John needs a licence will depend on whether the credit sales take place more than "occasionally." If they only took place at very long intervals, and if they formed a very small part of John's turnover, then no licence would be required.[2]

Even if there is a business, a licence will only be required if the trader makes *regulated* agreements. Thus, if a creditor only makes exempt agreements, or if the credit always exceeds £15,000 or the debtors are all companies, no licence will be required.

The above remarks also apply, *mutatis mutandis*, to a consumer hire business, but when we turn to the five other types of business defined in section 145 (the Act uses the term *"ancillary credit business"*) we find that there is one significant difference—the concept of "regulated agreement" is not critical. Thus, for example, an estate agent who introduces clients to an insurance company will require a licence as a credit-broker, even though his clients make (a) agreements which are not consumer credit agreements at all (because the credit exceeds the statutory ceiling) or (b) agreements which are exempt under section 16.[3]

A local authority does not require a licence[4] even though the agreements which it makes may be regulated by the Act.

---

[2] The mere fact that a licence is not required does not exempt the agreements themselves from statutory control, *e.g.* the formality rules (*post*, pp. 324–329) would apply.
[3] *Ante*, p. 306.
[4] See s.21.

Nature and duration of licences

A licence is personal and non-assignable.[5] The licence period was reduced from 15 years to five years from June 1, 1991. The first licences started to come up for renewal in August 1991, as licensing began in 1976. Since then over 300,000 applications have been made.[6]

The criteria and the wide powers of the Director General

The onus is on the applicant to prove to the Director General that he is a fit person to engage in activities covered by the licence.[7] In considering the application the Director General must consider any circumstances appearing to him to be relevant.[8] Section 25 sets out a non-exhaustive list of relevant matters including offences involving dishonesty or violence, contravention of the Act or certain other legislation, sex and race discrimination and undesirable business practices. In all these cases the section refers not merely to the trader himself but also to his employees, agents and associates (past or present). It is important to appreciate that the conduct in question need not involve any breach of the law, e.g. certain types of high-pressure salesmanship. As an alternative to refusing a licence the Director General may limit the licence to specified activities.[9]

If the Director General is "minded to refuse" an application[10] he must invite the applicant to make written representations and to give notice, if he thinks fit, that he wishes to make representations orally. Appeal against refusal lies to the Secretary of State who delegates his powers to certain appointed persons.[11] Further appeal lies to the High Court on a point of law. The above procedure is also followed in cases involving variation, suspension and revocation.[12] It will be seen that these provisions provide a potent weapon for the consumer. If a licensed trader is guilty of breaches of the Sale of Goods Act or of the Trade Descriptions Act, or continues to exhibit void exemption clauses, these matters may come to the attention of the Director General via trading standards inspectors or via the courts.[13] Even a letter from an individual consumer will be relevant in building up evidence against the trader and such evidence can, in appropriate cases, lead to refusal, suspension or revocation of the licence.[14] The

[5] See s.22(2).
[6] O.F.T. Press release, April 10, 1991.
[7] s.25(1)(a).
[8] s.25(2).
[9] See s.23(2).
[10] So far this has happened in 2,900 cases: see n.6.
[11] See s.41 and S.I. 1976 No. 837.
[12] See ss.31–33.
[13] See s.166.
[14] In 1990 the licences of 26 motor traders were revoked and 25 refused, usually because of clocking: O.F.T. Press release, April 16, 1991.

very existence of these provisions can have a salutary effect; thus they may induce the trader to alter his business practices before he applies for a licence.

Contracts by or through unlicensed traders

An unlicensed trader who engages in any activity for which a licence is required commits an offence for which the maximum fine on summary conviction is £2,000. If he is convicted on indictment the maximum penalty is two years imprisonment or a fine or both.[15] It may well be, however, that the most effective sanction is the unenforceability of agreements. Thus by section 40 a regulated agreement made by an unlicensed trader is only enforceable if the Director General makes a validating order. The Director General must consider (*inter alia*) the extent to which debtors and hirers have been prejudiced, the degree of culpability and whether or not he would have granted a licence to the trader if he had applied for it. He can limit the order to specific agreements and he can impose conditions.

These sanctions are a powerful deterrent against unlicensed trading. Section 149 goes one step further; in effect it places the creditor or owner under a duty to ensure that the credit-brokers with whom they do business are themselves licensed. The creditor or owner has a strong incentive to check on this; the section provides that a regulated agreement made by a debtor or hirer who, for the purpose of making that agreement, was introduced to the creditor or owner by an unlicensed credit-broker is only enforceable against the debtor or hirer if the Director General makes a validating order. Thus a finance company might be unable to enforce a hire-purchase agreement if the debtor was introduced to them by an unlicensed dealer.

Section 148 contains a similar "unenforceability" provision where an agreement is made for the services of an unlicensed person carrying on an ancillary credit business. Such a person can only enforce the agreement if the Director General makes a validating order. The wording of the section is not entirely clear. If we take the case of an estate agent whose business includes that of being a "credit-broker," does the unenforceability apply solely to an introduction fee payable to him by the borrower, or does it mean that he cannot sue the seller for his commission? On principle the former view should prevail—the sanctions imposed by the Act should be confined to his activities *qua* credit-broker and the words "agreement for the services of a person carrying on an ancillary credit business" should be construed accordingly.

In considering these provisions it must be borne in mind that consent by the debtor or hirer is as effective as a validating order (see s.173(3)).

---

[15] See Sched. 1.

2. Advertisements and Quotations

We have already seen that the very nature of credit carries the danger that the consumer may overcommit himself. The likelihood of this is greatly increased if the creditor is allowed to exhibit a misleading advertisement with words like "five years to pay" in bold type and a very high interest charge tucked away in the small print.

Advertisements and the consumer

Before embarking on a brief examination of the scope and content of advertisement regulation it may be relevant to consider what rights accrue to the consumer as a result of a defective advertisement. There are three overlapping possibilities:

(1) If he is induced by a misleading advertisement to make a contract with the advertiser, he may have a civil claim under the general law for misrepresentation or for negligence. (See Chapters 3 and 7.)

(2) If an advertisement contravenes the Act, the regulations or other legislation (e.g. the Trade Descriptions Act 1968[16] or the Control of Misleading Advertisement Regulations 1988 which were discussed in Chapter 14), the criminal court can exercise its general power to award compensation under the Powers of Criminal Courts Act 1973. (See Chapter 13.)

(3) There is the ever-present possibility of a complaint to the Office of Fair Trading which could, in the last resort, lead to the suspension or revocation of a licence.

Scope of advertisement control

The advertising provisions stand apart from the rest of the Act; in some respects the controls are wider and in some narrower. Thus:

(1) The controls are not restricted to "regulated agreements" (ante, p. 301). If, for example, a credit agreement is to be secured on land, the statutory advertising controls will apply even where the credit exceeds the statutory ceiling of £15,000. On the other hand, the controls will not apply if the advertisement indicates that the credit is only available to a body corporate (see s.43(3)(b)).

(2) The effect of the Consumer Credit (Exempt Advertisements) Order (S.I. 1980 No. 53 (as amended)) is to take many—but not all—types of exempt agreements outside the advertising controls.

---

[16] Ante, p. 195.

(3) When we turn to the Advertisement Regulations themselves (S.I. 1980 No. 54) we find one of the few distinctions between private and business transactions. These regulations will not apply to an advertisement which (1) clearly states that the credit or hire facilities are available for the purposes of a person's business and (2) does not indicate that the facilities are available for non-business purposes (see reg. 2(2)).

The definitions

It is clear from section 189 that the concept of "advertisement" is extremely wide and is not confined to visual forms. It can therefore include anything from a catalogue or brochure to films, radio and television commercials and even sales patter. It is also important to note that "the advertiser" is not necessarily the person who causes the advertisement to be inserted; it is the person who is indicated in the advertisement as willing to provide the credit, hire or credit brokerage facilities.

False advertisements

By section 46 an offence is committed if an advertisement is false or misleading in a material respect. Thus an "APR nil" advertisement has been held to be false where the trader made a hidden charge by giving a lower part-exchange allowance to instalment buyers than to cash buyers: *Metsoja* v. *H. Norman Pitt & Co. Ltd.*[17]

The advertising regulations

These deal in some detail with the form and content of advertisements falling within their scope. Thus (a) the statutory information must be clear and easily legible; (b) (subject to exceptions) it must be presented together as a whole; (c) due prominence must be given to the APR (*ante*, p. 309) where this is stated; and (d) the advertisement must contain a prescribed form of "health warning" in cases involving foreign currency mortgages or mortgages over a borrower's home. As regards content the regulations divide controlled advertisements into three types—simple, intermediate and full.[18] The advertiser must study the regulations carefully and then make sure that the advertisement does not contain either too little information or too much. For example, an advertisement "A. Smith—Moneylender" is a simple advertisement and must not indicate any price or any other willingness to enter into credit agreements. The Office of Fair Trading has

---

[17] (1989) 153 J.P.N. 630.
[18] Full advertisements are subdivided into those aimed at *new* customers and those offering variations of existing agreements.

published some helpful booklets (complete with cartoons!) to illustrate what the advertiser can and cannot do.

Quotations

As part of the policy of giving customers pre-contractual information the Act enables quotation regulations to be made (see sections 52 and 152) and the Consumer Credit (Quotations) Regulations 1989 (S.I. 1989 No. 1126) have been in force since February 1, 1990.

Scope

Like the Advertisement Regulations the Quotation Regulations go beyond the rest of the Act, because they apply not only to consumer credit or consumer hire but also to all agreements for the provision of credit (regardless of amount) to individuals secured on land. Unlike the Advertisement Regulations (see above) there is no distinction between private and business customers.

The trader's obligations

The regulations deal with the situation where a trader receives a request[19] from an individual asking for written information about the terms on which the trader is prepared to do business with the customer in relation to a particular transaction. In such a case the trader must (presumably within a reasonable time, although the regulations do not say so) provide the necessary information in the form set out in the regulations. The information is similar in many respects to that required in a full advertisement; indeed the request need not be complied with at all if, *inter alia*, it is made in writing at the business premises of the creditor or credit-broker where a full advertisement is conspicuously displayed. In addition it must contain a "health warning" in the following form (as appropriate):

BE SURE YOU CAN AFFORD
THE REPAYMENTS [PAYMENTS]
BEFORE ENTERING INTO A
CREDIT [HIRE] AGREEMENT.

Quotations and contracts

If the quotation, on its true construction, is an offer the consumer can accept the offer in the usual way whereupon a binding contract on the terms of the quotation will come into existence. The regulations make it clear, however, that the quotation need not take this form; regulation 2(2) provides that:

---

[19] See reg. 4(1)(*b*) as to the form of the request.

every [quotation] . . . may be framed as an offer or in any other way.

Accordingly there may be cases where it is the consumer who makes the offer. In such a case the creditor may (1) accept the offer on the terms of the quotation or (2) reject the offer completely or (3) make a counter-offer on different terms. A creditor or credit-broker who fails to comply with the regulations commits an offence (s.167(2)) but presumably this will not apply where the creditor or credit-broker can show that the quotation was totally accurate but that he subsequently (perhaps after the results of references or searches) changed his mind about the transaction.

3. CANVASSING

Section 49 follows the precedent set by the Moneylenders Acts by prohibiting the canvassing of debtor-creditor agreements, *e.g.* personal loans, off trade premises.

When is an offence committed?

The canvasser must be an individual and must solicit the debtor into the making of a regulated agreement by making oral representations to the debtor, or to any other individual, during a visit by the canvasser to non-trade premises. The visit must have been for the purpose of making such oral representations, so that a crime is not committed if one individual makes representations to another individual while they are both guests at a party. On the other hand, a social visit can be caught if the underlying intention was to make representations leading to the debtor-creditor agreement.

Previous request

No offence is committed if the visit was in response to a request made on a previous occasion, provided that the request was in writing signed by or on behalf of the person making it.[20] Presumably the person making the request need not be the debtor.

Trade premises

For *this* purpose the term trade premises is defined[21] as any premises where a business is carried on (whether on a permanent or temporary basis) by (a) the creditor or owner, or (b) the supplier, or (c) the canvasser's employer, or (d) the debtor.

Overdrafts

The Director General has made a determination[22] which exempts

---

[20] s.48(1)(*b*) and 49(2).
[21] *Cf.* cancellation *post*, p. 333.
[22] On June 1, 1977.

the soliciting of an agreement enabling the debtor to overdraw on specified types of current account, provided that the debtor already keeps an account with the creditor. This could be relevant where a bank manager invites his customer, ostensibly for a meal or a game of golf, but in reality to offer him overdraft facilities.

Circulars to minors

Minors (persons under 18) are particularly vulnerable to blandishments of "easy credit" and accordingly section 50(1) makes it an offence for a person, with a view to financial gain, to send to a minor any document inviting him or her to (a) borrow money or (b) obtain goods on credit or hire or (c) obtain services on credit or (d) apply for information or advice on borrowing money or otherwise obtaining credit or hiring goods. A defence is available where the person sending the circular did not know and had no reasonable cause to suspect that the addressee was a minor (s.50(2)) but the following subsection makes this defence somewhat difficult to raise if the document is sent to a school! Any such offence will not invalidate any resulting agreement[23] and such an agreement will be governed by a combination of common law rules, the Minors Contracts Act 1987, section 3 of the Sale of Goods Act 1979 and the Act.

[23] s.170(1), *ante*, p. 298.

CHAPTER EIGHTEEN

"I CAN'T REMEMBER WHAT I SIGNED"

In the previous chapter we examined vitally important provisions relating to the control of business activities.

We now turn to the other main form of control—the regulation of individual agreements. The law is to be found in Parts V–IX of the Act and much of it is modelled on the previous hire-purchase legislation. This chapter is concerned with formalities and copies.[1] The object of the legislation is to make sure that the debtor or hirer is made aware of his rights and obligations and that he can obtain further information if, for example, he has failed to keep a record of his payments. Once again a large amount of the detail is contained in regulations.

Sanctions for non-compliance

The sanctions are potentially severe. If the creditor or owner fails to comply with the various formalities, the agreement is said to be *"not properly executed."* By section 65 the creditor or owner cannot enforce such an agreement against the debtor or hirer unless (a) the court makes an enforcement order[2] or (b) the debtor or hirer consents to enforcement (s.173(3)).[3] What happens if the creditor or owner, in defiance of section 65, enforces the agreement by retaking the goods? If the repossession amounts to the tort of trespass or conversion, the creditor or owner will be liable for this. If, however, the repossession is only unlawful because it contravenes section 65, it seems that the only remedy of the debtor or hirer is to apply for a mandatory injunction to restore the status quo.[4] That leaves merely the administrative sanction of taking action which can put the licence of the creditor or owner in jeopardy.

The purpose of the sanctions is to put the creditor or owner at a disadvantage if they do not comply with the rules designed for the protection of the consumer. The agreement is not invalidated[5]: it becomes *unenforceable by the creditor or owner.* From the point of view of the debtor or hirer it is still valid and fully enforceable. For

---

[1] ss.58–65 and 77–80.
[2] *Post*, pp. 351–354. Sometimes no such order can be made at all (*ibid.*).
[3] *Ante*, p. 298.
[4] *Ibid.*
[5] *R.* v. *Modupe, The Times*, February 27, 1991 (total price omitted; liability to repay continued, though unenforceable).

example, if goods held under a hire-purchase agreement are defective, the debtor can bring a claim under the Supply of Goods (Implied Terms) Act 1973 even though the agreement is "improperly-executed."

Pre-contractual information

As part of the policy outlined above, section 55 enables regulations to be made whereby specified information must be disclosed to the prospective debtor or hirer before a regulated agreement is made. No regulations have so far been made.

Special pre-contract formalities in land mortgage cases

We have already seen that many land mortgage cases are outside the main control provisions because (i) the credit exceeds the statutory ceiling[6] or (ii) the agreements are exempted under section 16 or by regulations.[7] If, however, the agreement is a regulated agreement (*e.g.* a loan not exceeding the statutory ceiling granted by a non-exempt lender) section 58 lays down a special pre-contractual period of reflection and isolation; the reason for this is that the post-contractual cancellation provisions do not apply to any agreement secured on land.[8]

In two cases, however, the special reflection rules do not apply, namely (a) a restricted-use agreement to finance the purchase of the mortgaged land and (b) an agreement for a bridging loan in connection with the purchase of the mortgaged land or other land. In these two cases the debtor will have neither reflection rights nor cancellation rights.

Let us suppose that John, a moneylender, is prepared to lend George £4,000 on the security of George's house. The reflection and isolation rules can be summarised as follows:

(1) At least seven days before sending the agreement for signature, John must give to George a copy of the agreement (and of any document referred to therein) containing a notice in the prescribed form indicating George's right to withdraw from the transaction.[9]

(2) When seven days have elapsed, John can post the agreement for signature unless he has received a notice of withdrawal.[10]

(3) John must not approach George in any way during the "*consideration period*" except at George's specific request. The consideration

---

[6] £15,000 for agreements made on or after May 20, 1985.
[7] See *ante*, p. 306.
[8] s.67 *post*, p. 334.
[9] s.58(1) and 61(2). Thus a copy of the proposed mortgage would have to accompany the reflection copy which refers to it.
[10] s.61(2) and (4).

period begins when the "reflection copy" is sent[11] and ends seven days after the sending of the agreement for signature[12] or, if earlier, its return by George duly signed.

Regulations have now been made relating to the wording of the "reflection copy." Thus the heading of a prospective credit agreement must be as follows:

> Copy of proposed credit agreement containing notice of your right to withdraw
> DO NOT sign or return this copy.

The document must also contain an explanatory box containing the following words:

YOUR RIGHT TO WITHDRAW

This is a copy of your proposed Credit agreement which is to be secured on land. It has been given to you now so that you may have at least a week to consider its terms before the actual agreement is sent to you for signature. You should read it carefully. If you do not understand it you may need to seek professional advice. If you do not wish to go ahead with it you need not do so.

If you decide NOT to go ahead with the agreement you should inform   or, if you prefer, any supplier or broker involved in the negotiations. You can do this in writing or orally for example by telephone. If the agreement arrives for signature and you have decided NOT to go ahead DO NOT SIGN IT. Then you will not be legally bound by the agreement.

Finally the agreement itself must contain the following box:

YOUR RIGHTS

Under the Consumer Credit Act 1974 the creditor should have given you a copy of this agreement at least seven days ago to allow you time to consider whether to go ahead. If he did not, the agreement cannot be enforced without a court order.

The above also apply to a regulated consumer hire agreement secured by land mortgage.

Formalities of the agreement itself

Sections 60 and 61 enable regulations to be made to ensure that the

[11] See (1) above.
[12] See (2) above.

debtor or hirer is made aware of his rights and duties, the amount and rate of the total charge for credit and the protection and remedies available to him under the Act. The detail is to be found in the Consumer Credit (Agreements) Regulations 1983 which specify the information which must be included, having regard to the particular type of agreement.[13] Thus the debtor under a hire-purchase agreement must be made aware of (*inter alia*) his right of termination,[14] and the restriction on the creditor's right to repossess protected goods.[15] The regulations (not surprisingly) require that the information should be easily legible and of a colour which is easily distinguishable from the colour of the paper.[16] They also specify the prominence to be given to particular parts of the agreement, and the place where the debtor or hirer must sign and the words to be contained in the signature box. The financial and related particulars (description of goods, deposit, credit, cash price, APR, total charges, repayments, etc.) must be shown together as a whole and not interspersed with other information.

The Act itself lays down three broad requirements in section 61:

(a) a document in the prescribed form itself containing all the prescribed terms[17] and conforming to regulations under section 60(1) is signed in the prescribed manner both by the debtor or hirer and by or on behalf of the creditor or owner, and

(b) the document embodies all the terms of the agreement, other than implied terms, and

(c) the document is, when presented or sent to the debtor or hirer for signature, in such a state that all its terms are readily legible.

The wording of para. (a) makes it clear that the debtor or hirer must sign *personally*. It is also clear that a signature on a blank form, with the details filled in later, would not be sufficient.[18]

Copies

Sections 62–63 contain copy provisions which are similar, but not identical, to the provisions in the Hire-Purchase Act 1965. The basic rule is that the debtor or hirer is always entitled to at least one copy of the agreement; in many cases he is entitled to two copies.

The provisions are complex but they can be conveniently divided into (a) cases where the agreement is presented to the debtor or hirer for signature, (b) cases where it is sent to him for signature and (c) cases where it is neither presented nor sent.

---

[13] See S.I. 1983 No. 1553, regs. 2–5.
[14] *Post*, p. 339.
[15] *Post*, p. 358.
[16] Reg. 6(2).
[17] See reg. 6 and Sched. 6 of the Agreements Regulations for the meaning of this term.
[18] Consider *Eastern Distributors* v. *Goldring* [1957] Q.B. 600, a decision on a slightly different provision in the Hire-Purchase Act 1938.

(a) *Agreement presented to debtor or hirer*

In the vast majority of cases in practice the document which he signs will be *"an unexecuted agreement,"* i.e. a document embodying the terms of a prospective regulated agreement. In other words, the document is an offer by the debtor or hirer and there will be no concluded agreement until the document is signed by the creditor or owner thus accepting the offer. In this situation one copy must be given to the debtor or hirer immediately after he has signed[19] and, in addition, a copy of the executed agreement must be delivered or sent to him within seven days after the making of the agreement.[20]

In the less likely situation where the creditor or owner has already signed, signature by the debtor or hirer will convert the document into an *"executed agreement"*, i.e. a contract; in that situation a copy of that agreement must be given to him there and then. In this situation no further copy is required.[21]

(b) *Agreement sent to the debtor or hirer for signature*

Here again the position is somewhat similar to that mentioned above. In all cases the agreement which is sent to the debtor or hirer for signature must be accompanied by a copy.[22] If the document becomes an "executed agreement" when he signs, no further copy need be sent to him.[23] Usually, however, the document which the debtor or hirer signs is an offer to the creditor or owner and will not become an "executed agreement" until a later date—i.e. until it is signed by the creditor or owner. In that situation a copy of the executed agreement must be delivered or sent to the debtor or hirer within seven days of the making of the agreement.

(c) *Cases where the prospective agreement is neither delivered nor sent*

The situations contemplated here are those where the debtor completes an application form which he sees in a newspaper or which he picks up from a dispenser. In this situation the creditor or owner must deliver or send a copy of the executed agreement within seven days of the date on which it is made.[24]

(d) *Cancellation cases*

Special provisions apply in cancellation cases.[25]

[19] s.62(1).
[20] s.63(2).
[21] ss.63(1) and (2)(*a*).
[22] s.62(2).
[23] s.63(2)(*b*).
[24] s.63(2).
[25] *Post*, p. 334.

(e) *Form and contents of copies*

This matter is dealt with in considerable detail in the Consumer Credit (Cancellation Notices and Copies of Documents) Regulations 1983.[26] A failure to comply with these formalities will mean that the agreement is "not properly executed" (see ss.62–65 read with s.182(2)) and the consequences for the creditor or owner can be very serious.[27]

(f) *Other documents*

The duty to supply a copy includes a duty to supply a copy of every other document referred to in the agreement. Read literally this would require the creditor or owner to supply a copy of the Consumer Credit Act merely because the agreement referred to it. Fortunately the regulations make it clear that this is not necessary.[28]

Post-contractual information

Additional information on request

The copy provisions are supplemented by sections 77–79 which, as already stated, are designed to assist the debtor or hirer who has failed to keep a record of his payments (alternatively, he may have mislaid either or both of the copies referred to above). In each of these cases the debtor or hirer must make a written request and send the sum of 50 pence. To ensure that the creditor or owner is not put to unreasonable trouble, the sections require him to send to the debtor or hirer, within the prescribed period,[29] a copy of the executed agreement and a signed statement containing certain particulars (*e.g.* as to sums paid, due and payable) "according to the information to which it is practicable for him to refer." Further, to prevent the creditor or owner from being inundated with such requests, the information need not be given at all if the request was made within one month of a previous request having been complied with.

The sanctions for non-compliance are two-fold. Thus (a) while the default continues the creditor or owner cannot enforce the agreement and (b) if the default continues for one month he commits an offence.

Additional information without request

In the case of a running-account credit agreement, other than a small agreement,[30] the creditor must send to the debtor periodic statements containing the information required by regulations.[31]

---

[26] S.I. 1983 No. 1557.
[27] See *ante*, p. 323 and *post*, pp. 351–354.
[28] S.I. 1983 No. 1557, reg. 11(e).
[29] Twelve working days (S.I. 1983 No. 1569, reg. 2).
[30] *Ante*, p. 305.
[31] s.78(4) and S.I. 1983 No. 1570 which deal with form, contents and time limits.

Information as to the whereabouts of the goods

So far all the provisions have required information to be given *by* the creditor or owner, but section 80 is concerned with the reverse situation. It provides that where a regulated agreement requires the debtor or hirer to keep goods in his possession or control, he must within seven working days after receiving a written request from the creditor or owner tell the creditor or owner where the goods are. If the information is not given within 21 days of receiving the request the debtor or hirer commits an offence.

Transitional matters

The various sections discussed in this chapter came into force on May 19, 1985 and sections 77–79 are retrospective—they apply to agreements made before that date which would have been regulated if made on that date.[32]

Guarantees

Formality and copy provisions also apply to guarantees of regulated agreements.[33]

---

[32] See Sched. 3, para. 17(2), read with the Eighth Commencement Order.
[33] See ss.105–110 and S.I. 1983 No. 1556.

CHAPTER NINETEEN

"CAN I GET OUT OF THE AGREEMENT?"

We have seen that a debtor or hirer may commit himself too heavily (perhaps aided by an over-enthusiastic salesman). In this chapter we shall consider his right to resile from a regulated agreement and the financial consequences of his doing so. The subject will be considered under four headings, namely:

1. Withdrawal
2. Rescission and Repudiation
3. Cancellation
4. Termination.

The above topics must be distinguished from the problem which arises where the consumer wants to perform the agreement ahead of time. This matter is considered in Chapter 22—*post*, p. 354.

1. WITHDRAWAL

On general contractual principles a prospective debtor or hirer can withdraw from the transaction at any time before his offer has been accepted by revoking his offer. In the case of a regulated agreement his position is strengthened by section 59(1) which provides that an agreement is void if it binds a person to enter, as prospective debtor or hirer, into a prospective regulated agreement. This provision may, however, be cut down by regulations but the only regulations so far made are confined to certain types of business credit.[1]

Section 57, which deals with withdrawal, provides that no special form of wording is required[2] and the notice of withdrawal can be written or oral. Two important points should be noted:

(1) The list of persons to whom notice of withdrawal can be given is surprisingly wide. It includes not only the credit-broker or supplier but also "any person who, in the course of a business carried on by him, acts on behalf of the debtor or hirer in any negotiations for the agreement."[3] Thus if, for example, the prospective debtor had

---

[1] See S.I. 1983 No. 1552.
[2] s.57(2).
[3] s.57(3).

instructed a solicitor to negotiate on his behalf, a notice given by him to that solicitor would be sufficient. Such a deemed agent is under a deemed contractual duty to transmit the notice to his deemed principal (the creditor or owner) forthwith.[4]

(2) Withdrawal has the same effect as cancellation. Thus (a) the prospective debtor or hirer can recover all payments made by him to the creditor or owner (*e.g.* a pre-contract deposit, or a payment made for a survey of the house); (b) the withdrawal will also terminate any linked transaction[5] and sums paid under it become repayable; (c) under a three party D-C-S agreement[6] the creditor and the supplier are jointly liable to repay the sums paid by the debtor; and (d) the prospective debtor or hirer will have a lien over the goods until sums repayable to him have been repaid.[7]

One final point: the Act does not cut down the general rule that the revocation of an offer must be communicated to the offeree before acceptance. Thus if the consumer uses the post he runs the risk that his letter of withdrawal will be lost in the post or will only reach the creditor or owner after acceptance. In either of these cases the withdrawal is ineffective.[8]

2. RESCISSION AND REPUDIATION

Again on general contractual principles a debtor or hirer may have a right to rescind an agreement for misrepresentation or to treat it as repudiated by a breach by the creditor or owner. One example of this is considered in the next chapter. The deemed agency provisions referred to above also apply to rescission.[9] The principal distinction between rescission and accepting a repudiation is that the former is retrospective and the innocent party is treated as if the agreement had never been made. In the latter case obligations arising before the acceptance of repudiation remain enforceable, although they can usually be reduced or extinguished by a claim for damages.

3. CANCELLATION

We have already seen that a "consumer" will have cancellation rights in cases covered by the Consumer Protection (Cancellation of Contracts Concluded away from Business Premises) Regulations 1987—

---

[4] s.175.
[5] For the meaning of this term see *ante*, p. 310.
[6] *Ante*, p. 304.
[7] The consequences of cancellation are considered in more detail on pp. 336–338.
[8] See Goode, *Consumer Credit Legislation*, Vol. I, para. 575, where a similar view is taken.
[9] See s.102.

ante, p. 81. A somewhat similar cancellation right is available under sections 67–73 of the Act (for a somewhat wider class of "consumer") and this is considered below. Although the 1987 Regulations do not expressly exclude overlap between the two rights, this is the effect of regulation 4; in other words the cancellation rights under the regulations will not apply if the consumer has cancellation rights under the rules discussed below.

The cancellation provisions in sections 67–73 are modelled on those in the Hire-Purchase Act 1965, although there are significant differences between them. The object of the legislation is clear enough—to give the debtor or hirer a chance for second thoughts (*i.e.* a "cooling-off period") in a case where he may have been pressurised by a doorstep salesman into signing an agreement. The matter can be considered under the following headings:

(1) What agreements are cancellable?
(2) The copy provisions
(3) The time for cancellation
(4) How is cancellation effected?
(5) Effect of cancellation
(6) Duty to return goods
(7) The part-exchange allowance

(1) What agreements are cancellable?

A regulated consumer credit or hire agreement is cancellable if two conditions are satisfied, namely, (a) oral representations were made by or on behalf of the negotiator in the presence of the debtor or hirer; *and* (b) the unexecuted agreement was not signed by the debtor or hirer at premises where a business was carried on by (i) the creditor or owner or (ii) any party to a linked transaction (other than the debtor or hirer or a relative of his) or (iii) the negotiator in any antecedent negotiations.

Let us suppose that John, a trader, goes to a car dealer to buy a new car. The transaction is financed by a loan from a finance company who require John to take out a life policy with an insurance company. The car dealer (the negotiator) makes oral representations in John's presence. If John signs the agreement at the office of the dealer, finance company or insurance company, he will have no right of cancellation. On the other hand, if he signs at his own home, or at his own business premises, then cancellation is available. Thus, the definition of business premises does *not* include the business premises of the debtor or hirer.[10] The place where the representations were made is immaterial. They must, however, have been made in the *presence* of the debtor or

---

[10] Contrast the canvassing rules, *ante*, p. 320.

hirer. Representations made on the telephone would not give cancellation rights. If no oral representations were made at all (*e.g.* a mail-order purchase) there is no right of cancellation.

In the case of land transactions the concept of post-contractual cancellation can result in considerable administrative problems. Accordingly, the cancellation provisions do not apply to (a) an agreement secured on land, or (b) a restricted-use agreement to finance the purchase of land, or (c) a bridging loan in connection with the purchase of land. It will be recalled that in case (a) above the prospective debtor or hirer will have a pre-contractual period of reflection and isolation.[11]

Two other types of agreement are not cancellable. They are (a) a non-commercial agreement[12] and (b) a "small" debtor-creditor-supplier agreement for restricted-use credit.[13]

> Let us suppose that a doorstep salesman induces Mrs. Smith to buy a children's encyclopaedia at a price of £45 payable by nine instalments of £5. Nothing is said about the passing of property. (i) This is a "small" agreement[14]; (ii) since the supplier of the goods and the supplier of the credit are the same person it is "debtor-creditor-supplier"; (iii) since Mrs. Smith cannot get her hands on the credit it is "restricted-use"; (iv) therefore no cancellation is possible.

(2) The copy provisions

The basic rules in sections 62 and 63[15] are modified in three respects by section 64. Thus:

(a) each copy must contain a notice in the prescribed form indicating the right of cancellation, how and when it is exercisable and the name and address of a person to whom notice of cancellation may be given[16];

(b) in cases where a second copy is required it must be sent *by post*[17] (s.63(3));

(c) in cases where a second copy is not required a notice, containing the information mentioned in (a) above, must be posted to the debtor or hirer within seven days of the making of the agreement.[18]

We shall see that the usual "unenforceability" sanction can be particularly severe in these cases.[19]

---

[11] *Ante*, p. 324.
[12] *Ante*, p. 305.
[13] s.74(2).
[14] *Ante*, p. 305.
[15] *Ante*, p. 326.
[16] s.64(1)(*a*) read with the Consumer Credit (Cancellation Notices and Copies of Documents) Regulations 1983 (S.I. 1983 No. 1557).
[17] s.63(3).
[18] s.64(1)(*b*).
[19] See *post*, p. 353.

Exemptions

The Director General can grant exemption from the duty to send a cancellation notice in certain specified cases if he is satisfied that this requirement can be dispensed with without prejudicing the interests of debtors or hirers (see s.64(4) and the Consumer Credit (Notice of Cancellation Rights) (Exemptions) Regulations 1983 No. 1558).

(3) The time for cancellation

The cancellation period starts when the debtor or hirer signs the unexecuted agreement and ends five days after the debtor or hirer *receives* the statutory second copy or notice.[20] Thus, if the second copy is received on a Friday the cancellation period runs out at midnight on the following Wednesday. If the second copy is delayed in the post the cancellation period will, to that extent, be prolonged since the period only starts to melt away when the debtor or hirer *receives* the second copy. What happens if the second copy is not received at all and the creditor or owner then sends a further copy? Alternatively, what happens if the second copy or notice is sent off more than seven days after the making of the agreement? The wording of the Act is ambiguous. If the third copy or the late copy could be regarded as given "under" section 63, then it would start the five day period running. On the other hand it could be argued that a notice is only given "under" section 63 if it is posted within seven days; if this is correct then the effect of delay or non-receipt would be that the right of cancellation would remain permanently available. This seems so absurd that the court is likely to prefer the former view.

(4) How is cancellation effected?

By section 69 the agreement can be cancelled if the debtor or hirer serves a notice of cancellation on (a) the creditor or owner or (b) the person specified in the copy or notice or (c) the agent of the creditor or owner (including his deemed agent).[21] No special form of wording is required but it is clear from the definition of "notice"[22] that it must be in writing. If it is posted it takes effect as from the date of posting and the mere fact that it is not received by the creditor or owner is immaterial (this is in marked contrast to the second copy or notice which only triggers off the count-down of the cancellation period when it is received).[23] The regulations require that the second copy or the notice (see (2) above) must include a cancellation form which the debtor or hirer can use to cancel the agreement.[24]

---

[20] s.68.
[21] See *ante*, pp. 331 and 332.
[22] s.189.
[23] Notice of cancellation (effective when posted) can also be contrasted with notice of withdrawal—see *ante*, p. 332.
[24] S.I. 1983 No. 1557, regs. 5 and 6 and Sched., Pts. IV and VI.

(5) Effect of cancellation

Subject to two exceptions the general effect of cancellation is to treat the agreement, and most linked transactions,[25] as if it had never been made.[26] Thus the debtor or hirer can recover his payments and is discharged from liability to make further payments. In the case of a three-party D-C-S agreement[27] for restricted-use credit the creditor and supplier are jointly and severally liable to repay sums paid by the debtor or a relative. The debtor, hirer or relative has a lien over the goods until repayable sums are repaid to him. Thus, if Albert paid a £200 deposit to buy a £2,000 car and the remaining £1,800 was paid by a creditor who had "arrangements" with the seller, the effect of a cancellation of the loan agreement would be that (a) the sale contract, as a linked transaction, would also be cancelled (b) the seller and creditor would be jointly and severally liable to repay the £200 to Albert and (c) if the £1,800 were paid direct to the supplier he would have to repay it to the creditor.[28]

Two exceptions

(1) The first exception is in section 70(2) and deals with a debtor-creditor-supplier agreement for restricted-use credit to finance (a) the doing of work or supply of goods to meet an emergency or (b) the supply of goods which have become incorporated in any land or thing before service of the notice of cancellation. Since the debtor is unable to return the goods, it would clearly be wrong to allow him to avoid payment simply by serving a notice of cancellation. Accordingly, in this type of case the cancellation will wipe out the credit part of the agreement but the debtor will remain liable to pay the cash price for the goods or work.

(2) The second exception is to be found in section 71 and it deals with a case where the credit has already been advanced by the creditor before the expiry of the cancellation period. Here the strict application of the cancellation provisions would cause hardship. On the one hand, since the agreement is treated as never having been made, the creditor might be able to bring an action to recover money lent. On the other hand the debtor might try to avoid all liability in reliance on section 70(1)(b) which provides that any sum payable by the debtor or his relative shall cease to be payable. To deal with these problems section 71 starts by providing that cancellation of a regulated consumer credit

---

[25] By S.I. 1983 No. 1560 certain linked transactions (insurance, guarantee of goods, deposit accounts and current accounts) will survive the cancellation of the main agreement.
[26] s.69(4).
[27] *Ante*, p. 304.
[28] s.70(1)(c).

agreement (other than a debtor-creditor-supplier agreement for re-stricted-use credit) shall not destroy the obligation to repay the credit and interest. The words in brackets are inserted because, as we have seen, this type of transaction does not raise the type of problem at which section 71 is aimed—the supplier merely repays the credit to the creditor. The section then goes on to provide a complex formula. First of all it provides that if the whole or part of the credit is repaid within one month of cancellation, or not later than the first instalment repay-ment date, no interest is chargeable on the amount repaid. In other words, the consumer will have had the use of the money interest-free. It then goes on to deal with credit which is repayable by instalments where any part of the credit is still outstanding after the first repayment date. In such a case the creditor must serve a notice[29] recalculating the instalments over a period starting when this notice is served and ending with the final contractual repayment date. This shortening of the repayment period will often mean larger instalments.

(6) Duty to return goods

Let us remind ourselves at this point of the distinction between debtor-creditor-supplier agreements and debtor-creditor agreements:

(a) Where the debtor under a debtor-creditor agreement uses the credit to buy goods, the sale contract is *not* a linked transaction and is not affected by cancellation of the credit agreement.

(b) In the case of a debtor-creditor-supplier agreement the supply of the goods is either an integral part of the credit agreement itself (*e.g.* hire-purchase) or it is a linked transaction under section 19 which is cancelled along with the credit agreement. In either case the debtor will have to restore the goods to the other party under the rules set out below.

Section 72 deals with a case where a debtor-creditor-supplier agree-ment for restricted-use credit, a consumer hire agreement or a linked transaction (to which the debtor, hirer or a relative is a party) is cancelled after the debtor, hirer or relative has obtained possession. In such a case the possessor is under a duty to restore the goods to the person from whom he got them and in the meantime to retain posses-sion and to take reasonable care. The duty to restore the goods is merely a duty to redeliver them at *his own* premises on receiving a written request from the other party. The duty is also discharged if the possessor delivers the goods (whether at his own premises or else-where) to any person to whom a notice of cancellation could have been sent other than the "deemed agent."[30] Alternatively, he can send the

---

[29] See S.I. 1983 No. 1559 which sets out the form of the request.
[30] See *ante*, pp. 331 and 332.

goods to such a person, but in this case he must take reasonable care to see that they are received by the other party and are not damaged in transit. The duty to take reasonable care comes to an end 21 days from cancellation unless within that time the possessor has received a written request for redelivery and has unreasonably failed to comply with it.

There is, however, a sting in the tail. The duty to restore does not apply to emergency or incorporation cases where, as we have seen, the debtor remains liable to pay the price.[31] Nor does it apply to perishable goods, nor to goods which by their nature are consumed by use and were so consumed before cancellation—a classic case of having one's cake and not having to pay for it![32]

Any breach of section 72 is actionable as a breach of statutory duty.

(7) The part-exchange allowance

Section 73 deals with a case where, as part of a cancelled agreement, the negotiator agreed to take goods in part exchange and those goods have been delivered to him. The effect of section 73(2) is to give the debtor or hirer a right to recover the part-exchange allowance from the negotiator unless within 10 days of cancellation the goods were returned to the debtor or hirer in substantially the same condition. If the negotiator was the supplier in a three-party debtor-creditor-supplier agreement, the negotiator and the creditor are jointly and severally liable to repay the allowance and the lien of the debtor or hirer[33] extends to cover the return of the goods (during the 10 day period) or the part-exchange allowance.

4. TERMINATION

If there is no right of withdrawal, rescission or cancellation the final possibility (apart from any contractual right of termination) is a right of termination under sections 99–101. These are limited in scope; sections 99–100 only apply to regulated hire-purchase and conditional sale agreements while section 101 relates to regulated consumer hire agreements. In either case the statutory rights cannot be cut down by agreement; on the other hand if the agreement is *more* favourable to the debtor or hirer he can take advantage of it.

---

[31] s.69(2)(*b*) *ante*, p. 336.
[32] Thus the hirer of a motor vehicle would not have to pay for petrol consumed before cancellation.
[33] *Ante*, p. 336.

(1) **Hire-purchase and conditional sale**

The provisions of sections 99–100 are very closely modelled on the corresponding provisions in the Hire-Purchase Act 1965, although modifications have had to be made because the 1974 Act extends to land as well as goods. The right to terminate a hire-purchase or conditional sale agreement is available at any time before the last instalment falls due. It can be exercised by giving notice to any person who is entitled or authorised to receive payments. However, there are two cases in which the right to terminate is not available. The first is where, under a conditional sale agreement relating to land, title has passed to the buyer. The second is where, under a conditional sale of goods, the property has become vested in the buyer and has then been transferred to a third person, *e.g.* a sub-buyer.

Termination only operates for the future, so that sums which have *accrued due* remain payable.[34] The effect of termination may well be to leave the creditor with heavily depreciated goods. In order to provide some measure of compensation section 100(1) requires the debtor to pay such further sum (if any) as will bring the total payments up to *one-half* of the total price. If, however, in any action the court is satisfied that a smaller sum is adequate to cover the creditor's loss, the court may order such smaller sum to be paid. This could clearly be relevant if, for example, a hirer bought a car with a hire-purchase price of £3,000 and then wished to terminate the agreement after only a few week's use. He would presumably tender a sum falling far short of one-half, leaving it to the creditor to take court proceedings. The court has no discretion with regard to sums which have already accrued due.

The debtor may also have to pay damages if he is in breach of an obligation to take reasonable care of the goods[35] and he must allow the creditor to retake them.[36]

If the creditor agrees to carry out any installation and if the cost of the installation forms part of the total price, it is clearly reasonable that he should be paid for this in full. Accordingly, the reference to one-half is a reference to the installation charge in full and one-half of the balance.[37]

Example

A television set is let out on hire-purchase at a price of £300, including a £30 installation charge. The debtor pays a £50 deposit and one instalment of £10 is outstanding. He now wishes to terminate the agreement. He must first of all pay the £10. Then (unless otherwise ordered) he must bring his payments up to one-half of the total price:

[34] s.99(2).
[35] s.100(4).
[36] s.100(5).
[37] s.100(2).

$$\text{one half} = £30 + \frac{270}{2} \qquad = £165$$

$$\text{less sums paid and due} \qquad = \quad 60$$

$$\text{further sums payable}[38] \qquad = £105$$

(2) Consumer hire

Section 101 gives the hirer a new and non-excludable right to terminate the agreement, but the earliest termination date is 18 months after the making of the agreement (unless the contract provides for an earlier termination date).[39] Once again termination only operates for the future and sums which have accrued due are not affected. The hirer must give a termination notice equal to the shortest payment interval, or three months, whichever is less. Thus, if rentals are payable monthly, the hirer can end the agreement by giving one month's notice at the end of month 17.

The exercise of a right of termination can often cause financial problems to the owner, especially where the owner leases out commercial equipment. Accordingly, section 101(7) provides that in three cases the statutory right of termination is not available at all. These are:

(a) where the total payments (disregarding sums payable on breach) exceed £900 in any one year;

(b) where goods are let out for the hirer's business and were selected by the hirer and acquired by the owner, at the hirer's request, from a third party;

(c) any agreement where the hirer requires the goods to re-let them in the course of a business.

Apart from these special cases the Director General has a general power to exclude the operation of section 101 from agreements made by a particular trader.[40]

The section does not mention damages for failure to take reasonable care but on principle the hirer owes a duty of reasonable care as a bailee at common law and will be liable to pay damages for breach of that duty.

---

[38] s.100(1).
[39] s.101(3).
[40] See s.101(8) as amended by the Consumer Credit (Increase of Monetary Amounts) Order 1983—S.I. 1983 No. 1571.

CHAPTER TWENTY

"THE GOODS ARE DEFECTIVE"

In Part I of this book we considered the terms implied by sections 12–14 of the Sale of Goods Act 1979, and we also dealt briefly with hire-purchase and hiring agreements. In this chapter we shall consider these problems again in the context of credit transactions. The basic point can be made very briefly at the outset—the differences between cash and credit transactions are very slight. It is proposed to consider this topic under five headings and for convenience the term "connected lender" will be used in preference to "creditor with whom the supplier had arrangements." The five headings are:

1. Cash sale—unconnected lender
2. Cash sale—connected lender
3. Credit sale and conditional sale
4. Hire-purchase
5. Hire

1. CASH SALE—UNCONNECTED LENDER

Let us suppose that Robert borrows money from his bank and uses it to buy a car. The loan is a debtor-creditor agreement and, as we have seen, the purchase of the car is not a linked transaction. As between seller and buyer, the position is governed by the Sale of Goods Act 1979, and this has been fully discussed in Chapters 3 and 4. Alternatively, if the seller was guilty of misrepresentation Robert may be entitled to rescind the contract or to claim damages.[1] As between Robert and his bank the bank are not affected by any breach of contract on the part of the seller. It follows that Robert will have to continue to repay the loan and his sole remedy is against the seller. If he cannot afford the repayments his sole right as against the bank is to wait for a notice of default[2] or for proceedings to enforce the loan agreement and then apply to the court for a time order.[3]

2. CASH SALE—CONNECTED LENDER

Let us now suppose that the seller introduces Robert to a finance

---

[1] *Ante*, p. 97.
[2] *Post*, p. 356.
[3] *Post*, p. 357.

company with whom the seller has arrangements. The finance company makes a loan to Robert to finance the sale. This is a three-party debtor-creditor-supplier agreement. As between Robert and the seller, the position is exactly the same as in the previous example. As regards the position between Robert and the finance company there are two overlapping provisions of considerable practical importance which may enable Robert to hold the finance company responsible for the seller's default.

Section 56

The first provision is section 56 of the Consumer Credit Act which applies (*inter alia*) to antecedent negotiations with the debtor conducted by the supplier in relation to a transaction financed by a debtor-creditor-supplier agreement.[4] The key provision is section 56(2) which reads as follows:

> Negotiations with the debtor . . . shall be deemed to be conducted by the negotiator in the capacity of agent of the creditor as well as in his actual capacity.

In other words, if the seller made a misrepresentation (*e.g.* as to credit terms or the quality of the goods), he will have made it as *agent* for the finance company. Thus Robert could bring proceedings against the finance company, or he could merely discontinue his payments, wait to be sued and then counterclaim. It remains to add that section 56(3) makes void a clause (a) purporting to make the negotiator the agent of the dealer or (b) relieving a person from liability for acts or omissions of any person acting as, or on behalf of, a negotiator. This raises a problem in relation to a clause in a contract between creditor and debtor excluding liability for all misrepresentations, including those made by the dealer. Would such a clause automatically be void under section 56(3) or would it still be subject to the reasonableness test under section 3 of the Misrepresentation Act 1967?[5] It is felt that a carefully drafted clause should be given the latter construction—it would seem strange that the creditor should be in a worse position merely because the misrepresentation was made by the dealer rather than by the creditor himself or by some other agent.

Section 75

The second provision affecting three-party debtor-creditor-supplier agreements is section 75. In this situation it is provided that:

> (1) if the debtor . . . has . . . any claim against the supplier in respect of a

---

[4] s.56(1)(c).
[5] As redrafted by s.8 of the Unfair Contract Terms Act 1977, *ante*, p. 138.

misrepresentation or breach of contract, he shall have a like claim against the creditor, who, with the supplier, shall accordingly be jointly and severally liable to the debtor.

Subsection (3)[6] lays down two limitations.

Subsection (1) does not apply to a claim—
    (a) under a non-commercial agreement, or
    (b) so far as the claim relates to any single item to which the supplier has attached a cash price[7] not exceeding £100 or more than £30,000.

As already stated there is substantial overlap between sections 56 and 75. If the "negotiator" makes a misrepresentation, the buyer/borrower may well have a claim against the creditor under either section. In two respects, however, section 56 is wider; it is not limited to three-party D-C-S agreements and it is not subject to the section 75 upper and lower limits.[8]

The real importance of section 75(1) lies in the words "or breach of contract." It means that the creditor will be liable not merely for the misrepresentation or for breach of express terms but also for breach of the *implied* terms, *e.g.* under the Sale of Goods Act 1979.[9] This seems reasonable enough; finance companies who finance the transaction by letting the goods out on hire-purchase have been responsible for the quality of the goods ever since 1938. The effect of section 75 is to place them in basically the same position if they choose to finance the transaction by means of a loan. From the debtor's point of view the effect of section 75 can be very favourable. In an extreme case he might have a claim against a solvent finance company whereas a person buying with his own money, or with money borrowed from an unconnected lender, might only have had a claim against an insolvent seller. It will be appreciated that the amount of the claim can be far greater than the amount of the credit.

Credit cards

In the example above[10] we took the case of a car buyer, dealer and connected lender. Another situation where section 75 is highly relevant is in relation to buyer, credit card company and approved supplier. If goods bought with a credit card prove to be defective and cause enormous damage (*e.g.* death or personal injury), the buyer (or his personal representatives) will have a claim against the credit card company for the full amount of the damage.

---

[6] As amended by the Consumer Credit (Increase of Monetary Limits) Order 1983 (S.I. 1983 No. 1878).
[7] This is the *cash* price of the item, *not* the credit advanced.
[8] See above.
[9] See *ante*, Chaps. 3 and 4.
[10] *Ante*, p. 342.

In the previous edition of this book reference was made to credit cards issued before July 1, 1977 (when section 75 came into force) and renewed after that date: the question of whether the section applied turned on the true nature of a credit card agreement—was it a standing offer or a single contract or a new contract at each renewal.[11] This point still awaits a final decision but one further point has recently been decided: a credit card payment by the consumer gives him an absolute discharge and he cannot be made to pay again if the credit card company becomes insolvent before it has paid the retailer.[12]

As a modern example of section 75 in operation, many holiday-makers used Access and Barclaycard to book holidays with tour operators which went into liquidation before the holidays had been completed. The credit card companies have been resisting section 75 claims against them on the ground that the holiday-makers should look to the special fund set up by the tour operators. Not surprisingly tour operators took a different view! Similarly a buyer placing a deposit when ordering, say, furniture, curtains or domestic electrical equipment would be well advised to pay by credit card; then if the retailer goes bust, the buyer can recover the deposit from the credit card company. One word of warning: if the credit card arrangement involves paying the *travel agent* under his own credit card facility, the credit card company would not have section 75 liability for breaches of contract by the *tour operator*.

As between creditor and supplier the creditor is entitled to join the supplier as a party to the proceedings and to claim an indemnity from him.[13]

Some further points on s.75

Clearly section 75 is of great importance to consumers (even though in 1983 the lower cash limit in section 75(3) was raised from £30 to £100—thereby taking many credit transactions outside the section 75 protection). It must however be appreciated that section 75 can only be used by the consumer if the relevant credit agreement was a "regulated agreement" (*ante*, p. 301). If, for example, he books a holiday and pays with his American Express or Diner's Club charge card, the credit agreement is within the "single repayment" exemption (*ante*, p. 307); accordingly it is not a regulated agreement and section 75 will not help the consumer.

It is also important to note that a consumer who has a claim against the supplier has "a like claim" against the creditor. In a Scottish case[14]

---

[11] We prefer the third view.
[12] *Re Charge Card Services* [1988] 3 W.L.R. 764.
[13] s.75(2) and (5).
[14] *U.D.T.* v. *Taylor* (1980) S.L.T. 18.

it was held that a breach of the sale contract gave the consumer a right to rescind not only that contract but also the connected loan contract. It is thought that this reasoning cannot be correct since the two claims are not identical. The court could have reached the same (and correct) result by a different route—namely to allow the consumer to sue the supplier and the creditor for the return of the price of the goods which he had rejected.

3. Credit Sale and Conditional Sale

A dealer may sell goods and allow the customer to pay by instalments. If nothing is said about the passing of property, it will pass as soon as the contract is made[15] and the sale will be a credit sale. If, however, the passing of property is postponed it will be a conditional sale.[16] In either case the obligations of the seller with regard to the goods are to be found in the Sale of Goods Act 1979. It will be recalled that a notification of purpose to a credit-broker will be as effective as if it had been notified to the seller (see *ante*, p. 55).

There are just three further points. First, the relevant provisions of the Sale of Goods Act apply even though the agreement is outside the Consumer Credit Act (*e.g.* because it is a debtor-creditor-supplier agreement with four or fewer instalments). Secondly, a trader who buys goods on credit for his trade will not be "dealing as consumer" and therefore an exemption clause which satisfies the reasonableness test will be binding on him. Thirdly, section 11(4) of the Sale of Goods Act (*ante*, p. 104) does not apply to a "consumer" conditional sale agreement.

4. Hire-Purchase

In the case of a hire-purchase agreement (*whether or not it is regulated by the Consumer Credit Act*) the implied obligations with regard to the goods are contained in sections 8–11 of the Supply of Goods (Implied Terms) Act 1973 as redrafted by the Consumer Credit Act 1974.[17] The terms are virtually identical to those for the sale of goods and they include notification of purpose to a credit-broker.[18]

In practice, the dealer will frequently sell the goods to the finance company, which will then let the goods out on hire-purchase. If the hire-purchase agreement is a regulated agreement the dealer will be a "credit-broker" or "negotiator" and section 56[19] will apply. In other words, any representations made by the dealer are treated as made as

[15] *Ante*, p. 85.
[16] *Ante*, p. 299.
[17] *Ante*, p. 104.
[18] *Ante*, p. 55.
[19] *Ante*, p. 342.

agent for the finance company as well as in his personal capacity. Thus, the debtor has two concurrent remedies; he can bring a claim against the finance company which is bound by the dealer's representations. He can also bring a claim against the dealer, either in negligence[20] or on the basis of a collateral contract.[21]

5. Hire

The statutory implied terms have already been considered[22] and the law is not affected in any way by the Consumer Credit Act.

---

[20] *Hedley Byrne & Co. Ltd.* v. *Heller and Partners Ltd. ante*, p. 32. There can also be liability without any statement under the general law of negligence which was discussed in Chap. 5.

[21] *Andrews* v. *Hopkinson* [1957] 1 Q.B. 229. The dealer was also liable in negligence. See above n. 20.

[22] *Ante*, p. 57. See also Law Commission Report No. 95.

CHAPTER TWENTY-ONE

"I HAVE LOST MY CREDIT CARD"

The credit token, and especially the credit card, is of great importance as a form of consumer credit and the 1974 Act brings them within the ambit of control.

The Act contains a number of provisions relating to "credit tokens" and "credit token agreements" and these provisions will be considered in this chapter.

What is a credit token?

The term is defined in section 14(1) as a card, check, voucher, coupon, stamp, form, booklet or other document or thing given to an individual by a person carrying on a consumer credit business who undertakes:

(a) that on production of it (whether or not some other action is also required) he will supply cash, goods and services (or any of them) on credit, or

(b) that where, on the production of it to a third party (whether or not any other action is also required), the third party supplies cash, goods and services (or any of them), he will pay the third party for them (whether or not deducting any discount or commission) in return for payment to him by the individual.

Thus the term clearly includes credit cards and trading checks used in a form of credit known as "check trading." It does *not* include a cheque card, because the bank issuing a cheque card merely promises to honour cheques. Debit or switch cards fall outside the term, as the bank does not provide any credit. Nor does it cover trading stamps or free gift vouchers (*e.g.* on the back of a cereal packet), because the customer will not receive goods *on credit*.

Unsolicited credit tokens

The mass-mailing of Access cards provoked widespread criticism and now section 51 makes it an offence to give a person a credit token if he has not asked for it. The request must be in writing and signed by the person making it, unless (a) the credit token agreement is a small debtor-creditor-supplier agreement or (b) the card is renewed.

What is a credit token agreement?

By section 14(2) (read with section 189) it is a regulated consumer

347

credit agreement for the provision of credit in connection with the use of a credit token. Thus the term will not apply to an agreement where (a) the credit exceeds the statutory ceiling or (b) the debtor is a body corporate or (c) the agreement is exempt. It will be recalled that agreements involving the use of Diner's Club or American Express cards are exempt agreements, because they are debtor-creditor-supplier agreements for running-account credit and the indebtedness over a period has to be discharged by a single payment.[1]

Modification of formalities

The formalities required for a regulated agreement were considered in Chapter 18. They are modified in two minor respects in the case of a credit token agreement. The first relates to the sending of the second copy; by section 63(4) it need not be given within seven days following the making of the agreement if it is given before or at the time when the credit token is given to the debtor. The second relates to the notice setting out cancellation rights; by section 64(2) it need not be posted within seven days following the making of the agreement if it is posted to the debtor before the credit token is given to him, or if it is sent by post with the credit token.

Additional copies

Where, under the credit token agreement, the creditor issues a new token to the debtor he must at the same time give the debtor a copy of the executed agreement (if any) and of any document referred to in it. Failure to do so has the usual consequences, i.e. the creditor cannot enforce the agreement while the default continues and, if it continues for one month, he commits an offence.[2] The section does not apply to a small agreement.[3]

Liability of debtor

We come now to the problem which is likely to be the most troublesome one in practice—the extent of the debtor's liability if the token is used by someone else without the debtor's authority. This matter is primarily governed by sections 66 and 84. By section 66 the debtor under a credit token agreement is not liable for use made of the token by another person unless (a) the debtor had previously accepted the token or (b) its use constituted an acceptance by him. The debtor accepts a credit token when he or a person authorised by him to use it under the terms of the agreement:

---

[1] *Ante*, p. 307.
[2] s.85.
[3] *Ibid.*

(a) signs it, or
(b) signs a receipt for it, or
(c) uses it.

If the token has been accepted under section 66 we can turn to section 84 to consider the debtor's liability for its misuse by someone else. The provisions of this section can be summarised as follows:

(1) The underlying principle is that the debtor should give notice of the loss or misuse as soon as possible. Accordingly, the credit token agreement must contain, in the prescribed manner,[4] particulars of the name, address and telephone number of a person to whom notice of loss, etc., can be given. If the agreement does not contain this information the debtor will not be liable for misuse at all.[5]

(2) The debtor is not liable for any loss arising after the creditor has been given written or oral notice that the token has been lost or stolen or is otherwise liable to misuse.[6] The notice takes effect when received, but if it is given orally the agreement may provide that it is not effective unless confirmed in writing within seven days.[7]

(3) Subject to (1) and (2) above, the debtor's liability depends on the person by whom the token was misused. If it was misused by a person who acquired possession of the token with the debtor's consent, he is liable *without limit*.[8] In other cases (*e.g.* loss or theft) his liability is limited to £50,[9] or the credit limit if lower, for misuse in a period beginning when the token ceased to be in the possession of an authorised person and ending when the token is once again in the possession of an authorised person.[10]

Thus the moral is clear: the onus is on the debtor to notify the loss to the creditor without delay.

Cancellation

If the debtor cancels a credit token agreement he can only recover a sum paid for the token, and he will only cease to be liable for such a sum, if the token has been returned to the creditor or surrendered to a supplier.[11]

Some further points on misuse

There has been massive publicity concerning the enormous losses

---

[4] *i.e.* prominently and so as to be easily legible (see Consumer Credit (Credit-Token Agreements) Regulations 1983 (S.I. 1983 No. 1555), reg. 2).
[5] s.84(4).
[6] s.84(3).
[7] s.84(5).
[8] s.84(2).
[9] See S.I. 1983 No. 1571; the limit was formerly £30.
[10] s.84(1).
[11] s.70(5).

sustained by credit card companies through credit card frauds—
although the companies have largely themselves to blame by agreeing
to honour transactions where goods are ordered over the telephone
without a signature by the customer. Consumers are urged to be very
wary in giving their card number over the telephone. In any event the
consumer should always check his statement carefully and immediately report any unauthorised transactions.

CHAPTER TWENTY-TWO

"I CAN'T AFFORD TO PAY"

In practice there are two main areas where a debtor is likely to seek legal advice. The first is where he is dissatisfied with the goods. This has been considered in Part I of this book and in Chapter 20. The second is where, for one reason or another, he finds himself in difficulties with his payments. The legal adviser can approach the problem by asking a number of preliminary questions:

(1) Is there a contract at all?

If, for example, the document signed by the debtor was merely an offer, revocation is possible before it has been accepted.[1]

(2) Is the contract voidable for misrepresentation?

If so, it can be rescinded, and money recovered, if it is not too late.[2]

(3) Has the debtor a claim for breach of contract against the creditor?

If so, he may be able to treat the contract as repudiated, or he may have a claim for damages which he can set against the instalments.[3]

(4) Is the agreement cancellable?

If so, the debtor may be able to serve a notice of cancellation under provisions which have already been discussed.[4]

(5) Was the agreement "improperly executed"?

We have seen that if the creditor fails to comply with the statutory formalities as to contents, signature and copies (and pre-contractual reflection in certain land mortgage cases) the agreement can only be enforced against the debtor or hirer on an order of the court[5] or with the consent of the debtor or hirer given at the time.[6]

---

[1] See also s.57, *ante*, p. 331.
[2] See *ante*, pp. 96–98 and 332.
[3] *Ante*, p. 99.
[4] *Ante*, p. 332.
[5] s.65.
[6] s.173(3).

One of the features of the legislation is the very wide power given to the court to rewrite the agreement or to postpone its enforcement. If the creditor or owner brings proceedings for an enforcement order, the court must consider the degree of culpability for the defect and the prejudice (if any) which it has caused to any person.[7] The court can then do any of the following things:

(a) it may make an enforcement order;
(b) it may make a "time order" under section 129[8];
(c) it may modify the agreement as set out below and then make an enforcement order relating to the agreement as modified; or
(d) it may dismiss the application—but only if it considers it just to do so having regard to the matters mentioned above.[9]

There are, however, three cases where an enforcement order *cannot* be made and these are considered below.

Power to modify agreement

Section 127(2) provides that:

> If it appears to the court just to do so, it may in an enforcement order reduce or discharge any sum payable by the debtor or hirer or any surety, so as to compensate him for prejudice suffered as a result of the contravention in question.

We must also consider sections 135 and 136 which are not confined to proceedings for an enforcement order but apply to any order made by the court in relation to a regulated agreement. By section 135(1) an order may include a provision:

(a) making the operation of any term of the order conditional on the doing of specified acts by any party to the proceedings;
(b) suspending the operation of any terms of the order until such time as the court subsequently directs or until the occurrence of a specified act or omission (*e.g.* default).

These very wide powers cannot be used to suspend an order requiring a person to deliver up goods unless the court is satisfied that they are in that person's possession or control.[10] In the case of a consumer hire agreement the section cannot be used to extend the period for which the hirer is entitled to possession.[11]

---

[7] s.127(1).
[8] *Post*, p. 357.
[9] s.127(1).
[10] s.135(2).
[11] s.135(3).

We must also mention certain special powers available to the court in the case of hire-purchase and conditional sale agreements. These are considered later.[12]

Finally, the court has a general power under section 136 to amend any agreement or security in consequence of a term of the order.

It is likely in practice that these wide powers will only be exercised if the court feels that the debtor or hirer has been prejudiced by the failure to comply with the formalities. If the breach is only a technical one (*e.g.* the second copy sent a few days late) the court is likely to waive the breach entirely.

Three special cases

There are, however, three cases where the court has *no* power to make an enforcement order at all. In these cases the fortunate debtor or hirer can retain possession and cannot be sued for any instalments or other payments. These three cases are dealt with in sections 127(3) and (4) and can be summarised as follows:

(a) If the agreement was not signed as required by section 61(1)(*a*) no enforcement order can be made, unless some other document, containing all the prescribed terms (*ante*, p. 326), was signed by the debtor or hirer (whether or not in the prescribed manner).

(b) In a cancellation case the court cannot make an enforcement order if sections 62 or 63 (copy provisions) are not complied with, and if the creditor or owner did not give a copy of the executed agreement (and of any other document referred to in it) to the debtor or hirer before the commencement of the proceedings.

(c) The court cannot make an enforcement order in a cancellation case if the provisions of section 64(1) were not complied with. It will be recalled that section 64(1) deals with the duty to include cancellation information in the copies, and also in certain cases requires a notice to be posted to the debtor or hirer within seven days of the making of the agreement.

In the case of contravention the debtor or hirer may sometimes have a double right—the agreement cannot be enforced against him and (if the defect relates to the second copy or notice) it may well be that the right of cancellation remains open.

What happens if the creditor or owner purports to terminate the agreement and repossesses the goods? If it involves entry on premises without the consent of the debtor or hirer there may be liability for

---

[12] *Post*, p. 358.

breach of statutory duty.[13] Apart from this there may be very little that the debtor or hirer can do about it, because of the "no sanctions" rule in section 170.[14] The section does not however prevent the grant of an injunction[15] and it is just possible that a mandatory injunction could require the goods to be returned to the debtor or hirer. Apart from this, the only sanction is the ever-present administrative sanction of reporting the matter to the Director General of Fair Trading.

Despite the unenforceability of the agreement for defective formalities (see above) there is no doubt that the creditor or owner can sue the debtor or hirer in tort if, for example, the debtor or hirer wrongly disposes of the goods.[16] Similarly the sanction of not allowing enforcement of "the agreement" would not apply where, for example, the agreement has expired by effluxion of time so that the creditor or owner has a common law right to repossess which he can, it is thought, enforce by action.

(6) Can the debtor terminate the agreement?

This has already been considered. (See *ante*, p. 338).

(7) Can the debtor pay off early and obtain a rebate?

The debtor may be able to find another source of credit which is less expensive to him. In the case of hire-purchase the debtor may be better advised to settle early, become the owner of the goods and re-sell them. Section 94 gives the debtor a non-excludable right to complete the agreement ahead of time on service of a notice on the creditor and on payment of all sums due, less any statutory rebate of the charge for credit.[17]

In calculating the total charge for credit the critical factor is the time during which the creditor will be kept out of his money. Accordingly, it is clearly reasonable to allow for a rebate where the debtor pays off early, because the creditor will be able to earn fresh interest on the repaid amount. Section 95 enables regulations to be made for the calculation of this rebate, which will apply in any case of early settlement—whether by reason of re-financing, breach or for any other reason. How then is the rebate to be calculated? Three points must be borne in mind:

(a) the total charge for credit should be spread actuarially over the

---

[13] s.92(3) *post*, p. 358.
[14] *Ante*, p. 298.
[15] s.170(3).
[16] See *Eastern Distributors Ltd.* v. *Goldring* [1957] 2 Q.B. 600.
[17] Where sums are due from a debtor who has made only a partial early payment, the creditor can get judgment for the (unrebated) sum due: *Forward Trust Ltd.* v. *Whymark* [1989] 3 W.L.R. 1229 (C.A.).

repayment period and the debtor should get a rebate corresponding to the proportion of the total charge for credit which would have accrued after the settlement date;

(b) where capital is being constantly repaid (as in the case of mortgages and hire-purchase agreements) the proportion will reflect the fact that the interest payable at the beginning of the agreement is much greater than it is at a later stage when the outstanding capital is much lower;

(c) a completely even actuarial spread would be unfair to the creditor because certain expenses are incurred at the beginning of the transaction (legal fees, survey fees, stamp duty, etc.).

The Regulations (S.I. 1983 No. 1562) are exceedingly complex but they do reflect the principles set out above. Thus:

1. The regulations seek to meet point (c) above by allowing the settlement date (on which the rebate calculation depends) to be notionally deferred. If the credit is repayable on, or at the end of, a period of more than five years the deferral is one month; if the period is five years or less the deferral is two months (see reg. 5 with reg. 6).

2. The regulations also assist the creditor by allowing him to exclude from the rebate calculations (a) taxes and duties and (b) sums payable or paid under a linked transaction.

The regulations contain no less than five formulae and the correct choice depends upon the contractual repayment provisions (lump sum repayment, repayment by equal instalments, repayment by unequal instalments) etc. and upon the settlement arrangements. If, for example, the credit is repayable at equal intervals the amount of the deferred rebate (see above) is calculated by applying the so-called "rule of 78"; the name is derived from the fact that a loan for one year repayable with interest by equal monthly instalments can be said to represent a series of 12 (reducing) monthly loans and the total of the 12 months $(1 + 2 + 3 + 4 + 5 + 6 + 7 + 8 + 9 + 10 + 11 + 12)$ comes to 78.

Example (taken from the Regulations)

A loan of £1,000 is agreed to be repaid by 36 monthly instalments of £48 starting one month after the date of the loan. The consumer settles the loan at the end of the 30th month with 6 instalments still outstanding.

The statutory formula is $\dfrac{m\,(m\,+\,1)}{n\,(n\,+\,1)} \times k$

where m = the (deferred) number of future repayments,
　　　 n = the total number of repayments, and
　　　 k = the total charge for credit on which the rebate is to be
　　　　　 allowed, *i.e.* (36 × £48) − £1000 = £728

The formula produces the following result:

$$\frac{4(4 + 1)}{36(36 + 1)} \times £728 = £10.93 \text{ rebate}$$

If a debtor is contemplating making an early settlement, he can in writing ask the creditor to give him a statement containing the settlement figure.[18] If the creditor fails to comply within 12 working days the usual consequences will follow.[19]

(8) If the debtor or hirer is unable to withdraw, rescind, cancel, terminate or settle early, and if all the formalities have been complied with, the next possibility is to apply for a "time order"

Apart from section 127[20] the debtor or hirer can apply for a time order (a) after he has been served with a notice of default[21] or (b) where the creditor or owner brings proceedings to enforce a regulated agreement or any security or to recover possession of any goods or land to which a regulated agreement relates.[22]

Notice of default

The agreement may provide that, on default by the debtor or hirer, the creditor or owner shall become entitled to take certain action, *e.g.* to terminate the agreement, or to demand early payment of any sum, or to recover possession of any goods or land, or to enforce any security, or to treat any right conferred on the debtor or hirer (*e.g.* an option to purchase in the case of a hire-purchase agreement) as terminated, restricted or deferred. The effect of section 87 is that such a provision will not be enforceable unless the creditor or owner first serves on the debtor or hirer a notice of default in the prescribed form.[23] The notice must contain the following information[24]:

(i) it must specify the breach;

---

[18] s.97. The contents of the statement and the calculation of the settlement date are contained in the Consumer Credit (Settlement Information) Regulations 1983 No. 1564.
[19] See *ante*, p. 328.
[20] *Ante*, p. 353.
[21] See County Court (Amendment) Rules 1985 No. 566, Ord. 49, r. 4(5).
[22] s.129.
[23] See Consumer Credit (Enforcement Default and Termination Notices) Regulations 1983 No. 1561.
[24] s.88.

(ii) if the breach is capable of remedy (*e.g.* default in payment) the notice must indicate what action has to be taken to remedy it and the date before which it must be done;

(iii) if the breach is incapable of remedy (*e.g.* causing permanent damage to the goods) what compensation (if any) is required and the date before which it is to be paid;

(iv) the consequences of non-compliance; and

(v) in appropriate cases the restrictions on the creditor's right to repossess "protected goods" (*post*, p. 358).

The date in (b) and (c) above must be not earlier than seven days after the service of the notice of default. Presumably, if the notice is posted on February 1 it can specify February 8 as the date before which the act must be done.

Effect of notice

If, before the specified date the debtor or hirer takes the steps specified in the notice, the default is treated as never having taken place.[25] Alternatively, as already stated, the debtor or hirer can apply under section 129 for a "time order." Such an order may contain either or both of the following provisions:

(a) a provision that any sum owed by the debtor or hirer or any surety shall be payable at such times as the court, having regard to the means of the debtor or hirer and any surety, considers reasonable;

(b) a provision that a breach by the debtor or hirer (other than the non-payment of money) shall be remedied within such period as the court may specify.

Effect of repossession

The Act does not specify what remedies are available if the creditor or owner repossesses the goods or land without a default notice. The section provides that the creditor or owner is not *entitled* to repossess, etc. without serving a notice of default. It may well be, therefore, that non-compliance could be actionable as trespass to goods or conversion or there might be a breach of the implied warranty for quiet possession. There may also be liability for breach of statutory duty if there is unauthorised entry on premises[26] and the "snatch-back" of protected goods[27] will lead to the severe sanctions set out in section 91.[28]

[25] s.89.
[26] *Post*, p. 358.
[27] *Post*, *Ibid.*
[28] *Post*, *Ibid.*

(9) Additional protection in hire-purchase and conditional sale cases

The notice of default provisions are backed up by four other provisions aimed at what is known as "snatch-back"—the repossession of goods or land without an order of the court.

(a) *Entry on premises*

In the case of a regulated hire-purchase or conditional sale agreement the creditor or owner cannot enter any premises to repossess the goods without an order of the court.[29] Clearly, a contractual provision conferring such a right would be void[30] but a consent at the time of entry would be effective.[31]

(b) *Land*

If the debtor is in breach under a conditional sale agreement relating to land the creditor cannot recover possession of the land from the debtor, nor from any person claiming under him, without an order of the court.[32] The point relating to the debtor's consent will be equally relevant here.

In both (a) and (b) above section 92(3) does provide a sanction—any entry in contravention of either of these provisions is actionable as a breach of statutory duty.

(c) *Protected goods*

In the case of hire-purchase and conditional sale it is clearly inequitable that the debtor, having paid a substantial part of the price, should have the goods snatched away (with no credit for his payments) merely because he gets into arrears. Accordingly, section 90 gives him protection if (a) he is in breach and (b) he has not terminated the agreement and (c) he has paid to the creditor one-third or more of the total price and (d) the property in the goods remains in the creditor. In such a case the goods are called *"protected goods."* The creditor cannot recover possession of the goods from the debtor without an order of the court.

These provisions are modelled upon the provisions in the Hire-Purchase Act 1965 and both Acts impose serious sanctions for contravention. By section 91 if goods are recovered by the creditor in contravention of section 90 the agreement, if not already terminated, will terminate, the debtor is released from all further liability and he can recover from the creditor all sums paid by him under the agreement. A number of points arise under this very important provision.

(i) Where the agreement requires the creditor to carry out any

[29] s.92(1).
[30] s.173(1).
[31] s.173(3).
[32] s.92(2).

installation work, and if the cost of this work forms part of the total price, then the fraction of one-third is calculated by taking the installation charge in full and adding one-third of the balance.[33] Thus, if the price of £300 includes an installation charge of £30 the fraction of one-third will be:

$$£30 + \frac{270}{3} = £120$$

(ii) A dealer might be tempted to avoid the "protected goods" provisions in one of two ways. First of all there might be an agreement for a television set with a price of £150, of which £60 has been paid. If the customer then comes in for a £300 music centre the dealer might say "let us cancel the original agreement and make a new one for both items (£450) with a credit for sums already paid (£60)." Secondly, if the original agreement (with payments exceeding one-third) related to a tape recorder and a camera, he might suggest that the tape recorder should be treated as fully paid up and that a new agreement should be made relating solely to the camera. In either case the debtor starts inside section 90 and ends up outside it—because he has not paid one-third under the new agreement. To prevent such avoidance the effect of section 90(3) is to bring the new agreement within the section, even though one-third has not been paid.

(iii) Repossession of the goods from the debtor without a court order kills the agreement. Thus, on the one hand, the debtor cannot claim the return of the goods[34] while on the other hand the creditor cannot breathe any fresh life into the agreement by returning the goods to the debtor.[35]

(iv) Section 90 only prohibits recovery of possession "from the debtor." Thus, if the creditor seizes the goods which the debtor has abandoned the section is not infringed.[36] A similar principle would apply where the creditor seizes the goods from a third party to whom the debtor has purported to sell them.[37]

(v) A consent by the debtor given at the time is as effective as an order of the court[38] but the court is likely to examine the facts closely to make sure that there was a true and free consent.[39]

(vi) If the debtor chooses to terminate under section 99,[40] the goods are not protected.

---

[33] s.90(2). Similar to s.100(2), *ante*, p. 339.

[34] *Carr* v. *Broderick & Co. Ltd.* [1942] 2 K.B. 275.

[35] *Capital Finance Co. Ltd.* v. *Bray* [1964] 1 W.L.R. 323.

[36] *Bentinck Ltd.* v. *Cromwell Engineering Co. Ltd.* [1971] 1 Q.B. 324.

[37] Consider *Eastern Distributors Ltd.* v. *Goldring* [1957] 2 Q.B. 600.

[38] s.173(3).

[39] The matter could be raised if the debtor took proceedings alleging a breach of section 90 and denying his consent to the repossession. See *Chartered Trust plc* v. *Pitcher* [1988] RTR 72 (C.A.).

[40] *Ante*, p. 339.

(d) *Additional powers of the court*

In any proceedings for an enforcement order, or for a time order, or in proceedings by the creditor to recover possession, the court may (in addition to its other powers) make (i) a return order or (ii) a transfer order.[41] A return order, as the name implies, requires the debtor to return the goods to the creditor. A transfer order is, in effect, a "split" order, in that it orders the debtor to return *some* of the goods to the creditor and it vests in the debtor the creditor's title in the remainder. This is subject to a ceiling set out in section 133(3), namely, that the maximum transferable to the debtor is found by deducting from the sum paid one-third of the unpaid balance. Thus, if the debtor had paid £80 out of a total price of £200, the court can vest in the debtor goods to the value of:

$$£80 - \left[\frac{200 - 80}{3} \right] = £40$$

In practice, the court frequently makes a return order and then exercises its powers under section 135 to suspend the operation of the order on condition that the debtor pays the balance by instalments fixed by the court.

(10) Additional protection in consumer hire cases

A number of provisions which are relevant to consumer hire have already been considered earlier in this chapter. They include section 65 (improperly executed agreements), section 87 (notice of default), section 92 (no entry on premises without court order) and section 129 (time orders). In addition section 132 provides that where the owner recovers possession otherwise than by action the hirer may apply to the court for an order (a) extinguishing any further liability to make payments in whole or in part or (b) requiring the owner to repay sums paid by the hirer in whole or in part. The court can also include such a provision when it makes an order for delivery to the owner. Such a power could be exercised where, for example, the hirer has paid a year's rental in advance and then finds it necessary to terminate the hiring after only a few weeks or where the owner retakes the goods following the hirer's default.

It will be recalled that the general power to make a "suspended" order under section 135 cannot extend the period for which the hirer is entitled to possession.[42]

(11) Appropriation of payments

A debtor or hirer may have two or more separate regulated agree-

---

[41] s.133.
[42] *Ante*, p. 352.

ments with the same creditor or owner. If he finds himself unable to pay a sum to cover all the sums due, he can send in a smaller amount and section 81 allows him, on making the payment, to appropriate it to one or more of the agreements in such proportions as he thinks fit. If he fails to appropriate at the time of payment, then section 81(2) may come into play. It provides that where one or more of the agreements is a hire-purchase, conditional sale, consumer hire or secured agreement, the payment shall be appropriated in the proportion which the sums *due* bear to each other.

Example

£20 is due under a hire-purchase agreement relating to a dishwasher and £10 is due under a hire agreement relating to a television set. The debtor/hirer sends in a cheque for £12. If he fails to appropriate at the time of payment, £8 will go towards the dishwasher and £4 towards the television set.

Finally, if the debtor fails to appropriate in a case to which section 81(2) does *not* apply (*e.g.* if he has two debtor-creditor agreements with the same creditor) the general law will apply and the creditor will have the right of appropriation.

EXTORTIONATE CREDIT BARGAINS

The final weapon available to a debtor who finds himself unable to pay is to claim that the agreement is extortionate. The law is to be found in sections 137–140 of the Act.

Scope

These provisions are wider than most of the rest of the Act because they apply to a "credit bargain." This is defined as (a) an agreement whereby a creditor provides an individual (the debtor) with credit of *any amount*, plus (b) any other transactions which must be taken into account in computing the total charge for credit (*e.g.* a linked transaction). Thus these provisions will apply even though the credit exceeds the statutory ceiling and even though the agreement is an "exempt agreement." The only feature common to the whole Act is that the debtor must not be a body corporate.

What bargains are extortionate?

Section 138 provides that a bargain is extortionate if it requires the debtor or a relative of his to make payments which are grossly exorbitant or otherwise grossly contravenes ordinary principles of fair dealing. The section then sets out a non-exhaustive list of relevant factors which include:

(a) prevailing interest rates at the time when the bargain was made[43];

(b) factors affecting the debtor such as age, health, business capacity and the extent to which he was under financial pressure;

(c) factors affecting the creditor, such as his relationship with the debtor and the degree of risk undertaken by him;

(d) the extent to which a linked transaction was reasonably required for the protection of the debtor or the creditor.

How and when can the matter be raised?

The debtor or a surety can take proceedings to have the bargain re-opened[44]; in the case of a regulated agreement such proceedings must be brought in the county court.[45] Alternatively, the debtor or surety can raise the matter (a) in any proceedings to which the debtor and creditor are parties, being proceedings to enforce the agreement or any security or any linked transaction, or (b) in other proceedings where the amount paid or payable under the credit agreement is relevant. This could include bankruptcy proceedings, or proceedings where the debtor's wife brings a claim for financial provision, or where the judge investigates the means of the debtor as a preliminary to the enforcement of a judgment against him. Section 171(7) provides that if the debtor or surety alleges that the bargain is extortionate, the onus is on the creditor to prove that it is not. It is likely, however, that the court will require some evidence from the debtor or surety before putting the creditor to proof.

Powers of the court

The court has wide powers to (a) direct accounts to be taken (b) set aside obligations imposed on the debtor or a surety (c) order sums to be repaid to the debtor or a surety (d) order property given as security to be returned and (e) re-write the terms of the agreement of any security instrument.[46]

Conclusion

A great deal will depend on how the courts will exercise these sweeping new powers and how they will interpret the factors listed in section 138. What about the debtor who is old, ill, inexperienced and under great financial pressure from many sources? On the one hand

---

[43] The court can rely on its own knowledge of prevailing interest rates even if no evidence is presented: *Castle Phillips Finance Co. Ltd.* v. *Williams* [1986] Consumer Credit Law Reports 43.

[44] s.139(1).

[45] s.139(5).

[46] s.139(2).

the creditor must not take an unfair advantage of such a person, and if he does so the courts may well treat the bargain as extortionate. On the other hand, the risk undertaken by the creditor in this type of case is unusually high and may well justify an interest rate which reflects this added risk.[47]

---

[47] The leading case is *Ketley* v. *Scott* [1981] I.C.R. 241 where a lender agreed to lend £20,500 (with interest at a nominal annual rate of 48 per cent.) to a prospective house buyer at a few hours notice. Foster J. rejected the borrower's argument that the bargain was extortionate. See also *Coldunell* v. *Gallon* [1986] Q.B. 1184.

CHAPTER TWENTY-THREE

"I WANT TO SEE MY CREDIT FILE"

At the beginning of Chapter 15 we drew attention to the explosion of credit business. A credit transaction can, of course, cause problems at both ends. The consumer may overreach himself and may plunge into debt. The creditor may supply goods or services on credit terms and then suffer substantial financial loss if the consumer fails to pay the sums due.[1] To protect himself the creditor will frequently consult a credit reference agency[2] as to the financial standing of the prospective debtor. If the debtor then finds that his application for credit has been rejected, or has been granted on unfavourable terms, he may well suspect that the credit reference agency may have passed on unfavourable information. The Act contains provisions—which stand apart from the remaining provisions of the Act—giving the debtor a right:

1. to ask for details of any credit reference agency consulted by the creditor or credit-broker;
2. to obtain a copy of his file from the agency; and
3. to have errors corrected.

It is now proposed to conclude this Part of the book by looking briefly at these three matters. It can be said at the outset that a company which keeps its own credit records of customers would not of itself be a credit reference agency; the reason is that the statutory controls only apply where the activities of the credit reference agency is carried on as a business (see section 145(8)).

Duty to disclose name and address of agency

The debtor or hirer can make a written request to the creditor, owner or negotiator asking for the name and address of any credit reference agency to which the creditor, owner or negotiator applied for information as to his financial standing at any time during the antecedent negotiations. The creditor, etc., must then give him notice containing this information within seven working days of receiving the

---

[1] In many cases the creditor will take security from the debtor or from a third party and Part VIII of the Act contains provisions which regulate security arrangements. The term "security" includes a guarantee.
[2] Such an agency will require a licence under the Act—see s.145(1)(e).

request (see section 157(1) and the Consumer Credit (Credit Reference Agency) Regulations 1977, reg. 3).[3] The debtor or hirer must, however, act quickly because the duty to supply him with the information does not arise where his request is received more than 28 days after the end of the antecedent negotiations (whether on the making of the regulated agreement or otherwise).[4]

In practice the consumer will often be dealing with a credit-broker (as for example with a car dealer who arranges to finance the transaction through the creditor). Accordingly any request is likely to come from the consumer to the credit-broker. The regulations seek to ensure that the credit-broker will be able to pass on to the consumer the names of the agency or agencies consulted by the creditor as well as the agencies which he himself consulted. Accordingly, they provide that the creditor must give this information to the credit-broker not later than the date on which he informs him that he is not willing to make a regulated agreement.[5] The credit-broker must then include this information in the section 157 notice which he gives to the debtor or hirer.[6]

A creditor, owner or negotiator who fails to give the notice within the seven-day period commits an offence (see s.157(3)).

Duty on agency to disclose filed information

We turn now to the obligations of the agency itself. An individual who suspects that a credit reference agency has information on him can make a written request for that information ("the file") together with a fee of £1. On receipt of the request and fee and such particulars as the agency may reasonably require to identify the file the agency must within seven days supply him with a copy of the file together with a statement in the prescribed form[7] informing him of his rights under section 159 (as to which see below). It may well be that the file is not readily intelligible (perhaps because it is computerised). In any such case the consumer's right to a "copy of the file" is a right to a transcript reduced into plain English (see section 158(3)).

It may be of course that the agency has no file on the consumer; in that case they must give him notice of that fact but they need not return any fee paid (see section 158(3)).

An agency which contravenes any provision of section 158[8] commits an offence.

[3] S.I. 1977 No. 329.
[4] See s.157(2).
[5] Consumer Credit (Conduct of Business) (Credit Reference Agencies) Regulations 1977 No. 330, reg. 2.
[6] Ibid. reg. 3.
[7] Consumer Credit (Credit Reference Agency) Regulations 1977 No. 329, reg. 2 and Sched. 1.
[8] See also section 160 which lays down an alternative procedure for "business consumers."

Correction of wrong information

A consumer may realise that the file disclosed under section 158 (*supra*) contains an entry which is incorrect—perhaps that he is an undischarged bankrupt or that he has an outstanding unsatisfied judgment against him. If the consumer considers that an entry is incorrect, and that he is likely to be prejudiced if it is not corrected, he may give notice to the agency requiring them to remove the offending entry or to amend it. The agency must then within 28 days send the consumer a notice stating that they have (a) removed the entry or (b) amended it or (c) taken no action (see section 159(2)). In case (b) above the notice must include a copy of the amended entry (*ibid.*).

If the notice is given under (b) or (c) above (or is not given at all within the 28 day period) the consumer is given a further right under section 159(3). In any such case he can within 28 days serve a further notice on the agency requiring it (a) to add to the file an accompanying notice of correction, not exceeding 200 words, drawn up by himself and (b) to include a copy of it when furnishing information included in or based on that entry. On receiving this further notice the agency has a choice. It can either (a) comply with it and inform the consumer that it has done so or (b) it can apply to the Director General on the grounds that it would be improper for it to publish a notice of correction because it is incorrect or unjustly defames any person or is frivolous or scandalous or is for any other reason unsuitable (s.159(5)). Conversely, the consumer may apply to the Director General[9] on the ground that he has not received a correction notice within 28 days of requesting it (*ibid.*). The Director General after considering the relevant facts and the documentation[10] can make such order as he thinks fit.

The consumer may have one further problem; the correction of an erroneous entry may be all very well for the future but what about the past? What can be done to correct damage which he may already have suffered as the result of the erroneous information having been passed on to an enquirer? The regulations deal with this problem.[11] If the agency agrees to remove or amend an entry, or if it is ordered to do so by the Director General, the agency must notify each person to whom it furnished information relevant to the financial standing of the consumer at any time within six months before it received the section 158 request, particulars and fee (see *ante*, p. 365). This must be done within 10 working days after the notice of removal or compliance or after the expiry of the compliance period specified by the Director General under section 159(5) (see above).

[9] Form CC 314/77 must be used for such an application.
[10] See S.I. 1977 No. 329, reg. 4; the consumer must state why the information is false and why it is likely to prejudice him.
[11] S.I. 1977 No. 330, reg. 5.

Data Protection Act 1984

No discussion of this topic would be complete without a brief mention of this Act. The Act only applies to *computerised* personal data held by a data user or bureau. Taking the relevant provisions in the order in which they came into force the position is as follows:

1. Where an individual who is the subject of personal data held by a data user or bureau suffers damage by reason of the loss, unauthorised destruction or unauthorised disclosure or access, the individual can obtain through the courts (1) compensation for his losses—including damages for distress in appropriate cases and (2) erasure of the data. The data user/bureau will, however, have a defence if it can show that it took all such care as was reasonably required to prevent the loss, destruction or access. The matter is governed by section 23 of the 1984 Act.

2. Section 22 gives the individual a right to compensation (subject to the same defence as above) if he or she has suffered damage as a result of data being inaccurate. Once again damages for distress can be included.

3. Section 21 gives the individual a right similar to that under section 158 of the Consumer Credit Act (*ante*, p. 366)—namely (a) a right to be informed by the data user/bureau whether the data held by him include personal data of which that individual is the data subject and (b) a right to be supplied with information constituting any such personal data. Where such information is not intelligible without explanation, the information supplied to him must be accompanied by an appropriate explanation. If the data user/bureau fails to supply the information, etc., within 40 days of receiving a written request the individual can apply to the court for an order requiring it to comply with the request. Section 21 does not apply (*inter alia*) where the data is within section 158 of the Consumer Credit Act and any section 21 request will be treated as a request under section 158.

CHAPTER TWENTY-FOUR

THE EEC DIMENSION

1. THE TREATY OF ROME

On January 1, 1973, the United Kingdom became a member of the European Economic Community. Any book on consumer law would be incomplete without some mention of the activity of the Commission of the European Communities in the consumer protection field in the past decade or so. The matters discussed in this chapter do not, at present, give new rights and remedies to the consumer but they indicate how things might develop in the years ahead.

To set the scene let us consider four Articles of the Treaty of Rome which set up the EEC in 1957.

Article 2, which corresponds to the "main objects" clause of a company memorandum, provides that:

> The Community shall have as its task, by establishing a common market
> ... to promote throughout the Community a harmonious development of
> economic activities, a continuous and balanced expansion, an increase in
> stability, an accelerated raising of the standard of living and closer rela-
> tions between the States belonging to it.

This then is the central aim—the treatment of the Member States as one single market, with an unrestricted flow of goods, persons, services and capital, and a system to ensure that competition is not distorted. Article 3(h) specifies as one of the activities of the Community:

> the approximation of the laws of Member States to the extent required for
> the proper functioning of the common market.

Articles 100 and 235

Article 3(h) leads us on directly to Article 100:

> The Council shall, acting unanimously on a proposal from the Commis-
> sion, issue directives for the approximation of such provisions laid down
> by law, regulation or administrative action in Member States as directly
> affect the establishment or functioning of the common market.
> The European Parliament and the Economic and Social Committee
> shall be consulted in the case of directives whose implementation would,
> in one or more Member States, involve the amendment of legislation.

Article 100 has been the mainstay of the EC Commission in its justification for intervention in the consumer protection area. It may seem strange that the EEC Treaty does not contain a specific legal basis for consumer legislation, but it should be remembered that it was drafted at a time when the consumer movement in Europe was in its infancy. An example of Article 100 being used by way of justification is the Directive on Liability for Defective Products mentioned above.

Article 235 can be brought into play where a proposal does not fit within the ambit of Article 100. Article 235 reads:

> If action by the Community should prove necessary to attain, in the course of the operation of the common market, one of the objectives of the Community and this Treaty has not provided the necessary powers, the Council shall, acting unanimously on a proposal from the Commission and after consulting the European Parliament, take the appropriate measures.

It can be seen that this wide-ranging provision gives the Council power to take measures to attain a Community objective where the Treaty of Rome does not contain the power elsewhere.[1] Article 235 was approved as an appropriate legal basis by the Heads of State and Governments in 1972 when they gave the green light to the Consumer Protection Programme.

Completing the Internal Market

In June 1985 the EC Commission presented to the European Council the White Paper *Completing the Internal Market* which proposed the famous "1992" deadline.

This was followed within a year by the Single European Act which came into force on July 1, 1987. The Act made a number of significant amendments to the Treaty of Rome. Article 13 introduced a new Article 8A setting the ambitious date for establishing the internal market by December 31, 1992, and stating:

> The internal market shall comprise an area without frontiers in which the free movement of goods, persons, services and capital is ensured in accordance with the provisions of this Treaty.

We saw earlier that Article 100 provides the primary basis for the EC consumer protection policy, but has the drawback that directives must be adopted unanimously. (For this reason the Directive on Liability for Defective Products took more than a decade to see the light of day). A crucial change made by Article 18 of the Single European Act

---

[1] See Close, "The Legal Basis for the Consumer Protection Programme of the EEC and Priorities for Action," in Woodroffe (ed.), *Consumer Law in the EEC* (1984), Chap. I, where Arts. 100 and 235 are discussed as bases for the Programme.

was to permit the adoption of a proposal by a "qualified majority." The amendment appears in the new Article 100A:

1. By way of derogation from Article 100 and save where otherwise provided in this Treaty, the following provisions shall apply for the achievement of the objectives set out in Article 8A. The Council shall, acting by a qualified majority on a proposal from the Commission in co-operation with the European Parliament and after consulting the Economic and Social Committee, adopt the measures for the approximation of the provisions laid down by law, regulation or administrative action in Member States which have as their object the establishment and functioning of the internal market.
2. Paragraph 1 shall not apply to fiscal provisions, to those relating to the free movement of persons nor to those relating to the rights and interests of employed persons.
3. The Commission, in its proposals envisaged in paragraph 1 concerning health, safety, environmental protection and consumer protection, will take as a base a high level of protection.

It is noteworthy that paragraph 3 contains an express reference to consumer protection and aims at "a high level of protection."

The importance of the qualified majority procedure can be gauged from the fact that all three proposals discussed later in this chapter rely on Article 100A as their justification.

The Consumer Protection Programme

We have already commented upon the fact that in 1972 the Consumer Protection Programme was approved on the basis of Article 235. In the following year the Consumers' Consultative Committee was set up by a Commission Decision which stated in its preamble that close and continuous contact with consumer organisations at Community level could contribute to the achievement of the aims of the Treaty.

In 1975 the Commission drew up an ambitious programme of measures for consumer protection and information. In 1981 a second Consumer Protection Programme was adopted which placed consumer interests into five basic groups of rights:

(1) the right of protection of consumers' health and safety;
(2) the right of protection of their economic interests;
(3) the right of redress, help and assistance in judicial and para-judicial proceedings;
(4) the right to information and education;
(5) the right to be heard on matters affecting consumers' interests.[2]

This programme has no binding force but it gives an indication of the

---

[2] See Kraemer, "European Consumer Protection—A Progress Report," *ibid.* Chap. II.

Commission's thinking. No doubt the preparation of the programme was partly inspired by the desire to improve the image of the EEC amongst its 320 million consumers. Under this programme it has submitted draft directives to the Council on a number of important topics. The draft directives are discussed by the Ministers of the Member States who make up the Council of Ministers and may eventually decide, unanimously or by a qualified majority, to adopt the directive. It is therefore vitally important for United Kingdom lawyers to study the draft directives at the formative stage, decide how far they are appropriate to trading conditions in this country and make representations to the United Kingdom representatives.

In previous editions of this book we discussed various proposals which had not progressed beyond the stage of being draft directives. Since then the Directive on Liability for Defective Products has been adopted in 1985 and passed into the law of the United Kingdom as Part I of the Consumer Protection Act 1987 (analysed in Chapter 5, p. 63). The Control of Misleading Advertisements Regulations 1988 implemented the 1984 Directive on Misleading Advertisements (considered in Chapter 14, p. 289). The Doorstep-Selling Directive of 1985 has been incorporated into United Kingdom law by the Consumer Protection (Cancellation of Contracts Concluded away from Business Premises) Regulations 1987 (see Chapter 6, p. 81). The Package Travel Directive has yet to be implemented (see Chapter 9, p. 182).

We now propose to consider briefly three new draft directives which are likely to be adopted within a year or so. They are concerned with:

> Unfair Contract Terms
> General Product Safety
> Suppliers of Services

2. THREE DRAFT DIRECTIVES

Unfair Terms in Consumer Contracts

The 1970s saw a proliferation of legislation on unfair contract terms throughout Europe. It is no surprise that there was considerable divergence in the approach adopted in various Member States. This divergence is put forward as one of the reasons for intervention in this area in the preamble to the draft directive on Unfair Terms in Consumer Contracts proposed by the EC Commission in the autumn of 1990. The preamble also points out that the importance of safeguarding consumers in relation to unfair contract terms was underlined in the 1975 and 1981 Consumer Protection Programmes. The EC Commission justifies its proposal by virtue of Article 100A and sets as the deadline for its coming into force in the Member States that inevitable date, the last day of 1992. In our discussion of its contents we shall pay particular attention to the similarities and distinctions between the draft directive and the United Kingdom Unfair Contract Terms Act 1977.

Consumer contract

The draft directive is concerned only with contracts between business suppliers and *consumers*, whereas the 1977 Act contains provisions protecting business customers too. The definition of "consumer" is given in Article 2.3 as "a natural person who ... is acting for purposes which can be regarded as outside his trade, business or profession." This bears some similarity to the definition in the 1977 Act[3] and will doubtless raise similar problems. In contrast to the 1977 Act, however, it does not exclude any type of contract from its control, *e.g.* insurance.[4]

Unfair terms

It has been suggested by lawyers on both sides of the Channel that the draft directive adopts too narrow a perspective in concentrating on the fairness of the "term" rather than of the contract or bargain as a whole. Yet this approach reflects the approach adopted in the United Kingdom legislation and so is more likely to be acceptable to suppliers, whatever consumer lobbyists may think.

In one major respect it is more limited in its ambit: it applies only to contractual terms, whereas the 1977 Act embraces non-contractual notices and so applies to tort as well as to contract claims.[5]

What terms are unfair?

There was considerable debate before the proposal was drafted as to whether to impose a general test of fairness or to have a "black list" of prohibited types of clause. In the end the draft directive chooses both routes.

Article 2.1 encapsulates the broad brush approach in providing that a term is unfair if it causes "to the detriment of the consumer a significant imbalance in the parties' rights and obligations ... or the performance of the contract to be unduly detrimental to the consumer ... or significantly different from what the consumer could legitimately expect" or finally if it is "incompatible with the requirements of good faith."

Two comments will suffice. First, phrases such as "significant"

---

[3] *Ante*, p. 131.
[4] *Ante*, p. 127.
[5] *Ante*, p. 126.

imbalance, "unduly" detrimental and "significantly" different mean that the consumer will be unable to sidestep a clause without consideration being given to the fairness of the whole contract. Yet, as we commented earlier, the proposal purports to be concerned only with the term itself. This interaction between the individual term and its wider contractual context is bound to cause problems in practice. Secondly, Article 2.1 commences with the words, "A contractual term is unfair if, of itself or in combination with another term or terms. . . ." This raises exactly the same issue—the term cannot be assessed in isolation.

The Annex

Following this general provision is Article 2.2 which states "The Annex contains a list of types of unfair terms." The Annex itself commences, "The following types of terms are unfair if they have the object or effect of:" There then follows a three page list of the prohibited terms. During the consultation process a number of commentators, including the Law Society and the Law Society of Scotland, pointed out that it is unclear whether the Annex contains an exhaustive list of prohibited terms or whether it is meant to be merely illustrative of Article 2. The latter is probably the position, but this drafting ambiguity needs to be clarified before the proposal is finally adopted.

There are significant similarities between the types of terms included in the Annex and the types of terms covered by the 1977 Act. For example, a term excluding or limiting liability for death or personal injury is prohibited.[6] One major difference, though, is that the draft directive does not confine its attention to exemption clauses. In particular it would allow the courts to interfere where a seller increases the price of goods between the date of contract and the date of delivery—the 1977 Act does not help in these cases.

Void

Where a term is unfair—and like the Act of 1977 the test is applied at the date of the contract—Article 3 provides that it "shall be void." This is so even in relation to supplies of services.[7] To remove any doubt as to whether the rest of the contract is enforceable, it states expressly that the "remaining terms of the contract shall continue to be valid."

New rights and remedies?

The wording of the Annex is far from straightforward. On a quick

---

[6] *Ante*, p. 130.
[7] *Cf.* ss.2(2) and s.3(2) of the 1977 Act, *ante*, pp. 130 and 131.

reading it appears to interfere with the law relating to supplies of goods and services by implying both rights and remedies, rather than confining its attention to attempts to exclude them. For example, it refers to replacing and repairing the goods—remedies not available under English law. This impression has clearly been gained by representatives of industry to judge by their responses to the D.T.I.'s consultation exercise. Such a reading is mistaken. The proposal outlaws only those terms which remove a right or remedy otherwise available to the consumer under the relevant national law. It does not compel Member States to introduce new rights and remedies.

Thus the Annex begins, "The following types of terms are unfair if they have the object of effect of. . . . denying the consumer the right . . . to require the seller . . . (i) to reimburse the whole of the purchase price, or (ii) to replace the goods."[8] If the contract contains a term "denying" such a right, the term is void. The question must then be asked what the consumer's rights are in the absence of such a term. The answer in England would be a refund of the price, but not replacement; so (ii) is irrelevant. Here again we hope that a redraft of the proposal will make its effect more obvious!

Public interest action

Another provision which will be welcomed by the consumer movement appears in Article 4.2. This obliges Member States to empower "persons or organisations, if regarded under national law as having a legitimate interest in protecting consumers" to institute court proceedings to determine whether certain contract terms fail to comply with the draft directive. This has already met opposition from the Retail Consortium and other branches of industry, but has been welcomed by the Consumers' Association.

A prognosis

As we have suggested earlier, many of the provisions of the draft directive do little more than reflect the existing United Kingdom position as found in the Unfair Contract Terms Act 1977. However, to the extent that it goes beyond the current position it is bound to meet heavy criticism from commerce and industry. Particular areas of dispute are likely to be the provisions relating to prices and the opportunity for public interest actions.

It can also be surmised that the Government will need to be persuaded that harmonisation of the law of the 12 Member States ought to be undertaken in this area and, even if it is necessary as part of the programme of completing the internal market, that the approach contained in the draft directive is the correct one. Further, the European Parliament could well take the view that the proposal is too

---

[8] *Annex*, para. (*c*)(1).

wide in its scope and should be limited to standard form contracts, but if limited in that way should protect business customers too. From the consumers' point of view this would not be too restrictive, since most contracts which they make are "contrats d'adhésion" and not individually negotiated.

General Product Safety

As we saw in Chapter 12, the policy of ensuring that the consumer is protected from dangerous goods has been implemented in the United Kingdom by taking two complementary routes. First, legislation was introduced enabling regulations to be passed to regulate particular kinds of products which were inherently hazardous, *e.g.* paraffin heaters or foam furniture.[9] Such "vertical legislation" copes only with narrow sectoral problems which are attacked piecemeal, leaving the holes in the dyke to be plugged as and when they appear. So the second route was taken of introducing "horizontal legislation" with the imposition of a general safety requirement (GSR) by the Consumer Protection Act 1987.[10] Of course, such problems exist at the European level too and can be met with similar solutions.

The importance of safety was emphasised in point 72 of the EC White Paper *Completing the Internal Market* which stated that the health and safety of workers and consumers were interests which should be taken into account in the 1992 programme. This very same point was referred to in July 1985 when the Commission submitted to the Council a Communication concerning a *"New Impetus for a consumer protection policy."* This Communication gave a special priority to consumer safety and was followed in May 1987 with another Communication on *"Safety of Consumers in Relation to Consumer Products,"* which ended with the promise: "The Commission shortly intends to submit to the Council a proposal for a general directive on consumer safety in relation to consumer products."

This ambition was not realised until June 1989 when the EC Commission submitted its proposal for a directive on General Product Safety. The draft directive was circulated by the Department of Trade and Industry for consultation in the autumn. An amended proposal was submitted in June 1990 on which our comments below are based.[11] It is certain to be altered again before its adoption by the Council, as various amendments are in the pipeline emanating from national Governments and the European Parliament, but its essential structure should survive unscathed. This is explicable partly on the basis that

[9] *Ante*, p. 244.
[10] *Ante*, p. 246.
[11] O.J. 1990 C156/8.

horizontal legislation already exists in such other influential countries as France and Germany.

(1) Like the draft directive discussed above, this proposal finds its justification in Article 100A; so only a qualified majority is required for its adoption.

(2) The preamble to the draft directive argues that the absence of horizontal legislation throughout the Community is liable to create a barrier to trade and to distort competition within the internal market. The difficulty then arises as to how to dovetail specific Community or national rules relating to particular products or product sectors into the general safety duty. We would argue that there is nothing novel in overlaying specific requirements with a general duty and that the specific and general duties should not be mutually exclusive. Nevertheless, the approach adopted in the draft directive is clearly stated in the preamble: "Whereas, in the absence of more specific safety provisions covering the products concerned, the provisions of this Directive are to apply." This presumption is contained in Article 4, which states that "suppliers shall be deemed to have complied with" the GSR when the product conforms with the specific legal rules of the Community or, if none, of the Member State where the product is in circulation.

(3) Although the original plan was to include only consumer products in the proposal as the 1987 Communication stated, the scope of the draft directive turned out to be much wider and encompasses all products (whether manufactured or agricultural or new or used).[12] This contrasts with the general safety requirement in the Consumer Protection Act 1987 which applies only to new consumer goods. Another difference is that there are no exclusions from the draft directive, whereas the United Kingdom Act contains a number of exclusions for goods covered by other legislation, *e.g.* crops, food and vehicles.

(4) The general duty to ensure that only safe products are placed on the market is contained in Article 3. That raises the question as to what is a "safe product"? The answer is given in a complex definition in Article 2: briefly it means that the product must not present an unacceptable risk to health and safety. Factors to be taken into account will include its instructions for use and its intended use. No product can be absolutely safe, so that the broad test is whether the risk has been reduced to an acceptable level. Although the definition of "safe" does not follow exactly the definition of "defective" in the Product Liability Directive,[13] we forecast that the definitions will give rise to similar wrangles.

(5) Much of the proposal is concerned with monitoring compliance

---

[12] Art. 2(*a*).
[13] *Ante*, p. 67.

with its provisions and ensuring that, if dangerous products reach the market, action is taken by the appropriate Member State to have them withdrawn from the market.[14] This last obligation will be a novel one in the United Kingdom, where there is no power for any public authority to order the recall of unsafe products.

The onus lies on the Member States to make appropriate monitoring arrangements and to establish or nominate appropriate authorities to effect compliance by suppliers with the GSR.[15] Presumably this time-consuming and expensive task will be added to the already onerous responsibilities of trading standards departments in the United Kingdom.

(6) Emergency procedures are specially built into the proposal. Where there is a grave and immediate risk, the authorities should serve a prohibition notice, effective for only three months, to prohibit the supply of the unsafe product.[16] (This resembles the emergency procedures set out in the 1987 Act.[17]) In similar circumstances the Member State must ensure that there is a "rapid exchange" of information between its own authorities and, if the grave risk is not merely local, immediately inform the EC Commission.[18] In limited circumstances the Commission may take the initiative[19]—there was some anxiety in a number of countries that the Brussels bureaucracy, as they saw it, would be too keen to interfere and "flex its muscles." Such a "rapid exchange system" is a cornerstone of the system in that nothing can be more important than the prompt recall of a product once it is discovered to be unsafe. The Commission will be assisted by a new Committee on Product Safety Emergencies.[20]

(7) The proposal contained as its date for implementation January 1, 1991. That has already passed.

Suppliers of Services

Finally, we turn to the third and latest of the Commission's proposals. The draft directive on the Liability of Suppliers of Services[21] was presented to the Council in December 1990 and should be in place by the end of 1992. Like the Product Liability Directive it is concerned with civil liability and intended to compensate consumers for injury or damage to private property. The Explanatory Memorandum accompanying the proposal underlines its connection with that Directive[22]:

---

[14] Art. 6.1(*i*).
[15] Arts. 5(*a*) and (*e*), 6.1(*a*) and (*d*).
[16] Art. 6.1(*j*).
[17] *Ante*, p. 252.
[18] Art. 7.
[19] Arts. 8 and 9.
[20] Arts. 10 and 11.
[21] COM(90)482 Final.
[22] Para. II, 2.

There is already a general Directive covering the liability of manufacturers of defective products. So that consumers can take advantage not only of the internal market in products but also of the internal market in services under the best possible conditions, it is necessary to have a similar Directive on liability of suppliers of services.

Like the two proposals discussed earlier in this chapter this one is also based on Article 100A because it relates to the completion of the single market. Its aim is to remove discrepancies in this area of the law in the various Member States. For example, in the United Kingdom and Italy a customer of services must generally prove that the supplier was at fault to succeed in a claim, *i.e.* that the supplier had broken a duty of care. However, in some Member States the burden of proof is reversed in favour of the consumer. The Commission's original intention was to establish a system of no fault or strict liability in respect of services to align it with supplies of goods. However, they were forced to abandon this radical reform because it would have increased the responsibility of suppliers in most countries so that "some of the interest groups concerned had misgivings about such a Directive," as the Explanatory Memorandum reveals. In the end the proposal comes down firmly in favour of reversing the burden of proof only.

Burden of proof

The major change from the point of view of the British consumer is this reversal of the burden of proof so that, provided the consumer can prove that the damage was caused by the performance of the service, "the burden of proving the absence of fault shall fall upon the supplier of the service," as Article 1.1 states.

Service

The wide definition of "service" in Article 2 draws a distinction between services and goods by including "any transaction ... which does not have as its direct and exclusive object the manufacture of movable property." This covers such obvious services as dry cleaning, hairdressers, furniture removals and leisure centres. However, it extends further to include contracts for work and materials such as the repair of vehicles, watches, televisions or washing machines and the supply and installation of equipment such as electric showers or central heating systems.

As the aim of the proposal is to protect "the health and physical integrity of persons or the physical integrity of movable or immovable property,"[23] it does not extend to pure economic loss caused by poor advice on financial, investment or insurance matters; nor does it cover

[23] Art. 1.1.

package travel or waste services which fall within other EC legislation.[24]

Supplier of services

Liability is imposed on a "supplier of services," defined by Article 3 as "any natural or legal person ... who, in the course of his professional activities or by way of a public service, provides a service." Clearly this covers the ordinary business supplier as well as a public authority such as the National Health Service. However, public services "to maintain public safety" are excluded, *e.g.* the police and fire services.[25]

Damage

The definition of "damage" in Article 4 closely follows the definition of the same word in the Product Liability Directive. So a claim may lie for death or personal injury or damage to private property, including land. Damage to property also covers damage to the subject-matter of the service itself, *e.g.* a torn suit at a dry cleaners or car damaged at a garage while parked or being repaired.

Disclaimers

The supplier is prevented by Article 7 from excluding or limiting his liability. This overlaps the attack on exemption clauses launched by the draft directive on Unfair Terms.[26] It strengthens the law for British consumers in outlawing such a clause rather than imposing merely a reasonableness test.[27]

Limitation and cut-off periods

Here again the Product Liability Directive is followed in that both limitation periods and cut-off periods are included. The limitation period is the same—three years from the day when the plaintiff became aware of the damage; so time runs against the consumer from the "discoverability date" of the breach of contract or tort. In addition there is a five year cut-off period starting from the date on which the supplier provided the service.

To cater for the special problems faced by the consumer in building disputes where defects may not come to light for many years, longer periods are chosen where the service relates to the design or construction of buildings—a 10 year limitation period and a 20 year cut-off period.

---

[24] Art. 2. The Directive on Package Travel is discussed on pp. 182–184.
[25] *Ibid.*
[26] *Ante*, p. 372.
[27] *Cf.* Unfair Contract Terms Act 1977, s.2(2): *ante*, p. 130.

Finale

It remains to be seen whether the EC Commission's ambitious programme for *Completing the Internal Market* is realised by the last day of 1992. We hope that it is not too optimistic to anticipate that the proposals discussed in this chapter will have become part of the substantive law of the United Kingdom by the time the fourth edition of this book is due for publication.

THREE SELECTED CODES OF PRACTICE

1. CODE OF PRACTICE FOR THE MOTOR INDUSTRY*

1.1 **1 New Car Sales**
Dealers must bear in mind that in sales of goods to consumers they are responsible under the Sale of Goods Act 1979 for ensuring that the goods are of merchantable quality and fit for the purpose for which they are required. Statements whether oral or in writing which are in apparent conflict with this principle must be avoided.

1.2 Manufacturers relying on dealers to carry out a standard Pre-Delivery Inspection shall provide dealers with a standard check list for the particular model of car. Dealers must ensure that these inspections are carried out properly and a copy of the PDI check list shall be given to the customer.

1.3 The car must be delivered in condition which is to the manufacturer's standard. Each car must conform fully to all legislation affecting its construction, use and maintenance. This paragraph does not affect any legal responsibilites which may be placed on manufacturers and users to ensure this.

1.4 The benefit and limitations of any treatment over and above that already provided by the manufacturer which is recommended by the dealer in order to inhibit the growth of rust or other corrosion should be explained to the customer.

1.5 Order forms are intended to help both parties to the contract by spelling out the terms and conditions on which business is being done. Such terms and conditions must be fair and reasonable and set out clearly, together with a statement of the circumstances under which the order can be cancelled.

1.6 All documents must be legible.

* Published with the permission of: Retail Motor Industry Federation, in association with the Society of Motor Manufacturers and Traders and the Scottish Motor Trade Association.
Revised March 1981.

1.7   Order forms must contain details of all charges additional to the car price so that the customer may understand clearly the total price he has to pay to put the car on the road.

1.8   Manufacturers and dealers should ensure that the manufacturer's handbook relating to the model of car being sold is available to the customer at the time of sale of the car and for a reasonable length of time thereafter.

1.9   The terms of the manufacturers' warranties should be drawn to the attention of the customer and any relevant document published by the manufacturer must be handed over to him.

2 Car Manufacturers' Warranties (or Guarantees hereafter called Warranties)

2.1   A manufacturer's warranty is a simple and straightforward way for the customer to have faults of manufacture appearing within certain times (or before the car has done a certain mileage) put right at little or no cost to the customer without the necessity of his pursuing legal rights against the seller.

2.2   The warranty must not adversely affect the consumer's remedies against the seller under the Sale of Goods Act 1979 and must include a statement making this clear to the customer.

2.3   The warranty must include a statement advising the customer that it is in addition to any other remedies he may have under the contract of sale.

2.4   The warranty will not extend to cover defects arising from a failure by the customer to have the car serviced in accordance with the manufacturer's recommendations.

2.5   The terms of the warranty must be easily understandable particularly in relation to any items specifically included in or excluded from its provisions. Manufacturers and dealers should also give advice to customers as to who is responsible and what to do if they have a problem regarding parts and accessories not covered by the manufacturer's warranty.

2.6   The manufacturer should permit the transfer of the unexpired portion of any warranty to a second or subsequent owner.

2.7   The manufacturer should make clear that rectification work may be done under warranty by any of his franchised dealers. Manufacturers and dealers will take steps to ensure that warranty work is carried out rapidly and effectively.

2.8   Manufacturers will operate fair and equitable policies to permit the extension of warranty in the event of a car being off the road for an extended period for rectification of warranty faults, or of the repetition outside warranty of a fault which had previously been the subject of rectification work during the warranty period.

Vehicle off road for warranty work

2.9   There is no automatic right to a loan car or contribution towards hiring charges in circumstances where a customer's own car is off the road for repair under warranty. Whether there is any such right will depend on the normal legal rules relating to damages.

2.10   Manufacturers must give clear advice to their dealers as to the circumstances in which a loan car or contribution towards hiring charges should be provided. Such guidance should take full account of the legal position and be made available to customers on request.

2.11   Where a loan car is made available, this will merely be as reasonable alternative transport rather than an exact replacement for the car which is off the road.

3 Used Car Sales

3.1   Used cars sold to customers must conform to legislation affecting the construction and use of cars and should, where appropriate, be accompanied by a current Department of Transport Test (MoT) Certificate.

3.2   Dealers must bear in mind that sales of used cars are subject to the Sale of Goods Act 1979 and attention is specifically drawn to the conditions of merchantable quality and fitness for purpose contained in this Act. If, however, defects are specifically brought to the attention of the customer or the customer examines the car before the contract is made there is no condition of merchantable quality as regards those specific defects or ones which that examination ought to reveal. Dealers should therefore reveal defects on an approved checklist. See 3.5. The format and use of the checklist are determined and approved by the trade associations or the manufacturer of the car concerned. Dealers should provide all reasonable facilities to enable prospective customers or their nominees to carry out an examination of the car prior to sale, in order that any defects which ought to be revealed at the time of sale are made known to both parties.

3.3   Dealers are reminded of the legal requirement that when selling a used car subject to a printed guarantee or warranty, that guarantee or warranty must not purport to take away or diminish any rights which the consumer would otherwise enjoy in law. The warranty document must also include a statement advising the consumer that the warranty is in addition to his statutory or common law rights.

3.4   If a printed guarantee or warranty is not used, then any specific promises which the dealer is willing to make in relation to the used car should be set out in writing.

3.5   Used cars will be subject to a pre-sales inspection in accordance with an approved checklist. The checklist must be completed before the car is offered for sale and displayed in a prominent place in the car. A copy of the checklist shall be given to the customer for his retention.

3.6   All descriptions, whether used in advertisements or in negotiations regarding the sale of used cars should be honest and truthful. Terms which are likely to be misunderstood by the customer or which are not capable of exact definition should be avoided.

3.7   Copies of relevant written information provided by previous owners regarding the history of cars should be passed on to the customer. This may include service records, repair invoices, inspection reports, handbooks and copy of warranties, as applicable.

3.8   Reasonable steps will be taken to verify the recorded mileage of a used car and dealers will use their best endeavours to obtain a signed statement from the previous owner as to the car's mileage. Dealers should pass on any known facts about an odometer reading to a prospective customer.

3.9   Unless the dealer is satisfied that the quoted mileage of a used car is accurate, such mileage should not be quoted in advertisements, discussions or negotiations or in any documents related to the supply of the used car. Where the car's mileage cannot be verified the customer should be informed. The law requires that any disclaimer used must be as bold, precise and compelling as the car's mileage reading itself and as effectively brought to the prospective customer's attention.

4 Replacement Parts, Accessories and Petrol

4.1   Dealers must bear in mind that in sales of goods to consumers they are responsible under the Sale of Goods Act 1979 that the goods are of merchantable quality and fit for the purpose for which they are required. Statements, whether oral or in writing, in apparent conflict with this principle must be avoided.

4.2   Whenever goods are offered for sale a clear indication of cash price must be available to the customer.

4.3   Terms must not be used in advertisements if they are likely to be misunderstood by the customer or if they are not capable of exact definition.

4.4   With offers of promotions or trading stamps, any restrictions which are attached to sales other than cash sales must be clearly stated.

4.5   A dealer must not display any notices or make any statements which might mislead a consumer about his legal rights in relation to the purchase of faulty goods.

5 Repairs and Servicing (excluding work carried out under a car manufacturer's warranty)

5.1   Dealers must bear in mind that when supplying parts or accessories in connection with repairs or servicing work for consumers, they have a similar responsibility to that which exists under a contract for the sale of goods to ensure that the goods are of merchantable quality and fit for the purpose for which they are required and that work is performed in a proper and workmanlike manner.

5.2   Manufacturers accept a responsibility for ensuring the reasonable availability of spare parts to the distribution chain.

5.3   Spare parts should be readily available from the manufacturer from the time that a new model is offered for sale continuing throughout its production and for a reasonable period thereafter.

5.4   Dealers will provide at least an estimate of the cost of labour and materials for all major repairs and manufacturers' recommended servicing. A firm quotation should be offered wherever possible. It must be made clear to a customer whether an estimate or quotation is being made and whether it is inclusive of VAT and where applicable the rate at which this is chargeable. Quotations should always be in writing identifying the dealer. If requested, estimates will be in writing. It should be remembered that an estimate is a considered approximation of the likely cost involved whereas a quotation constitutes a firm price for which the work will be done. If a charge is to be made for the estimate or quotation this must be made known to the customer before his instructions are accepted. Any dismantling costs which are necessary to arrive at such estimates or quotations should be notified to the customer in advance on the clear understanding whether or not dismantling costs are to be charged on an estimate or quotation which is refused. If, during the progress of any work, it appears that the estimate will be exceeded by a significant amount, then the customer should be notified and asked for permission to continue with the work.

5.5   Parts replaced during service or repair will be made available for return to the customer until the customer has taken delivery of the car unless a warranty claim is involved or unless the parts have to be submitted to the supplier because replacement parts are being supplied on an exchange basis. Dealers should notify customers in advance of work being done what their arrangements are in regard to retention and disposal of parts replaced.

5.6   Invoices should be clearly written or typed and give full details of the work carried out and materials used. The amount and rate of VAT should be clearly indicated. Dates and recorded mileages should always be noted where applicable.

5.7   Dealers should exercise adequate care in protecting customers' property while it is in their custody, and must not seek by disclaimers to avoid their legal liability for damage or loss. Dealers should carry adequate insurance to cover their legal liability and should strongly advise customers to remove any items of value not related to the car.

5.8   Repairs must be guaranteed against failure due to workmanship for a specific mileage or time period which should be stated on the invoice. Dealers are advised to ensure that they are adequately insured against consequential loss claims arising from any such failure.

5.9   A dealer's rules as to the method of payment he will require on completion of the work should always be notified to the customer before the work is accepted.

5.10   When it is necessary to sub-contract work, the dealer will agree to be responsible for the quality of the sub-contractors' work. Any estimate given to the customer must include the sub-contracted work and in the event of any increase in charge for the work, the principles in paragraph 5.4 must apply.

5.11   Dealers must make it clear whether or not servicing will be carried out in accordance with the appropriate manufacturer's recommended service schedule.

5.12   While a dealer's contractual responsibility is limited to the exact terms of the customer's instructions or, for standard services, the schedule prepared by the manufacturer or other body or person, he should make it a general rule to advise the customer of any defects which may become apparent while the work is being carried out.

6 Advertising

6.1   All advertising by manufacturers and dealers must comply with the codes and standards set by the Advertising Standards Authority and the Independent Broadcasting Authority, and with the requirements of the Trade Descriptions Act and the Energy Act (*e.g.* concerning fuel consumption figures). In particular, references to credit facilities must conform to the appropriate legal requirements current at the time.

6.2   Advertisements must not contain any references to guarantees or warranties which would take away or diminish any rights of a customer nor should they be worded as to be understood by the customer as doing so.

6.3   Advertisements must not contain the words "guarantee" or "warranty" unless the full terms of such undertakings as well as the remedial action open to a customer are either clearly set out in the advertisement or are available to the customer in writing at the point of sale or with the product.

6.4   Claims and descriptions in advertisements should not be misleading. In particular any comparison with other models of different manufacturers should be based on a similar set of criteria and should not be presented in such a way as to confuse or mislead the customer.

6.5   In principle, a price quoted should be a price at which the customer can buy the goods. Manufacturers and dealers should therefore quote prices for new cars, whether in advertisements or in showrooms, inclusive of the price of any extras known to be fitted to the car together with the appropriate VAT (quoting the rate applicable) and Car Tax. If the price excludes delivery charges or number plates, such exclusions must be clearly specified.

6.6   Advertisements for used cars must quote prices inclusive of VAT and they should state that the prices are inclusive.

6.7   In the description of used cars, terms likely to be misunderstood by the customer or which are not capable of exact definition should be avoided. For example, if the word "reconditioned" is used, the nature of the reconditioning must be carefully explained.

6.8   In the description of a used car, any year must be either:

(a) the year of first use, or

(b) the year of the first registration, or

(c) the last year that the car complied with the manufacturer's specification of a model sold as new during that calendar year whichever is the earliest.

6.9 Where an advertisement quotes the price of one model in any model range but depicts another, the actual price of that other model should also be shown.

6.10 Where a manufacturer advertises a rust-proofing process, information about the process and its limitations should be made freely available.

7 Handling Complaints

7.1 Manufacturers and dealers must ensure as appropriate that effective and immediate action is taken with a view to achieving a just settlement of a complaint. To this end there will be, from the point of view of the customer, an easily identifiable and accessible arrangement for the reception and handling of complaints. In addition, manufacturers must give every assistance to their dealers in handling complaints under warranty, or those in which the manufacturer is otherwise involved.

7.2 When complaints are raised through a third party (*e.g.* the Automobile Association, the Royal Automobile Club, a Trading Standards Officer or a Citizens Advice Bureau), willing guidance must be given to that body and every attempt should be made to re-establish direct communication with the complaining customer and to reach a satisfactory settlement with him.

7.3 In the event that a complaint is not resolved, manufacturers and dealers must make it clear to a customer that he has a right to refer the complaint to the appropriate trade association.

7.4 Manufacturers and dealers will give every assistance to the association concerned while it is investigating a complaint. The SMMT, the RMI and the SMTA will establish liaison as necessary.

7.5 Where conciliation has failed to resolve a dispute the SMMT, the RMI and the SMTA have agreed to co-operate in the operation of low cost arbitration agreements which will be organised by an Independent Panel of Arbitrators. Details of the arbitration arrangements are set out in the Appendix. Customers must always be advised that they have the option of taking a claim to the Courts.

7.6 The award of the arbitrator is enforceable in law on all parties.

8 Monitoring

8.1   As subscribers to the Code of Practice, dealers should ensure by the clear display of appropriate symbols or other means that customers are informed of dealers' adherence to the industry's Code of Practice.

8.2   All manufacturers and dealers should maintain an analysis of justified complaints relating to any of the provisions of the Code of Practice and should take action based on this information to improve their service to the customer.

8.3   The SMMT, the RMI and the SMTA will analyse all complaints about the Code or matters referred to the association for conciliation or arbitration. The results of such analyses will be published in the Annual Report of the relevant association.

Appendix: Complaints and Arbitration

1. A customer who has a complaint about the quality of the goods or service to his motor car should in the first place and at the earliest opportunity refer it to the dealer concerned.

2. The complaint, preferably in writing, should be addressed to a senior executive, a director, a partner or the proprietor. Some dealers will have an executive especially appointed to deal with complaints.

3. If the complaint relates to warranty on a new car and the dealer is unable to resolve the matter, the customer should take his complaint direct to the manufacturer concerned.

4. If attempts to reach a satisfactory solution fail, the customer has a right to refer his complaint to one of the trade associations who subscribe to the Code of Practice for the Motor Industry, if the dealer concerned is a member of that association. Any such complaint must be in writing.

   (a) if the complaint refers to a manufacturer's warranty or lies against a dealer who is a member the address is:
   The Customer Relations Department, Society of Motor Manufacturers & Traders Ltd., Forbes House, Halkin Street, London SW1X 7DS.
   (b) if the complaint lies against a dealer who is a member situated in any part of the United Kingdom except Scotland the address is:
   The National Conciliation Service, Retail Motor Industry Federation, 9 North Street, Rugby CV21 2AB.
   (c) if the complaint lies against a dealer who is a member situated in Scotland, the address is:
   Customer Complaints Service, Scottish Motor Trade Association, 3 Palmerston Place, Edinburgh EH12 5AQ.

5. All complaints referred to the appropriate trade association (SMMT, RMI or SMTA) within a reasonable time of the cause for complaint arising will be considered.

6. If the trade association fails to resolve the complaint, its members will agree to go to arbitration except in those cases where the trade association is of the opinion that it would be unreasonable for the member to be required to do so.

7. Parties to arbitration will be asked to pay the registration fee laid down by the Chartered Institute of Arbitrators. When, later, the arbitrator makes his award, he will consider whether the registration fee should be returned to the successful party.

8. The parties will also be asked to sign an application for arbitration which will be sent, together with the registration fee, to:
The Independent Panel of Arbitrators, c/o Retail Motor Industry Federation, 9 North Street, Rugby CV21 2AB.

9. In order to keep costs as low as possible, the arbitration will normally rely on documents. In these cases, none of the parties to the dispute may be present nor may they be represented by any other person.

10. The trade association will submit to the Chartered Institute of Arbitrators all the documentary evidence in their possession that they consider relevant to the case. The Chartered Institute of Arbitrators will advise the parties to the dispute of the written evidence they have available on which to base their judgment and invite the parties to submit any further evidence which they consider relevant.

11. The President of the Chartered Institute of Arbitrators will appoint a single arbitrator and will make all the necessary arrangements for the arbitration to be conducted as speedily as possible.

12. In suitable cases, the Arbitrator has the right to conduct an oral arbitration and the parties may then attend to present their evidence. Legal representation may only be employed if the Arbitrator so directs.

13. The Arbitrator will have the power to direct any party to provide him and to the other party(ies) any additional document or information he considers to be relevant to the matter under dispute.

14. The award of the Arbitrator will be published in writing to the parties to the dispute and to the relevant association.

15. The award of the Arbitrator is enforceable in the Courts by any party.

Retail Motor Industry Federation, 201 Great Portland Street, London W1N 6AB.

The Society of Motor Manufacturers & Traders, Forbes House, Halkin Street, London SW1X 7DS.

The Scottish Motor Trade Association, 3 Palmerston Place, Edinburgh EH12 5AQ.

2. ABTA Tour Operators' Code of Conduct*

All members of the tour operators' class (hereinafter referred to as tour operators) shall comply with this Code of Conduct.

AIMS

To ensure that the public receive the best possible service from tour operators.

To maintain and enhance the reputation, standing and good name of the Association and its membership.

To encourage initiative and enterprise in the belief that properly regulated competitive trading by and between tour operators will best serve the public interest and the well-being of the travel industry.

To ensure that the public interest shall predominate in all considerations of the standards of competitive trading between tour operators.

To encourage growth and development of the travel industry, consistent with the above aims.

PRINCIPLES

This Code is designed to regulate the activities of tour operators between themselves and members of the public; between themselves and their travel agents; and between themselves.

This Code recognises and embodies the relevant parts of those Acts of Parliament and Government Regulations which relate to Trade Descriptions and Civil Aviation and the Codes or Regulations of recognised organisations or associations such as the Advertising Standards Authority, the Code of Advertising Practice Committee, the Independent Broadcasting Authority, the Independent Television Companies Association and the Association of Independent Radio Contractors which regulate the standards and practices of tour operators in relation to advertising.

This Code embodies measures for the regulation of the standards and

---

* Published with the permission of: The Association of British Travel Agents Ltd., 55–57 Newman Street, London W1P 4AH.
There are two codes dealing separately with Tour Operators and Retail Agents. Only the Tour Operators' Code is reproduced here.

practices of tour operators generally. These measures are included in recognition of the need to regulate competitive commercial practices where such practices are considered by the Association to conflict with the public interest.

This Code embodies definitions of commercial practices and nomenclature used by tour operators. These definitions are designed to specify and clarify beyond reasonable doubt the intentions of the Code.

This Code recognises the necessity for enforcement of its standards and practices and embodies measures and procedures by which tour operators can uphold observance of the Code under the authority of the Tour Operators' Council.

This Code provides facilities to deal with consumer complaints by a system of conciliation and arbitration.

1. DEFINITIONS

For the purposes of this Code, definitions are as follows:—

Brochures: brochures are publications which specify the contents of a tour, holiday or travel arrangement offered by a tour operator.

Advertising: advertising is a means of promoting tours, holidays or travel arrangements by publication other than a brochure as defined above.

Incentives: incentives are offers in cash or kind to an ABTA member company to sell a holiday.

Promotions: promotions are activities designed to stimulate the sale or purchase of a tour, holiday or travel arrangements offered by a tour operator by means other than incentives or advertising as defined above.

Representatives: representatives are persons, whether in direct employment or not, acting as the company's agent to assist customers to further their enjoyment of the holiday, tour or other travel arrangements.

Force Majeure: force majeure means circumstances where performance and/or prompt performance of the contract is prevented by reasons of war or threat of war, riot, civil strife, industrial dispute (as defined below), terrorist activity, natural or nuclear disaster, fire or adverse weather conditions.

Industrial Dispute: is defined as a dispute between a person, other than the tour operator, supplying services comprised in a package holiday and

(a) his employees and/or

(b) any other person whose services affect the performance of the package holiday.

which the tour operator cannot reasonably be expected to overcome by substituting comparable alternative arrangements.

United Kingdom (UK): is defined as England, Scotland, Wales and Northern Ireland.

Foreign Inclusive Holiday: foreign inclusive holiday means a prearranged combination of **transport** taken by clients to a destination outside the UK originating in the UK, Channel Islands and the Isle of Man and not less than one of the following when organised for the benefit of the client at a global price all or part of which is payable in advance of departure and marketed as such:

(a) **accommodation** and/or

(b) **other services not ancillary to transport or accommodation**.

The expression "package holidays," "package tours" and "package travel" shall be deemed to have an identical meaning.

2. CONDUCT BETWEEN TOUR OPERATORS AND MEMBERS OF THE PUBLIC

2.1 Minimum Standards on Brochures
A Tour Operator shall ensure that his brochure complies with the spirit as well as the principles, rules and procedures contained in "ABTA Standards on Brochures" as published by the Association from time to time.

2.2 Statutory Requirements for Brochures
Every brochure published by or in the name of a tour operator shall observe the requirements of the Trade Description Act 1968, the Misrepresentation Act 1967, the Civil Aviation Act 1971 (including any regulations made thereunder) the Unfair Contract Terms Act 1977, the Control of Misleading Advertisements Regulations 1988 and the Consumer Protection Act 1987, or any amendment or re-enactment thereof in accordance with the second principle of this Code.

2.3 Cancellation of Tours, Holidays or other Travel Arrangements by the Tour Operator

(i) A tour operator shall not cancel a tour, holiday or other travel arrangements after the date when payment of the balance of the price becomes due unless it is necessary to do so as a result of force majeure, or unless the client defaults in payment of such balance.

(ii) If a tour operator cancels a previously confirmed tour, holiday or other travel arrangements

    (a) for any reason whatsoever prior to the date on which payment of the balance of the price becomes due or

    (b) for reasons of force majeure at any time prior to departure

he shall inform agents and direct clients without delay and shall offer clients the choice of an alternative holiday, if available, or a full refund of all monies paid. Such refund shall be sent to agents within 10 clear days and to direct clients within 14 clear days of the client's decision being notified to the tour operator.

(iii) Notwithstanding clause 2.3 (i), if the cancellation is made for reasons *other than force majeure* on or after the date when payment of the balance of the tour price is due the tour operator shall also offer clients reasonable compensation. Such compensation shall be in accordance with a rising scale of payments geared to the length of time prior to departure at which the cancellation is made, *i.e.* the nearer to departure, the higher the level of compensation.

2.4 Material Alterations to Tours, Holidays and other Travel Arrangements by Tour Operators

(i) Except for reasons of force majeure, a tour operator shall not make a material alteration to a previously confirmed tour, holiday or other travel arrangements unless he does so in time to inform agents and direct clients not less than 14 days before the departure date of the tour, holiday or other travel arrangements.

(ii) If a tour operator makes a material alteration to a previously confirmed tour, holiday or other travel arrangements.

    (a) for any reason whatsoever prior to the date on which payment of the balance of the price becomes due or

    (b) for reasons of force majeure at any time prior to departure

he shall inform agents and direct clients without delay and shall offer clients the choice of either accepting the alteration or of cancelling the tour, holiday or other travel arrangements and receiving a full refund of all monies paid. Such refund shall be sent to agents within 10 clear days and to direct clients within 14 clear days of receipt of the notification to cancel.

(iii) Notwithstanding Clause 2.4(i), if the material alteration is made for reasons *other than force majeure* on or after the date on which payment of the balance of the price becomes due, the tour operator shall also offer clients reasonable compensation. Such compensation shall be in accordance with a rising scale of payments geared to the length of time prior to departure at which the material alteration is made, *i.e.* the nearer to departure, the higher the level of compensation.

2.5 Cancellation of Tours, Holidays or Other Travel Arrangements by Clients

A tour operator shall clearly state in his booking conditions the amount of, or the basis for calculating, the cancellation fees which the client shall be liable to incur, as well as the terms and conditions under which the client shall be liable to incur such fees.

2.6 Overbooked Hotels

(i) A tour operator shall exercise reasonable care and skill to ensure that tours, holidays or other travel arrangements are not cancelled or altered as a result of overbooking.

(ii) Where tours, holidays or other travel arrangements are cancelled or altered as a result of overbooking by a hotel, a tour operator shall only be deemed to have exercised reasonable care and skill to prevent the cancellation or alteration if he can show that the overbooking occurred for reasons beyond his control.

(iii) If, despite sub-paragraphs (i) and (ii) above, a hotel is overbooked and a tour operator knows this before the departure of the affected clients, he shall immediately inform those clients and shall offer them the choice of an alternative holiday of at least comparable standard, if available, or a full and prompt refund of all money paid.

(iv) If, despite sub-paragraphs (i) and (ii) above, a hotel is overbooked and a tour operator does not know this before the departure of affected clients, such clients shall on arrival at their destination be offered alternative accommodation and shall also be offered reasonable compensation for "disturbance" where the location and/or facilities of the alternative accommodation can reasonably be regarded as inferior to that originally booked.

(v) For the purpose of the above sub-paragraphs, hotels include accommodation of other kinds such as apartments, villas, guest houses and camping sites.

2.7 Building Works

Where a tour operator becomes aware of building works which may reasonably be considered to seriously impair the enjoyment of a holiday he must, without undue delay, notify clients of the situation and afford them an opportunity to transfer to an alternative holiday at the price pertaining to that holiday or to cancel without penalty. Furthermore he must ensure that all prospective clients are alerted to the situation.

2.8   Tour Operator's Liability

(i) Tour Operators shall include as a term of any contract for the sale of their foreign inclusive holidays or tours a provision accepting responsibility for acts and/or omissions of their employees, agents, sub-contractors and suppliers. In addition, tour operators shall indicate acceptance of responsibility should the services which the operator is contractually obliged to provide prove deficient or are not of a reasonable standard save that tour operators shall not be responsible nor accept liability for death, bodily injury or illness caused to the signatory to the contract and/or any other named person on the booking form except as provided by Clause 2.8(ii) below. Where the services in question consist of carriage by air or by sea, the tour operator shall be entitled to limit his obligations and liabilities in the manner provided by international conventions in respect of air or sea carriers.

(ii) A tour operator shall include, as a term of any contract for the sale of foreign inclusive holidays or tours, a provision accepting responsibility for the negligent acts and/or omissions of:

(a) his employees or agents,

(b) his suppliers and sub-contractors, servants and/or agents of the same whilst acting within the scope of, or in the course of their employment (other than air and sea carriers performing any domestic, internal or international carriage of whatsoever kind)

in respect of claims arising as a result of death, bodily injury or illness caused to the signatory to the contract and/or any other of the named persons on the booking form.

(iii) A tour operator shall include as a term of any contract for the sale of a foreign inclusive holiday provisions stating that, where appropriate and subject to the tour operator's reasonable discretion:

(a) General assistance shall be afforded to clients who, through misadventure, suffer illness, personal injury or death during the period of their holiday arising out of an activity which does not form part of the foreign inclusive holiday nor of an excursion offered through the tour operator.

(b) Where legal action is undertaken by the client, with the prior agreement of the tour operator, initial legal costs associated therewith shall be met by the tour operator, always provided clients request such assistance within 90 days from date of misadventure.

(c) The aggregate costs for the tour operator in respect of Clause 2.8(iii)(a) and (b) above shall not exceed £5,000 per booking form. Furthermore, in the event either of there being a successful claim for costs against a third party or there being suitable insurance policy/ies in force, costs actually incurred by the tour operator shall be recoverable from the clients.

(iv) A tour operator shall ensure that he obtains adequate liability insurance to cover claims made by clients under Clause 2.8(ii) of this Code.

(v) A tour operator shall not include as a term of any contract relating to the sale of any travel arrangements, clauses which purport to:

(a) exclude or limit liability for misleading statements made by the tour operator, his employees or agents; and

(b) exclude or limit liability for the tour operator's contractual duty to exercise care and skill in making arrangements for a package holiday; and

(c) exclude liability for any alleged cause of dissatisfaction by stipulating that such cause must be made known to the tour operator within a fixed period unless that period is at least 28 days from completion of holiday.

(vi) A tour operator shall indicate that claims under Clause 2.8 shall in respect of both liability and quantum fall within the exclusive jurisdiction of the courts in the country in which the contract was entered into.

2.9 Complaints and Correspondence from Clients

In the event of a dispute between a client and a tour operator all correspondence relating to client's complaints shall be dealt with by the tour operator within the following time limits:

(i) not later than 14 days from receipt for an acknowledgement to be sent and;

(ii) not later than 28 days from receipt for a full reply to be sent or a reply containing a detailed explanation for the delay;

(iii) the final date for dealing in full with the aforesaid correspondence shall be 56 days.

2.10 Correspondence from the Association

All correspondence from the Association about complaints and compliance with the Articles of Association and this Code shall be dealt with within the same time limits shown in paragraph 2.9 above.

2.11 Conciliation and Arbitration

(i) In the event of a breakdown in communication or a serious disagreement between the tour operator and the client, ABTA is prepared to intervene to give help and impartial guidance and to offer the facilities of conciliation.

(ii) A tour operator shall include as a term of any contract relating to the sale of his inclusive holidays or tours a provision whereby any dispute arising out of, or in connection with, such sale which is not amicably settled, may be referred to arbitration under a special scheme devised for the travel industry by the Chartered Institute of Arbitrators.

It shall also be stated that:—

    (a) the scheme provides for a simple and inexpensive method of arbitration on documents alone with restricted liability of the client in respect of costs;

    (b) the scheme does not apply to claims for an amount greater than £1,500 per person or £7,500 per booking form or to claims which are solely or mainly in respect of physical injury or illness or the consequences of such injury or illness;

    (c) details of the scheme will be supplied on request.

(iii) Where a client indicates in writing that he wishes to refer an unresolved dispute to arbitration, the tour operator shall reply to the Association within 21 days enclosing payment and documents and shall comply with the terms of the Arbitration Scheme referred to in sub-paragraph (ii) above and in particular with all the relevant rules and regulations of the Chartered Institute of Arbitrators for the time being in force.

Note: A recommended clause for inclusion in booking conditions is set out in the ABTA Standards on Brochures.

2.12 Advertising

(i) All advertising by tour operators shall observe the requirements of all such Acts of Parliament as may be enacted from time to time and in particular, with the Trade Descriptions Act 1968, the Misrepresentation Act 1967, the Civil Aviation Act 1971, the Control of Misleading Advertisements Regulations 1988, and the Consumer Protection Act 1987 (including any regulations made thereunder) and of any amendment or re-enactment thereof.

(ii) Where a tour operator is convicted of an offence or judgment is entered against him in respect of a proven breach of any of the statutory provisions as contained in paragraph 2.12(i) above he shall be deemed to be in breach of this Code.

(iii) All advertising by a tour operator shall comply with the Codes or Regulations of the recognised organisations or associations. Where a tour operator is reported to have breached such Codes or Regulations, the Code of Conduct Committee retains the right to reconsider the alleged complaint and to decide in their view if the tour operator has or has not breached this Code.

(iv) A tour operator shall not advertise in such a manner as to suggest that other members of the Association are or may become insolvent.

(v) A tour operator shall show his ABTA number in all his press advertisements for travel business, but shall not be obliged to do so where these advertisements are in classified run-on form unless such advertisements contain any reference to ABTA.

2.13 Surcharges—ABTA Standards

A tour operator shall ensure that his conduct complies with the principles, rules and procedures contained in "ABTA Standards on Surcharges" as published by the Association from time to time.

2.14 Airport and Seaport Taxes

A tour operator shall include airport and seaport taxes in the prices quoted in brochures and advertisements for all inclusive holidays except in respect of taxes which cannot be paid in advance by the tour operator.

2.15 Misleading Use of ABTA Symbol

A tour operator shall not, directly or indirectly cause, permit, assist or encourage a company or firm trading as a tour operator or travel agent which is not a member of the Association to represent itself as a member by the use of the ABTA symbol or by any ABTA number on brochures or other documents or by any other means which may give the false impression to the public that such company or firm is a member of the Association, or in relation to travel business be connected to or associated in any way (including through any of its proprietors, shareholders, officers or personnel) with any such company or firm which so misrepresents itself.

2.16 Representatives

A tour operator shall ensure that all his representatives can communicate clearly in English and are familiar with their company policies in

order that they can comprehend and perform within written
procedures.

3. CONDUCT BETWEEN TOUR OPERATORS AND TRAVEL AGENTS

3.1 Confirmation of Bookings, Tickets and other Documentation

It shall be the duty of a tour operator to pass on without undue delay to
the travel agent confirmation of bookings, tickets and other relevant
documents appertaining to the tour, holiday or travel arrangement
booked, to enable the agent to transmit these to the client within a
reasonable period before departure.

3.2 Accounts and Refunds

A tour operator shall settle accounts and refunds without undue delay
or, if applicable, within the period previously agreed in writing between the parties concerned.

3.3 Incentives

Any incentives as defined in 1. above shall only be offered by a tour
operator to the head office of a member travel agent and shall not be
offered direct to a travel agent's staff.

3.4 Promotions

Promotions as defined in 1. above may take place between tour
operators and travel agents or between tour operators and members of
the public and shall comply with all relevant paragraphs of this Code.

4. PAYMENT OF ACCOUNTS

A tour operator shall settle all accounts and refunds without delay or,
if applicable, within the period previously agreed in writing between
the parties concerned.

5. NOTIFICATION OF TRADING NAMES

Before employing a trading name (which for these purposes means a
name which is not either the correct corporate name or in the case of an
unincorporated business, the name under which ABTA membership is
enjoyed) a tour operator shall ensure that he has notified ABTA of
such trading name in compliance with ABTA's regulations for such
notification.

6. SERVICE

All members shall ensure that the public receive the best possible
service and shall take no action that might adversely affect the reputation, standing and good name of the Association and its members.

7. INFRINGEMENT AND ENFORCEMENT

7.1 If any infringement of this Code of Conduct is alleged against a tour operator, the facts shall be reported to the ABTA Secretariat for preliminary investigation.

7.2 The tour operator against whom the allegation has been made shall provide, at the request of the Secretariat, such further information and/or documents as may be required within such a period as may be specified.

7.3 If, after preliminary investigation, the facts alleged against the tour operator appear to the Secretariat to constitute a prima facie infringement of this Code, the facts shall be dealt with in accordance with paragraph 7.4 below or submitted to the Code of Conduct Committee of the Tour Operators' Council (hereinafter called the Committee) in accordance with paragraph 7.5 below.

7.4
(i) Where the Secretariat after due investigation have reason to believe that a tour operator has committed a fixed penalty offence as set out below, the Secretariat may issue the tour operator with a fixed penalty notice in respect of the offence.

(ii) the following breaches of this Code by a tour operator constitute a fixed penalty offence and attract a fine of £200 which may be increased by Tour Operators' Council from time to time.

2.1	Brochure Standards
2.5	Cancellation Fees
2.9	Complaints/Correspondence from Clients
2.10	Correspondence from the Association
2.11	ABTA Arbitration Scheme
2.12(v)	Requirements to show ABTA No. in advertisements
2.13	Standards on Surcharges—failure to include one of the mandatory paragraphs
3.1	Passing on of documentation
5	Notification of Trading Names

Breaches of the remaining paragraphs of this Code of Conduct are not fixed penalty offences and therefore shall be referred to the Committee in accordance with 7.5 below.

7.4
(iii) The Secretariat has at all times the discretion to refer directly to the Committee in accordance with the procedures laid down in paragraph 7.5 below all alleged breaches of this Code including repeated breaches which would normally constitute a fixed penalty offence.

(iv) Where the Secretariat issues a fixed penalty notice in the standard form as set out in the appendix attached hereto indicating what Clause has been breached, the fine that is to be levied and the time period in which the fine must be paid, the tour operator may:—

    (a) Pay the fine within 28 days as set out in the fixed penalty notice

    (b) Request in writing to the Secretariat that the matter be referred to the Committee

  (v) Where the tour operator fails to pay the fine within the specified fixed period notice, or requests that the matter be referred to the Committee, or fails to respond to the fixed penalty notice, the Secretariat shall refer the matter to the Committee in accordance with the procedure laid down in paragraph 7.5 of this Code. The Secretariat shall not refer the matter to the Committee until the period specified in the fixed period notice has expired.

7.5 Where the Secretariat after due investigation has reason to believe that the facts alleged against the tour operator constitute a prima facie infringement of this Code, the facts shall be submitted to the Committee who shall give the tour operator at least 14 days notice in writing of the time and place of hearing of the complaint. The tour operator shall be entitled to make representations at the hearing either personally (with or without legal representation) or in writing. The Committee shall have the power to impose a reprimand or a fine or recommend suspension/termination of membership.

7.6 In cases where the Committee decide that the appropriate penalty for the alleged breach of the Code is termination or suspension of membership, the decision shall be submitted to the Tour Operators' Council which may ratify the decision or impose an alternative penalty.

7.7 The Committee or Tour Operators' Council, as appropriate, shall notify its decision to the tour operator, whereupon the tour operator shall have the right, exercisable within 14 days after the service of the notice upon him, to appeal against such decision to the Appeal Board who shall make such arrangements as it thinks fit for the conduct of the appeal.

The decision of the Tour Operators' Council to terminate or suspend the membership of a tour operator or to impose a fine or reprimand shall take effect on the expiration of the period allowed for appeal. If the tour operator has not then appealed, he shall thereupon cease to be a member, be suspended as a member, be liable to pay the fine or sustain the reprimand.

7.8 If the tour operator shall appeal against a fine or reprimand or termination or suspension of membership, the decision shall not take effect unless and to the extent that it is confirmed or varied by the Appeal Board, which shall determine the appeal by exercising the powers of the Tour Operators' Council in such manner as in its discretion it thinks fit.

7.9 The Appeal Board shall be constituted in accordance with Article 17 of the Articles of Association.

7.10 After the decision of the Appeal Board has been made known to the appellant, that decision shall be communicated to the Tour Operators' Council.

7.11 The Tour Operators' Council shall arrange for decisions to penalise a tour operator and the reasons therefore to be published in the ABTA News.

8. DIRECT SELLING BY TOUR OPERATORS

8.1 A tour operator who sells his tour, holiday or travel arrangements direct to the public shall in addition, conform so far as is applicable to the Travel Agents' Code of Conduct in respect of such sales as if he was a member of the travel agents' class.

8.2 A tour operator shall pass onto clients, without undue delay, confirmations of bookings, tickets and other relevant documents appertaining to the tour, holiday or other travel arrangements provided that the appropriate payment has been received from the clients.

8.3 A tour operator shall settle accounts and refunds without undue delay.

R.E.T.R.A.

3. CODE OF PRACTICE FOR THE SELLING AND SERVICING OF ELECTRICAL AND ELECTRONIC APPLIANCES*

1 Pricing

1.1 All goods to be sold will have a clear indication of the cash price at which they are offered for sale.

1.2 The retailer will at all times do everything possible to ensure that any customer who may have been charged too high a price arising from an error in his shop will have any excess charge refunded.

---

* Published with the permission of: The Radio, Electrical and Television Retailers Association (R.E.T.R.A.) Ltd., R.E.T.R.A. House, 57–61 Newington Causeway, London SE1 6BE.

2 Discounts

2.1 Where a discount is offered the retailer will ensure that it is clearly understood and easily verified by the customer. Imprecise comparisons with claims of "worth," "value" and "price elsewhere" are not to be used.

2.2 The retailer shall at no time attempt to confuse or mislead the customer or falsely describe any of the goods he offers for sale.

3 Refunds

3.1 Although the retailer is under no obligation (subject to the provisions of the Hire Purchase Acts and the Consumer Credit Act) to refund payments when a customer has changed his mind or simply does not like the goods, retailers may in these circumstances give a full cash refund at their discretion.

3.2 The retailer shall advise customers at the time of sale of any special conditions that he wishes to apply to the sale of goods or the use of credit cards or credit tokens and to the exchange or return of goods sold. Where possible, a notice should be displayed to this effect.

4 Deposits

4.1 Any retailer who accepts an advance payment or deposit for goods shall indicate the period during which the delivery of the goods will be made to the customer. If delivery is not made to the customer within this period then the retailer shall offer the customer the option of a refund.

4.2 Failure by the customer to perform his contractual obligation to pay the balance of the purchase price may give the retailer the legal right to retain some or all of the deposit to compensate for his loss.

5 The Sale

5.1 The retailer will give the customer as much information as possible about the goods and this will normally include such items as:

> Correct method of unpacking
> Correct pre-usage checks
> Correct method of installation
> Correct usage
> Details of additional guarantees and service
> Indication of the correct mains plug fuse value

The retailer will provide the manufacturer's handbook or instructions wherever possible.

5.2 The retailer will make clear at the point of sale the exact terms of the contract for the goods including any additional costs for delivery, installation and commissioning of the goods.

5.3   When work is not carried out by the retailer or by his appointed agent the retailer will advise his customers of the limitation of his responsibility for loss or damage resulting from such matters as faulty installation.

5.4   The retailer should provide customers with documentary evidence of proof of purchase and the date. Customers are to be advised to keep such documentary evidence and if possible to produce it when asking for service or making any complaint about the goods.

5.5   The retailer will ensure that the goods he stocks are manufactured to the relevant safety standards. When an item is found to be electrically or mechanically dangerous the retailer will, wherever possible, take steps to contact customers so that the merchandise can be modified or exchanged.

6 Retailer's Guarantee

6.1   Without detracting from the customer's legal rights including those under the Sale of Goods Act 1893 as amended by the Supply of Goods (Implied Terms) Act 1973, the retailer shall guarantee new goods for both parts and labour for a period of not less than 12 months from the date of purchase and this shall apply even if the manufacturer's guarantee is for a shorter period.

The retailer's guarantee given under 6.1 does not apply in the following respects:

   (a) Damage or faults caused by customer misuse, negligence or failure to adhere to the manufacturer's or retailer's instructions.
   (b) Certain goods and replaceable parts that may have a limited life span (*e.g.* low cost transistor radios, styli, fuses, lamps, drive belts and batteries).

6.2   The terms of any guarantee given will be clearly set out at the time of sale.

6.3   If during the guarantee period the retailer is unable to effect a repair within 15 working days from date of notification of defect, he will by the expiration of such period, endeavour to lend the same or a similar item to the customer. This obligation does not necessarily apply where the retailer is not the service agent. If the retailer finds that it is impracticable to lend such an item, he shall always extend the period of the original guarantee by the period of time during which the customer was without the use of the item.

6.4   Where a customer moves outside the retailer's normal service area, the retailer may not be in a position to implement effectively all guarantees and services normally offered. Where possible, however, the retailer will transfer any servicing or guarantee arrangement to a local retailer in the customer's new area if the customer so requests. R.E.T.R.A. operate a National Rental and Service Transfer Scheme that may be used for this purpose.

7 Advertising

The retailer's advertisements shall be clear and honest and in accordance with any statutory requirements and the British Code of Advertising Practice and in particular the attention of the retailer is drawn to the unacceptable practice of "switch selling" set out in Section 4 thereof.

8 Repairs and Servicing

8.1   The retailer will make clear the exact terms of the contract for any repairs or servicing work to be carried out. Invoices should be clearly presented showing details of the work carried out, the materials used and VAT charged.

8.2   The retailer will accept for repair or service goods that he has sold but may not be able to accept for repair or service goods purchased from other sources (but see 6.4 above). The retailer will encourage customers to return faulty goods to his workshop where practicable. If the customer requests a visit to his home, the retailer shall ask the customer to provide as much of the following information as possible in order to identify these goods, expedite the repair and minimise costs:

　　(i) make of appliance
　　(ii) model number
　　(iii) serial number
　　(iv) description of fault
　　(v) name of purchaser
　　(vi) address where the equipment is located (indicating any special difficulties)
　　(vii) a suitable time for the engineer to call, giving working day alternatives am/pm
　　(viii) whether it is an in-guarantee fault, out of guarantee fault or service call for maintenance.

8.3   The retailer will provide service and spares to the best of his ability but where he is unable to provide such a service he will give the information listed in 9.2.

8.4 Where goods are handed in or collected for repair or service, the retailer shall provide the customer with a receipt where requested.

8.5 Many retailers offer a same day service. However, when a customer requests a service visit (and the retailer supplies the service) under normal conditions the initial call will be offered to be made within three working days after receiving the request.

8.6 When a request for service is received from the customer, the retailer shall advise the customer of any minimum service charge which is to be made. At the same time the customer shall be informed of payment arrangements for any service call, inspection or repair.

8.7 Should the fault fail to be repaired either in the workshop or *in situ*, the engineer or retailer will report the suspected fault to the customer and the reasons why a repair has not been effected. Reference should be made to one or more of the following categories:

    (i) lack of spare parts
    (ii) the equipment requires major repair
    (iii) unable to trace defect
    (iv) several other important defects are apparent
    (v) appliance unsafe (mechanical, electrical, electronic or physical)
    (vi) appliance unrepairable
    (vii) appliance not worth repairing (age or hazardous)

The provisions of section 6 of this Code apply in the case of in-guarantee repairs on goods referred to therein.

8.8 Retailers will, upon request, advise customers of their own conditions for the servicing and repair of products. Field service repairs which cannot be completed at the time of the first visit should be completed normally within 15 working days from the date of the first visit. In the case of workshop repairs, manpower and facilities should be calculated to achieve completion of 80 per cent. of all repairs within five working days from the date of receipt of the product in the workshop. Completion of repairs will be dependent upon availability of spares, normal working conditions and the maintenance of electricity supply and transmissions.

If the retailer finds there will be an undue delay in performing the repair, he will notify his customer of this giving the reason for the delay.

9 Where the Retailer is not the Service Agent

9.1   Some manufacturers allow only their service engineers to perform in-guarantee work. Where this situation arises although the retailer fully accepts his responsibility under the law, he is not in a position to provide service.

9.2   The retailer undertakes where in-guarantee service is required to provide the customer with the name, address and telephone number of the manufacturer or service agent.

In appropriate circumstances the retailer will accept the goods brought in by the customer for return to the manufacturer or service agent for service.

9.3   The retailer also undertakes, where the manufacturer fails to provide an adequate service to his customer to use his best endeavours to procure such a service for his customer and if necessary to enlist the assistance of the R.E.T.R.A. Conciliation Service.

10 Delayed, Cancelled or Abortive Calls

10.1   Where the retailer has agreed to an appointment which has to be cancelled through circumstances beyond the normal running of the retailer's business, he will endeavour to advise the customer, where practicable, of any change in call times.

10.2   Retailers shall advise customers of the inconvenience and expense that can be caused by the customer's failure to cancel or rearrange appointments.

11 Guarantee of Repairs on Products Outside Normal Guarantee Period

A specific repair performed by the retailer will be guaranteed both in parts supplied and fitted and workmanship for a minimum period of three months. This guarantee shall not detract from the legal rights of the customer.

12 Estimates

If requested, the retailer shall offer to provide customers with estimates of the cost of all major repairs. The customer shall be advised in advance whether or not the estimate is free and that circumstances may require its variation. The customer shall be advised that if the equipment is beyond economic repair, or if he is unable to accept the estimate, the retailer may not be able to return the goods in the condition in which they were originally received. Where a quotation for repair work is provided, as distinct from an estimate, it should be realised by both parties that the acceptance of a quotation constitutes a contract embodying the terms of the quotation.

13 Life Expectancy

13.1 The economic life expectancy of any product is difficult to determine as some products which have been cheap and basic in manufacture, may in some instances far outlive the normal expected life of such a product.

13.2 Functional parts are electrical and mechanical parts which are essential to the continued operation and safety of the appliance. To assist customers in determining whether or not a product is repairable the following table on the availability of functional parts after the date on which the production of the appliance ceases, has been prepared by the Association of Manufacturers of Domestic Electrical Appliances.

Small appliances	5–8 years
Cleaners, direct acting space heaters, refrigerators and freezers, spin and tumble driers and wash boilers	8 years
Cookers, dishwashers, washing machines	10 years
Thermal storage space heating	15 years

13.3 It is important for retailers to advise that the availability of spares quoted for any particular group of appliances does not make all appliances repairable or economic to be repaired.

14 Life Expectancy—Electronic Equipment

Most electronic equipment can be expected to last about seven years and in certain cases this period may be longer. Customers should be advised, however, that non-functional parts may not be available for this length of time.

15 Spare Parts

15.1 Retailers will make every effort to keep a comprehensive stock of commonly used parts. With the increasing complexity of modern goods and a vast overall range of spares, the retailer, unless exceptional circumstances prevail, will be unable to stock all spares.

15.2 Spares other than these will therefore be drawn from the retailer's suppliers and the retailer will use his best endeavours to ensure a swift delivery.

15.3 Non-functional parts may only be available by special order from the manufacturer and the retailer may request payment with order for replacement on goods out of guarantee.

15.4 Retailers should ensure that products they sell can be serviced during their normal life expectancy. Where they cannot ascertain this they should advise the customer accordingly.

16 Conciliation Services

16.1   There is no doubt that the vast majority of sales and or service calls are performed satisfactorily. Situations will arise, however, when either the customer or the retailer feels he has been unfairly treated by either the other party or by a supplier.

16.2   Customers with a complaint should always be encouraged to return to the retailer or service agent. The retailer or service agent should examine the matter speedily and sympathetically and must take decisive action if justification is established.

16.3   Disputes are usually local matters and customers who are dissatisfied with the retailer can be referred to the local Trading Standards Officer, Consumer Advice Centre or Citizens' Advice Bureau. Each customer or retailer, however, shall also have the right to apply for assistance, in writing, to the Secretary of the Association assisted if necessary by the R.E.T.R.A. Customer Conciliation Panel.

16.4   The objective of the R.E.T.R.A. Conciliation Service is to provide prompt and informal conciliation where the retailer and the customer cannot resolve their dispute.

16.5   The customer should indicate the nature of the complaint in writing in the first instance, to the Secretary of R.E.T.R.A.

16.6   If the Secretary is unable to resolve the complaint it may be referred to the R.E.T.R.A. Conciliation Panel. The Panel consists of:

  (i)   an independent chairman
  (ii) a Trading Standards Officer
  (iii) a Consumer representative
  (iv) a member of the R.E.T.R.A. Council
  (v)   a representative of such manufacturers' association as is appropriate.

The Panel will be able to ask R.E.T.R.A. to obtain as much information as is necessary to assist it in its task. The retailer or the customer may, if required, attend the meeting of the Panel but in the majority of cases the Panel should be able to reach its decision on the basis of documentary evidence.

16.7   The retailer and the customer will be advised of the Panel's decision and any award or action recommended by the Panel will be honoured by the member of R.E.T.R.A. within 15 days, provided that the customer also fully accepts the recommendations of the Panel.

16.8   The Secretary of R.E.T.R.A. will prepare an annual report on the disputes referred to the Panel. Copies of the report will be submitted to the R.E.T.R.A. Council and to the Office of Fair Trading.

17 Use of Courts

The customer can of course at any stage pursue his normal legal rights and seek redress from the County Courts in England and Wales or the Sheriff Court in Scotland. The simple arbitration procedure now available in the County Courts in England and Wales may be suitable for settling the dispute if the customer is not satisfied with the award or action recommended by the R.E.T.R.A. Conciliation Panel. R.E.T.R.A. will advise him of the availability of the courts to resolve the complaint.

18 Monitoring

The Association will monitor the compliance of its members with the Code of Practice and discuss with a member any persistent breach of any provisions. Each year details of cases dealt with will be made available to the Office of Fair Trading.

ADDRESSES OF TRADE ASSOCIATIONS SPONSORING CODES AGREED WITH THE O.F.T.

Caravans

British Holiday and Home Parks Association Ltd.,
Chichester House,
31 Park Road,
Gloucester GL1 lHL.

National Caravan Council,
Catherine House,
Victoria Road,
Aldershot,
Hants GU11 1SS.

Cars

Retail Motor Industry Federation Ltd.,
201 Great Portland Street,
London W1N 6AB.

Society of Motor Manufacturers and Traders Limited,
Forbes House,
Halkin Street,
London SW1X 7DS.

Scottish Motor Trade Association Ltd.,
3 Palmerston Place,
Edinburgh EH12 5AQ.

The Vehicle Builders & Repairers Association,
Belmont House,
102 Finkle Lane,
Gildersome,
Leeds LS27 7TW.

Credit

Finance Houses Association,
18 Upper Grosvenor Street,
London W1X 9PB.

The Consumer Credit Trade Association,
Tennyson House,
159/163 Great Portland Street,
London W1N 5FD.

The Consumer Credit Association of the United Kingdom,
Queen's House,
Queen's Road,
Chester CH1 3BQ.

The National Consumer Credit Federation,
98/100 Holme Lane,
Sheffield S6 4JW.

London Personal Finance Association,
"Hill Top",
Bargers Hill,
Wooburn Common,
High Wycombe HP10 0JP.

Direct Marketing

Association of Mail Order Publishers Ltd.,
1 New Burlington Street,
London W1X 1FD.

British Direct Marketing Association,
Grosvenor Gardens House,
35 Grosvenor Gardens,
London SW1W 0BS.

Direct Selling

The Direct Selling Association Ltd.,
29 Floral Street,
London WC2E 9DB.

Double Glazing

Glass and Glazing Federation,
44–48 Borough High Street,
London SE1 1XB.

Dry Cleaners and Laundries

Textile Services Association Ltd.,
7 Churchill Court,
58 Station Road,
North Harrow,
Middlesex HA2 7SA.

Electrical Goods

The Association of Manufacturers of Domestic Electrical Appliances,
Leicester House,
8 Leicester Street,
London WC2H 7BN.

The Radio, Electrical and Television Retailers' Association (RETRA) Ltd.,
RETRA House,
St John's Terrace,
1 Ampthill Street,
Bedford MK42 9EY.

Funerals

The National Association of Funeral Directors,
618 Warwick Road,
Solihull,
West Midlands B91 1AA.

Furniture

Branded Furniture Society,
Blakemere,
Frieston,
Grantham,
Lincs NG32 3BY.

British Furniture Manufacturers Federation,
30 Harcourt Street,
London W1H 2AA.

British Shops & Stores Association,
Middleton House,
2 Main Road,
Middleton Cheney,
Banbury,
Oxon OX17 2TN.

National Bed Federation Ltd.,
251 Brompton Road,
London SW3 2EZ.

Mail Order

The Mail Order Traders' Association of Great Britain,
25 Castle Street,
Liverpool L2 4TD.

Motor Cycles

Motor Cycle Association of Great Britain Ltd.,
Starley House,
Eaton Road,
Coventry CV1 2FH.

Scottish Motor Trade Association Ltd.,
3 Palmerston Place,
Edinburgh EH12 5AQ.

Retail Motor Industry Federation Ltd.,
201 Great Portland Street,
London W1N 6AB.

Photography

The National Pharmaceutical Association,
Mallinson House,
40–42 St Peter's Street,
St Albans,
Herts AL1 3NP.

The Association of Photographic Laboratories,
9 Warwick Court,
Grays Inn,
London WC1R 5DJ.

The British Institute of Professional Photography,
2 Amwell End,
Ware,
Herts SG12 9HN.

Master Photographers Association (MPA),
Hallmark House,
97 East Street,
Epsom,
Surrey KT17 1EA.

The Association of British Manufacturers of Photographic, Cine
and Audio-Visual Equipment (BPEG),
1 West Ruislip Station,
West Ruislip,
Middlesex HA4 7DW.

Professional Photographic Laboratories Association (PPLA),
9 Dean Avenue,
Timperley,
Altrincham WA15 7DR.

The British Photographic Association,
Carolyn House,
22–26 Dingwall Road,
Croydon,
Surrey CR0 9XF.

The British Photographic Importers' Association,
Carolyn House,
22–24 Dingwall Road,
Croydon,
Surrey CR0 9XF.

Shoes

The Footwear Distributor's Federation,
Bedford House,
69/70 Fulham High Street,
London SW6 3JW.

The National Association of Multiple Shoe Repairers,
60 Wickham Hill,
Hurstpierpoint,
Hassocks,
Sussex BN6 9NP.

The Society of Master Shoe Repairers,
St Crispin's House,
Station Road,
Desborough,
Kettering,
Northants NN14 2SA.

Travel

Association of British Travel Agents,
55–57 Newham Street,
London W1P 4AH.

THE INSURANCE OMBUDSMAN'S BUREAU

THE INSURANCE OMBUDSMAN'S TERMS OF REFERENCE

1. The Ombudsman shall (subject to the supervision of the Board and of the Council) have the power to incure expenditure in accordance with his current financial budget as approved by the board. The Ombudsman shall exercise no power of the Bureau expressly assigned to the Board or the Council or any other person pursuant to the Articles of Association ("the Articles").

2. (a) Subject to clauses 4 and 5 hereof, the Ombudsman shall receive references in relation to complaints, disputes and claims made in connection with or arising out of policies of insurance effected or proposed to be effected with Members of the Bureau or ancillary Members appointed in accordance with the Articles.

   (b) Subject to clauses 4 and 5 hereof, the Ombudsman shall facilitate the satisfaction, settlement or withdrawal of the complaints, disputes or claims comprised in such references by the making of awards or by such other means as seem expedient.

   (c) Subject to clauses 4 and 5 hereof, the Ombudsman may act as counsellor, conciliator, adjudicator or arbitrator in relation to any such reference as is specified in paragraph (a) of this clause and (subject to the general or specific consent of the Council) may appoint (on such terms as to remuneration or otherwise as he shall think fit) any other person who seems to him to be suitably qualified (whether as a professional adviser or as an expert) to act as aforesaid in conjunction with him.

   (d) The Ombudsman may, in relation to any complaint, dispute or claim comprised in a reference, make an award against any Member named in such reference and in making any award he shall have regard to the terms of the contract, and act in conformity with any applicable rule of law or relevant judicial authority, with general principles of good insurance or marketing practice, with these Terms or Reference, with the Statements of Insurance Practice and Codes of Practice issued from time to time by the Association of British Insurers and with the Rules made from time to time by the board of directors of

Lautro Limited but shall not otherwise be bound by any previous decision made by him or by any other Ombudsman or by any predecessor in any such office. In determining what are the principles of good insurance or marketing practice he should where he considers it appropriate consult within the industry.

(e) Such an award shall comprise a money sum and shall be binding upon the Member against which it is made:

   (i) if it is made in respect of a reference the subject of which is a policy of insurance of Permanent Health business under which the basic benefits insured at the date of the policy do not exceed £10,000 per annum; or

   (ii) if it is made in any other case and does not exceed £100,000. In both cases the limits may be altered from time to time by ordinary resolution of the Bureau in general meeting.

(f) Where such an award exceeds the relative monetary limit prescribed by paragraph (e) above, it shall not be binding upon the Member against which it is made but shall constitute the Ombudsman's recommendation to that member of an equitable solution to the complaint, dispute or claim comprised in the reference.

(g) The Ombudsman may, in relation to any complaint, dispute or claim comprised in a reference (but without prejudice to the exercise of the powers conferred by paragraph (d) of this clause) make such recommendations or representations to the persons named in the reference or to the Council as he shall think fit.

3. The Ombudsman shall:

   (a) in relation to references entertained by him of the kind specified in clause 2(a) hereof have the power to charge such fees to all or any of the persons named therein as the Council shall from time to time prescribe; provided that the Ombudsman shall have power, if in his absolute discretion he considers it expedient or appropriate, to remit the payment of any fee or to return any fee paid as aforesaid;

   (b) have the power to request the provision, within a reasonable period of time, of information concerning the subject matter of any such reference as aforesaid from any Member named therein which is, or is alleged to be, in possession of such information; provided that where such Member admits possession of the said information but refuses or fails to supply it within a reasonable period of time the Ombudsman shall forthwith give particulars of such request and refusal to the Council with copies for information to the Board;

   (c) be available to attend each meeting or part of a meeting of the

Council as required by the Council and thereat to make such reports and give such information and assistance to the Council as the Council shall from time to time direct and, on giving reasonable notice to the Council, have the power to attend any meeting or part of a meeting of the Council in order to address the Council on a matter specified in that notice, and have regard to these Terms of Reference and to any assistance and guidance of a general nature offered or given by the Council;

(d) without prejudice to paragraph (c) of this clause, submit to each Council Member not less than fourteen days before each Annual Meeting of the Council a copy of his Report, for a period co-extensive with the accounting reference period (as defined in Section 224 of the Companies Act 1985) of the Bureau last ended, such Report to be in such form and to contain such information and recommendations on such subjects relative to the affairs and business of the Bureau during such period, as the Council shall from time to time direct and upon each occasion when he submits copies of his Report to Council Members, submit additional copies of the same to each Member and to each member of the board; and

(e) subject to the approval of the Board and the Council and to these Terms of Reference, have the power to delegate to a deputy all or any of the powers and duties assigned to an Ombudsman in clause 2 and paragraphs (a) and (b) of this clause and shall exercise such power if directed to do so by the Council with the approval of the Board.

4. Without prejudice to clause 5 hereof, the Ombudsman shall not entertain any reference of the kind specified in clause 2(a) hereof unless he is satisfied that:

(a) the subject matter of the reference has been considered by the senior management of any Member named in the reference, but the observations made, or any conditions of settlement or satisfaction offered, by that Member to any other person named in that reference have proved unacceptable to that person;

(b) where any party to the complaint, dispute or claim comprised in the reference has instituted proceedings in any court of law or has made a reference to arbitration in relation thereto, the proceedings have been discontinued or the reference to arbitration withdrawn prior to final judgment or award;

(c) the reference contains no subject matter any part of which was comprised in any previous reference made to any Ombudsman appointed in accordance with Article 65 of the Articles (provided that with the leave of the Council the Ombudsman may entertain a reference if he is satisfied that new evidence is now available in relation to the reference which was not available at the time the previous reference was entertained); and

(d) the reference is received by him not later than six months or such later time as may be agreed by the Member after the date of observations or offer referred to in paragraph (a) of this clause.

5. Without prejudice to clause 4 hereof, the Ombudsman is not empowered to entertain or comment upon any reference of the kind specified in clause 2(a) hereof which:

(a) is made other than by the person who effected the policy which is the subject of the reference or by some person who has acquired (not for value) the legal title thereto;

(b) relates to a policy of insurance other than one effected by or on behalf of or for the benefit of natural persons (not being partnerships or unincorporated persons consisting of or including natural persons);

(c) relates to a policy of insurance in respect of which the performance by the Member of any of his obligations under the contract evidenced thereby would constitute the carrying on by the Member of insurance business of any class other than in the United Kingdom, the Isle of Man or Channel Islands (as defined in the Articles);

(d) is made in respect of ordinary long term insurance business (as defined in the Insurance Companies Act 1982) of a Member to the extent that such reference concerns those actuarial standards, tables and principles which that Member applies to its ordinary long term insurance business including in particular (but without being limited to) the method of calculation of surrender value and paid up policy values, and bonus system and bonus rate applicable to the policy in question; provided that this paragraph shall not preclude any reference concerning the application of any of the Rules made from time to time by the board of directors of Lautro Limited; or

(e) relates to any policy of insurance, to the extent that such reference concerns any question or disputes between the person making the reference and any person other than the Member relative to which the reference is made, as to title to the proceeds of the policy which is the subject of the reference.

INDEX

A.B.T.A.,
  codes of conduct, 179–184, 393–405
ACQUISITION OF TITLE. *See also* TITLE.
  estoppel, by 10, 11–12
  voidable title, where, 10, 16–17
ADMINISTRATIVE CONTROL, 265 *et seq.*
ADVERTISING,
  Advertising Standards Authority, 288
  business, 280–281
  cars,
    code of practice, 389–390
  compensation, 259–260
  consumer credit and, 317–320
  electrical goods,
    code of practice, 408
  mail order, 278–280
  misleading, 286 *et seq.*
    EC Directive, 287–288
    exclusions, 291
    injunctions, in respect of, 289–291
    meaning of, 289, 290
  self-regulation, 288
  trade descriptions, and, 207–208
  travel agents, by,
    code of conduct, 400–401
  regulations,
    consumer credit law, 318–319
AGENT,
  mercantile. *See* MERCANTILE AGENT.
ARBITRATION, 184–186
  agreement for,
    unfair terms, whether, 129
  codes of practice, under, 153
  consumer agreements, 185–186
  County Court, 187–189
  motor industry code of practice,
    391–392
  travel services,
    code of conduct, 400

BARGAIN OFFERS, 230–231
BRITISH STANDARDS INSTITUTE, 4
BUSINESS,
  "consumer credit business,"
    meaning, 314
  consumer credit controls, 313 *et seq.*
  licensing for consumer credit, 313–316
  meaning of,
    consumer credit, in, 314

BUSINESS—*cont.*
  meaning of—*cont.*
    exemption clauses, in, 127, 130–131
    sales of goods, in, 44–45
    trade descriptions law, under,
     197–198
  unfair traders, 283

CARAVANS,
  code of practice, 159–160
  trade associations, 415
CARS,
  accessories,
    code of practice, 386–387
  advertising,
    code of practice, 389–390
  body repairs, 162–163
  breach of statutory duty, 263
  car dealer,
    negligence, liability in, 74
  codes of practice, 160–163, 383–393
    monitoring of, 391
  complaints, 162
    arbitration, 391–392
    handling of,
     code of practice, 390–391
  defective,
    consumer credit remedies, 341–342
  guarantees of manufacturer,
    code of practice, 384–385
  loan for, consumer credit law, 341–342
  manufacturers' warranties, 160
    code of practice, 384–385
  mechanical breakdown insurance,
    code of practice, 163
  merchantability of,
    guarantee, effect of, 48–49
    minor defects, 47–48
    second-hand, 49–50
  new, 160
    code of practice, 383–384
    trade descriptions, 213–214
  odometer offences, 206–212
    disclaimers, effect of, 209–211
    due diligence defence, 223
  petrol,
    code of practice, 386–387
  repairs,
    code of practice, 387–389

CARS—*cont.*
  replacement parts,
    code of practice, 386–387
  second-hand,
    merchantability of, 49–50
  servicing, 161
    code of practice, 387–389
  trade associations addresses, 415
  used, 160–161
    code of practice, 385–386
CAVEAT EMPTOR, 42–43
CITIZEN'S ADVICE BUREAU, 147, 152
  complaint to, 267
CODES OF PRACTICE, 148 *et seq.*
  A.B.T.A., 179–184, 393–405
  addresses of associations, 415–420
  advantages of, 149–150
  arbitration, 153
  caravans, 159–160
    letting of, 159
    selling and siting of, 159–160
  cars, 160–164. *See also* CARS.
    monitoring of, 162
  conciliation procedures, 152–153
  credit, 163–164
  direct marketing, 164–166
    definition of, 165
    mail order selling and, 165
  direct selling, 166–167
  double glazing, 167–168
  dry cleaners, 168–169
  electrical goods, 169–171, 405–413
    monitoring of, 413
  electricity board, 171–172
  enforcement, 150–152
  examples, 148–149
  funerals, 172–173
  furniture, 173–174
  launderers, 168–169
  leaflets on, 154
  mail order, 174–175. *See also* direct
    marketing, *above.*
  mechanical breakdown insurance,
    163–164
  Motor Industry Code, 160–164,
    383–393. *See also* CARS.
    odometers, concerning, 206–212
  motorcycles, 175
  non-compliance sanctions, 150–152
  photography, 175–177
  Post Office, 177
  prices, 239–240
  publicity, 153–154
  R.E.T.R.A., 405–413
  sanctions for non-compliance, 150–152
  shoes, 177–179
  travel, 179–184
COMPENSATION, 257 *et seq. See also*
  DAMAGES.
  assessment, 260–261

COMPENSATION—*cont.*
  breach of contract, for, 111–115
  civil rights,
    interrelation with, 261–262
  enforceability of order, 261
  how to apply for, 261
  maximum, 258–259
  means of defendant, 261
  type of loss, 259–260
CONCILIATION SERVICES,
  codes of practice, 152
  electrical goods,
    code of practice, 412–413
  travel services,
    code of conduct, 400
CONDITIONAL SALE, 85. *See also*
  CONSUMER CREDIT.
CONSUMER,
  arbitration agreements, 185
  credit file on,
    duties of disclosure, 365–368
  criminal law, and, 193 *et seq.*
  data protection, 368
  "deals as consumer,"
    definition, 131–135
  healt and safety,
    EEC provisions, 371
  meaning, 1, 4, 74, 296–297
  protection legislation. *See* CONSUMER
    PROTECTION LEGISLATION.
  safety. *See* CONSUMER SAFETY; GOODS,
    dangerous, unsafe.
    Green Paper, 243–244
    regulations, 252–253
  safety legislation, 244–245. *See also*
    GOODS, unsafe; CONSUMER
    PROTECTION LEGISLATION.
    general requirement, 249–251
CONSUMER ADVICE CENTRE, 147, 152
CONSUMER COMPLAINTS, 267, 268–269.
  See also CONSUMER PROTECTION
  ADVISORY COMMITTEE.
  analysis of, 155–158
CONSUMER LAW,
  history, 1–2
CONSUMER CREDIT, 295 *et seq.*
  administrative sanctions, 298
  advertisements, 28, 317–320
    definitions, 318
    false, 318
    regulations, 318–319
    scope of control, 317–318
  agreements, 301 *et seq.*
    additional information, 328–329
    budget accounts, 303
    cancellation, 327, 332–338
      copy provisions, 334–335
      duty to return goods, 337–338
      effect of, 336
      effected, 335

CONSUMER CREDIT—*cont.*
  agreements—*cont.*
    cancellation—*cont.*
      exemptions, 335
        part-exchange allowance, 338
        time limit, 335
    copies, 326–328
    credit token, 347–348
    exempt, 306–310
    debtor-creditor, 303–304
    debtor-creditor-supplier, 303–304
    fixed sum credit, 303
    formalities of, 325–326
    improperly executed, 351–352
    meaning, 302
    modification, 352–353
    non-commercial, 305
    overdrafts, 303
    partially-regulated, 305–306
    regulated, 301–305
    related documents and, 328
    repudiation, 332
    rescission, 332
    running-account, 303
    small, 305–306
    termination, 338–340
      debtor, by, 354
    types of, 301–302
    unsigned, 351
    withdrawal from, 331–332
  associate,
    meaning, 299
  background, 295–296
  budget accounts, 303
  business activities, 313 *et seq.*
  cancellable agreements, 333–334. *See also under* agreements, *above.*
  cancellation regulations and, 81, 332–333
  canvassing, 320–321
    circulars to minors, 321
    previous requests, 320
  check trading, 347
  conditional sale agreements, 302
    appropriation of payments, 361
    termination, 339–340
    meaning, 299
    snatch-back provisions, 358–359
  consumer, definition of, 296
    EEC draft Directive, 373
  consumer hire agreements, 304–305
    termination of, 340
  control of business activities, 313 *et seq.*
  credit bargains,
    extortionate, 361–363
  credit card agreements, 302
  credit cards, 296, 347 *et seq.*
    date of issue, relevance of, 344
    defective goods bought with, 343
    fraud, 349–350

CONSUMER CREDIT—*cont.*
  credit cards—*cont.*
    loss of, 347–350
  credit files, 365–368
  credit reference agency, 365. *See also* CREDIT REFERENCE AGENCY.
  credit sale agreements, 302
  credit tokens, 347 *et seq.*
    acceptance by debtor, 348
    agreements, 347–348
      cancellation of, 349
    debtor's liability, 348–349
    definition, 347
    loss adjustment rules, 339
    loss of, 347–350
    unauthorised use, 348–349
    unsolicited, 347
  criminal sanctions, 194, 298
  Crowther Report, 9–10, 267, 295
  defective goods, 341 *et seq.*
    cash sale, where, 341–345
    conditional sale, 345
    connected lender, where, 341–345
    credit card purchase, 343
    credit sale, 345
    hire-purchase, 345–346
    hired, where, 346
    unconnected lender, where, 341
  deposit/current account agreements, exempt, 311
  duty to disclose credit information, 366
  early payment, 354–356
    statutory formula, 355–356
  enforcement orders, 352–353
  exempt agreements, 297, 306–310
  extortionate credit bargains, 361–363
  false advertisements, 318
  guarantees of goods exempt, 311
  hire-purchase agreement, 302
    "credit," meaning of, 302
    meaning, 299
    termination of, 339–340
  "individual," meaning of, 297
  individual agreements, 323 *et seq.*
    copies, 326–328
      form and content of, 328
    formalities of, 325–326
    pre-contractual information, 324
    related documents and, 328
    sanctions, 323
  information on whereabouts of goods, 329
  insurance contracts exempt, 311
  land mortgage loan agreements, 302
    pre-contract formalities, 324–325
  legislation, commencement of, 297
  licensing, 4, 298, 313–316
    Director General's role, 315–316
    duration of, 315
    nature of, 315

CONSUMER CREDIT—*cont.*
linked transactions, 310–311
notice of default, 356–357
overdraft agreements, 302, 303
canvassing for, 320–321
personal loan agreements, 302
pledges, 302
protected goods, 358–359
quotations, 319–320
scope, 319
trader's obligations, 319
rebates, 354
regulated agreements,
commencement of legislation, 344
credit cards, and, 343
relative,
meaning, 299
repossession of goods, 344
effect of, 357
snatch-back provisions, 358–359
"restricted-use,"
meaning, 299–300
sanctions, 299
snatch-back provisions, 358–359
surety, meaning of, 297
termination, 338–340
time orders, 356
total charge for credit, 302, 308–310
annual percentage rate, 309–310
calculation of, 354–356
items excluded, 308–309
rebates and, 354
unexecuted agreements, 327
unincorporated traders, 297
unlicensed traders, 316
"unrestricted-use,"
meaning, 299–300
CONSUMER PROTECTION AGENCIES, 3 *et
seq.*
government departments, as, 3
CONSUMER PROTECTION ADVISORY
COMMITTEE, 269
adverse trade practices role, 269 *et seq.*
speed of procedure, 272–273. *See also*
CONSUMER TRADE PRACTICE.
order, the, 274 *et seq.*
penalties and enforcement, 271–272
references, to,
business advertisements, 280–281
mail order transactions, 278–280
procedure, 270–271
VAT exclusive prices, 281–282
void exemption clauses, 273–276
written statements of rights, 273–274,
276–277
restrictions on statements, 273–278
CONSUMER PROTECTION LEGISLATION,
civil liability, 63 *et seq. See also*
PRODUCT LIABILITY.
criminal liability, 245 *et seq.*

CONSUMER PROTECTION LEGISLATION—
cont.
criminal liability—*cont.*
enforcement, 254
enforcement notices, 253
general safety requirement, 249
goods, definition of, 248
notices, 253–254
penalties, 254
safe, definition of, 247
supply, definition of, 248
EEC Treaty, 369–370
consumer protection programmes,
371–372
prices, 219–220
safety regulations, 252–253
EEC Draft Directive, 376–378
emergency procedures, 252
safety standards, 250–251
CONSUMER SAFETY. *See also* CONSUMER,
safety legislation; CONSUMER
PROTECTION LEGISLATION.
Consultative Document, 243–244
CONSUMER TRADE PRACTICE, 270. *See
also* CONSUMER PROTECTION
ADVISORY COMMITTEE.
adverse, 270 *et seq.*
complaints procedure, 270–271
speed of, 272–273
penalties and enforcement, 271–272
persistently unfair traders, 282 *et seq.*
business advertisements, 280–281
definition, 270
exchange of goods, 277
exemption clauses, 273, 274–276
mail order transactions, 278–280
restrictions on statements, 273
VAT-exclusive prices, 281–282
written statements, 273–274,
276–277
CONSUMERS' ASSOCIATION, 5
CONTRACT,
breach of,
misrepresentation, and, 99
refund of money, 101 *et seq.*
remedies for, 99 *et seq.*
supplier, by, 79
cancellation regulations, 81–84
agreements caught, 81–82
consumer credit and, 81, 332–333
exceptions, 82–83
notice, 83
time limits, 83
collateral,
guarantee, as, 60
misrepresentation and, 30
consumer credit agreements. *See*
CONSU CREDIT, agreements.
contractual terms, 27
contra proferentem rule, 123–124

CONTRACT—*cont.*
 disclaimers,
  trade descriptions law, and, 208–212.
   See also DISCLAIMERS.
 exchange, of, 24, 40, 41
 exemption clause in, 99, 117 *et seq. See
   also* unfair terms, *below.*
  construction of, 125
  contra proferentem rule, 123–124
  criticism, 118
  death/personal injury, for, 243
  dry cleaners, 168–169
  examples, 117
  fundamental breach and, 125
  inconsistent oral promise overrides,
   124
  incorporation of, 119–123
  judicial control of, 118–125
  justification for, 117–118
  launderers, 168–169
  Law Commission and, 118, 126,
   131
  limitation clause, as, 125, 142
  misrepresentation overrides,
   124–125
  onerous conditions, 121–122
  privity of contract and, 123
  reasonableness test, 139–142
  referred to C.P.A.C., 264–266
  signature, where, 119
  strict construction of contract,
   123–124
 frustration of, 92
 fundamental breach, 125
 guarantees,
  unfair term, whether, 137–138
 hire, of, 40, 41, 57
 holidays. *See also* TRAVEL AGENTS.
  damages for breach, 114–115
 indemnity,
  unfair term, whether, 137–138
 insurance, of, 127–128
 late performance of, 91–92
  repudiation for, 92
 limitation clause, 125, 142
 liquidated damages clause,
  unfair term, whether, 129
 misrepresentation. *See*
   MISREPRESENTATION.
 onerous conditions, 121–123
 performance of,
  late, 91–92
 price in, 92–93
 privity of, 43–44, 123, 129
 quotation,
  consumer credit law, 319–320
 reasonableness test, 139–142
 repudiation of, 28, 79 *et seq.*
 revocation,
  acceptance, prior to, 351

CONTRACT—*cont.*
 sale of goods, for, 41. *See also* SALE OF
   GOODS.
  late performance, 91–92
  unsatisfactory performance, 90–91
 services, for,
  specific performance inappropriate,
   99–100
 severable, where, 104
 specific performance, 99–100
 standard form, 54, 117
 strict construction of, 123–124
 supply of, 55–57
  right to reject goods, 109
  unfair terms, 136–137
 terms, 35–36, 101–103
  innominate, 36
  unfair. *See under* unfair terms, *below.*
  warranty and, 36, 102
 unfair terms, 61, 117, 126–145. *See
   also* exemption clauses, *above.*
  arbitration agreement, as, 129
  bargaining power, 141, 143
  business liability, 127
  case law, 142–145
  consumer, dealing as, 132–135
  EC Draft Directive, 372–376
  guarantee, whether, 137–138
  implied terms, 135–137
  indemnity, whether, 137
  insurance contracts exempt, 127
  land, concerning, exempt, 127
  legislation, scope of, 126
  limitation clause, as, 142
  liquidated damages clause, and, 129
  misrepresentation and, 138–139
  negligence, defined, 129–130
  private sales, 136
  privity of contract, and, 129
  relevant factors, 143
  reasonableness test, 139–144
  supply contracts, 136–137
 voidable,
  misrepresentation, for, 351
 voidable or void, 16–17
 warranty, 35
 work and materials, for, 24, 40, 41,
   55–57
COSTS,
 enforcement proceedings, in, 187
COUNTY COURT,
 arbitration in, 187–189
 enforcement proceedings, 186–187
CREDIT,
 code of practice, 163–164
 trade associations, 416
CREDIT-BROKER, 55
 code of practice, 164
CREDIT CARDS. *See under* CONSUMER
   CREDIT.

CREDIT FILE, 365–368. *See also* CREDIT
REFERENCE AGENCY.
CREDIT REFERENCE AGENCY,
correction of information, 367
duty to disclose information, 366
duty to disclose name/address, 365–366
CREDIT TOKENS. *See under* CONSUMER
CREDIT.
CRIMINAL OFFENCES, 193 *et seq.*, 257 *et
seq.*
accessories,
unfair trading, to, 286
adverse trade practices, 269–282
breach of statutory duty, 262–264
compensation for. *See* COMPENSATION.
consumer credit,
canvassing, 320–321
unlicensed trading, 316
criminal courts, powers of, 258–262
dangerous goods, 254
defences, 254
defences,
dangerous goods, 254
trade descriptions law, in. *See under*
TRADE DESCRIPTIONS.
multiple prosecutions,
trade descriptions law, under, 228
powers of criminal courts, 258–262
private prosecution,
trade descriptions law, under, 227
statutory duty,
breach of, 262–264
supplier, by, 61
time limit for prosecution,
trade descriptions law, under, 227
trade descriptions. *See* TRADE
DESCRIPTIONS.
unfair trading, 284–285
unlicensed trading, 316
unsolicited goods, for, 80–81
vicarious liability,
trade descriptions law, 223

DAMAGES,
breach of contract, for, 111–115
builders, from, 115
condition, breach of, for, 111
cost of repair, 77
dry cleaners, from, 115
extent of loss, 111
general principles, 112
hire-purchase contracts, in, 114
holiday contracts, 114–115
limitation clauses, 142
mental distress, for, 113–114
mitigation of, 112
negligence, 77
non-delivery of goods, for, 112–113
remoteness, 111

DAMAGES—*cont.*
set-off, 91
warranty, breach of, for, 113
DATA PROTECTION, 368
DEATH,
compensation for, 243
DEBTORS, 351 *et seq.*
appropriation of payments,
360–361
compensation for prejudice, 352
early payment by, 354–355
statutory formula, 355–356
enforcement order, 352–353
rebate for, 354
snatch-back provisions, 358–360
special cases, 353–354
time orders, 356–357
DEPARTMENT OF TRADE AND INDUSTRY,
consumer protection role, 3
DESCRIPTION. *See* SALE OF GOODS;
TRADE DESCRIPTIONS.
DIRECT MARKETING,
associations, 416
code of practice, 164–166
DIRECT SALES,
association, 416
code of practice, 166–167
DIRECTOR GENERAL OF FAIR TRADING,
consumer credit licensing,
role in, 315–316
powers and duties of, 3–4
DISCLAIMERS, 208 *et seq.*
cars,
code of practice, 212
defences, 212
documents, in, 210–211
effect of, 208–209
notices, in, 211
oral, 210
DISPOSITION. *See* SALE.
DOUBLE GLAZING,
code of practice, 167–168
federation, 417
DRY CLEANERS,
association, 417
code of practice, 168–169

EEC, 369 *et seq.*
advertising, misleading, Directive,
287–288
consumer protection programme, 3,
371–372
Draft Directives,
general product safety, 376–378
suppliers of services, 378–381
unfair contract terms, 372–376
internal market, 370–371
misleading advertising,
Directive, 287–288

ELECTRICAL GOODS,
associations, 417
code of practice, 169–171, 405–413
monitoring of, 413
ELECTRICITY BOARD,
code of practice, 171–172
ENFORCEMENT, 147 *et seq.*
adverse trade practices, 271–272
arbitration. *See* ARBITRATION.
codes of practice. *See* CODES OF
PRACTICE.
consumer protection laws, of, 254
costs, 187
county court proceedings, 186–189
trade descriptions law, of, 226–227
weights and measures, inspectors,
duties of, 226–227
ESTIMATE, 93
ESTOPPEL, 10, 11–12
EVIDENCE,
circumstantial, 75
negligence actions, in, 76–77
EXCHANGE OF GOODS, 277
contract of, 27, 40, 41
EXEMPTION CLAUSES. *See under*
CONTRACT.
EXTORTIONATE CREDIT BARGAINS. *See*
CONSUMER CREDIT, *passim*

FAIR TRADING, 267 *et seq.*
Director General, 267. *See also*
DIRECTOR GENERAL OF FAIR
TRADING.
sanctions, 194. *See also* UNFAIR
TRADERS.
FEDERATION OF CONSUMER GROUPS, 5
FILM PROCESSING,
code of practice, 176–177
FITNESS FOR PURPOSE. *See* SALE OF
GOODS.
FOOD,
quality control, 193
FUNERALS,
association, 417
code of practice, 172–173
FURNITURE,
associations, 417
code of practice, 173–174

GOODS. *See also* SALE OF GOODS.
absence of title in, 108–109
acceptance of, 104–109
intimation of, 105
accidental damage to, 84–89
ascertained, 87, 100
cancellation of contracts, 81–84
consumer credit transactions,
defective goods, 341 *et seq.*

GOODS—*cont.*
damage to,
accidental, 84–89
damaged,
seller's risk, where, 89
dangerous, 63 *et seq. See also*
under unsafe, *below;* CONSUMER,
safety legislation; CONSUMER
PROTECTION LEGISLATION;
PRODUCT LIABILITY.
agricultural, exclusion, 66–67
general safety requirement, 249
notice to warn, 253–254
offence, 249–250
prohibited, 244, 253
suspension notices, 245, 253
defective. *See also* SALE OF GOODS,
merchantable quality.
consumer credit transactions, 341 *et
seq.*
manufacturers' guarantees, 59–62
meaning of in tort, 67–69
right to reject, 103
delivery of unordered, 79–81
description of. *See* SALE OF GOODS;
TRADE DESCRIPTIONS.
destruction of,
accidental, 84–89
total, 88–89
duty to return,
cancellation of credit agreement,
337–338
exchange of. *See* EXCHANGE.
false description of, 200–202
information on whereabouts,
consumer credit law, in, 329
loss or damage pre-delivery, 84–89
negligent damage to, 106
perished, 88–89
price of, 92–93, 197
VAT-exclusive, 281–282
prohibition notices, 244–253
protected,
snatch-back provisions, 358–359
rejection of, 103–110
part rejection, 110–111
repair/replacement rights, 101
repossession of, 356–357
no default notice, where, 357
snatch-back provisions, 358–359
retention of, 106–108
reasonable time, 106–107
risk of loss, 84–89
safe,
definition, 246–247
sale of. *See* SALE OF GOODS.
second hand, 49–50
self-service, 37–38
specific,
transfer of property in, 85–86

GOODS—*cont.*
  trade descriptions and, 195 *et seq. See*
      TRADE DESCRIPTIONS.
  transfer of property in, 84–85
  unascertained,
      definition, 84–85
      perishing of, 89
      transfer of property in, 87–88
  unordered, 79–81
  unsafe, 243 *et seq. See also*
      under dangerous, *above*;
      CONSUMER, safety legislation;
      CONSUMER PROTECITON
      LEGISLATION.
  unsolicited, 79–81, 82
      civil remedies, 80
      criminal remedies, 80–81
GREEN FORM SCHEME,
  civil proceedings, in, 187
GUARANTEE,
  collateral contract, as, 60
  "consumer guarantee", proposal for,
      62
  exemption clauses in, 137–138, 273–274
  extended, problems of, 62
  manufacturers', 59, 60–62
  reform proposals, 61–62
  statutory provisions, 61
  transferable, whether, 62
  unmerchantable goods, and, 48–49

HIRE, 57. *See also* CONTRACT; CONSUMER
      CREDIT, *passim.*
HIRE PURCHASE, 22. *See also* CONSUMER
      CREDIT *passim.*
  agreements, 302
  damages under, 114
  dangerous goods,
      safety legislation, 248
  description of goods, 40
  early payment advisable, 345
  implied title, 24
  legislation, history of, 296
  meaning,
      consumer credit law, in, 299
  repossession,
      protection from, 358–360
  termination of agreement, 339–340
  unfair terms, 136
HOME OFFICE,
  consumer protection role, 3

IMPROVEMENTS AND REPAIRS, 24–25,
      101
INDEMNITY,
  exemption clause in, 137–138
INSURANCE,
  Ombudsman, 421 *et seq.*

LAND,
  mortgages,
      regulated agreements, where,
          324–325
  repossession of, 358
LAUNDERERS,
  association, 417
  code of practice, 168–169
LAW COMMISSION,
  defective goods, report on, 103
  exemption clauses,
      report on, 117, 118, 126, 181–182
  right to reject goods,
      report on, 103, 109
LEGAL AID,
  civil proceedings, in, 186–187
LICENSING,
  consumer credit, for. *See under*
      CONSUMER CREDIT.
LOCAL AUTHORITIES,
  consumer advice role, 4–5
  consumer protection department, 147
  trading standards officer,
      complaint to, 267
      conciliation, role in, 152
      enforcement by, 227

MAIL ORDER,
  associations, 418
  codes of practice, 174–175
  prepayment for goods, 278–280
  property in goods, 88
MANUFACTURERS,
  guarantees, 59, 60–62. *See also*
      GUARANTEES.
      codes of practice, 61, 62
      statutory provisions, 61
  liability of, 7, 59 *et seq.*
      EEC, in, 63
      law reform proposals, 61–62
      negligence, in, 73–77
      United States, in, 2
  negligence, liability in, 73–77
  product liability, 63 *et seq.*
  strict liability and, 76
MARKET OVERT,
  sale in, 10, 14–16
MERCANTILE AGENT,
  disposition by, 10, 12–14
MERCHANTABLE QUALITY. *See under*
      SALE OF GOODS.
MISLEADING ADVERTISEMENTS, 286 *et*
      seq. See also ADVERTISING.
MISREPRESENTATION, 27, 29–30
  breach of contract, and, 99
  consumer credit, in,
      defective goods, where, 342
  collateral contract, where, 30
  contract voidable for, 351

MISREPRESENTATION—*cont.*
  damages for, 30
  defective goods, where,
    consumer credit law, in, 342
  description of goods, 36–40
  exclusion clauses, 99, 138–139
    overrides effect of, 124–125
  fact or opinion, of, 30
  fraudulent, 16
    remedies for, 96
  innocent, 96, 99
  mere puff, or, 28
  negligent,
    remedies for, 96–97
  remedies for, 95–99
  unfair terms law, and, 138–139
  voidable contract and, 16
MITIGATION, 112
MOLONY REPORT, 1, 2
MOTORCYCLES,
  associations, 418
  code of practice, 175
MOTOR VEHICLE,
  disposition on hire-purchase, 10, 20–22.
    See also CARS.

NATIONAL CONSUMER COUNCIL,
  powers of, 4
  "Service Please" report, 90
NEGLIGENCE,
  causation, proof of, 75, 77
  duty of care, 32
  defectiveness of product,
    need to prove, 75
  economic loss, causing, 32, 73
  intermediate examination, 74
  liability for, 31–35
    auditors, of, 32, 34
    surveyors, of, 33
  manufacturers' liability in, 73–77
  need to prove, 44
  "neighbour" test, 31
  onus of proof, 76
  proof of, 75
  repairers and assemblers,
    liability of, 74
  sale of goods,
    strict liability, 44
  special relationship, where, 32–35
  unfair terms legislation,
    defined in, 129–130
NEMO DAT RULE, 10

OFFICE OF FAIR TRADING, 3, 61, 147,
  268
  codes of practice. *See* CODES OF
    PRACTICE,
  complaint to, 269

OMBUDSMAN, 5
  insurance,
    Terms of Reference, 421–424
OWNERSHIP,
  transfer of, 84–88

PERSONAL INJURY,
  compensation for. *See* COMPENSATION.
  defective product,
    caused by, 65
PHOTOGRAPHY,
  associations, 419–420
  code of practice, 175–177
POST OFFICE,
  code of practice, 177
PRICE. *See also under* TRADE
    DESCRIPTIONS.
  accommodation, 237–238
  bargain offers, 49, 231
  code of practice, 239–240
  consumer protection, 229 *et seq.*
  contract, in, 92–93
  defences, 240–242
    by-pass, 242
    due diligence, 241
  definition, 234
  electrical goods, 405
  misleading, 235–237
  new homes, of, 238–239
  offences, 232–233
  overcharging, 230–231
  previous, 230
  recommended, 230
  services and facilities, 237
PRIVITY OF CONTRACT, 43–44, 123, 129
PRODUCT LIABILITY, 63 *et seq. See also*
    MANUFACTURERS; CONSUMER
    PROTECTION LEGISLATION.
  basic rule, 64
  burden of proof, 64
  defective products, 67–69
  defences, 70–72
    development risks, 71–72
    relevant time, 71
  EEC Directive 63, 376–378
  excluded cases, 73
  legislation, commencement of, 73
  liability, 69
  limitation periods, 72–73
  product, definition of, 66
  small claims, excluded, 65
  supply, definition of, 71

REMEDIES, 95 *et seq.*
  appropriation of payments, 360–361
  arbitration. *See also* ARBITRATION.
    motor industry complaints, 391–392
  breach of statutory duty, 262–264

REMEDIES—*cont.*
  compensation. *See* COMPENSATION.
  consumer credit, 298
    time orders, 356
    unlicensed trading, 316–317
  consumer safety legislation,
    civil remedies, 254–255
  criminal law,
    compensation. *See* COMPENSATION.
  damages. *See* DAMAGES.
  debtors, for, 351 *et seq.*
  equitable, 88
  extortionate credit bargains, 361–363
  misrepresentation, for. *See*
    MISREPRESENTATION,
  products, defective, where, 89
  refund of money, 101 *et seq.*
  rejection of goods, 102 *et seq.*
    part rejection, 110–111
  repair, right of, 101
  replacement, right to, 101
  repossession of goods,
    protected goods, 358–359
  repudiation of contract, 79 *et seq.*
  rescission of contract, 16, 97–99
    misrepresentation, for, 95–97
    statutory restriction, on, 98–99
  Restrictive Practices Court, 285
  severance, 104
  specific performance, 99–100
  statutory duty, breach of, for, 262–264
  supply of goods, 27 *et seq.*
  tort, in, 115
  trade descriptions law, in,
    civil, 228–229
  unfair traders, against, 285–286
  unsolicited goods, for, 80
REPAIRS AND IMPROVEMENTS, 24–25, 101
RES IPSA LOQUITUR, 76–77
RESTRICTIVE PRACTICES COURT, 285
RISK. *See* GOODS.

SALE,
  auction, 15–16
  business, course of, in, 42
  buyer in possession after, 18–20
  court order, under, 10
  estoppel, by, 10, 11–12
  market overt, in, 10, 14–16
  mercantile agent, by, 10, 12–14
  motor vehicle, of,
    hire-purchase, on, 10, 20–22
  owner's consent, with, 10
  possession, relevance of, 17–18
  voidable title, under, 10, 16–17
SALE OF GOODS, 42 *et seq. See also*
  GOODS.
  acceptance of goods, 108–109
  agent, 42–43

SALE OF GOODS—*cont.*
  breach of implied terms,
    consumer credit law and, 343
  business,
    definition of, 44–45
  business, course of, in, 44–45
  caveat emptor principle, 42–43
  conditional sale, 85
  consumer credit, and,
    breach of implied terms, 343
  credit-broker, 55
  damage to goods,
    negligent, 106
  description of goods, 36–40
  description, sale by, 36–38
    self-service, 37–38
    special meaning, 39
  exceptions to general rule, 51–52
  fitness for purpose, 39–40, 53–55
    credit-broker, 55
    implied condition, 54
    reliance, 54
    single-purpose goods, 54
    special purpose goods, 54
    warnings and instructions, 54–55
  goods supplied, 44, 45
  guarantee, effect of, 48–49
  hire-purchase, 55
  implied terms,
    exemption clause, 135–136
  merchantable quality, 44–53, *See also*
      unmerchantable, *below.*
    acts before use, 50
    duration of, 50–51
    exceptions to rule, 51–52
    Law Commission's proposals, 52–53
    manufacturers' guarantees, 59–62
    strict liability, 44
  minor defects, 46, 47–48
  negligence, need to prove, 44
  private sales, 136
  private seller, 42–43
  privity of contract, 43–44
  retention of goods, 106
  right to reject goods,
    loss of, 104
  sample, by, 36
  sale by description, 36–38
    special meaning, 39
  "sale" goods, 47
  second-hand goods, 46, 49–50
  shoes, 177
  spare parts, 51
  standard form contract, 54
  strict liability, 44
  supply contracts, 55–57
  title,
    absence of, 108–109
  trade, meaning of, 44–45
  unmerchantable goods, 45–50

SALE OF GOODS—*cont.*
  unmerchantable goods—*cont.*
    guarantee, effect of, 48–49
SERVICES. *See* CONTRACT; SUPPLY OF
    SERVICES; WORK AND MATERIALS.
SHOES,
  associations, 420
  code of practice, 177–179
SMALL CLAIMS COURT, 187–189
SOLICITOR, 147
  bill unsatisfactory, 93
SPARE PARTS, 51
STATUTORY DUTY,
  breach of, 262–264
STRICT LIABILITY. *See* MANUFACTURERS;
    SALE OF GOODS.
SUPPLY OF GOODS,
  business supply, 248
  dangerous goods,
    safety legislation, 249 *et seq.*
  description of goods, 36–40
  false description of goods, 202–203
  offer to supply, 202–203
  remedies, 27 *et seq.*
  rejection of goods, 104 *et seq.*
SUPPLY OF SERVICES,
  additional work, where, 93
  bargain offers, 231–232
  cancellation regulations, 81–84
  consumer protection, 232 *et seq.*
    definition, 237
  EEC Draft Directive, 378–381
  estimates, 93
  false statements, 197
  future services,
    trade descriptions law, 218–219
  late performance, 91–92
  price, 93
  quotation, 93
  statutory obligations, 90
  trade descriptions law, 214 *et seq. See
    also under* TRADE DESCRIPTIONS,
    services, supply of.
  unsatisfactory, 90–91

TITLE,
  acquisition of, 9 *et seq. See also*
    ACQUISITION OF TITLE; GOODS
    passim.
  implied,
    hire-purchase agreements, in, 24
  voidable, 16–17
TORT,
  conversion, of,
    unsolicited goods and, 79–80
  deceit,
    misrepresentation, as, 95, 96
  interference with goods, 25
  negligence. *See* NEGLIGENCE.

TORT—*cont.*
  negligent misstatement, 27, 31–35
  remedies in, 115
TRADE. *See* BUSINESS.
  meaning of, 45
TRADE ASSOCIATIONS,
  addresses, 415–420
  consumer protection role, 5
TRADE DESCRIPTIONS, 195 *et seq.*
  advertisements, 207–208
    special defence, 226
  bargain offers, 231
    competitor's prices, 229
    future prices, 229
    previous prices, 228
    recommended prices, 229
    reduced prices, 228
    services, 231–232
  business, course of, in, 197–200
  civil remedies, 228–229
  defences, 220 *et seq.*
    act or default, 221–222
    advertisements, 226
    "by-pass" provision, 224–226, 242
      default defence, and, 225–226
      review recommendations, 226
    consumer protection legislation,
      240–242
    default, of,
      'by-pass" provision, and, 225–226
    due diligence, 222–224, 241
    general defence, 220–221
    mistake, 221
    odometer cases, 212, 223
    reasonable precautions, 221
    sampling, 223–224
    suppliers, of, 224
    vicarious liability, 221–222
  definition orders, 205
  description. *See* false description,
    below.
  disclaimers, and, 208 *et seq. See also*
    DISCLAIMERS.
  enforcement, 226–227
  examples, 212–214
  false description,
    application of, 201–202
    knowledge of, 203
    meaning of, 205–207
    supplying goods with, 202
  fines for contravention, 228
  goods, 200 *et seq.*
    business suppliers, 200
    strict liability, 200
  legislation,
    history of, 196
  meaning, 203–205
  merchandise marks, 196
  milometers, and, 208, 211–212
  Molony Committee, 196

TRADE DESCRIPTIONS—*cont.*
  odometers, and, 208, 211–212
  penalties, 227–228
  price of goods, 197, 229 *et seq.*
    business, in course of, 233
    code of practice, 239–240
    comparisons, 237
    consumer, definition of, 233
    defences, 240–242
    definition, 234
    indication of, 234–235
    misleading, 235–237
    new homes, 238–239
    offences, 232–233
    "offer to supply," 202–203
    overcharging, 230–231
    previous prices, 230
    recommended price, 230
    requlations, 240
    services, of, 237
  private prosecution, 227
  remedies, civil, 228–229
  Review recommendations, 220, 226
  sanctions, 194
  services, supply of, 214 *et seq. See also*
    SUPPLY OF SERVICES.
    "facilities," 219–220, 237
    false statement,
      knowledge of, 216–218
      timing of, 218
    future services, 218–219
    knowledge of falsity, 216–218
    prices of, 219–220, 237
    reckless statement, 215–216
    Review recommendations, 220
TRADING STANDARDS DEPARTMENTS. *See*
  LOCAL AUTHORITIES.
TRADING STANDARDS INSPECTORS, 4–5
TRAVEL AGENTS,
  advertising,
    code of conduct, 400–401
  association, 420
  brochures, minimum standards,
    395
  cancellation by,
    code of conduct, 395–396, 397

TRAVEL AGENTS—*cont.*
  code of practice (A.B.T.A.), 179–184,
    393–405
    enforcement, 403–404
  credit cards, payment by, 344
  disciplinary procedures, 181–182
  material alterations, 396–397
  overbooking,
    code of conduct, 397
  surcharges,
    code of conduct, 401
  tour operators' code of practice, 393 *et
    seq.*
  trade descriptions law,
    false statements, 218
TREATY OF ROME, 369–370

UNFAIR TRADERS,
  accessories, 286
  court proceedings, 285–286
  persistent, 283 *et seq.*
    meaning, 284–285
  remedies against, 285–286
  Restrictive Practices Court, in, 285
  unfair, meaning of, 284–285
  written assurance by, 282–285
UNITED STATES,
  consumer protection in, 2–3
UNSOLICITED GOODS. *See under* GOODS.

VAT-EXCLUSIVE PRICES, 281–282
VOLUNTARY BODIES,
  consumer protection role, 5

WARRANTY,
  contractual terms, and, 35
  damages for breach, 113
  implied, 22
WEIGHTS AND MEASURES,
  control over, 193–194
WORK AND MATERIALS,
  contract for, 24, 40, 41, 90–91
  strict liability, 55–57